Let Freedom Swing

Let Freedom Swing

Collected Writings on Jazz, Blues, and Gospel

Howard Reich

Foreword by Ellis L. Marsalis Jr.

Northwestern University Press
Evanston, Illinois

Northwestern University Press
www.nupress.northwestern.edu

Printed in the United States of America

10 9 8 7 6 5 4 3 2 1

Library of Congress Cataloging-in-Publication Data

Reich, Howard.
Let freedom swing : collected writings on jazz, blues, and gospel / Howard Reich.; foreword by Ellis L. Marsalis, Jr.
p. cm.
Collected articles, previously published.
ISBN 978-0-8101-2705-0 (pbk. : alk. paper)
1. Jazz—History and criticism. 2. Jazz—Illinois—Chicago—History and criticism. 3. Jazz musicians. 4. Blues (Music)—History and criticism. 5. Blues musicians. 6. Gospel music—History and criticism. I. Title.
ML3506.R45 2010
781.64—dc22
2010008959

∞The paper used in this publication meets the minimum requirements of the American National Standard for Information Sciences—Permanence of Paper for Printed Library Materials, ANSI Z39.48-1992.

For the memory of Robert Reich, my dad,
whose love of music became mine.

And for Pam Becker, my wife,
who travels with me through music, and life.

Contents

XIV Farewells: Final Parting from the Masters

Foreword

Ellis L. Marsalis Jr.

In 1953 Jesse Bell, my friend and schoolmate at Dillard University in New Orleans, decided to go to Chicago. It was August and, just before starting our junior year, we thought it would be a good idea to take the City of New Orleans train to Chicago. We had many classmates from Chicago and Detroit, and we timed it so we would all come back to school together. This was the year that Chicago became one of my favorite cities for all time.

I was eighteen and looked and acted sixteen, which caused me to get tossed from the Crown Propeller nightclub with a poorly doctored draft card. However, we were more successful getting to hear Nat "King" Cole downtown.

There was more than a bit of nostalgia reading Howard Reich's *Let Freedom Swing*. He captures the essence of the Pilgrim Baptist Church in a manner that expresses a dilemma that is yet to be resolved. This church, which laid the foundation for the gospel music developed by Thomas A. Dorsey (aka "Georgia" Tom), shares a problem with many of its sister churches throughout the United States, both north and south—being trapped between the old ways and an uncertain future.

Reich also speaks to the secular side of black lifestyle in south Chicago through the music teachers at DuSable High, such as the legendary Walter Dyett. The level of concern they demonstrated for their students fueled the discipline necessary to get the desired results without the apprehension of parental lawsuits.

Reich introduces us to the likes of McKinley Morganfield (aka Muddy Waters), Charley Patton, Robert Johnson, Blind Willie Johnson, Blind Lemon Jefferson, and the bluesmen and women from the Mississippi

Delta who have come and gone, leaving only a few recordings for dedicated lovers of the original blues.

Reich also addresses the demise of older black blues players, with a major emphasis on the support recording companies currently give to young white blues players. The testimony of Muddy Waters and the discussion of a play entitled *I Was There When the Blues Was Red Hot* (written by a thirty-six-year-old singer and guitarist named Fernando Jones about the decline of the South Side blues in Chicago) illustrate these changes. "The blues are a true picture of life," says Roebuck "Pops" Staples. The various testimonies found in Reich's book speak loudly to the inequities experienced by many bluesmen who emigrated from the Mississippi Delta to Chicago's South Side.

Reich also touches on the St. John Coltrane African Orthodox Church in San Francisco and its trials and tribulations to stay afloat. He examines Coltrane's spirituality through his album notes from *A Love Supreme* and his upbringing in High Point, North Carolina. Reich writes about a former student of mine, Fred McCray, who has the dubious distinction of being the only black jazz pianist in Salt Lake City. This is a city whose NBA basketball team retained the name "Jazz" when it relocated from New Orleans but has yet to embrace the music. This is somewhat of a paradox, but there are other American cities that are paradoxical in their own ways. I happened to be in New York City working at the Carnegie Tavern restaurant when the only jazz station in the city went country-and-western overnight in the summer of 1979.

There is much, much more to *Let Freedom Swing* than I have mentioned. Reich allows the people and the music to speak for themselves. With very little editorializing, we get more of a historical perspective than a popular point of view. He has the ability to write thought-provoking articles with a historical bent instead of being an apologist or a cheerleader when confronted with high levels of mediocrity. This book is a must-read for the connoisseur or one who has broad interests in America's indigenous music, especially jazz and its root sources. Enjoy!

Preface

You don't see or hear jazz on TV much anymore, at least not on the networks or major cable channels, where America defines its popular culture. Nor does the music turn up on leading radio stations—or even minor ones, unless you count low-wattage outlets at the bottom of the dial, nobly broadcasting to a handful of devoted souls.

Much the same kind of cultural obscurity has been accorded blues, gospel, Afro-Caribbean, and various forms of "world" music, most of it permanently marginalized—at least in the United States—by the mass-appeal, mass-merchandising apparatus that sells sounds by the click. Even as the pop-music marketplace itself has been splintered by iPods and the Internet, by file sharing and YouTube, music beyond a narrowly defined mainstream has become increasingly peripheral to American life. Without high-profile exposure on TV and radio, without muscular advertising and promotional push, long-standing musical art forms have scant chance of reaching an ever-fragmenting audience. The sheer onslaught of easy-to-digest, commercially marketable music makes it virtually impossible for somewhat more rarefied sounds to reach the young and uninitiated who disseminate culture faster and wider than anyone else.

And yet this nonpop music, often with roots dating back to African antiquity, thrives, albeit in out-of-the-way places: in obscure jazz clubs on the South Side of Chicago, in urban cathedrals and storefront churches dotting America, in back alleys and town squares of crumbling Havana, and, above all, in the hearts and lungs of the musicians who helped invent it. Venture away from the din of the late twentieth and early twenty-first centuries, and you'll see—and hear—musical rituals of tremendous majesty unfurling before audiences hungry to receive them.

For more than three decades, that's how I have spent my professional life, reveling in music largely discarded (or worse, ignored) by the culture at large. From the outset of my writing career in the mid-1970s, I have been struck by a stark but pervasive paradox: music of exceptional vitality and sophistication moves listeners of all ages and backgrounds but figures less and less on TV, in film, and on the pages of our newspapers.

Yet this disconnect only has enhanced the thrill of searching out undeservedly obscure music, then sharing that experience in print (and, of course, online). For insofar as readers haven't yet encountered the free radicals of the Chicago avant-garde, the jazz pioneers of Panama, or the ecstatic parishioners of San Francisco's St. John Coltrane African Orthodox Church, it has been my great joy to introduce them. Journalists live to share stories, after all, and the lesser known, the better.

This collection pulls together some key pieces from the *Chicago Tribune,* where I have been writing since 1977, and *DownBeat,* where I have contributed since the 1980s. In so doing, it journeys from the New Apartment Lounge, on Chicago's East Seventy-fifth Street, to the chic boites of Paris's 1st Arrondissement; from the riches of a gospel recording session in Alexandria, Indiana, to the cultural cataclysm of post-Katrina New Orleans; from the rise and fall of Chicago's Pilgrim Baptist Church, where modern gospel music first emerged, to the revelations of current jazz visionaries such as Patricia Barber, Kurt Elling, and Ken Vandermark—iconoclasts whose fiercely unconventional art quite naturally burst forth from Chicago. For in Chicago, a redoubt far from the recording-industry capitals of New York and Los Angeles, eccentrics flourish. Always have, in fact, at least since Ferdinand "Jelly Roll" Morton came here from New Orleans, in 1910.

Not all the works in this collection, however, are blow-by-blow descriptions of music as it is being created, perceived, and reviewed. Many of the articles were fashioned as musical reportage: chronicles of forays into Cuba and Panama; dispatches from a culturally devastated New Orleans after Hurricane Katrina; historical perspectives on the musical roots of the South Side of Chicago; and profiles of far-flung masters, from the inextinguishably youthful Herbie Hancock to the mature-beyond-his-years young ragtime genius Reginald Robinson.

Nor are all of these writings devoted to tantalizingly obscure artists. But in essays on Frank Sinatra and Dizzy Gillespie, Ornette Coleman and Lena Horne, I have aspired to look and listen in personal ways. Essentially, I've strived to regard these innovators not so much as cultural icons but as working musicians grappling with harmony, rhythm, and phrase. The music, after all, matters most.

Whatever the form of the article, however, the quest has been essentially the same: to decode the music, understand how and why it was made, and try to calibrate where it fits in our lives. The place where music and society converge long has been a source of fascination, which is why I've explored not only clubs and concert halls but also urban street corners and high school band rooms, followed parades and funeral processions, and focused on the big screen and the small one. Every song has a story, and the setting and context often complete the tale.

Certainly I'll never forget the rumbling baritone of Cuban troubadour Compay Segundo, expounding on the glories of bolero and *son* as he spoke on the veranda of Havana's Hotel Nacional. Nor the thunder that the jazz ensemble of DuSable High School—where South Side Chicagoans from Dinah Washington to Von Freeman learned their art—unleashed one afternoon during a processional on Chicago's South Side. Nor the triumphant beats that the marching band of St. Augustine High School in New Orleans ignited on the football field, not long after Katrina had wounded both the school and its fabled music program.

The incendiary sounds of Duke Ellington's long overlooked civil-rights manifesto *My People* still echo in my ear, shattering commonly held notions that Ellington ignored the great racial struggles of the 1960s. So does the famously raspy voice of Louis Armstrong, fervently denouncing racism and the U.S. government on reel-to-reel tapes he made; the recordings show a man obtusely deemed an Uncle Tom by those who never bothered to look past his smiling facade.

These are the sounds that resonate between this book's covers, and I believe they disprove Stravinsky's famous assertion that "music is powerless to express anything." When the music "bubbles up from the streets," as pianist Ellis Marsalis has poetically described the rhythms of New Orleans, it expresses plenty about race, culture, society, and life.

Why call this book *Let Freedom Swing*? Not simply because that's the title of a column included here on a historic moment in jazz history: Wynton Marsalis winning the first Pulitzer Prize in Music given to a jazz composition, in 1997, for his epic *Blood on the Fields.*

More important, an inescapable motif runs through most of the music that resonates in this book: freedom. Jazz, blues, gospel, and related genres have all signified a kind of liberation to the creators. In retrospect, it must have been the creative freedom of jazz improvisation, the expressive freedom of early-generation blues, and the spiritual freedom of gospel that attracted me—and generations of others—to this music. Surely it's apparent to everyone that these chords and melodies, these longing harmonies and crashing dissonances, speak eloquently of freedom: freedom from the printed score, freedom from European musical conventions, and, of course, freedom from racial injustice.

Sadly, this heroic music has not often brought its practitioners the great fortunes it has generated for others. Yet, on strictly musical terms, it has enriched uncounted lives, especially mine.

Listen with me to the music that much of America has tuned out—to its everlasting loss—and hope that the culture that produced these sounds will revere them once more.

Howard Reich
Chicago, 2010

Acknowledgments

So many people have guided me in music and in writing. Among journalists, I thank Frank Alkyer, Pam Becker, Robert Blau, Geoff Brown, Zbigniew Bzdak, Carmel Carrillo, Richard Christiansen, Aaron Cohen, Yorke Corbin, Robin Daughtridge, Ed Enright, Jack Fuller, William Gaines, Jane Hirt, Gerould Kern, Rick Kogan, Jason Koransky, Ann Marie Lipinski, James O'Shea, George Papajohn, Scott Powers, Sid Smith, Howard Tyner, Phil Velasquez, Nancy Watkins, Randy Weissman, and Joyce Winnecke. Among teachers, I treasure the memory (and lessons) of musicologist Arrand Parsons, critic Thomas Willis, and pianists Wanda Paul and Mary Sinclair. In addition, I am grateful to my colleagues at Northwestern University Press, including Serena Brommel, Rudy Faust, Jenny Gavacs, Marianne Jankowski, and Mike Levine. As always, thanks to Jennifer Joel, my inspired agent at ICM. Finally, my family makes everything else possible, so thanks to Pam Becker, my wife; Sonia Reich, my mother; Barbara-Reich Abramovitz, my sister; and her indispensable family: Lou, Robbie, Aaron, and Amanda Abramovitz.

Let Freedom Swing

I

Born on the South Side

Exploring Chicago Gospel, Jazz, and Blues—Then and Now (in Three Parts)

Chicago's South Side nurtured musical forms—gospel, jazz, and blues—that eloquently addressed the black experience in America. This is the first in a series of three articles in the Chicago Tribune Sunday *magazine that looks at the role the music now plays in South Side life.*

Can Music Save the Church That Gave Birth to Gospel?

At two months shy of 101, Mary Lewis does not climb up to the choir loft easily, but it's not only the years that weigh her down on this Sunday morning.

As she looks out onto the congregation of Pilgrim Baptist Church, where she has spent virtually every Sunday morning since 1923, Lewis sees a stark and depressing sight. The pews, which in the old days were packed with parishioners dressed to the nines, are more than half empty. The huge, horseshoe-shaped balcony, which once was so crowded that it seemed a miracle that just a few pillars held it up, is vacant, except for a couple of children and their parents. Worse, once Lewis and the choir begin to sing, the sounds she hears around her—a thin and uneven collection of about a dozen rough-hewn voices—hardly suggest a church choir at all. Where is the beat, the drive, the resplendent sound of sixty-odd voices singing at full tilt to the greater glory of God?

Such exultant moments seem barely a memory now, a remarkable turn of events considering that this is not just any South Side church. This is Pilgrim Baptist, the sacred place where—it is no exaggeration to say—gospel music was born.

In this massive stone edifice, at Thirty-third Street and Indiana Avenue, the legendary Mahalia Jackson, Sallie Martin, Roberta Martin, and Clara Ward learned to sing the then-new, soul-stirring music. James Cleveland, the Edwin Hawkins Singers, Albertina Walker's Caravans, the Barrett Sisters—all owed their fame to this place, which now stands just a few blocks east of a vast public housing complex stretching for miles along south State Street and including the Robert Taylor Homes.

But on this Sunday morning, Mary Lewis—the oldest living member of the church that changed the sound of black music in America—does not feel light of heart.

"You can see, there's no choir here now," says Lewis, bluntly, after the Sunday service has ended and the church faithful have trickled outside, into the gray afternoon.

"I'm so old, I just want to stay here as long as God lets me sing. But when I joined Pilgrim, they had seven thousand members. On Sunday, there were people standing alongside all the walls. All the seats upstairs were filled, and they put chairs down in the aisles.

"If you weren't in church by ten o'clock in the morning [for the 11:00 A.M. service], you wouldn't get a seat," adds Lewis, who came to Chicago from Alligator Lake, Mississippi, in 1923.

"You see how it is now."

~

In another room, just across the street from Pilgrim Baptist, a more exuberant scene unfolds a couple of days later.

Inside a converted garage, which Pilgrim uses as its community center, you would think some kind of carnival was under way, with music and the riotous sound of kids at play echoing everywhere. In this space the children of Pilgrim, and of the public housing nearby, meet every Tuesday night, order in pizza, sing songs, and blow off steam. At the moment, they're preparing for their singing debut, which will take place in a few weeks, during Sunday services at Pilgrim.

The kids don't realize it, Mary Lewis across the street may not realize it, but they may be Pilgrim's best—and only—chance for survival.

At the front of the room, a remarkably patient and soft-spoken woman who says she was saved by gospel music is trying to do the same for these kids. It is not going well.

"Calm down, pipe down, pay attention," she implores the children, who range from toddlers to teens. Miss Howard, as everyone in the neighborhood calls her, is trying to make a gospel choir out of this rambunctious lot. She has been sent here by Pilgrim's pastor, Floyd W. Davis. Not long ago, Davis threw open the church community center to

CAPS, the Chicago Alternative Police Strategy, a program in which local officers and residents team up to give neighborhood kids an alternative to street life.

Though there are CAPS programs in neighborhoods across the city, the one at Pilgrim tries to reach the children in the same way Pilgrim has always saved souls: through music.

And if anyone can use gospel to show kids the way, it is Miss Ellanoyes Howard.

"Gospel music is what pulled me through," she says during a break in the proceedings, recalling her childhood in the Chicago Housing Authority's Altgeld Gardens in the 1960s.

"My grandmother used to listen to gospel music and sing it all the time, and I learned to sing it from her. Those gospel songs truly saved me, because you know how cruel children can be. . . .

"My skin happens to be real dark, so I couldn't connect with the [other] teenage children. I was a monster to them. They would say, 'If you touch me, I will turn black.' "

To console herself, the teenage Ellanoyes found younger kids who hadn't yet learned about black-on-black prejudice and taught them to sing gospel. They were so grateful for the attention, she remembers, that they followed her wherever she went, giving her the only companionship she knew in her adolescence.

"It was really the children that brought me through," says Miss Howard, "because through gospel music I was able to give them something: I taught them to sing."

~

Two settings, two struggles: a fading church where children rarely go, a gritty community center where children seek refuge from the streets. In these two places you can see the crisis facing both Pilgrim Baptist Church and the troubled neighborhood around it. Long gone are the days when Thirty-third and Indiana pulsed with the sounds of black Chicago coming to worship on Sunday morning, in the process inventing a new music that the world eventually would embrace as gospel. All that remains is a fraction of that congregation toiling to keep Pilgrim afloat and hoping to save a few young souls across the street.

The tragedy is not unique to this corner; it's being played out in neighborhoods across the South Side. But Pilgrim may have an edge in facing hard times: its identity in music. After all, gospel's exultant chords have resonated in this church, and in the lives of its congregants, for nearly seven decades.

Perhaps no church in America more thoroughly epitomizes the significance of music in black life. If gospel music ever lifted spirits and inspired churchgoers to keep the faith, it did so from the confines of this church.

Pilgrim Baptist created gospel music as an expression of the black struggle in America. The question is: Can gospel music save Pilgrim? More specifically, can the music lure back the children and perhaps help to restore a community?

Music at Pilgrim, in other words, is much more than just a passing entertainment on Sunday mornings. Rather, it is the measure of where the congregation has been and where it is going. Listen to the sounds coming out of Pilgrim—how they are evolving as the church and its neighborhood change—and you can learn where a community is headed.

This is the place, after all, that was a spiritual home for waves of black migrants who came from Mississippi, Alabama, Louisiana, and other points due south of Chicago. This is where black Chicago went to worship, to organize, to use the telephone for finding jobs.

And Mary Lewis, the chorus centenarian, isn't the only one who remembers Pilgrim in its heyday. Ask anyone who witnessed the ascent of this church, and you'll learn that life on the South Side once seemed inconceivable without it.

"They used to have loudspeakers so that the people who couldn't get in could stand on the steps and hear the sermon being preached," remembers church deacon Lewis D. Samuel, who has belonged to Pilgrim since his family moved here shortly after he was born in Shreveport, Louisiana, in 1917.

"In those early days, church was the No. 1 thing for blacks. There was no television. There were no stores open in those days; there was no such thing as Sunday shopping," he says.

Moreover, with a growing black population pouring into Bronzeville—the cultural heart of the South Side—churches such as Pilgrim barely could keep up with demand. The journey north may have begun slowly in the early part of the century, but from 1940 to 1970—the years of the Great Migration—five million black people headed north, more to Chicago's South Side than to any other place.

They came by bus, train, and thumb, many lured by stories in the *Chicago Defender*, which told of a place where southern blacks could escape the burden of poverty in the South.

Once here, though, the newcomers—alone in an unfamiliar and dangerous city—yearned for a sense of community and consolation, and they found it in four churches that soon dominated life in the South Side's black community: Pilgrim, Olivet Baptist (at Thirty-first and South Park Way, as King Drive then was known), Ebenezer Baptist (Forty-fifth Street and Vincennes Avenue), and Quinn Chapel AME Church (which, in the previous century, had served as a stop on the Underground Railroad, at Twenty-fourth Street and Wabash Avenue). Confined to the tight boundaries of Bronzeville, people connected. They knew one another from back home in the South, from family ties, from work, play, school, and—above all—from church.

Among these magnificent places, Pilgrim Baptist Church stood out for the brilliant oratory of its pastor, Reverend J. C. Austin, and the daring new music developed there by a former blues-jazz pianist named Thomas A. Dorsey. Known as "Georgia Tom" throughout the South, Dorsey, son of a Baptist minister and grandson of a slave, had hit on the revolutionary idea of applying the jazz and blues vernacular to music for the church.

"I wanted to get the feeling and the moans and the blues into the songs," Dorsey said in 1976. "Before that, they would sing 'Spiri-tu-al-fellow-ship-of-the-Jor-dan land.' Jubilee songs. Wasn't nothing to them. But then I turned those blues moans on, modified some of the stuff from way back in the jazz era, bashed it up and smoothed it in. It had that beat, that rhythm. And people were wild about it."

The church fathers, however, were not, and Dorsey found sanctuary doors slammed in his face throughout the 1920s. It wasn't until Austin invited him to Pilgrim, after Dorsey's brief residency at Ebenezer, that the new music took root, beginning in 1932.

In that year, Dorsey wrote "Precious Lord, Take My Hand," which not only became the most famous of all gospel songs, but also signaled the birth of gospel music (a term Dorsey had coined as early as the 1920s). Devastated by the death of his wife and baby in childbirth, Dorsey had turned away from jazz-blues and toward the church, where he would go on to write such indelible songs as "If You See My Savior," "There'll Be Peace in the Valley," "If You Ever Needed the Lord Before," and nearly four hundred more.

Together, Dorsey and Austin turned Pilgrim Baptist into a place of theater, music, religion, and spiritual balm.

"Reverend Austin would give an electrifying sermon, and the gospel choir would come right back and electrify the audience with their singing," remembers Lena McLin, Dorsey's niece and now pastor at Holy Vessel Baptist Church on East Fifty-third Street. "They didn't have all these instruments; they didn't have the tambourines and the drums and all that kind of stuff.

"In Uncle Ted's [Dorsey's] chorus, nobody was yelling, nobody stood out, but everybody was soulful. It wasn't like today where they stomp and scream and all of that.

"It was like a well-trained choir—you heard all four parts [soprano, alto, tenor, and bass]—but with soul.

"And the lyrics had a message. So first you got the message in the preaching, then you got the message in the song, and that's what made it. . . .

"People would hear the choir preach those words:

Things we do in the dark
Will often come to light
And the wrong will soon or later yield to right,
The old story and we all know
You must reap just what you sow,
Without a doubt be sure your sins
Will find you out.

"And people would just start pouring down the aisles, rushing to the front and joining in the refrain:

Find you out,
Your sins will find you out,
No matter how you pray, sing and shout."

—"Your Sins Will Find You Out," by Thomas A. Dorsey, 1946

"Everyone wanted to be there," says McLin. "It was a happening."

The churches that had sent Dorsey packing—the churches that "showed their opposition" and "preached against it," as Dorsey told *Black World* magazine in 1974—saw congregants flock to Pilgrim as to no other church on the South Side.

"The more they listened to it, the more they could see that it was really in them to want to hear this swing, and swing with it, so it wasn't long before it took root," remembers Austin's daughter, Dorothea Austin.

"Dorsey's songs made them know how important music is to a spiritual growth, because not only are you taking the words and thinking on them, but at the same time your body responds to something, to some rhythm, that is already there. There is something in the body of everyone that wants to sway and swing."

As the migration of blacks to the North gained momentum in the 1930s through the '50s, Pilgrim's stature rose. Dorsey's gospel choir and the Sanctuary choir, which sang traditional hymns and classical pieces, gave the newcomers cause for exultation.

They needed it. Though they had improved on their lot in the South, earning, for example, twenty-five dollars a week butchering cattle in Chicago's stockyards compared with six dollars picking cotton on southern plantations, their lives were anything but comfortable. Bronzeville became dangerously overcrowded, with hundreds of thousands of migrating blacks crammed into its tight borders (Twenty-sixth Street on the north, Fifty-first Street on the south, Cottage Grove Avenue on the east, and State Street on the west). Multiple families shared one- or two-room apartments; workers toiled day and night at two or three jobs to make ends meet.

"Dorsey was able to give people an escape," says Davis, who took over as senior minister of Pilgrim Baptist in 1992. Because Davis is the nephew of J. C. Austin Jr., who headed Pilgrim after the death of his father in 1968, Davis is only the third pastor since the arrival of Dorsey and the dawning of gospel music at the church.

"You went to Pilgrim," McLin says, "because you were struggling with finances or social problems or the most terrible things, but after Sunday morning in church, you felt that maybe you could go on.

"It was like a filling station, where you came in and got filled up for the week."

Church and its uplifting music alone, however, could not hold this community together. Not after the riots that followed the assassination of Reverend Martin Luther King Jr. in 1968, not after middle-class blacks and whites moved to other areas of Chicago and to suburbia on newly built expressways.

Those who remained in what once was Bronzeville tended to be the poorest of the poor, and the high-rise public housing built to shelter them virtually destroyed what sense of community remained. Inevitably, Pilgrim Baptist Church, once at the center of black life, found itself pushed toward the periphery.

"There was a time when 98 percent of the membership of this church lived in this area," says Davis. "Now maybe 8 percent does. A lot of people moved out of this area, and the other folks who moved in were churched already."

Indeed, in the 1960s and '70s new waves of black migrants from the South established their own ministries, often creating tiny storefront churches that served small, extremely localized constituencies. With the death of Austin Sr. at age eighty-one in 1968 and Dorsey's retirement in the 1980s, Pilgrim's membership dwindled. Austin Jr. acknowledged that he never could match the fiery oratory of his father, and no minister of music ever could compete with the legacy of Dorsey.

"When Reverend Austin Jr. came, that was the beginning of the real decline of the church," says Davis. "Pilgrim got to the point, when I first came here [in 1992], where you wouldn't have fifty people on a Sunday morning.

"When I arrived here, the median age at Pilgrim was seventy. We were doing more funerals than baptisms. It was frightening."

What's more, the music itself was changing. The gently swung gospel songs of Thomas Dorsey, performed to the simple accompaniment of piano or organ, had long since been eclipsed in many churches by a rowdy counterpart. With the ascendancy of rock 'n' roll in the 1960s, electric guitars, drums, horns, vibes, and a battery of percussion were turning church music into something decidedly more exhibitionistic.

"The way some of the churches started going, you might as well be going to see the Rolling Stones," says Pauline Austin-Keller, Dorothea Austin's daughter (and Reverend J. C. Austin's granddaughter). "But that's what the young people started wanting to hear."

Through the 1980s and the early '90s, Pilgrim Baptist clung to the good old Dorsey songs, but, alas, not many youngsters cared to hear them. Most, in fact, probably didn't even know who Thomas A. Dorsey was.

Neither Pilgrim nor its pastor, however, was going down without a fight. From the moment he stepped to the altar, in April 1992, Davis virtually declared war on the lethargy of a fabled church on the decline.

The future of both Pilgrim and its neighborhood, he reasoned, belonged to its youth. Bring in the kids, and there might be hope yet for the church, its legacy and its gospel songs.

And though Davis tried to lure youngsters in a variety of ways, including laying plans for a day-care center that will open in May, he made his boldest move in music. By disbanding the old choirs and starting a fledgling one, he sought to bring new voices to the altar at Pilgrim. And by opening the church's community center to the CAPS program and sending Miss Howard there to fill it with gospel songs, Davis hoped to entice kids back to the church and, perhaps, begin to restore at least a measure of community to this neighborhood.

Miss Howard, however, is discovering firsthand how difficult a task she has been assigned. For weeks, she works toward a more modest goal: simply getting the twenty-plus kids to pay attention. By asking them to tell stories about their own lives, she eventually teaches them how to use a microphone and finally persuades them to read printed song lyrics that she has passed out.

The kids aren't exactly hitting the tune Miss Howard is trying to teach them, but at least they're reciting the lyrics as a bona fide group, in preparation for their performance at Pilgrim, now just a few days away.

With considerable lung power, they shout out:

Love lifted me,
Love lifted me,
When nothing else could help,
Love lifted me.

They don't know it yet, but they're learning one of the most beloved of the church songs, "Love Lifted Me," a 1912 hymn that helped prepare the way for Dorsey's gospel songs. Its verses easily could serve as a prayer for these children:

Souls in danger, look above,
Jesus completely saves;
He will lift you, by His love
Out of the angry waves.

No sooner have the children mastered the lyric than a group of Chicago police officers comes into the room, armed with drums, guitar, and bass. Instantly, the kids stop what they're doing and flock to the men holding the instruments.

The officers lay down an easy backbeat, and after a minute or two, teenagers Donnie Fuller and Jabari Montgomery step to the fore. They had heard through friends that some music was going to be happening on this Tuesday night, and they wanted to check it out.

Before long, Fuller and Montgomery begin rapping to the backbeat the cops are playing. Their original lyrics, it turns out, are not of the "gangsta" variety, extolling guns and drugs, but, rather, a kind of gospel rap.

Never mind that the teenagers have never met these musicians before. Never mind that police officers are not exactly heroes in the gangsta rap lyrics that these young people hear daily on the radio and on the streets. For this remarkable moment, kids and cops are making an appealing and danceable music together.

"Every word you heard, those were our words," says Fuller, smiling after an exuberant jam session that lasts about twenty minutes. "Me and Jabari write up our own words. There's a lot of Christian rap artists out there, but I don't know of any real gospel rappers—that's what we are."

Montgomery concurs. "I've been rapping since I was eight or nine," he says. "Growing up in the environment I grew up in, rap was like the culture. What we're doing is rapping to praise the Lord. We spend eight hours a day, four days a week practicing our raps."

Miss Howard, thankful that the teenagers even showed up, decides to make the gospel rap part of the church performance. She figures she has to.

"I've tried getting the older kids to come in here to sing gospel songs, but they just won't do it," she says. "You've got to let them rap. That's the cool thing to them, so that's what we're letting them do."

After a couple more Tuesdays, the cops, the rapping teens, and Miss Howard's kids' choir are beginning to blend as an ensemble, though a somewhat ragged and unwieldy one. The music-making may be a little crude, but the joy it brings to the young people is unmistakable.

"As you can see, these kids are no different than kids anywhere else; it's the circumstances that they have to deal with that are totally different," says Calvin Strong, a veteran Chicago police officer who is also a seasoned jazz percussionist.

"These kids know what a drive-by is; they know what the gangs are doing, even though some of [the children] are so small you might not think they do. But look what happened after we walked in here. Inside of ten minutes, they had their own music going; they found their rhythmic groove.

"Despite the circumstances that you get down here in this neighborhood, you can find your way through, with music. By making music, Donnie and Jabari are making a statement. They're saying: 'I ain't no dope slinger; I'm hip and I'm the best.'

"Now these are supposedly destructive, terrible kids, right? You'll notice that some of them put my drums back into the bag when we finished. I did not tell them to do that.

"They just value what we have here."

~

The neighborhood surrounding Pilgrim Baptist Church has changed momentously since Thomas A. Dorsey—who died five years ago, at age ninety-three—and Mary Lewis and Deacon Lewis D. Samuel were young. The once-bustling Bronzeville is now an odd mixture of tenement public housing and exquisitely restored brownstones, of dilapidated old apartments and $280,000 town houses springing up near Thirty-first Street. Still, empty lots and abandoned buildings dot the landscape.

"A long time ago, you could go anywhere—you could sleep in the park," says Mary Lewis, the century-old choir member who has seen the entire history of Pilgrim Baptist and Bronzeville unfold before her eyes.

"Now a person will just drive by and shoot you. I don't go out. The deacon takes me shopping in the church van and he takes me to church, and that's the only places I go.

"Now it's better living down South," she adds, referring not to the South Side of Chicago but to the South she left seventy-five years ago.

"For homes and people, it's all down South now. I don't think people are as ornery there, or will hurt you like they will here."

Lewis already knows what sociologists are only beginning to discover: a reverse migration is under way.

"Between 1990 and 1996, for the first time in any five-year period, the South saw net gains of black migrants from the Northwest, Midwest, and West," writes William Frey of the University of Michigan in the February edition of *Population Today*, a magazine published by the independent, Washington-based Population Reference Bureau.

During that time the South gained 368,000 black migrants, while the Northeast lost 233,600 blacks, the Midwest lost 106,500 and the West lost 28,700.

In other words, the Great Migration that created Pilgrim Baptist Church and the gospel music it nurtured appears to have turned back on itself. The struggle to rebuild this church and this community only becomes more arduous as residents pick up and leave.

"This is a hard time for Pilgrim and for this neighborhood," concedes Pastor Davis. "But I believe the church has to lead the way. . . . I can't save all the youth, but I'm trying to do what I can for those I can touch."

As far as the old-timers at Pilgrim are concerned, however, Davis may be facing a challenge too great for anyone to overcome.

"I would love to see Pilgrim just survive into the twenty-first century," says Deacon Samuel. "The black church in America stems from slavery time, from the times when black people didn't have nothing else to do but get together and praise the Lord and talk to the Lord, ask for his help and believe that he would give it to you, and he did. But now we can't get 350 people in there on a Sunday morning.

"We have a very good minister. He preaches very well, but the spirit is not there. That's what it is; I've got to put it like that.

"It's hard to say just why, but there's something wrong. The spirit could be—the whole spirit of the church and the Lord could be hurt. . . .

"Something had to happen that killed the spirit in Pilgrim."

Perhaps. Or perhaps the spirit at Pilgrim is just barely staying alive against unbelievable odds. Perhaps Pilgrim, its community center, and its music are the only hopes remaining for the spirit of this place.

~

Whether Pilgrim survives into the next century can only be answered on high. What's certain, though, is that just as the neighborhood and the times have changed, so must the music. Yesterday's songs can't speak for today's generation, which helps explain why the Dorsey songs that Pilgrim made possible no longer seem to attract churchgoers as they once did.

If those songs expressed the struggle and yearnings of black America on the eve of the Great Migration, perhaps a new music will have to address the lives that the children of Pilgrim now lead.

Considering that the kids Miss Howard has been coaching can't read music or play instruments or sing as a group, the prospects might not seem bright. And yet something unexpected takes place during another Sunday service, with the choir and congregation bearing witness. It happens just a few weeks after Miss Howard, Officer Strong, Donnie Fuller, Jabari Montgomery, and the children's choir begin rehearsing together in the Pilgrim Baptist Community Center.

As Mary Lewis, who has just celebrated her 101st birthday, looks on from the choir loft, the two teenagers lead an army of pint-sized performers up to the altar.

Fuller and Montgomery have created an audiotape accompaniment for the occasion. They turn on their boom box, and a catchy instrumental riff suddenly resonates through the old and venerable church. (What would Thomas Dorsey think of that?)

After a few beats, the children begin chanting the words to "Love Lifted Me"—they still haven't learned the melody—and everyone in the congregation breaks into a smile on hearing their high-pitched voices.

Between refrains, Fuller and Montgomery pick up a microphone and offer their homemade gospel rap. Its lines are enough to break your heart.

Even though I know it's hard to stay strong
And easy to do wrong
The Lord don't let it last long.
Every day is a struggle, a hustle, and test
Just make the man upstairs happy
Before you are put to rest.

When they're done, Fuller tells the congregation, about three hundred strong, "Everybody say, 'Amen,'" and the congregation pauses for a moment, as if in stunned silence, before letting loose with the loudest, happiest "Amen!" that has been heard inside these walls in a long time.

If music is indeed a measure of life at Pilgrim—and its neighborhood—then perhaps its parishioners have witnessed the glimmer of a new beginning.

Certainly the youngsters' performance suggests that music may yet bring new blood and new ideas into this old church. Though one of the deacons complains that the kids don't even know how to sing a tune, Pastor Davis steps up to the podium—visibly moved—and sums up what almost everyone in the congregation must be feeling.

"You know, sometimes our young people express themselves a little bit differently than we express ourselves," he says, referring to the rap music that has just rumbled in the house of Dorsey.

"That doesn't mean that God doesn't hear them."

March 29, 1998

On January 6, 2008, Pilgrim Baptist Church burned down. Workers repairing its roof accidentally set the fire; what remained were four exterior walls and many broken hearts. A community effort to raise $37 million to replicate the building at the same site—and to build two additional edifices—is under way. The congregation, comprising a few hundred souls, now meets in a *church community center across the street—the same converted garage where the kids of Pilgrim Baptist Church gathered after school to practice their rap songs. No one knows if the congregation ever will return to the birthplace of modern gospel music. Or if Pilgrim Baptist ever will be reborn.*

Chicago's South Side nurtured musical forms—gospel, jazz, and blues—that eloquently addressed the black experience in America. This is the second in a series of three articles in the Chicago Tribune Sunday *magazine that looks at the role the music now plays in South Side life.*

The Drill Sergeant of DuSable

With a whistle around his neck and a rasp in his throat, the fellow barking orders at the front of Room 345 sounds more like a platoon leader than a music teacher.

In fact, it's difficult to say which is worse—the piercing scream of his whistle or the steel in his voice. Either way, his attempts at coaxing music from his students are not exactly genteel. "If you want to talk, take your butt out of my room," he snarls at a couple of kids who have been snickering over some private joke. "You'll never be a musician. You'll never learn how to be a musician, because you don't listen. You can't listen with your mouth wide open."

With that, he smacks his baton on his music stand, abruptly signals the downbeat and . . . glowers as students continue trickling into the room five, ten, fifteen minutes late.

"This is your last chance in life that anyone's going to tolerate you walking in late," he says, his voice rising with anger. "If you go to a nonblack college, you're going to be all by yourself; no one's going to help you find your place and get started.

"You'll be on your own. You will not survive."

Newsome Oatis, the high school music teacher with venom in his veins, knows a few things about survival. A sharecropper's son, he has endured an impoverished youth in Mississippi, eye-opening combat in Vietnam, and an ongoing struggle to make himself a jazz trumpeter in Chicago.

Right now, though, he's attempting what may be the most daunting task of his life: turning a bunch of indifferent South Side kids who are poorer even than he was in Mississippi into a legit concert band and, ultimately, into a roaring, swinging jazz ensemble. No one has been able to do it at DuSable High School since the glory days of the 1930s, '40s, and '50s, and maybe no one ever will again.

The irony of this situation is not lost on Oatis, who knows all too well that in this same rehearsal room—where today his students keep hitting clinkers—some of the greatest musicians in the world once learned their art. Dinah Washington, Johnny Hartman, Dorothy Donegan, Von Freeman, Johnny Griffin, Gene Ammons, Eddie Harris—they and scores more became virtuosos at DuSable, perhaps the most famous high school in the history of jazz.

Or at least it was until the mid-1960s, when the towers of public housing abruptly went up across the street from DuSable, working-class blacks fled, the poorest of the poor remained, and jazz—a music that came of age on the South Side nearly a century ago—all but vanished from the halls of DuSable High.

Can even a thick-skinned, hard-headed, take-no-prisoners taskmaster such as Oatis return jazz to the corridors from which its greatest stars once emerged? Or should he even bother trying?

Ask most of the kids at DuSable, and you'd get a resounding "Who cares?" for an answer. Jazz is about as meaningful to their lives as Mozart or Beethoven, and no more comprehensible. Outside the school, the kids listen to boom boxes that churn out heavy bass beats with a stream of raunchy hip-hop lyrics firing away on top.

You don't need instruments, written music, rehearsals, or a pain-in-the-rear teacher to make the kinds of sounds that the kids listen to these days. A simple tape loop with a backbeat, plus a cheap microphone to rap into, will suffice.

So who needs to lug around some prehistoric instrument, get hassled for it by your friends, spend hours practicing it every day, and then get yelled at every morning for not being able to play it right?

Who needs it? So far as Newsome Oatis is concerned, every kid in this crumbling school does, especially those who know least about the legacy of black jazz in America. If they haven't heard of Duke Ellington and Louis Armstrong, Oatis reasons, if they've never listened to Ella Fitzgerald and Sarah Vaughan, if they've never grappled with the challenging music of Dizzy Gillespie and Charlie Parker and Miles Davis, surely they don't understand the majesty of black culture and the enormous imprint it has left on life in twentieth-century America. Deny these kids that information, and they have been robbed of a cultural identity that is their birthright.

"When Charles Mingo [DuSable's principal] called me a couple of years ago to ask if I would teach at this school, I hesitated," recalls Oatis, who had created an award-winning jazz band at the Gershwin Elementary School, on south Racine Avenue. "I had such a good program going at Gershwin, but I finally made the decision to come to DuSable when he told me that jazz will be lost—that got to me.

"We can't lose our music. I tell the kids all the time that there are some bands in Texas—I don't like to say what color they are, but you may have one black kid in the band—and those kids are chopping, they are blowing, they are swinging seriously. That's Texas!

"Now you've even got the kids at New Trier playing jazz," says Oatis, who can barely stomach the notion that privileged white teenagers in Winnetka are mastering a black music that most DuSable students couldn't care less about, let alone play.

"We can't lose our music," he says again, though he knows that the kids already have.

~

No one can cite the exact day that jazz died at DuSable, but it had to be somewhere in the late 1960s, when the South Side started imploding. With Chicago's public schools in perpetual free fall, musical tastes in constant flux, and musical illiteracy rapidly on the ascent, the intricate, elusive, and demanding art of jazz was not likely to survive.

Worse, music at DuSable never recovered from the death of the man who first taught the school how to swing, the feared and revered Captain Walter Dyett (he had earned the title as a bandleader in the army, where he presumably acquired his disciplinarian's manner).

From the mid-1930s to the late '60s, Dyett, a veteran with one glass eye and two acutely sensitive ears, transformed DuSable into the Juilliard of jazz through sheer force of will. Though many of his kids weren't much more affluent than the students are now, and though DuSable stood then—as it does today—in a tough part of town (Forty-ninth Street and Wabash Avenue), the man effectively arm-twisted, cajoled, and bullied his students into attaining greatness.

"He was the strong, authoritarian type. The more talent you had, the harder he was on you, and he could curse like crazy," recalls Fred Hopkins, a Chicago bassist who played in Dyett's band in the early 1960s.

"It was like psychological warfare. He would push you beyond your limits. He made us very angry, because, as teenagers, we didn't want to take orders.

"Once, after I had left DuSable but had come back to visit, one kid wanted to lip him and said, 'Hey, man, screw you,' and Dyett went over and jumped the guy.

"Now you realize, this is a man who recently had his foot amputated, but he gets up from the desk, with his cane, and jumps all over this guy. And I'm thinking, 'Nope, the old man hasn't changed a bit.' "

With his imperious manner, booming voice, considerable physical strength, occasionally violent temper, and obvious musicianship and erudition, Captain Dyett ruled Room 345 of DuSable as if it were his own private fiefdom. It was.

"In that band of a hundred, Captain Dyett could hear a single wrong note and cuss you out for it," remembers Chicago author Dempsey Travis, who played piano in Dyett's DuSable band in the late 1930s. "That man could hear a fly spit on cotton, and he punched it to you."

So every South Side kid who could blow into a horn or wield a set of drumsticks set his sights on DuSable. Long before the education bureaucrats had dreamed up the concept of magnet schools, Dyett turned DuSable into one of the most powerful draws in the Chicago public school system.

It was a place where the students' annual musical revue—the legendary "Hi-Jinks" shows—attracted ticket-paying audiences from across the city.

At its peak, in the 1940s to the '60s, the school was jammed with more than four thousand students (today it's just over a thousand). It was a population so large that the school held two graduation ceremonies—winter and spring—to accommodate everyone, says music teacher Doris Smith.

And the sounds that poured out of Room 345 were astonishing to feel, virtuoso music-making matched by the incredible energy of youth.

"I was amazed when I first heard Captain Dyett's band; I thought I was listening to music on a radio," recalls Betty Stell, a veteran DuSable music teacher and a mentor to her colleagues through the city's Teachers for Chicago program. "I was blown out of my mind with the tone, the music coming out of battered instruments. I remember seeing a tuba that had been hammered back into shape, and yet the tone of that thing, the sound of that band, was magnificent."

But it wasn't just the band room that resonated with the sounds of brilliant young musicians at work. Because DuSable even at its peak never could afford individual practice rooms for its students, the kids rehearsed in every corner and crevice they could find. Scales, arpeggios, chords, riffs, and whatnot rumbled through the building, so much that "I wondered at first how the other kids in the school were even able to concentrate on their work," says Stell. "I guess they just got used to it."

The place was alive with music, and Dyett's kids played everything from Bach and Beethoven to Gershwin and Grofe. But to Dyett, the concert band that toiled in 345 was something more than just an exceptional student ensemble: it was an outsize talent pool from which he picked the crème de la crème to play in a separate jazz band.

If you were invited to work in Dyett's Booster Band, as he called the jazz outfit, you were on your way to a professional career in music, perhaps even to jazz immortality.

"You had to pass an audition to get in the musicians' union back then, but after working with Captain Dyett, those auditions were nothing; they were a joke," says Tim Galloway, a 1960s veteran of the Dyett Booster Band and former DuSable music teacher. "We were pros before we graduated. I played in the Regal Theater band when I was still a junior."

Career progress and artistic prestige, however, were not the only reasons that talented young musicians flocked to Dyett and DuSable. For black kids growing up in a veritable Chicago Jazz Age, music was more than an art form or a means of personal expression—it was a ticket out of one of the poorest neighborhoods in Chicago, Bronzeville.

"Music in that period, beginning in the late 1920s and '30s, was what basketball became in the 1980s and '90s—an out," Travis explains. "If you were a player, you were working in tuxedos when everyone else (in the neighborhood) was working in overalls at the stockyards or in a blue uniform with the post office, if you were lucky enough to get a job like that.

"You have to keep in mind that within a radius of three miles of DuSable High School, there must have been thirty-five clubs, and they all hired entertainers. You would see Duke Ellington or Bill 'Bojangles' Robinson or Louis Armstrong walking down the street.

"When you went to school in the morning, you'd see people coming out of the clubs in their fancy clothes, and you'd think, 'Damn, that's a good life, to be cabareting all night and then go out and get some breakfast.'"

Perhaps that's why the kids who flocked to Room 345 would put up with whatever grief Captain Dyett dealt them. If it hadn't been for his hard-driving ways, jazz in America surely would have been less than it is, for its most luminous stars might never have realized that excellence was within their reach.

Even Dyett, however, might have had a tough time at the school that DuSable started to become in the late 1960s.

To make way for the Robert Taylor Homes, across State Street from DuSable, the city leveled hundreds of homes, wiped out neighborhoods, drove away commerce and working-class blacks, and devastated the community that had made DuSable great.

City government called it "urban renewal." Its victims termed it "Negro removal."

"DuSable always had working-class kids, but it went from mostly lower middle class to rock-bottom poor," says Mingo, DuSable's principal for the last decade. "And, see, poor people have nothing; it takes all they can do just to exist. They have no give. They can't worry about making music.

"At least with the earlier generations, they might have been living in a kitchenette [apartment] on [south] Michigan Avenue, but you would sing in the choir, you'd go to church."

Or, as Emil Hamberlin, a longtime DuSable science teacher, expresses it, "They were poor kids, but they were not poor of spirit."

More than just the social structure came apart at the seams in the 1960s. Jazz itself all but disappeared from the South Side, its audience marginalized by the rise of rock 'n' roll and the shuttering of world-famous neighborhood spots such as the Club DeLisa, Dreamland Cafe, New Apex Cafe, Oriental Cafe, Parkway Ballroom, Regal Theater, Savoy Ballroom, Sutherland Show Lounge, and dozens more.

The merger of Chicago's black and white musicians' unions in 1963 sped the demise of jazz around DuSable, since it gave South Side musicians a shot at North Side wages for the first time in this century. They fled to the more lucrative gigs.

And by the 1970s, when someone stole most of Captain Dyett's immense and meticulously maintained library of orchestral scores—with their pristine versions of charts by Ellington and Basie—jazz at DuSable was dead and literally gone.

~

Perhaps it takes a chip-on-the-shoulder personality like Newsome Oatis to jolt DuSable back into action, for Oatis is nothing if not a man with something to prove.

Born fifty-three years ago in the small farm town of Prentiss, Mississippi, he rarely made it to school more than two or three days a week; there was too much cotton to be picked helping his sharecropping parents feed a family of eight boys and four girls. "It was called survival," Oatis says today.

He didn't touch a horn until he was in tenth grade, and he discovered it was too late to catch up with luckier kids who had been immersed in music their entire lives. Nevertheless, that beat-up old trumpet changed Oatis in ways he never anticipated.

"When I got that horn in my hands," he says, "I felt like I was middle class. I was poor as dirt, my family was poor, but with that trumpet, I felt like I was the richest boy in Mississippi."

Oatis eventually moved to Chicago, at age nineteen, and started making strides as a jazz trumpeter, getting a name around town, playing with such local giants as Von Freeman, Ari Brown, and Duke Payne, developing a style and a musical attitude of his own.

Unfortunately, just as he was beginning to hit his stride, the military draft got him, interrupting his performing career, which never regained momentum. But his harrowing experiences in Vietnam, where he was wounded by a land mine in his right arm and leg, taught him a few things about life and music.

"When I was in Vietnam, I told the Judge," says Oatis, surely referring to a higher power, "'I want to get back to the world and contribute.' By that I meant I wanted to survive, because I had this purpose, this goal. . . . I had to get back and do something positive and constructive. . . .

"In the war, when you'd see those B-52s coming through to drop that stuff, you'd see how powerful we are. Well, I see music as that kind of power. To me, music is almost a religion, a force for something so positive.

"A jazz band is a powerful thing. When you're in that band, you're in your own world, protected, safe, and nothing can happen to you. That's why we've got to get a great jazz band back going again in DuSable."

After several weeks of threatening, scolding, shouting, and otherwise imploring his kids to work hard and play smart, Oatis actually has made some progress with the band. The kids now can dispatch the old Ben E. King hit "Stand by Me" with nary a blooper. Granted, that's not quite so dramatic an improvement as Oatis had achieved at Gershwin Elementary School, where "we sounded like a kiddie band before Mr. Oatis took over," remembers saxophonist Kevin Nabors, who now attends Chicago

Vocational High School on east Eighty-seventh Street. "Within two years, we became a really good group, like a grown-up band."

But at least the DuSable kids have "Stand by Me," R. Kelly's "I Believe I Can Fly," and a few other tunes in their working repertoire, so Oatis believes they are ready to perform in the school's annual "Spring Fling" show—or about as ready as they're going to be.

In a quixotic attempt at recapturing a golden moment in DuSable history, the school's four music teachers are trying to stage a modern-day version of the old "Hi-Jinks" revue that used to draw standing-room-only audiences and "was so good they could have taken it on the road," as science teacher Hamberlin puts it.

On this spring afternoon, however, the show—optimistically subtitled "Club DuSable"—is not going well. The high schoolers in the audience are talking loudly and incessantly, the kids onstage can barely be heard, and some of the players in Oatis's band are mugging shamelessly for their friends in the crowd.

This is how far music, culture, and social behavior at DuSable have sunk.

"I would say many of the kids at DuSable are the most beautiful children . . . but then I would describe [others] as broken and damaged children," says Hamberlin.

"Because of the unstableness that they're surrounded with in the community and in the environment, many of the kids that we're dealing with, though not all, have to do a lot by themselves . . . without getting the [parental] support that they actually need, and it's basically cheating them."

So while the music teachers at more affluent schools are coaching kids on the fine points of Ellington and Basie, their counterparts at DuSable are working on decidedly different issues.

"A lot of the students are not optimistic about their futures," says Marea Rivers, a DuSable music teacher who graduated from the school in 1949. "They really take a doomsday attitude. I've heard some boys say, 'I probably won't be around two or three years from now.'

"I try to talk them out of it, show them some positives, but that is very, very hard. It's hard when their brothers have been run down and killed—two in one year, in one boy's case."

When the kids decide to go ahead and pick up an instrument anyway, despite everything else that's going wrong in their lives, they encounter a whole new series of battles.

"DuSable is a tough school," says principal Mingo, "because a kid just taking home a $300 trumpet will walk out of the building and be knocked in the head—and the trumpet is gone."

Moreover, many of the kids' parents don't want them practicing at home because it makes too much noise, say DuSable's music teachers. And unlike the days when jazz still was king, carrying a trombone case doesn't have quite the cachet these days as slam-dunking a basketball.

Despite the odds against any DuSable kid learning even the basics of playing an instrument—let alone the rigors of improvising bona fide jazz—a remarkable turn of events takes place at the end of the nearly anarchic "Club DuSable" show.

An unassuming student slowly walks onstage and begins to sing the opening phrases of "Summertime," from Gershwin's *Porgy and Bess,* and the bloom of her voice and poetry of her phrasing quickly bring the room to a hush.

By the time Sikisha Bramlett, a DuSable senior, finishes her glorious aria—reworking the phrases and the changing melody notes just as a jazz singer does—the young audience is on its feet. It's the kind of ovation you'd sooner expect the kids to give rapper Puff Daddy than Bramlett's extremely sophisticated take on, of all things, a Gershwin opera.

"I didn't even know I could really sing until I came to DuSable, in the middle of sophomore year," Bramlett says after the performance. "I didn't know how to read music, but they taught me how to read, how to sing from your stomach [or diaphragm] and how to hold long notes.

"Last year I sang Billie Holiday's 'God Bless the Child' here, and I put a lot of jazz in. I didn't sing it exactly the way she did it; I kind of jazzed it up to make it interesting."

So, in a school where jazz ostensibly expired years ago, a nascent jazz singer has stepped forth, and a potentially magnificent one at that. Furthermore, Bramlett and her "soul sister," Tiffany Hudson, shatter every stereotype about students in a tough, urban school, and the notions they hold about music and black culture.

Though Bramlett concedes that many kids while away the hours listening to "mix tapes" (in which a deejay has strung together a series of dance-oriented tunes), that's not the only sound playing in their minds.

"I think the old music is better than the music now," Bramlett says. "My friends in the [DuSable] choir already know there's a lot more to music than mix tapes."

Indeed, Hudson, a trumpeter and singer, adds: "I love jazz and Louis Armstrong and Duke Ellington, Billie Holiday and Erykah Badu, Stevie Wonder, Lionel Richie, all kinds of music. When I hear Dizzy Gillespie playing the trumpet, it's like something happens on the inside of me; it's indescribable.

"Today, the [rap] music is just up-front and forward and blunt [in its lyrics]: 'I want you to do this and do that,'" says Hudson, who considers much of the music that kids listen to today as a watered-down version of earlier styles.

"When Mary J. Blige sings 'You Are My Everything,' that's an Aretha Franklin beat. When they remade 'Love and Happiness,' that's an Al Green song.

"If the other kids in school went to music class, they'd know that. . . . They should open up more and see things for what they really are and search for different sounds.

"If you like something, you shouldn't be afraid to say that you like it."

No doubt Bramlett and Hudson are exceptions in a student population that has little interest in music older than last week and outside the rapmaster fashion of the day. That they have been able to transcend peer pressure to learn to read music and embrace a century of black musical tradition is testament to their strength of personality. But they are not alone.

"You'll always have some kids coming through who are going to be just great, in spite of all this stuff that's going on," says Oatis. "Some of us are a little tougher than others, so to speak; some fall by the wayside. But if the road was a little clearer, the others would make it as well."

The only way to save them, says Oatis, is to save them young. That's why, for the last couple of years, he has been bringing pupils from Farren Fine Arts Elementary School, three blocks south of DuSable, to play in his concert band. Look at the DuSable drum corps, and you'll see youths who stand nearly six feet tall playing alongside tykes barely tall enough to see the music stands.

What's more, Oatis has been spending the summer coaching elementary students from across the city, hoping that they can learn what Hudson and Bramlett know before entering DuSable.

"It's too hard to start a freshman in high school in music, because that kid is so self-conscious, so peer-pressured, it's hard to get him in there to make a mistake," Oatis says during a break in one of the summer rehearsal sessions. "Whereas the little kids, they will make a mistake and forget about it and jump in and make another mistake.

"If the kids get four years of music in elementary school and I have them for four years at DuSable, I can get them to play anything.

"It's like Mr. Mingo says: I'll get them to follow me into Lake Michigan, if they know how to play."

So Oatis sounds positively overjoyed when he learns, at the start of the summer, that the VH1 cable music channel has selected DuSable and Farren to participate in Save the Music, a pioneering program that will bring used instruments and cash support to public schools in desperate need of them.

"It's an excellent program; it should have been done many years ago," says Oatis, who regards Save the Music as a rare chance to get his kids the instruments they can't afford and the corporate support they never receive.

The venture, to begin in the fall and run for at least five years, will give both schools (as well as several others in the Chicago system) instruments that are in terribly short supply, as well as funds for scores, music stands, and other essential items. In all, the seven participating schools will receive about $350,000 worth of support annually.

Suddenly, Oatis, a man who was building his hopes on dreams alone, believes he may have a fighting chance to forge the jazz band that is his soul.

~

As the school year draws to a close, Newsome Oatis is hellbent on proving to the students, to the school, to himself, and to anyone who will listen that this band can make a great and glorious sound.

He has enlisted the band to play for the groundbreaking of the new Lou Rawls Cultural Center at Forty-seventh Street and Martin Luther King Jr. Drive, just a stroll southeast of the school, and he is going to get these kids to play if it's the last thing he does. So he blows his whistle for all it's worth—it's a wonder the windows in Room 345 don't shatter—and lines up his kids in marching-drill formation. With a megaphone at his lips, he begins to shout orders at a decibel level that is almost too much to bear.

"Get ready to march. Pick your chin up. Get off the walls. I don't want to hear nothing out of you but your instruments," Oatis shouts.

"When I blow this whistle, that is your name," he adds, blowing into the thing, its sound amplified a thousand times by the megaphone. "'Whistle' is your name, each and every one of you, and that's all you know."

With that, the newly anointed DuSable marching band/drill corps proceeds down three flights of stairs from the band room like some attacking army. When the students get outside and into the street, the band's horns begin to play with so much force and the drum corps lets loose such an avalanche of sound that car alarms begin going off as the band marches by.

The expressions on these kids' faces reflect surprise, pride, and awe at the sheer eruption of sound they are producing. Surely no band at DuSable has sounded this bold, this brashly aggressive since the days when Dyett himself lorded over the place.

As the kids march north on Wabash Avenue to Forty-seventh, then east toward King Drive, people are coming out of their houses, out of tiny storefronts and mom-and-pop restaurants to find out what in blazes is happening out there.

What they're hearing is not jazz, not by a long shot, but something that hauntingly suggests the very roots of jazz, the turn-of-the-century marching band music that propelled so many funeral processions and second-line struts in old New Orleans.

The DuSable drums, especially, bring home the point, firing off ebullient, almost swinging jazz rhythms that not only wake up the neighborhood but also suggest that Newsome Oatis may indeed be on the path he has spent decades seeking for jazz, for the kids, and for himself.

"I didn't know Mr. Dyett," he says later, "but I think my desire is a lot similar to his, because I want to be great. I want them to talk about me like that late old Mr. Dyett.

"That's the thing that drives me. I think we can top Walter Dyett."

And who would dare tell Newsome Oatis that his burning dream cannot come true?

September 6, 1998

~

Newsome Oatis left DuSable High School in 1999 and retired from the school system a few years later. In 2004, the Chicago Public Schools announced that DuSable—which had a poor academic performance record—would be broken up into several smaller schools. As of the 2008–2009 school year, the rechristened DuSable Leadership Academy High School served 383 students, its music program a footnote, at best. The school made news in June 2009, when a nineteen-year-old man was shot to death and another injured outside DuSable by someone firing at their blue Dodge Caravan. Neither casualty attended the school, though they were giving a ride to a student, who was not hit. Police said the gunfight was gang-related. The shooter fled.

Chicago's South Side nurtured musical forms—gospel, jazz, and blues—that eloquently addressed the black experience in America. This is the third in a series of three articles in the Chicago Tribune Sunday *magazine that looks at the role the music now plays in South Side life.*

Faded Blues

The few remaining disciples from the Delta fight to be heard over the North Side pretenders.

The thumping sound of the electric bass rumbles up and down the block, and inside the crowded North Side blues club it's nearly deafening.

Onstage, five youngish men—shirts untucked, jeans tattered, faces nearly expressionless—are reeling off "Sweet Home Chicago" for what must be the tenth time this week, the thousandth time this year. What they lack in musical ability and expressive detail they drown with volume, and the white, mostly young audience is lapping it up. The lyrics may be rendered nearly unintelligible by the souped-up amplification, but, by all appearances, the audience—college kids in jeans and T-shirts, businessmen in three-piece suits with ties loosened—believe they're hearing classic Chicago blues in a local landmark. They could hardly be more mistaken.

On the South Side of town, along a block of east Forty-seventh Street that once flourished as the commercial heart of black Chicago, a legendary but now mostly forgotten club sits practically empty.

In another era Muddy Waters, Quincy Jones, Count Basie, Dizzy Gillespie, James Brown, and other giants of black music practically lived at Gerri's Palm Tavern. They would rush in to catch a drink between shows at the Regal Theater, which was just across the street; they would unwind there after sets, catching up with old friends as the jukebox churned out tunes.

On this evening, however, the only signs of life come from Gerri Oliver, who has owned the struggling club since its heyday in the 1950s, and a few young actors rehearsing a play about the demise of South Side blues.

"After the Regal was torn down [in 1973], no musicians hardly came by anymore," says Oliver, who nevertheless has been unable to persuade herself to give up on the decaying place.

"Why did they tear down the Regal?" Oliver asks, then provides the answer. "If I want to kill your identity, what do I do? I tear down something that is you."

Perhaps more than any other sound, more even than jazz or gospel, the blues is at the core of the musical identity of black America.

Its vast lineage reaches back to the African chant that slaves, in chains, brought to America. In time, the incantatory phrases of ancient Africa became the field hollers that slaves uttered as they picked cotton, the rhythm of the music setting a tempo by which to endure excruciating work, the plaintive phrases expressing a deep sorrow that inevitably found voice in country blues.

By any name, however, this was a lamenting, profoundly autobiographical music nurtured in the Mississippi Delta, the fertile, slender stretch of flatland that runs alongside the Mississippi River from approximately Memphis in the north to Vicksburg in the south. Here, newly freed blacks toiled as sharecroppers, making pennies with backbreaking work and finding at least a measure of release in music.

You can hear as much listening to the haunting sounds of Charley Patton and Son House, two blues forefathers whose stunning recordings of the 1920s carry all the fervor and rough-hewn vocal delivery of the field hollers they sang as children. In fact, the distinctions between classic field hollers and early country blues are slight, and from this incredibly potent, declamatory music eventually blossomed gospel, jazz, swing, rhythm and blues, jump, soul, and virtually every other form of black musical expression invented in America and subsequently embraced around the world.

Yet as the twentieth century comes to a close, the original sound of the blues—the music that Patton, House, Tommy Johnson, and others recorded and that a thousand bluesmen and women developed first in the Mississippi Delta and then on the South Side of Chicago—has all but vanished.

It's rarely heard in North Side clubs, where mostly third-tier bands specialize in a rock-blues hybrid virtually unrelated to the sounds of the Delta pioneers, and it no longer draws crowds to the jukebox at Gerri's or to tiny barrooms in black neighborhoods across the South Side.

Though listeners around the world savor the rock-styled, rough-and-tumble "West Side blues" of Buddy Guy, though there's genuine lyric eloquence in the work of such gifted young Chicago bluesmen as guitarist-vocalist Johnny B. Moore and harmonica virtuoso Billy Branch, these remain distant offshoots of a glorious music that has virtually receded from memory.

Just ask the few remaining Mississippi Delta bluesmen who still sing this music as if they had grown up alongside Patton, House, and Johnson—which, indeed, they did.

"You got plenty folks can raise hell with a big, wide sound on electric guitar, but they ain't doin' any playin'," says David "Honeyboy" Edwards, at eighty-three still speaking in a dialect rich in the rhythms, cadences, and inflections of the Mississippi Delta where he was born. One of the last surviving Delta bluesmen, he lives on the South Side, as he has since 1954, spending most of his days in the tiny bedroom of a small basement apartment he shares with relatives and friends.

"It's too loud. I don't know why they have to do that," he adds, in an impromptu dissertation on the blues. "Remember, blues don't supposed to do that. Don't you know the lower it is, the better it sounds?"

Edwards, of course, is right. Virtually every genuine blues recording, from Patton's first in the late 1920s to Robert Johnson's in the '30s to Muddy Waters's classics of the '50s and '60s, stresses intensity of expression over mere amplification and arbitrary raucousness. Even at his most rambunctious, Waters played his electric blues in a soaring, poetic way that unmistakably evoked the sounds of his birthplace, the Mississippi Delta.

"Now some of the blues you do have to holler, just like a field holler, and you do have to scream a little bit," concedes Edwards. "But you have to be able to hold that pitch, and people really want to know what you're sayin', so you have to say the words as plain as you can say 'em, so somebody else can understand them too."

To underscore the point, Edwards picks up his red Gibson guitar and instantly evokes the deep southern blues of the turn of the century. He bends some notes, making them laugh or cry, and eases his metal slide up and back on the fingerboard, coaxing a haunting, throaty sigh from his instrument.

After a few bars, he begins to sing, and it's clear that the field hollers he learned in his native Mississippi still resonate in every cell of his body. Partly singing and partly speaking, rarely lingering on a single note but instead slipping languorously from one pitch to the next, Edwards is demonstrating a style of song as closely linked to Africa as anything recorded blues has to offer.

"They never get the blues [music] like we did, never," says Edwards, referring to latter-day performers who play for peanuts in the same Chicago blues clubs where the Delta masters refuse to work. Instead, Edwards and his peers play mostly out of town, at festivals and in concert halls.

"They're not playing the blues like we play 'em," he adds. "And those that can play 'em, they can't sing 'em. You got maybe one out of a hundred can sing. They learned how to imitate, how to mark somebody else.

"They tried it, they can't get it, because we already got it coming here [to Chicago]," says Edwards, pointing to an elusive musical tradition he and the other Delta bluesmen acquired in a world of southern rural culture that no longer exists.

"They ain't coming in like we was coming in."

Like Robert Johnson, the revered blues artist who collaborated with Edwards frequently in the mid-1930s, Edwards always regarded the blues quite literally as a music of freedom. Playing and singing from the vast blues repertoire offered escape from life on the farm.

Levee camps, street corners, country bars, backyard parties, big-city taverns—there wasn't a place that Edwards and his blues brethren wouldn't play if there was money to be made.

"Down in Mississippi we weren't making but fifty cents a day, three dollars a week picking cotton, chopping cotton and corn, putting in corn and potatoes; that was my job," remembers Roebuck "Pops" Staples, who, like most of the Delta bluesmen, is a self-taught master who came to the South Side in the 1950s.

"I was the thirteenth of fourteen children. We was farmers, and we would go in the field and work all day. It was hard, it was hard, it was hard, out in that hot sun all day long.

"Then we'd come home and didn't have anything to do after we eat but go to bed. We just had a very big yard, and so we'd go out in the yard and sing. At home we sang church songs, but when I was a boy, I had a chance to play some nightclubs and I sung the blues too.

"Not much difference between the blues and church songs but the words. The blues is a natural feeling and a true feeling. The blues is the truth; you hear them singing that 'you done broke my heart' and this and that—that's the naked truth."

Yet Staples, the founder of the esteemed Staple Singers gospel group, hastens to add that the brokenhearted blues songs by which the genre is mostly known today represent but one facet of a music that spans an immense range of human experience. Blues about faith ("Preachin' Blues"), disaster ("Southern Flood Blues"), trains ("Empire State Express") and transformation ("Prayer of Death") may not turn up very often on today's blues circuit, but they point to the expressive breadth of the form at its best.

"They got some songs, like 'Mississippi Blues,' 'Heavy Water Blues,' all those kinds that just tell what has been happening, just like it was," says Staples.

"The blues are the true picture of life."

Perhaps the depth of expression that Edwards and Staples have attained—and which their younger imitators cannot approach—owes to the extraordinary events they experienced. The stories they tell in the blues, in other words, are their own.

Edwards, for instance, in his youth was arrested more times than he can remember simply for walking down a southern street when the local sheriff didn't want him to. He often found himself either sent to jail or dispatched to a farm to do manual labor.

Similarly, when Delta piano player Pinetop Perkins—who came to the South Side in 1951—sings the blues, he does so as a man who has seen more than his share of pain. One night in 1942, for instance, an angry woman mistakenly blamed him for an offense her husband had committed and stabbed him in his left arm, severing the ligaments and promptly ending his dreams of becoming a famous guitarist.

"It was a freak accident," recalls Perkins, who, at eighty-five, lives in a South Side apartment he says is "falling apart." "When she did that, I just said, 'Well, you just cut me out of my career, that's all I can say.' It was hard to start over. It was kind of rough, but I just figured out playing the piano the best way I could."

Indeed, Perkins remade himself as one of the most accomplished blues and boogie-woogie piano players in the world, his virtuosity still quite something to behold. Little wonder he acquired the nickname "Pinetop" (he was born Joe Willie Perkins) for his tour-de-force version of Clarence "Pinetop" Smith's showpiece "Pinetop's Boogie Woogie."

Nevertheless, "I don't read music; it looks like dog droppings to me," he says. Yet even without reading music, Perkins, Staples, and uncounted others learned to play blues for every occasion and came to understand that the music is anything but the monolithic, twelve-bar chord pattern familiar today from countless TV ads, radio jingles, and modern-day recordings.

The Delta musicians learned that the blues is the spiritual incantations of Son House, the gravelly moans and wordless chants of Blind Willie Johnson, the guitar pyrotechnics of Robert Johnson, and the careening guitar lines of Blind Lemon Jefferson. They learned that the up-tempo blues could celebrate life as eloquently as the slow drag blues could bemoan it, that the blues could address any aspect of human experience.

Above all, they learned that the blues, in all its forms, was cathartic for both listener and player, at least for a while.

"The blues come about, like when you're lonesome or something like that, and if you can't play no music," says Perkins.

"We'd say all the time, 'You got the blues if you can't sing 'em.' And that's the way the blues start to come out. If something happen and you can't get nothing to act right, you got the blues if you can't sing 'em," adds Perkins, referring to a sense of grief or sorrow that lingers when it has no outlet.

So far as Perkins is concerned, Delta blues music emerged as a release for those sentiments, a kind of healing power that only a few players still know how to deliver.

~

To this day, the myth persists that after the southern bluesmen migrated to the South Side in the 1950s, they put down their battered old acoustic guitars, picked up electric instruments (and powerful amplifiers), and proceeded to play a scorching music that would become rock 'n' roll.

The tale makes for neatly convenient storytelling and gives an enviable musical pedigree to younger white performers in need of one, but it's only partly true.

For starters, musicians such as Edwards began acquiring their electric guitars in the early 1940s, yet that changed their music much less than popular mythology would have listeners believe. Yes, Edwards and other singing guitarists realized they could be heard more clearly playing electric guitar, especially when they were competing with the din of music and noise at Chicago's Maxwell Street market in its heyday.

But their music—sometimes still with acoustic guitar—continued to emphasize the vocals, the meaning of the song lyrics, and the art of storytelling above all else. The best of the old Delta musicians—such as Edwards, Staples, and Perkins—never sacrificed a whit of the melodic shading, rhythmic freedom, subtle dissonance, and musical intimacy they had learned in the Mississippi Delta.

In the Delta, after all, they were playing to fellow sharecroppers and didn't have to dilute their message to communicate. The blues, in other words, had not yet become a music for the masses.

The electric band of Muddy Waters (who was born McKinley Morganfield in Mississippi in 1915) stripped the music down to its essentials and thereby made it saleable to all of Chicago and then to the rest of the world. Waters indeed inspired rock 'n' roll performers such as the Rolling Stones, who took their name from Waters's blues dirge "Rollin' Stone."

But the popular ascent of the Stones and the rest of the British Invasion rock bands of the 1960s was no blessing for the real Delta and Chicago blues. Great artists such as Jimmy Rogers fell off the map, and blues legends such as Waters soon found themselves playing for a white audience that had little patience for the intricate vocal chants and richly textured instrumental accompaniments of Honeyboy Edwards, pianist Sunnyland Slim, and many more.

"I play in places now don't have no black faces in there but our black faces," Waters told Robert Palmer. Worse, he added, "ain't too many left that play the real deep blues. There's John Lee Hooker, Lightnin' Hopkins—he have the Texas sound, and Texas blues is very, very good blues—and, let's see, who else? Ain't too many more left. They got all these white kids now. Some of them can play good blues. They play so much, run a ring around you playin' guitar, but they cannot vocal like the black man."

Twenty years later, the sound of undiluted Delta and Chicago blues is even harder to come by, its expressive power and musical subtlety diminished by uncounted imitators in the modern blues and rock camps.

That's perhaps the main reason why a group of young black actors has converged this evening on Gerri's Palm Tavern. Led by a thirty-six-year-old singer-guitarist and fervent blues advocate named Fernando Jones, the actors are rehearsing a play Jones wrote about the decline of South Side blues, *I Was There When the Blues Was Red Hot.*

Jones does not mince words when reflecting on the plight of the music he lives to play.

"I think we have been tricked either by white folks or black folks that the blues do not exist," says Jones, who came to the music at age six. He has been playing, studying, and championing the blues ever since.

"I think that it's easier just to say, 'Oh, the blues is dead,' and too many of us think that way. Because some of us probably think that B. B. King is dead [he's alive and well at age seventy-three], and people believe that there is not a black blues musician under fifty years old alive. So we'll just say that there's only one left, John Lee Hooker [now seventy-eight]," adds Jones, referring to the only living Delta bluesman besides B. B. King who enjoys pop-icon status.

"We seem to believe that you have to be ninety-seven years old and outlive everybody to be a certified black blues artist, but you can be thirteen years old, and have some money put in back of you, and you are a white blues artist," says Jones, clearly pointing to Jonny Lang, the white, would-be blues prodigy who has been heavily promoted by the record industry.

"It's just like I say in the play, 'There will come a time when black men won't be able to get a black job being black anymore.'"

Though the casual observer might believe record industry hype that the music is enjoying a popular resurgence, the homogenized, commercialized, bowdlerized sounds of Lang, Bonnie Raitt, and other would-be blues saviors are such pale imitations of the real thing as to render them irrelevant to the artistic evolution of the music.

Furthermore, the neon-lit franchise known as the House of Blues (which generally features anything but the blues), the musical buffoonery of the Blues Brothers (on film and stage), and the gaudy impersonation of the music that thrives in clubs across the country are only the most obvious forms of sacrilege.

There's also the canonization of Robert Johnson as the patron sinner of the blues (the better to sell a boxed set of his recordings), even though Johnson himself revered such masters as Patton, House, Willie Brown, and Ike Zinneman; and the deification of the great John Lee Hooker by the pop record industry even as it neglects all of his contemporaries (such as Edwards, Staples, and Perkins).

These unfortunate facts gall everyone in the cast of Jones's play, and they vent their sentiments during a break in rehearsal.

"If you go to blues clubs today, most of the time you see white kids in the audience," says John LeMay, an ardent blues enthusiast who plays a nightclub emcee in the blues drama. "But when I was growing up on the South Side, blues clubs were filled with black people, partly because the option to go somewhere else did not exist.

"I've been running around this very block since I was a little kid. The Regal was across the street, the Metropolitan Theater was nearby, there was black music and black blues everywhere."

The implosion of the South Side in the 1960s, with upwardly mobile blacks moving out and the poorest of the poor moving in (to public housing), changed all that.

"All of a sudden the role models were gone," adds LeMay. "And they took with them all the culture that they brought when they migrated from down South. So these [South Side] kids now have this really hollow image of how they got to be where they are.

"They do not know about the blues."

LeMay barely finishes that sad observation before the youngest cast member, twenty-year-old Carl Vanoy, chimes in.

"When I first started working on the play, by me being so young I was totally blind to the blues," says Vanoy, who plays a character named Two Dollars, a moocher.

"We kids, all we wanted to hear was rap, that's what's hip. Some people may think the blues is dying because they are not hearing about it, and a young generation is not coming out to hear it, but they should, because for me it was an eye-opener. The blues ain't all that bad.

"It's not all sad songs. It's happy and it's sad. It gives you energy; it's a feeling."

That Vanoy has made that discovery and leap of faith while working on the show very nearly brings Jones—the blues musician-cum-playwright—to tears. And yet Jones knows that Vanoy's conversion is but one in a million, and that there aren't enough years in Jones's life to persuade every young black listener he needs to reach.

"Some people think we should hide away the blues, because it talks of a time when we weren't successful and we didn't have money and people didn't exactly think we were cool," says actor LeMay. "It's like Billie Holiday singing about how her man beats her up [in 'My Man']: it's not politically correct.

"But we had to go through that to get to be a congressman or a lawyer or a doctor or to drive whatever car.

"We are under this real false impression that we've come such a long way, that if we get rid of the things that people connote as being negative, that we're going to take another step up.

"Don't work that way. If you don't reach back, you can't go forward."

When it comes to the evening of the big performance, about a week later, Gerri's Palm Tavern, surprisingly, is almost filled. Word about the blues play apparently has spread through the neighborhood, and this is the first time since Gerri Oliver can remember that cars are double-parked along Forty-seventh Street.

Moreover, the music onstage is not some gross distortion of South Side blues but something closer to the real thing, at least in its fervency and economy of expression and its fidelity to the storytelling nature of bona fide black blues. Pinetop Perkins even swings by to catch the show, and remarks afterward, "That Fernando can play. He's got good time, I liked that. There's plenty young guys who don't know how to do that stuff. He jumped right in. I'm going to call him and give him a job."

The comment is remarkable if only because, just a few days earlier, neither Perkins nor Edwards nor Staples could name a musician under forty who had a clue about the musical origins and stylistic demands of the blues.

What's more, when Fernando Jones is onstage, whether coaxing laconic blues phrases from his guitar, singing a blues dirge, or acting the part of Dizz (loosely based on the late blues guitarist Lefty Dizz), he looks like a million bucks. He's dressed in a sharp suit that clearly has been pressed within an inch of its life—not precisely the image of the hard-luck blues martyr that pop culture typically demands.

"I think that we collectively, as black artists and black musicians, we think that if we live in a Cadillac, we have no health insurance, no teeth and women outside of our race, that we're really playing the blues," says Jones, later, of the modern myth of the blues musician.

"But you can't find one photo of Muddy Waters—that's not a personal photograph—that he didn't have on a suit. Or Willie Dixon without a white shirt. White shirt, shined shoes, hat, and union card: you had to have that.

"All I'm trying to do is let people know that you don't necessarily have to die from emphysema playing for twelve to fifteen dollars a night to be a bluesman. I'm trying to show that the blues is a celebration of Africans in America making something out of nothing."

By the end of the play, which mixes comedy and tragedy, sorrow and hope as only the blues can do, the audience comes to its feet, as if surprised by the power of the nickel-and-dime production and the searing, uncompromised beauty of its music.

But surely no one in the house, packed with about a hundred people, is moved more than Gerri Oliver, who has seen it all in roughly forty years at the Palm Tavern.

"If my life ends tonight," she tells a visitor afterward, "this would be the icing on the cake, what my life has been all about.

"Quincy Jones, that was his seat over there," she says, pointing to a booth. "Count Basie, that was his table over there. And these kids here are the continuity of all that, so this is a culmination for all the efforts that I have put into that world."

Even Vanoy, the young blues convert, knows what "Mama Gerri," as everyone in the cast calls her, is talking about.

"This place is almost like a character in the play," he says late in the evening, when the club is nearly empty. "To know that Sarah Vaughan has been here, Joe Louis courted his wife right over in that booth in here, Dizzy Gillespie, a ton of people have been in here.

"And to know that, and to be here, and to know that our ancestors are floating around in this room is a strong and mystical and spiritual thing."

Considering that these words come from a twenty-year-old who six months ago believed the blues dead at best, something to be ashamed of at worst, perhaps there's hope yet for the purest form of this music. If kids growing up on the South Side of Chicago are to know the sweep of black culture in America, they surely must hear the music that once flowered on the streets where they now live. That music—generations in the making—rose up from a culture that transformed deprivation into great art. To lose it now would be unspeakably wrong.

Surely everyone in this room prays that the tradition can survive, for artists such as Edwards, Perkins, and Staples have represented the true sound of the blues for the better part of a century—and the time will soon come when someone else will have to take their places.

December 27, 1998

Pops Staples died December 19, 2000, at age eighty-five, of a heart attack in his home in south suburban Dolton. Nonagenarians David "Honeyboy" Edwards and Pinetop Perkins continue to astonish the world performing their ancient Delta blues, among the last of their generation doing so. The origins of this music still live in their work, which has been documented on CDs such as Edwards's Delta Bluesman *(Earwig, 1992) and* Roamin' and Ramblin' *(Earwig, 2008) and Perkins's* After Hours *(Blind Pig, 1988),* Pinetop's Boogie Woogie *(Discovery, 1992), and* Pinetop Perkins and Friends *(Telarc, 2008). Staples's brief discography as featured performer includes* Peace to the Neighborhood *(Point Blank, 1992) and* Father, Father *(1994).*

II

Street Scenes

Music Bubbling Up from the Pavement

St. John the Saxist

San Francisco congregation finds spiritual comfort in the music of Coltrane.

SAN FRANCISCO—Just before noon on a recent Sunday, there was barely room to breathe—let alone sit—during the prayer service at St. John Coltrane African Orthodox Church.

By half past twelve, crowds were lined up outside, hoping to get at least a glimpse of this famously unconventional institution. The lucky hundred or so who squeezed inside witnessed a devotional service accompanied not by traditional hymns and chorales but by the searing music of jazz giant John Coltrane, the patron saint of a church that perhaps could have taken root only in this anything-goes city by the bay. Unfortunately, Coltrane devotees who have been flocking since 1972 to the shoebox-shaped storefront church on 351 Divisadero Street (near the Haight-Ashbury area) will have to pray elsewhere come Sunday. Pushed out by skyrocketing rents, St. John Coltrane African Orthodox Church will take up temporary quarters fifteen blocks away in St. Paulus Lutheran Church, 930 Gough Street.

To mark the end of one era and the start of another, church officials and followers will converge on the old address around 11:00 A.M. Sunday, then launch a grand processional to the new, temporary home.

"As John Coltrane would say, 'We look to the future optimistically,'" says Bishop Franzo Wayne King, who founded St. John Coltrane's with his wife, known to parishioners as Reverend Mother Marina. "But sometimes I feel like a pawn in this situation, with different parties battling over the church, and us caught in the middle."

Indeed, the plight of the church has become a symbol of recent tensions in San Francisco, where rents have been driven up by an influx of "dot.com" people—computer-industry folks whose riches are said to have elevated the price of real estate in a city where housing already is among the most expensive in the country. Using the exodus of St. John Coltrane as a rallying cry, television and print media have been all over the church, taking up its cause.

"I think they're using us to beat up the dot.com people, but we can handle this transition just fine," adds King. "I see it as a step forward, as the thorns in the eagle's nest. We must move, we must grow, we must expand, so it's time to take flight to higher heights."

In a way, it's a miracle that St. John Coltrane has survived in one location for as long as it has, since its very premise—a church that views a jazz musician as its guiding spirit—perturbs almost as many people as it delights.

"The whole idea, as far as I can see, is pretty ridiculous," says *San Francisco Examiner* critic Philip Elwood. "It's supposed to be spiritual, but it's kind of a novelty.

"I will say this—the musicians are quite good."

That much was apparent throughout the service, with a small jazz band playing Coltrane's music for all the fire and brimstone it held. To behold a tenor saxophonist unleashing the soaring lines of Coltrane's *A Love Supreme*—backed simply by a weathered upright piano, stand-up bass, and drums—was to hear this music anew. Stripped to its bare essence, and without the ostentatious solos and showy virtuosity that often drive the music at jazz clubs, Coltrane's music sounded fresh, urgent, and mercifully unadorned.

Moreover, the congregation hung on every note, as if savoring the opportunity to spend an afternoon in church hearing music not celebrating the European culture of two centuries ago but the American experience, here and now.

When Mother Marina asked the congregation if there were any out-of-towners in the house, she heard pilgrims shout out their places of origin: Holland, Australia, Denmark, Los Angeles, Italy, Wisconsin, Kansas City, Japan, Turkey. Clearly, the message of St. John Coltrane African Orthodox Church has spread far and wide.

Even so, skeptics wonder how a jazz musician came to be the focal point of a congregation.

"There were unexplainable events that happened in my life that made it very clear to me that the spirit of the Lord was leading me to proclaim John Coltrane as a medium for good," King explains, pointing to the life-altering experience of hearing Coltrane perform. It was a few months before the jazz visionary's death of liver cancer in 1967, and King to this day refers to it as his "baptism in sound."

Having already launched jazz listening sessions in their living room, King and his wife began devoting these neighborhood gatherings to music of Coltrane. The meetings eventually blossomed into an informal church with an expansive name—One Mind Temple Evolutionary Transitional Body of Christ—and with Coltrane as its inspiration.

But after studying in Chicago with Archbishop G. D. Hinkson of the African Orthodox Church—which grew out of the Eastern Catholic Church and traditions dating to Saint Peter the Apostle—King decided his storefront outpost needed affiliation with a larger organization. In 1982 King was appointed a bishop, and St. John Coltrane African Orthodox Church was born.

Not surprisingly, the services on any given Sunday represent an intriguing mixture of ancient and modern, Eastern and Western philosophies. Following a long prelude of Coltrane's music, played with fervor by church musicians, King alternates scriptural readings with freely improvised sermons on the perils and aspirations of modern life. But the musicians are front and center, playing almost constantly through a four-hour marathon.

To those who complain that Coltrane was a heroin addict unworthy of adoration, King counters that the man transcended his human failings. Indeed, after being fired from trumpeter Miles Davis's band in 1957 because of heroin addiction, Coltrane transformed his life, kicking the habit through sheer force of will.

This profound change not only precipitated Coltrane's maturation into one of the most important creators in jazz but led him to seek spirituality in music and life. As he wrote in the liner notes to the 1964 suite *A Love Supreme,* his transcendent work: "During the year 1957, I experienced, by the grace of God, a spiritual awakening which was to lead me to a richer, fuller, more productive life. At that time, in gratitude, I humbly asked to be given the means and privilege to make others happy through music. I feel this has been granted through His Grace."

For Coltrane, however, the journey of spiritual discovery did not come out of the blue. Both of his grandfathers were preachers, his mother was a church pianist, and his family was deeply involved in church activities in North Carolina, where Coltrane was born in 1926. Black religious music, gospel singing, and fire-breathing sermons defined the sounds that the future jazz revolutionary heard in his youth. If landmark Coltrane recordings such as *Giant Steps* (1959) and *Impressions* (1961) hinted at the spiritual fervor yet to come, *A Love Supreme* articulated it boldly.

As if to remind visitors of Coltrane's extensive comments on the subject of spirituality, the church walls are covered with handwritten posters quoting its namesake.

"My goal is to live the truly religious life and express it in my music," reads one banner. "My music is the spiritual expression of what I am—my faith, my knowledge, my being."

And another: "I know there are bad forces, forces out there that bring suffering and misery to the world, but I want to be the opposite force. I want to be the force which is truly for good."

It's worth noting, though, that the religious elements of Coltrane's music are not as unusual in jazz as casual observers might think. Jazz, after all, was born, at least in part, of the spirituals of African American culture, and no less than Duke Ellington wrote vast sacred scores that eloquently merged elements of jazz improvisation with spiritual devotion.

"For tourists, St. John Coltrane may be a novelty, but the people of the church take it very seriously," says Randall Kline, executive director of SFJAZZ, the city's leading jazz organization.

Kline also praises the church's musicians, a band staffed by King's children and various San Francisco jazz avant-gardists. The largest version of the church ensemble, which includes a nine-voice choir, goes by the name Ohnedaruth and the Sisters of Compassion and commands respect in San Francisco's vibrant jazz community. Part of its fame owes to the church's weekly radio broadcast, Tuesday afternoons on KPOO-FM 89.5.

To King, the music is really what the church is all about: the sense of spiritual quest that defines the music of the last part of Coltrane's career, and the inspiration it can give to those who listen.

"The music of John Coltrane is beyond all cultures, all prejudices, all ethnicities; it is beyond calendars and caskets," says King. "It has universal appeal, and so we want to be in every valley, every hillside, every village and town. In fact, we don't want to be just in the African Orthodox Church. We need to be in synagogues and mosques. We need to reach Buddhists and Muslims and even atheists," adds King, who dreams of extending the philosophy and music of St. John Coltrane Church outside the confines of the African Orthodox faith.

"And John Coltrane's music can do that."

April 28, 2000

Though St. John Coltrane African Orthodox Church has moved to 1286 Fillmore Street in San Francisco, its calling endures. Mass is said from noon to 3:00 P.M. *every Sunday, and all are welcome. The church continues to celebrate "the universality of John Coltrane's music and his philosophy" and believes "that his spirit and legacy does reach and touch the lives of people of many different faiths, creeds, and religions," observes Bishop Franzo Wayne King, in the church's mission statement. The goal is "to lift up the Name of Jesus Christ through Saint John Coltrane's music, knowing from personal experience and testimony, and from a great cloud of witness, that the Spirit of the Lord is in the Sound Praise as it is delivered from heaven through John." Though a sacred impulse has coursed through jazz since its inception—with church hymns as central to its musical identity as street songs, blues chants, and bordello piano riffs—no other jazz composer has inspired the sacraments accorded to John Coltrane.*

A Groovable Feast

A visiting American finds that, more than ever, Le Jazz is still a French preoccupation.

PARIS—As the train glided out of the Metro station at the Louvre, there was no mistaking the sweet sounds of an alto saxophone, bass, and drums riffing on W. C. Handy's "St. Louis Blues."

But the horn's tone was too hot to be coming from a boom box, and, sure enough, a young alto saxophonist soon emerged from the rear of the car. While the train sped from one subway stop to the next, the saxist unreeled one American jazz tune after another, playing karaoke style to a tape loop on a portable player nearby. In Paris, jazz is everywhere—in the Metro cars, on the radio, and deep inside cavernous clubs every night of the week. This European cultural capital may be famous for its art, food, and opera, but on Paris's streets, life sways to the unmistakable beat of bona fide jazz.

Moreover, none of America's predominant jazz cities—including Chicago, New York, and New Orleans—can rival the sheer number of jazz joints that make this city swing. There are at least a few jazz rooms in virtually every Paris arrondissement (or "district"), and they're as crowded on weeknights as they are on weekends.

"There are so many clubs, even I haven't been to some of them," said the otherwise omniscient concierge at Hotel le Loiret, near the Louvre. "It has been this way for as long as I can remember."

Even this feast of venues is not enough to slake Paris's thirst for jazz. Clubs continue to proliferate, with sleek new rooms opening alongside slightly dank old ones. Meanwhile, young musicians from across Europe flock to Paris the way their American counterparts gravitate to New York and Chicago.

Emerging Parisian musicians, though far from household names on either side of the Atlantic, attract a comparably youthful audience. An American scanning the crowd in a Paris jazz room might think he was in a rock club, judging by the predominance of young faces, spiky hairdos, and piercings of all kinds.

"Jazz gets a lot more attention and care in France than it does in the United States," says Dee Dee Bridgewater, the accomplished American jazz singer who has lived outside Paris for more than a decade. "You can feel it wherever you go, and I'm reminded of it whenever I come to the States."

Yet, at first glance, France's embrace of America's most distinctly autobiographical music might seem puzzling. This is the same country, after all, that has passed laws banning foreign words in advertisements and official documents while decreeing that a certain percentage of radio airtime must be devoted to French music. Though the legislation hasn't been particularly effective in keeping out American slang and Hollywood films, the French remain famously protective of their indigenous art.

Nevertheless, American jazz has become practically a second language to the French. In part, say Parisians, that's because of the American troops who liberated Paris during World War II and brought with them their passion for big band and hot-swing music (though some credit must go to guitarist Django Reinhardt and violinist Stephane Grappelli, who established a beachhead for Parisian jazz leading the Quintet of the Hot Club of France in the 1930s). Once the war was over, jazz exploded in Paris.

"The first records we received in France after the liberation were those Dizzy [Gillespie] made with Charlie Parker for Guild," remembered French jazz critic Charles Delaunay in Gillespie's memoirs, *To Be or Not to Bop* (with Al Fraser).

"And when these records arrived they were the talk of the city the very same day. So the news spread in twenty-four hours over all the music circles in Paris."

At the time, jazz clubs such as Caveau de la Huchette (in the Latin Quarter) and the Slow Club (near the Louvre) already were thriving, as they do to this day.

But there's a more profound reason that French musicians and audiences embrace jazz: the French played an integral, if barely credited, role in the creation of the music in the United States roughly a century ago.

Though no American metropolis can claim exclusive rights to the authorship of jazz, New Orleans—once governed by the French—provided the ideal setting for the eventual flowering of nascent American music. More racially tolerant than perhaps any other city in the United States as the nineteenth century segued into the twentieth, New Orleans brought French, Creole, Spanish, and black cultures into unprecedented proximity.

Thus jazz pioneers such as Ferdinand "Jelly Roll" Morton, Alphonse Picou, and George Baquet grew up hearing the Gallic arias that drew throngs to the French Opera House in the heart of New Orleans's French Quarter since 1850. The sublimely lyrical and melodically ornate quality of opera scores by the likes of Jean-Baptiste Lully and Jean-Philippe Rameau deeply influenced the first generation of Creole jazz artists and helped define the sound of the new music.

Little wonder that jazz began surfacing in Paris by at least the 1920s, when Darius Milhaud unveiled his jazz-tinged ballet *La Creation du monde* and Jean Wiener and Clement Doucet played two-piano jazz at the famous club Le Boeuf sur le Toit. By midcentury, American jazz players such as Sidney Bechet, Don Byas, Mezz Mezzrow, Kenny Clarke, and Bud Powell were celebrated in Paris, the city serving as a magnet for generations of expatriate black musicians escaping racism in the United States.

"I guess every Negro performer dreams of going to Europe," wrote Billie Holiday in her autobiography, *Lady Sings the Blues* (with William Dufty). "Some of them have gone over and never come back."

Even those who just visited were struck by what they saw and heard in a faraway culture.

"This was my first trip out of the country, and it changed the way I looked at things forever," wrote Miles Davis, recalling his Parisian outing of 1949, in *Miles Davis: The Autobiography.* "I loved being in Paris and loved the way I was treated."

Today, American jazz stars such as Bridgewater and saxophonist Johnny Griffin still call France home. Though each spends time in the United States, neither has returned permanently to America—their bond with the French seems destined to last a lifetime.

But not all of France's jazz stars are imported. Artists such as the aforementioned Grappelli, the venerable pianist Martial Solal, and the violinist Jean-Luc Ponty long ago gave France its own jazz icons. Today, the Belmondo Big Band is the talk of Paris nightlife.

French films, too, have long celebrated jazz, most notably Bertrand Tavernier's *'Round Midnight* (1986), starring American tenor saxophone giant Dexter Gordon and still the greatest jazz film ever made. Jazz aficionados also treasure Roger Vadim's *No Sun in Venice* (with a score by Modern Jazz Quartet founder John Lewis) and Louis Malle's *Elevator to the Gallows* (with a famous soundtrack by Miles Davis).

Not surprisingly, then, Parisians improvise jazz with utter naturalness and ease, though with an unmistakably French cadence. Like much of the culture's classical music, its jazz leans toward refinement of expression, subtlety of color, and elegance of melody.

Even more striking, the French don't look down on earlier periods of jazz history as many American listeners and critics mistakenly do. Go to a Parisian jam session and you're likely to hear music of bebop revolutionaries Charlie Parker and Thelonious Monk sharing the spotlight with vintage work by Morton and Louis Armstrong. All are considered equally important, at least judging by a recent sojourn through several of Paris's best clubs.

Most Parisian jazz lovers probably would concur that the top room—the equivalent of the Jazz Showcase in Chicago or the Village Vanguard in New York—is Duc des Lombards. Its facade, featuring images of jazz immortals such as John Coltrane and Duke Ellington, makes American visitors feel at home before they even walk inside.

Like virtually any Paris jazz club worthy of the name, Duc des Lombards is located below street level, its view of the stage interrupted by several pillars. But despite the somewhat cramped and funky quarters, the club earns respect as a serious listening room, with visitors barely breathing when the music is under way.

Recently, the French pianist Jean-Marie Machado led a superlative quartet in standards such as "Softly, as in a Morning Sunrise." Machado unabashedly merged classical and jazz techniques, and the enthusiastic response of the audience illustrated the French openness toward both traditions. Indeed, American musicians have long been seduced by the open-mindedness of French audiences. Gillespie, deemed a radical in the United States for championing complex bebop music in the 1940s, was astonished by his reception in France in 1948.

"The audiences were composed of a younger, wilder crowd, but they were ready for us," he later wrote. "And, of course, I hardly knew the place, it had changed so much since I'd been there with Teddy Hill almost eleven years before. But the music had changed too, and the French loved it."

To this day, the French savor adventurous music-making, as guitarist Philip Catherine proved one evening at Sunset, a club just a couple of doors away from Duc des Lombards. Catherine, an esteemed guitarist who grew up in Belgium but has long been associated with Parisian jazz, played harmonically daring, structurally complex music that never became loud, aggressive, or abrasive.

Even at its most daring, Catherine's trio refused to sacrifice gentility or grace. There was a lesson here for many American and other avant-gardists, who often mistake mere volume for energy and predictably grating dissonance for experimentation.

The toniest jazz room in Paris remains Le Bilboquet, a three-tiered restaurant-cabaret that has flourished in various guises since 1947. The club looks and feels as glamorous today as it must have during its postwar heyday, when "jazz mania invaded" France, as the club's fliers proclaim.

But that's not even the tip of the flame. Caveau de la Huchette, an underground club in the Latin Quarter, attracts young French swing dancers and American tourists; and the tiny, aptly named Petit Opportun features experimenters such as Blue Sphere, with pianist Alex Tcholakian and tenor saxophonist Jean-Pierre Thirault reinterpreting American standards in arcane and fascinating ways.

Yet the miracle of jazz in Paris is not in any one club but in the sheer wealth of them, as well as in the way French musicians address this music. Uninterested in merely mimicking American giants, they typically filter the techniques of jazz improvisation through their own European sensibility.

For listeners who revere French impressionists Claude Debussy and Maurice Ravel as much as American innovators Louis Armstrong and Jelly Roll Morton, French jazz epitomizes an alluring synthesis of both schools.

And no Parisian boulevardier can stroll far without finding it.

August 8, 2000

Landmark Paris jazz clubs such as Duc des Lombards, Sunset, Le Bilboquet, Caveau de la Huchette, and Jazz Club Lionel Hampton still thrive in Paris, which to this day reveres the music as few American cities do. Most arrondissements nurture one or more major jazz rooms; the music still pulses on the Metro; and the annual Paris Jazz Festival spotlights a range of European, African, and American artists every weekend in June and July. In essence, jazz is inextricably intertwined with the identity of this city. And because of the partially French roots of American jazz, Paris's robust jazz landscape simply reflects the musical links between two cultures.

In the Home of Jazz, Swing Definitely Not the Thing

But team's nickname sticks in the home of the Tabernacle Choir.

SALT LAKE CITY—In sports, names mean a lot. Our championship-bound Bulls evoke both the legendary Chicago stockyards of old and the stampeding capitalists of the Chicago Board of Trade.

Which makes you wonder whose idea of a practical joke it was to keep calling their clueless opponents—Utah's NBA franchise—the Jazz after it relocated from New Orleans in 1979.

This is, after all, Mormon country, a devout place no more hospitable to jazz than Fargo, North Dakota, is to klezmer music.

"We know it's rather odd," concedes Utah Jazz media relations manager Mark Kelly.

In fairness, Utah has no monopoly on bizarre monikers—just look at the Los Angeles Lakers, formerly of Minneapolis and the "land of 10,000 lakes."

Yet there might be more lakes in L.A. than there are jazz joints in Salt Lake City.

On a search for music here, the first stop was Zephyr, a downtown nightclub where, locals bragged, Wynton Marsalis once performed.

Alas, that was nine years ago. On this evening, a group of semitalented lads doing their best Nirvana impression held the stage.

Then there was the nearby Manhattan Club, a promising, subterranean room with a white neon skyline above its chrome-plated doors.

Surely this place would offer swank, urban sounds. Sadly, the joint was almost empty, with Fleetwood Mac playing softly on the sound system.

The quintessential Salt Lake City nightclub turned out to be The Bay, a place where there's no smoking, no drinking, and, at least on this night, no live music. Instead, up on the second floor, a few souls were dancing to 1970s disco.

The scene wasn't much livelier in the atrium of the Embassy Suites hotel, a space with the acoustics of an airplane hangar. "I think I may be about the only black jazz piano player in this town," says Frederick McCray, whom many consider the best jazz keyboardist in the city (though he faces scant competition).

"It's sure a lot different than New Orleans, where I grew up," adds McCray, who studied piano with Ellis Marsalis, father of Wynton, Branford, Jason, and Delfeayo.

Sure, he would love to play a bona fide jazz club. Unfortunately, there aren't any here.

Meanwhile, just a few blocks away, locals and tourists were standing in a line half a block long for nearly an hour, hoping to attend a rehearsal of the Mormon Tabernacle Choir in Temple Square.

The music was glorious, but it definitely did not swing.

When it comes to jazz, Salt Lake City certainly defines the music in intriguing ways.

Under the "jazz" category in one record store, one will find CDs by Mannheim Steamroller (a New Age band), Robert Cray (a blues musician), Spyro Gyra (an instrumental pop group), and Yanni (whom jazz musicians often call Yawnni).

Flip on the car radio, and you'll hear hours of Patti Page and Smashing Pumpkins before you encounter any Charlie Parker.

The University of Utah's radio station, KUER-FM, offers a smattering of jazz amid its classical and National Public Radio fare, but the selections lean toward the easy-listening variety.

Clearly, this is not a cutting-edge kind of town, though apparently that's the way the residents want to keep it. City ordinances require that any establishment that's not a restaurant obtain separate licenses to sell beer, wine, and liquor, a laborious and costly process that does not encourage entrepreneurs to open jazz rooms.

Even after acquiring the requisite licenses, however, owners have to operate the places as private clubs, selling yearly memberships. Since most folks can't afford to belong to more than a couple of these establishments, they do not proliferate.

"The private clubs just aren't the kinds of places where hip young singles want to go," says Christina Joslin, associate editor of *Salt Lake Magazine*.

"That's one of the main reasons there's no jazz scene here: the city makes it almost impossible for cafe culture to exist," adds Joslin, who moved here from the East Coast four years ago.

In fact, if you want to hear live jazz, or a rough approximation of it, you have to head to the hills, where most of the ski lodges employ cocktail pianists. Just don't show up in the wee hours of the morning.

"People around here tend to ski hard, have dinner, and go directly to sleep," says pianist Katie Kuhn, a transplanted Chicagoan who works the ski lodge circuit.

Well then, since jazz is a rare bird here, why not find a better name?

After all, when the Washington Senators moved to the Minneapolis–Saint Paul area, they had the good sense to change their name to the Twins. Similarly, when another incarnation of the Senators fled the capital, they were reborn as the Texas Rangers.

"When we first came out here, there was a lot of talk about changing the name, maybe to Utah Saints or Pioneers," Kelly says.

"[But] the NBA said we had to wait a certain amount of time before changing our name," he explains, "and, in the meantime, Jazz just kind of stuck.

"Maybe if we were doing as badly as the L.A. Clippers," quips Kelly, "we'd be eager to change our name, but not now."

June 8, 1997

In 2001 the first Salt Lake City International Jazz Festival emerged in a spectacular downtown setting, placing jazz front and center in a city that hitherto had been tone deaf to the music. Artists such as Dianne Reeves, Eddie Daniels, Wallace Roney, Dave Valentin, Jerry Bergonzi, and Barbara Morrison have brought credibility to an event that, alas, has also featured Debby Boone and Spyro Gyra. In jazz, it sometimes takes a while to get up to tempo.

Heavenly Choir

Kindred spirits gather to record the triumphs and trials of gospel's pioneers.

ALEXANDRIA, Indiana—They came from as far off as Honolulu and as nearby as the South Side of Chicago, and though each was a star in his or her own right, together they represented perhaps the greatest gospel choir ever assembled.

Imagine an opera company made up of Luciano Pavarottis or a string orchestra of Itzhak Perlmans, and you have a general frame of reference for the forces that converged last week on a tiny farm town fifty miles northwest of Indianapolis.

For three days and three nights, from sunup to nearly midnight, the foremost surviving pioneers of gospel music jammed into one room of PineBrook Studios and sang, swayed, laughed, wept, embraced, rejoiced, and, above all, implored the heavens. With camera lights burning hot and cameramen incessantly weaving through the crowd for this close-up or that long shot, the gospel stars—most in their sixties, seventies, and eighties—turned a marathon videotaping session into a sublime church service. True, there were no candles or Bibles in sight, no sermons or vestments, but the thunderous sound of this chorus and the poignance of its life-affirming, redemptory message led one gospel scholar to tell a fellow visitor, "Church is happening in here—they'll never get these singers to come out."

The occasion was the taping of a still-to-be-titled video documentary on the origins of gospel music, and virtually every major survivor of the genre's early years was in attendance: the Barrett Sisters (the most revered trio in gospel), Albertina Walker (founder of the world-renowned but long-defunct Caravans), Inez Andrews (one of the most eloquent gospel singer-songwriters), Dorothy Norwood (a former Caravan who went on to become the reigning storyteller in gospel), and scores more.

Anyone who could tell a story or sing a forgotten song from the old days had taken this pilgrimage to Indiana, in hopes of putting down for posterity what the music was originally meant to be.

"I can't tell you what it feels like to see everybody gathered up here," said DeLois Barrett Campbell, at sixty-seven still leader of the Barrett Sisters, which sings close harmony exquisitely enough to have been nicknamed, years ago, the "Sweet Sisters of Zion."

"I can only say that if I had wings, I could just rise up and fly."

Wings weren't really necessary, though, at least as far as musical flights were concerned. One by one each singer, each trio, each quartet stood up to improvise on one gospel standard or another, with upwards of 150 voices as backup.

Making no concessions to contemporary musical fashion or to commercial considerations, these exultant voices were accompanied by piano and organ alone—no synthesizers, no drum machines, no electric guitars. Nor were there any crossover lyrics aimed to reach wide audiences while diluting the message of faith.

As the three days of sessions unfolded, with voices increasingly hoarse but spirits undiminished, each of the singers took a few minutes here and there to slip out of the room and reminisce on camera about their lives, their hardships, and their personal triumphs. The spoken soliloquies will be used to complement the musical selections on the forthcoming video, scheduled to be released by Ed Smith Productions of Detroit and Bill Gaither Ministries of Alexandria this summer.

"The kids [in gospel] today don't know how easy they have it, or how tough it was on the pioneers," said veteran Indianapolis gospel singer and deejay Robert Turner, who has been leading his Silver Hearts vocal quartet around the country—in a station wagon—for nearly four decades.

"The young gospel singers think it's just something that's handed to you, but that's not how it was. The pioneers would drive [to church services, revival meetings, and concert dates] in old broken-down cars that would hardly move, and they'd end up in towns with no hotels where blacks were allowed to stay, so sometimes they'd sleep and eat and live in that car, too.

"I still drive six hundred miles a weekend, and even in the 1960s we'd get turned away from restaurants and hotels because we were black, so imagine how it was for the earlier gospel singers."

One didn't have to imagine, though, for Albertina Walker, today generally referred to as "the queen of gospel" and "the starmaker" (for her role in launching soloists such as Inez Andrews and Shirley Caesar via the Caravans), spelled it out.

"When I first started singing [professionally]" in the 1940s, recalled Walker, "you'd go to do some concerts for some promoter, and in the middle of the tour he'd tell you to just go home with whatever pennies you had. They just dropped you whenever they felt like it.

"And when we went on the road as the Caravans," the revolutionary, all-star, all-female ensemble that Walker founded in Chicago in the early 1950s, "we would get $250 tops, for all five or six of us, for a tour. And from that we had to get from Chicago to New York and pay for transportation and food and hotel and clean clothes and every single thing. So we weren't eating caviar. We were eating sardines and crackers.

"Or the promoters would tell us that the money would be divided 60–40, but he got the 60 and the five of us shared the 40.

"But you know what? What you don't have, you don't miss. The little we did have, we thought was plenty. We thought we were in the big time, we were seeing places in the country we never saw before.

"Young people say to me, 'I don't know how you made it.' Well, I know exactly how we made it. Through the grace of God. The Lord will keep you—if you want to be kept."

That unshakable faith in the face of adversity, the determination to persevere despite depressing odds, was not unique to Walker and her Caravans but absolutely integral to gospel from its first days, sixty-odd years ago.

Though traditional spirituals and hymns flourished in nineteenth-century black churches, the music took a dramatic turn in 1930, when the wife and infant of blues pianist Thomas Dorsey died during childbirth.

Disconsolate, Dorsey turned away from the blues life and searched for faith and healing in the church. The songs that he wrote, such as "Precious Lord, Take My Hand" and "Peace in the Valley," utterly redefined black church music.

And from Dorsey's organ at Pilgrim Baptist Church, at Thirty-third Street and Indiana Avenue on the South Side of Chicago, generations of young singers learned to sing the new gospel music, among them Mahalia Jackson, Roberta Martin, Sallie Martin (no relation), and, of course, DeLois Barrett Campbell.

Campbell recalled, "I sang in the choir of Thomas A. Dorsey" as a child, and it was Dorsey who taught her the essence of singing gospel: "That it's not just the beat, it's the message."

One gospel legend after another reiterated that sentiment during the taping sessions, as if pleading to young and future generations about what's important, and what isn't, in the making of real gospel music.

"Many young folks are caught up more in the sound than the substance of gospel," said Reverend Maceo L. Woods, a famed gospel organist and pastor at Christian Tabernacle Church on south Prairie Avenue, in Chicago.

"I tell our choir all the time: 'If your spirit is not right, it does not matter how good you sing. You've got to live it. This music should radiate, permeate, illuminate the room if your love of God is in it.'"

Woods, too, knows whereof he speaks, his life in gospel filled equally with peaks and valleys. Consider his solo organ recording of "Amazing Grace," possibly the most popular recorded instrumental in all gospel, with uncounted millions having been sold around the world.

The reason the millions are uncounted, at least as far as Woods is concerned, is because he drew only pocket change from the fortune the record must have earned.

When he made the record in his youth, recalled Woods, "I didn't know the mechanics and the legal aspects" of the music business. "So I don't know how many records were sold, but I do know the compensation was not what it should have been.

"But so be it. More important than the monetary gain is the joy of knowing that that music has touched some people. I'm mature and secure enough to know that nothing good is ever lost. It's a joy to know that whatever I might have done [such as 'Amazing Grace'] might have blessed somebody."

"Amazing Grace" also taught Woods some critical lessons on the ways of the world. Little wonder that the Christian Tabernacle Church, where he is pastor, produces and distributes its own recordings on its Gospel Supreme label. Nevermore would Woods or his congregation be shortchanged.

By the end of this gospel marathon, old friends were bidding each other farewell, kisses and hugs and tears were being exchanged generously. For every gospel pioneer in the house, the past three days had rekindled memories thought long forgotten and had released stories long left unspoken.

"A lot of people don't know this, but when I wrote my first song, in Birmingham, I was working as a domestic," Inez Andrews told a visitor, referring to "No Tears in Heaven," an enduring classic for which, alas, she was never credited or paid.

"I have to look at [young] people nowadays when they say, 'That's not enough money.'

"Well, try working six days a week, ten hours a day, for eighteen dollars a week, doing washing, ironing, cooking, keeping up the kids.

"One day, I was cooking some rice and brown beets, and I felt: 'This wasn't what I wanted to do with my life, this wasn't what I wanted to be.' I felt there was something else, something better.

"And I said to myself, 'Is this all God planned for me?'

"And as I began to say that, I got a pencil and brown paper bag, and I wrote 'No Tears in Heaven.'

"At that time," continued Andrews, "I didn't even know you could get money for writing a song, and Reverend Raspberry asked me to go sing it with him. And then next time I heard that song it was on a record by Sallie Martin. . . .

"So I hope this video they're making here will go into the Smithsonian, because people have to know what happened.

"Personally, I'd like to be remembered as a person who lived the life they sang about.

"And I would hope that my conduct in life would be such that someone would want to see me again on the other side."

February 3, 1994

The aging gospel pioneers continue to sing, though—inevitably—far less frequently than before. Albertina Walker celebrated her eightieth birthday in 2009 with a concert at West Point Baptist Church, on the South Side of Chicago, her spiritual home since her childhood. DeLois Barrett Campbell has been bedridden for years, yet she and the Barrett Sisters appear annually to mark her birthday, singing at the First Church of Deliverance—DeLois in a wheelchair. Inez Andrews performs only sporadically with the Caravans, but in 2006 she joined Walker, Dorothy Norwood, and Delores Washington in a Caravans reunion album, Paved the Way *(Malaco), a bookend to a glorious career.*

Night School

'Round midnight, Professor Von Freeman
teaches his pupils the three Rs:
the riffs, rhythms, and roots of jazz.

The clock just struck midnight, but with the crowds still pouring in and the booze flowing freely, it's clear that the night has only begun.

"Did I see some horn players in the audience?" asks Von Freeman, the legendary Chicago tenor saxophonist who's presiding over the Tuesday night bash at the New Apartment Lounge on the South Side. "Well, open those cases, bring out those instruments, and step forward. Vonski's jam session is now in order."

Before Freeman has finished the sentence, the young saxophonists, trumpeters, guitarists, bassists, and whatnot are noodling on their instruments, all the while making a beeline to the club's tiny stage. Though the cast of aspiring stars ranges from a twenty-year-old student to a seventy-ish retiree, most of the players are young, hungry, and more than a little nervous.

They've been waiting all week for a chance to sit in—however briefly—with one of the foremost improvisers in jazz, septuagenarian tenor master Freeman. For more decades than he probably cares to remember, Freeman has been holding these late-night soirees in one South Side bar or another, inviting all comers to step forward and show what they've got.

"OK, we're going to do 'Billie's Bounce' in B-flat—are you ready?—two, three, four," says Freeman, and with that the impromptu band hits the downbeat, letting out a great and joyous wail.

One by one, Freeman points to this player or that one, each taking a quick solo before slipping back into an ensemble. Some of the twenty-odd players who have turned out this night offer respectable statements, others fumble a bit, stumbling into unfortunate chord changes.

But the spirit of the music-making, its rhythmic exuberance and sonic roar, prove irresistible to the listeners crowded around the bar and packed into an adjoining room. The performance may not always be top-notch, the makeshift band sometimes may seem to be playing in a couple of keys at once, but the sheer spectacle of so many ebullient young musicians trying to keep up with the master makes for great entertainment.

"The first time I ever sat in here, I was really nervous," recalls twenty-year-old trumpeter and music student Donald Richard Jr. between numbers. "I mean, you're playing not only in front of an audience but in front of Von, and you really want to impress him.

"So you get kind of shaky, and after you're done, you go home and practice real hard. You don't want to embarrass yourself again.

"And it works. It makes you practice, it makes you mature, it really helps turn you into a musician."

For uncounted artists over the years, Freeman's midnight sessions have amounted to a kind of jazz finishing school of the most demanding sort. As all the players quickly discover, studying harmony and theory in a lesson or in a classroom is one thing, applying that knowledge to a live performance is quite another.

Despite their anxieties, though, the young musicians just keep on coming, hoping to pick up some wisdom on how to play this elusive, unscripted form of music.

"I've been coming here since June, because this is where you learn," says twenty-three-year-old bassist Eric Harper, who has worked a few professional engagements as a sideman.

"I had read in the paper that Von Freeman held these sessions, and I couldn't believe it. I had been listening to his records since I was a kid, and the chance to be on the same stage with him was too much to pass up.

"Even in these past few months I've learned a lot, in a basic way, about swing, how to project it, how to put ideas across to listeners. Like once when we were playing a blues in F, and I started to mess around with [melodic] ideas with the pianist, and Von said, 'No, no, just swing it, keep swinging.'

"In other words, Von didn't want any fancy passages here. He just wanted to keep the swing feeling going and not let it get bogged down, he wanted it strong, loud, and hard."

When Freeman issues these instructions, the players take his advice as if it were gospel, not only because of Freeman's instrumental virtuosity but also because of the man's artistic pedigree. As this century heads toward a close, there aren't many saxophonists still working who have traded riffs with Charlie Parker, Dexter Gordon, Gene "Jug" Ammons, and other first-generation beboppers.

In effect, Freeman simply is passing along what he learned firsthand from his own idols. His knowledge of phrasing, riffing, tonal inflection, harmonic development, and melody-making is unique and unavailable in the most prestigious music schools.

That Professor Freeman's coursework is free and open to the public makes it all the more tantalizing to young players.

"When you're sitting up there onstage with Von Freeman, it's like you're getting the real thing, the authentic sound," says twenty-five-year-old guitarist Dave Sampson, who has begun to make his living as a professional musician but still comes to study at the source.

"This may sound strange, but it's kind of like getting to play with Michael Jordan of the Bulls. It lifts you up just by standing next to somebody like that."

Even for top-notch professionals, such as twenty-seven-year-old bassist Rob Amster, who's part of Freeman's regular Tuesday night band, the experience is less a working date than a kind of jazz seminar for postgraduates.

"I can only say that when I get onstage with Von, it's like being transported to a different time," says Amster. "You just feel the history of the music with him."

As far as Freeman is concerned, he's doing his part to nurture the tradition.

"When I was a kid on the South Side of Chicago, I sat in with the late and great alto player of Count Basie's band, Tab Smith, and that knocked me out," says Freeman.

"I sat in once with [trumpeter] Hot Lips Page, and then later I worked with his group. I sat in with [trumpeter] Roy Eldridge, and later he hired me, too.

"I even got to sit in with Duke Ellington's band, way back in 1949, and I got to sit in with Bird [Parker] and all those people.

"But back in the late 1930s and '40s, the jam sessions were a big part of the music business—you'd even have tap dancers, singers, comedians come by and join in," adds Freeman, noting that in the 1960s and '70s the scene mostly faded away.

"Now it's coming back, and that's a real good thing," adds Freeman, "but I don't want it to feel like anything but a party."

As the clock pushes toward 1:00 A.M., the music is still going strong. Even when Freeman isn't offering a word of formal instruction or advice, he's teaching the young players about the right tempos for certain pieces, the best keys in which to achieve certain effects, the way to build a solo to a dramatic peak.

The players are absorbing some of these lessons without even knowing it, simply by modeling their performances on Freeman's. Thanks to sessions such as these, the jazz tradition courses virtually uninterrupted from earlier days of this century, when Parker and Dizzy Gillespie were sitting in with their heroes, to its closing moments.

When the young musicians finally hit a big, climactic chord, Freeman brings the set to a close, thanks everyone, and heads to the bar for a sip and a smoke. The youngsters hang around for a few minutes to talk about what just happened, their adrenaline clearly still running high.

"Man, I've got to practice some more," says one of the players to another, as they head out into the night.

"No kidding," answers his friend. "That tempo was brutal."

No doubt they'll be back next week to try again.

March 19, 1996

Remarkably, the eighty-seven-year-old Freeman not only continues to hold Tuesday night sessions at the New Apartment Lounge but, if anything, has made the engagement even more central to his artistic life. Touring less than before and focusing more of his activities at home, he appears more frequently at the New Apartment than anywhere else in the city, including such high-profile rooms as the Jazz Showcase, the Green Mill Jazz Club, and Andy's Jazz Club. And though Freeman remains one of the most tragically under-recorded of major Chicago jazz soloists, a late-in-life burst of activity has resulted in such critically acclaimed releases as Live at the Dakota *(2001),* The Improviser *(2002),* The Great Divide *(2004), and* Good Forever *(2006), all on Chicago-based Premonition Records. In addition, an indispensable boxed set gathering 135 minutes of the aforementioned music has been released under the apt title* The Best of Von Freeman on Premonition *(2007). For Freeman devotees, it's essential listening; for everyone else, it should be.*

III

Havana's Pulse

At the Nexus of Afro-Cuban Jazz

This is the first article of a two-part series entitled "Isolated Genius: How Cuba's Musical Revolution Is Being Muffled."

Homegrown Virtuosos

Even using battered instruments, the Cuban-Soviet system creates masters of jazz.

HAVANA—Without saying a word, teenager Yamile Cruz seats herself at the grand piano, places her slender fingers on the keyboard, and, after a brief pause, unleashes a torrent of sound one might expect from a virtuoso twice her age and size.

Though the battered, perpetually out-of-tune instrument—made ages ago in Moscow—sounds as if its strings might pop at any moment, though the din of traffic outside rushes in through open windows on a sweltering afternoon, the sixteen-year-old has tuned everything out to turn in a masterful performance of Saint-Saens's Piano Concerto No. 2.

Similar scenes are unfolding in practically every chaotic corner of the sprawling Amadeo Roldan Conservatory, a fabled institution in central Havana that has trained some of Cuba's most celebrated musicians. Guitarists, drummers, flutists, percussionists, pianists, you name it, they're making music well beyond their years in the classrooms and hallways and sun-drenched courtyard of a three-story walk-up that looks as if it hasn't had a new coat of paint since Fidel Castro took power, in 1959.

Yet in this decaying building, and others like it scattered across this impoverished city, Cuba is producing musicians of Herculean technique, many of whom have applied their intensive classical training to the art of jazz—and thus have come to tower over their counterparts around the world. Though the roots of Afro-Cuban music run deep in Havana, to the slave trade of centuries past, the last two generations have yielded larger-than-life jazz players whose mastery of their instruments and exalted level of musicianship enable them to conquer audiences wherever jazz is played.

Exactly why Cuban jazz musicians sound consistently brilliant may be a mystery to the outside world, but in Havana it is no secret: after Castro forged his alliance with the former Soviet Union in the early 1960s, the island quickly saw an influx of Russian and Soviet-bloc music teachers. They brought with them techniques that had been producing monumental classical virtuosos since the nineteenth century. And though the fall of the U.S.S.R. in the early 1990s meant that financial support from Moscow virtually vanished, the Russian methods had become integral to Cuban music education and remain so to this day.

The merger of Cuban musical tradition and rigorous Soviet teaching has produced some of the most imposing jazz players of the past forty years. Yet for every Chucho Valdes and Gonzalo Rubalcaba, who have broken through the United States' long-running embargo of Cuba to win acclaim in the States and beyond, uncounted others feel doomed to a lifetime of obscurity. Unable to bring their gifts to the international marketplace because they have great difficulty getting into the States, where most of the world's musical stars are merchandised, the Cuban giants languish well outside the spotlight.

These musicians—some old and tired of battling against the effects of the embargo, others young, poor, and frustrated by their inability to make contact with U.S. listeners—are creating a music as complex and profound as anything available in jazz today. But they were not featured in the *Buena Vista Social Club* film, which in 1999 popularized a small group of aged Cuban musicians, and few listeners outside Cuba get to hear today's exceptional players.

With political tensions between Washington and Havana on the rise during the past couple of years, and with the United States granting entry visas only sparingly to Cuban musicians, the Cuban jazz artists realize that their prospects are getting worse.

"If Cuban musicians would have a chance to enter the great distribution of the United States, we could show everyone that some of the most important music in the world is being made here, in Havana," says the esteemed Cuban bandleader Jorge Gomez. Gomez has toiled for thirty years in the Cuban music industry but was allowed into the United States to perform just once, in 1986.

"Without us, the world is losing one of the most important roots of music."

As well as some of the most formidable jazz artists working today.

Ernan Lopez-Nussa, a forty-four-year-old jazz pianist admired in Havana but virtually unknown in the United States (despite a brief tour in 1999), can see himself in the faces of the gifted youngsters making music at the Amadeo Roldan Conservatory.

It was in this building, near the intersection of two dusty, noisy roads in central Havana, that Lopez-Nussa spent more than a decade studying the harmonic intricacies of Bartok, the technical idiosyncrasies of Liszt, and the keyboard poetry of Chopin. Though Lopez-Nussa, like the students today, spent mornings studying math, science, and literature, in the afternoons he pored over musical scores, practiced ear-training exercises, and polished his technique at the piano.

He didn't realize it at the time, but Lopez-Nussa was coming of age at an extraordinary moment in Cuban culture, the mid-1960s and '70s, when the ancient traditions of folkloric Cuban music were being galvanized by the techniques of Soviet musicians who had been sent to the island by the Kremlin. Suddenly, students who attended the Amadeo Roldan Conservatory were not only being taught the noble works of Cuban composers such as Roldan and Ernesto Lecouna but were also being drilled in the ferociously difficult keyboard exercises of Anton Rubinstein, Nikolai Rubinstein, and other giant Russian pedagogues. To Lopez-Nussa, this Cuban-Soviet training seemed the most natural thing in the world, but it was unprecedented in Cuban history and laid the groundwork for a musical revolution yet to come.

"I cannot say that we students loved being here—we certainly never loved this building," says Lopez-Nussa, who's greeted with hugs and kisses from students and teachers alike as he makes an impromptu visit to the conservatory, which trains pre-university students.

"Even now, the conditions are terrible, the pianos are terrible, the noise from outside is terrible, the practice rooms are filled with distractions.

"To tell you the truth, I do not understand how the kids here learn to make music in such a difficult place.

"Yet somehow we forget about everything else and concentrate on the music."

In truth, the children have no choice, their teachers placing the same demands upon them as had been made on such earlier Russian super-virtuosos as Vladimir Horowitz, Sviatoslav Richter, Emil Gilels, David Oistrakh, Mstislav Rostropovich, and scores more.

"Something incredible happened in this building, and it continues to happen today," says Roberto Catala de la Hoz, director of the conservatory, which opened on October 2, 1903.

"When we got the great professors from Russia, and they joined with the great Cuban professors, the students started to play at an incredible level, unimaginable.

"The Russians have a tradition of tremendous technique—speed and accuracy and power on their instruments. And the Russian method became our method.

"It is very strict, very disciplined, and it is at the center of what happens here."

Adds Mayra Torralba, assistant director of the conservatory, "The Russians brought us the knowledge of how to study music, all the experience they had acquired in more than a century. And we adapted their methods into our reality."

That much is obvious in every studio in the conservatory, where young Cuban musicians still play from Soviet scores, the titles of works and the composers' names written in a Cyrillic alphabet that is impenetrable to the students. Moreover, the youngsters make music on grand pianos bearing the names not of Steinway or Baldwin but of Moscba (or Moscow) and Estonia. Compared with modern-day American and German instruments, the Soviet models sound dull, metallic, and poorly constructed.

Yet on these wrecks, as in Lopez-Nussa's youth, the students fire off scales with phenomenal speed and accuracy, meanwhile playing melodic phrases with a degree of sensitivity and introspection one does not associate with Russian-school training. In effect, the young Cuban musicians are reaping the best of two worlds: monumental Soviet technique and ardent Afro-Caribbean melodicism.

As Lopez-Nussa strolls through hallways of the Amadeo Roldan Conservatory, he knocks on individual practice-room doors, sticking his head in to hear one young musician bringing demonic rhythmic drive to a Bartok dance, another finding sublime lyricism in a Chopin ballade.

But these youngsters are practically beginners compared with the university-level students preparing to play on the international stage—should they ever get the chance.

Before Castro's revolution, the lush acreage along Calle 120, in an upscale neighborhood, was a country club, its rolling hills a golfer's paradise, its spacious main building a posh restaurant and plush hotel.

But after 1959 it was nationalized and transformed into the Instituto Superior de Arte (Institute of Superior Arts), the place where Lopez-Nussa obtained his artist's diploma and new waves of great Cuban musicians have been trained.

Here, the students—who play on instruments not much better than the ones at Amadeo Roldan—are old enough to have found their calling in jazz. You can hear it by strolling past some of the practice rooms, where swing rhythms and blue-note scales intermingle with Beethoven's trills and Liszt's arpeggios.

In one practice room, two young marimba players are firing off syncopated riffs so complex and fast-moving you might guess that American vibes masters Bobby Hutcherson and Stefon Harris were wielding the mallets. In another room, a group of percussionists is laying down gently swaying backbeats of the sort that could keep a mambo jam session going for hours.

And in yet another, a young pianist takes a pause from practicing a Chopin ballade to talk about his heroes—jazz pianists Oscar Peterson and Chucho Valdes.

"I have one goal for after I graduate—to have a jazz band of my own," says Alejandro Vargas, age twenty-one. "Everyone at the school knows it. My professor knows it, and he thinks it's great.

"But when I am in his studio, I am not supposed to play jazz. I am to play only classical—Beethoven and Chopin and Debussy."

Indeed, no one graduates without mastering the classical repertory, which means that aspiring jazz players like Vargas pick up the art of jazz improvisation in the same way that American jazz musicians long have done: by listening to records and repeating and transforming what they've heard on the bandstand.

Since the embargo prevents them from buying the CDs, the youngsters befriend professional musicians in the nightclubs, then go to their homes to listen to the American jazz CDs the musicians have picked up during European tours. Then the young Cubans try out the tunes in the streets.

When they play American jazz, however, they cannot help but redefine the music with the Cuban dance rhythms and song forms they have heard all their lives. Played by the young Cuban jazzmen, tunes such as Miles Davis's "So What" convey gorgeous layers of rhythm and counterpoint, as well as the fluid technique and sophisticated harmonic sense the youngsters have learned in the conservatory.

Thus when emerging Cuban musicians take turns riffing with pros such as pianist Danilo Perez during the recent Havana International Jazz Festival, the Americans are startled by what they hear.

"These kids have accomplished so much with so little," says Perez, after leading a master class with a roomful of gifted young players. "Their passion for this music is unbelievable."

In essence, the nascent Cuban jazz players are following an artistic path established by artists such as Valdes and Rubalcaba and Lopez-Nussa before them.

Valdes, above all, proved that the merger of Soviet-style technique and Afro-Cuban jazz could create a cross-cultural music so brilliant and powerful that it could pierce the wall separating Cuba and the United States. By establishing the great Cuban band Irakere in the 1970s and touring it first on the island, and then around the world, Valdes and his followers brought Cuban jazz musicians a prominence not seen since the days when artists such as percussionist Chano Pozo and bandleader Mario Bauza collaborated with Dizzy Gillespie in the 1940s.

But this time the Cuban jazz revolution was homegrown, based in Havana and not dependent on the cosponsorship of an American star such as Gillespie. Moreover, emerging Cuban musicians in the 1970s were blessed not only with conservatory training but with the deep vein of Cuban folkloric music that they grew up hearing. From fantastically accomplished *congueros* such as Tata Guines and Changuito they learned to hear and reproduce the multiple layers of rhythm that are at the heart of Cuban music. From elder pianists such as the late Frank Emilio—whose tune "Mandinga, Mondonga, Sandunga" holds a place in Cuban culture roughly equivalent to George Gershwin's "I Got Rhythm" in the United States—they learned that jazz and Cuban music were as compatible as rum and coke. Historic Cuban musical forms such as *danzon, son,* rumba, and cha cha cha were easily integrated into American swing rhythm.

Perhaps it's no coincidence that so many of the classically trained Cuban jazz musicians who conquered the music world came from families already steeped in folkloric Cuban music and American jazz. Valdes's father, pianist Bebo, led the sensational dance band at the Tropicana nightclub, which from 1939 to this day stands as the most opulent showroom in Havana. Rubalcaba's father, Guillermo, was widely applauded for the exquisite *charanga* dance bands he still leads around Cuba. And Lopez-Nussa was the fortunate son of a pianist mother who often traveled to Europe and brought back recordings of Louis Armstrong, Charlie Parker, Oscar Peterson, Art Tatum, Count Basie, and John Coltrane.

When Lopez-Nussa tells the young Vargas of the populist backgrounds of so many of the best Cuban jazz pianists, the twenty-one-year-old musician practically beams.

"My father plays in the jazz bands too," Vargas says. "Maybe I will be the next Lopez-Nussa."

He's not the only one who's nurturing big dreams. In a nearby practice room, a young musician is struggling with Cuban dance rhythm, slowly playing dance beats while counting aloud "One, two, three, four" in endless repetition. But this is no Cuban musician—it's an American who has come to Havana to study with the masters.

"Havana is the heart of Latin music, and there's no better place on earth to study rhythm," says Andrew Turpening, age twenty-eight, of Saint Paul.

"In a way, it's impossible to compete with the Cuban jazz musicians—their folklore and their training gives them the edge.

"I was lucky. I got a license to come here. When I get back to the States, the other musicians are not going to believe the rhythms that I'll be able to play. Then I'll have the edge."

The most remarkable music-making at the institute takes place not inside the great conservatory but outdoors, where the wind and brass students are playing to the heavens. This is the norm in Cuban music education, which encourages students to play outdoors so that they can sound big and as bold as possible.

Put these same players in a jazz club or concert hall, and they sound as if their lungs are twice normal size. Perhaps this is why Cuban trumpeters such as Arturo Sandoval and Jesus Alemany (of Cubanismo) sound as huge as all outdoors.

"When we're not in class, we're always out here, practicing, blowing, trying to make our sound big," says Kervin Barretto, a twenty-year-old trumpeter.

Then Barretto puts his horn to his lips and begins a lightning-fast version of "A Night in Tunisia," a tip of the hat to the great Gillespie, who wrote the tune.

Another young trumpeter a few feet away picks up the theme, the two quickly exchanging riffs as if having a conversation on the nature and meaning of jazz.

"This is the music that a lot of the students here want to play," says trumpeter Jorge Miguel Vistel Serrano, age twenty. "But sometimes we feel that everyone in the world is trying to stop us, that everything is against us."

But it won't be until later in the evening, when Serrano has left the school to play at a Havana jazz club, that the depth of his frustration and the hopelessness of his situation will become fully apparent.

Until then, he tilts his horn skyward and lets out a great blast of sound, a mighty horn call if ever there was one.

Lopez-Nussa listens admiringly, then shakes his head.

"Imagine what he could do if he could come to America."

February 2, 2003

This is the second article of a two-part series entitled "Isolated Genius: How Cuba's Musical Revolution Is Being Muffled."

"I May Never Get to the Heart of Jazz"

HAVANA—Just before showtime, a couple of aspiring young Cuban jazz musicians crowd into the cramped bathroom of a basement nightclub, place their horns to their lips, look dead ahead into a smudged mirror, and start blasting away.

Neither the brittle sound nor the harsh, fluorescent lighting of this makeshift rehearsal space is easy to take, yet by the time the two men emerge from the bathroom to stand before the microphones, they're on fire, playing John Coltrane's "Giant Steps" as if their lives depended on it.

For all the urgency and passion of their work, however, they're practically despondent after their first set, which they consider inadequate.

"Until I heard American jazz musicians performing live, I thought I was a good jazz player," says Jorge Miguel Vistel Serrano, a much talked-about twenty-year-old Cuban trumpeter who studies at one of the country's top conservatories, the Instituto Superior de Arte (Institute of Superior Arts).

"But after I heard [trombonist] Steve Turre and [trumpeter] Roy Hargrove in person, I realized how far I am from the truth of this music.

"If I can't come to America," adds Serrano, "I may never get to the heart of jazz."

Whether or not Serrano and his colleague, nineteen-year-old saxophonist Luis Deniz, need to be in the States to master the elusive art of improvising jazz is open to debate. Yet there's no question that Serrano and Deniz, as well as uncounted Cuban jazz musicians young and old, increasingly find themselves trapped on this island.

Beyond the embargo that the United States placed on Cuba in the early 1960s, nearly eliminating financial ties between the two countries, the States passed tough new visa laws in the wake of the terrorist attacks of September 11, 2001. Both the U.S.A. Patriot Act of 2001 and the Enhanced Border Security and Visa Entry Reform Act of 2002 added new hurdles for foreign nationals attempting to visit the States. And though the new rules blocked artists of many nationalities from performing in the States, the restrictions have been acutely felt by Cuban musicians, who already had experienced four decades of barriers.

"We're trying to enforce the law as aggressively as Congress intended," says Tony Fratto, a spokesman for the U.S. Treasury Department, which oversees U.S.-Cuba commerce under its Office of Foreign Assets Control.

While U.S. officials had loosened their interpretations of the embargo during the 1990s, leading to the busy American touring schedules of Cuban musicians in the *Buena Vista Social Club* film and recording, the tide turned dramatically with the arrival of the Bush administration.

"I don't want to speak for the previous administration and what it did, or if the nuances of its enforcement of the embargo were different," Fratto adds.

"When we came into Treasury, we looked at our jobs, and the job of the Office of Foreign Assets Control is to enforce the Cuban sanctions program, and we try to make sure to do that."

With the United States clamping down on interaction between the two countries, the opportunities for emerging talents such as Serrano and acknowledged giants such as pianists Chucho Valdes and Ernan Lopez-Nussa to visit America have diminished significantly. At the same time, American musicians and their managers have complained of increasing red tape in getting into Cuba, which has curtailed musical contact between the artists of two nations.

American and Cuban musicians alike lament the opportunities that have been lost, as well as the promising musical careers that never will get started. And they wonder why a decades-old political dispute between two nations can interrupt an artistic exchange that dates to the nineteenth century and has produced so much groundbreaking music.

"American music and Cuban music have been like sisters for very long," says Lopez-Nussa, an acclaimed Cuban jazz pianist who's virtually unknown in the States, where he has toured just once, in 1999.

"You can find in the ragtime music of New Orleans the same rhythms you hear in Cuban music, because in the nineteenth century people traveled between New Orleans and Havana all the time. The syncopated habanera rhythms of Spain and Cuba are not so far from the syncopated rhythms of Jelly Roll Morton.

"We speak similar musical languages, but now the conversation is being stopped."

~

A capacity crowd has gathered inside one of Havana's top jazz rooms, La Zorra y El Cuervo (The Fox and the Crow), enthusiastically greeting the young band that takes the stage.

Once trumpeter Serrano, saxophonist Deniz, and their rhythm section begin playing, it's clear not only that they have mastered their instruments but that they have carefully studied recordings that Miles Davis cut with John Coltrane in the 1950s and Wayne Shorter in the '60s. The wide-open, fervently lyrical character of Serrano's trumpet lines and the high-energy solos of Deniz's tenor saxophone represent a credible response to the groundbreaking work of Davis's great first and second quintets.

But Serrano and Deniz also have imbued their performance with the unmistakable influences of more recent American players, including the bravura trumpet playing of Roy Hargrove and Wallace Roney and the harmonically nimble tenor saxophone work of Joe Lovano and Branford Marsalis.

"I don't own any American jazz records, but I've listened to a lot of them," says Serrano, who has won several jazz competitions in Havana.

No amount of listening to recordings, however, prepared Serrano and Deniz for hearing American jazz musicians live, during the Havana International Jazz Festival in 2000 and 2002. The biennial event awakened the young men and their friends to the full glory of improvised jazz, an art form to which they already had decided to dedicate their lives.

But the encounters with America's jazz stars also showed them the artistic implications of being cut off from face-to-face contact with the United States.

"When I played with trombonist Steve Turre earlier today, I almost fell down from the excitement, and from realizing how much I still do not know," says Serrano, who participated in a master class at the Instituto Superior de Arte led by Turre, a brilliant New York jazz musician. "I realized that the only way to fuse our Cuban music with jazz is to play with the American musicians, just like the Americans learn Cuban rhythm by coming to Havana to play with us."

But Serrano knows full well that he has about as much chance of fulfilling his dream of coming to the United States to study at Boston's Berklee College of Music, arguably the top jazz conservatory in the States, as he has of finding $19,200 in annual tuition lying on Calle 23, the famed—if potholed—street on which La Zorra y El Cuervo is located. Even if, by some miracle, Serrano were to locate an American sponsor who might back him, the young Cuban trumpeter probably would not get into the States because of the new visa hurdles that he would have to finesse.

"Bringing Cubans to the United States became tremendously more difficult with the beginning of the Bush administration," says Bob Guild, a program director at New Jersey–based Marazul Charters, which facilitates travel between the two countries.

"Basically, the application process takes longer than it ever did before, and whether or not a Cuban musician finally is going to get a visa is totally unpredictable."

Treasury Department spokesman Fratta says that there has not been a slowdown in processing applications. But, he adds, "some people may have noticed an increase in the numbers of penalties for people who violate the embargo, and perhaps a slowdown in the processing of appeals of these penalties."

Some of the most pronounced effects of the chill in U.S.-Cuba relations have stemmed from the Enhanced Border Security and Visa Entry Reform Act of 2002, which went into effect last August and added new barriers to visitors from foreign nations considered state supporters of international terrorism. Cuba is on this list, along with Iran, Iraq, Libya, North Korea, Sudan, and Syria.

"Even if the slowdown in issuing is simply due to the backlog caused by the new legislation, the fact remains that it's getting harder for Cuban musicians to come to the States," says a Chicago attorney who specializes in these cases but declined to be identified.

Others point to the unfortunate case of Polo Montanez, an immensely popular Cuban singer who was going to tour major American cities last fall. When his managers realized the bureaucratic obstacles involved in bringing him to the United States, they canceled the tour.

~

On November 26, Montanez, whose real name was Fernando Borrego, was killed in an auto accident in Havana, at age forty-seven.

"Now no one in the U.S. will ever hear Montanez," said San Francisco immigration lawyer Bill Martinez, who was involved in making arrangements for the aborted U.S. tour.

"How many more opportunities to hear great music, how many more opportunities to speak with each other, are we going to miss?"

For a young Cuban musician such as saxophonist Deniz, the obstacles to getting to America have become virtually impossible to transcend.

"You see our problem," says Deniz, between sets at the jazz club.

"You can learn to be a great musician in Cuba, and you can get very good at playing a kind of Afro-Cuban jazz.

"But unless you come to play in the U.S., like Chucho Valdes and Gonzalo Rubalcaba did, even if it's for a short while, you never will become as good a jazz musician as you were meant to be.

"And you certainly will never be heard of by anyone in the U.S."

What Deniz, Serrano, and their young colleagues may not realize is that even Valdes, Lopez-Nussa, and others of their stature are having just as much trouble getting past the U.S. border.

During last year's Latin Grammy Awards, held in Los Angeles in May, twenty-two musicians from Cuba were not allowed into the United States to take part in the proceedings. Among those kept out was Cuba's most prominent jazz musician, Valdes, who came to America regularly in the 1990s but now has trouble getting in.

"We just finally succeeded in getting Chucho into New York a couple of weeks ago, but literally until the last minute we had no idea if he would be able to make his engagement at the Village Vanguard," says Martinez.

"Chucho was scheduled to leave on a Saturday morning, but his paperwork from the States did not come through until 3:55 P.M. on Friday, the day before," continues Martinez.

"Simply not knowing whether you'll be able to make an engagement in the U.S., not knowing whether the paperwork will come through on time, is enough to kill your career in the U.S., even if you're lucky to already have started one, like Chucho."

Indeed, after Lopez-Nussa received glowing reviews following his American debut engagement, in 1999, the pianist believed that his American career was off and running. Managers across the United States were queuing up to present the next great Cuban pianist, but two planned tours fell apart when Lopez-Nussa could not get permission to enter the States.

Since then, no American manager has been willing to take a chance on Lopez-Nussa, or his greatly accomplished colleagues, for fear that up-front costs spent on booking clubs and running advertisements will be lost when the United States decides not to provide a visa.

"When I played in the United States in 1999, it was one of the greatest experiences of my musical career," says Lopez-Nussa.

"I felt when I was playing in the Chicago Cultural Center, for example, that the people were with me every beat, that they understood what I was trying to do at the keyboard, that they felt and followed the development of the tune.

"But when the follow-up tours fell apart, the managers in the States weren't interested anymore."

Meanwhile, American musicians trying to travel to Cuba to share what they know and to learn about Afro-Cuban jazz are running into similar roadblocks.

At last December's Havana International Jazz Festival, many American performers and managers complained about the difficulty involved in clearing required paperwork through Washington on time. The strictures for Americans visiting and working in Cuba are based upon regulations issued by the United States in 1963 under the Trading with the Enemy Act. "The basic goal of the sanctions," reads a Treasury Department summation of the rules, is "to isolate the Cuban government economically and deprive it of U.S. dollars."

The recent, tough enforcement of this doctrine has made it increasingly difficult to obtain the licenses, say the American musicians.

"I never had it so hard getting into Havana as I did this time," Turre said.

Added Larry Clothier, a prominent manager of American jazz artists, "This may be the last time in a long time that you'll see American musicians coming to Havana in any numbers."

But it isn't just the bureaucratic hassles that express the icy state of U.S.-Cuba relations.

In past years, the American Interests Section in Havana—which serves as the U.S. mission there—planned lavish receptions for American and Cuban musicians playing at the Havana International Jazz Festival. In December, however, the American Interests Section didn't acknowledge the arrival of American jazz artists and their followers, let alone host them.

When asked to articulate American policy on travel to Cuba, an American Interests Section representative said that Americans visiting Cuba without the proper licenses would be subject to prosecution to the full extent of the law.

American musicians who have difficulty getting into Cuba face no significant damage to their careers, for they still benefit from the promotional muscle that American record companies and booking agencies provide them around the world.

The Cubans who cannot come to America, however, say they face a considerable hardship, because the U.S. embargo and tightened travel policies do more than just cut them off from the players they admire most and from the biggest, most lucrative market in the world. The embargo also chokes off their international performing and recording careers, they say.

"To be cut off from America is, in a way, to be cut off from most of the world's music industry," says Jorge Gomez, whose Moncada band holds a legendary stature in Cuba but is virtually unknown in the United States.

"When you go to Italy, you see America's MTV and VH1 on the television. But you don't see the Cuban artists on there, because of the embargo.

"So even though we can go to Europe, the effect is much smaller than if you have the promotion of the United States.

"When it comes down to it, if you want to make an impact on the world of Latin music, you always have to deal with executives in New York or Miami," adds Gomez. "If you can't get to them, you have problems."

Without the promotional push that American corporate interests can produce, however, a Cuban jazz musician is lucky if he sells a thousand copies of a CD, Gomez says.

Moreover, isolation from the United States, as well as the generally distressed state of Cuba's economy, has left Cuba's jazz musicians without the tools that their American and European counterparts take for granted. The latest microphones, synthesizers, musical instruments, and recording technology are well out of reach for most Cuban players, whose limited careers cannot support high-priced gadgetry.

Yet the Cuban musicians justly take pride in how much they have achieved without these tools, creating a music that remains more technically virtuosic and historically informed than that of any other jazz musicians in the world—even if the instruments often are dilapidated and the technology out of date.

Consider just a few recent examples. Though Americans haven't yet heard it, Lopez-Nussa's new band Habana Report merges ancient Afro-Cuban rhythms with sleek, contemporary jazz improvisation in astonishingly fluid, natural, and graceful ways. The music, superbly documented on the *Habana Report* CD (on the Unicornio label), eventually turned up on iTunes.

Gomez's band Moncado, meanwhile, performs with an ensemble precision and a joyous dance-beat fervor that might create a sensation in the United States—if they could be heard here (the band toured the States once, in 1986).

Why don't the Cuban musicians just defect to Europe, then make their way to the States?

"Why should I have to move outside of my country to be a Cuban jazz musician?" Gomez asks.

"Why should I have to become a European or an American?"

Adds Lopez-Nussa, "I need the Cuban life to play the music I play. If I went to live in Paris or New York or Chicago, not only my music would change but my life would change. I would need to do a hundred different things to make a living.

"Here I just make music. I need the beautiful old buildings and the traffic and the cigars and, most important, the other Cuban musicians to make the music I know. If I took myself away from this music and this place, it would not be me anymore."

Certainly the riches of Cuban culture are ample, as is apparent one afternoon during a music industry party at the Tropicana, Havana's most opulent nightclub.

On this occasion, however, the main attraction isn't the scantily clad dancers but Cuban singers and instrumentalists convening at an annual party hosted by BIS Music, a record label that has specialized in Cuban fare since 1995.

One by one, great artists such as the septuagenarian singer Omara Portuondo and the emerging singer-songwriter William Vivanco take the stage, their work collectively attesting to the vibrancy of Cuban jazz and jazz-tinged music to this day.

"Where else in the world are you going to hear music like this?" the Havana music journalist Guille Vilar asks a visitor.

Nowhere.

Yet these monumental artists languish in Cuba, revered by their fans, but increasingly cut off from the United States and overlooked wherever U.S. interests prevail.

Day to day, they live decent, if not luxurious lives, the best jazz artists typically enjoying the comforts of a two- or three-bedroom apartment, a Soviet car, a well-worn musical instrument, and, perhaps, a home computer. The most successful of the artists obtain satellite TV by buying the satellite dishes in Europe, assembling them in Havana, and planting them in their backyards, where the satellites pick up everything from CNN to Bravo.

Even the most prosperous musicians, however, endure some of the hardships that fall on most everyone in Havana, including the rolling blackouts in a city perpetually starved for electricity and paychecks in Cuban pesos, which are accepted nowhere else in the world (and therefore keep Cubans tied to the island).

But the musicians say they are willing to withstand these difficulties in order to preserve their identity as Cuban jazz artists.

Still, they yearn for the day when they can come to America as easily as they can travel to Europe or South America, and show the world what it has been missing.

"If I could come to America, everything would be possible," says Serrano, the talented young trumpeter.

"I do not see how I am such a danger to America."

February 9, 2003

During the course of the Bush administration, relations between the United States and Cuba—which had thawed in the 1990s—entered an increasingly deep chill. In addition to the continued impact of the aforementioned U.S.A. Patriot Act of 2001 and the Enhanced Border Security and Visa Entry Reform Act of 2002, Cuban musicians hoping to tour America encountered new obstacles in the Intelligence Reform and Terrorism Prevention Act of 2004; the Border Protection, Antiterrorism, and Illegal Immigration Control Act of 2005; the 2006 reauthorization of the U.S.A. Patriot Act; the Safe Port Act of 2006; and the 21st Century Emergency Communications Act of 2006. Inevitably, fewer Cuban musicians traveled north, and those who did appeared less frequently than before; and scant American musicians and listeners reciprocated. Even Chucho Valdes, perhaps the most internationally celebrated Cuban artist still touring, plays only sporadically in the States; and the next generation's stars, such as Ernan Lopez-Nussa, hardly at all. The Obama administration has eased some restrictions on Cuban-Americans who wish to travel to the island and transfer money there, but no cultural impact has yet been apparent.

Link to the Past: Compay Segundo Upholds the Traditions of a More Romantic Era

HAVANA—Seated comfortably on the balcony of the Hotel Nacional and savoring his ever-present cigar, singer-guitarist Compay Segundo begins to reflect on his ninety-three years. He hardly could have chosen a more appropriate setting.

Like the Nacional itself, the man looks every inch a holdover from a decidedly more romantic era. His impeccably pressed suit, suavely tilted straw hat, and silk handkerchief tucked neatly into a breast pocket recall an age when men dressed elegantly even for an afternoon smoke. In this era, couples routinely danced late into the night in the ballroom of the Nacional, a once-plush hotel that has faded since the days when Frank Sinatra and Nat "King" Cole stayed there during jaunts to the capital of Caribbean nightlife. If the hotel looks a bit worn, reflecting the poverty of a country still reeling under the United States' economic embargo, Compay Segundo surprisingly does not. His nimble wit, vivid memory, and expansive soliloquies certainly are not typical of men who have lived nearly a century.

"I am the oldest musician in the whole world," he says in his majestic bass-baritone, which will resonate in Symphony Center on Monday during a belated Chicago debut.

"Some people say I am the music."

And in a very real sense he is, for Compay Segundo helped develop the poetic musical form that he symbolizes to listeners around the world, the *son*. Though its melodies are easily singable and its harmonies comparatively straightforward, the *son* carries an expressive power much deeper than its simple structure might suggest. Like the blues in the United States, it is a musical form that achieves added profundity when delivered by its most accomplished practitioners.

When Compay Segundo sings this music—accompanying himself on guitar, *tres,* or *armonica* (a seven-string instrument that's a kind of cross between guitar and *tres*)—there's no question that listeners are hearing the genre in the purest form possible.

Moreover, from his pen came some of the most beloved songs created on the island and exported around the world, including "Chan Chan" and "Te Apartes de Mi." Both are likely to turn up during his Chicago concert, an event he is looking forward to "because everyone in Cuba knows Chicago, the great city of jazz and blues."

Yet Compay Segundo, who was born Francisco Repilado Muñoz in the Cuban city of Siboney (province of Santiago), hastens to note that he does not claim to be the inventor of a musical tradition that resonated on the island long before he was born. Rather, he extends into a new millennium the music of the early Cuban *trovadores* he has revered since his youth, when he heard masters such as Sindo Garay.

"My music, my inspiration comes from this group of *trovadores,* they were like our mentors," he says. "I was inspired by them to play my music. It is a music I learned in the streets and only later learned by studying."

That mixture of streets and sophistication, of oral tradition and diligent study, long has distinguished many idioms of Cuban music, from hyper-virtuosic Afro-Cuban jazz to unabashedly populist ballroom dance. Somehow, several generations of Cuban musicians have been able to seduce a broad public while creating music of extraordinary emotional depth and melodic subtlety.

But for Compay Segundo, stardom has come surprisingly late in life. Though he played *tres* and clarinet in the early 1920s and toiled for years as an instrumentalist in such notable bands as El Conjunto Matamoros, he didn't really begin to attain recognition until 1942, when he and Lorenzo Hierrezuelo formed Los Compadres. The duo, which thrived for more than a decade, not only put both vocalists on the map but gave an emerging star his nickname, Compay Segundo—a reference to the "second voice" bass line that he sang.

When the two singers parted ways in 1953, Compay Segundo performed sporadically as a soloist, though devoting most of his time to working in a cigar factory and raising five children. Nevertheless, his own band, Compay Segundo y sus Muchachos (Compay Segundo and His Boys), gave the man an opportunity to continue to mature as a singer and songwriter.

By the time he retired from rolling cigars, a distinctly Cuban art that he still regards as seriously as any tune he sings, Compay Segundo was hardly seeking international acclaim. But the ardor of his singing and its fidelity to earlier *trova* traditions was making him a known quantity in Latin American culture, inspiring an invitation to play the Smithsonian Institution in 1989 and increasing touring thereafter.

Even so, the man never contemplated the kind of fame he would achieve as a result of his appearance in the film and recording of the *Buena Vista Social Club*, which made a nonagenarian acoustic musician into an unlikely pop star.

"When I walk down the street in Cuba, it is almost impossible for me, because everyone seems to know me," he says, speaking through an interpreter. "When I was in Madrid, the police pulled over my car and the driver thought he had made a violation. But the officer said, 'I stopped you because this is Compay Segundo, and I wanted to meet him.' "

Yet there may be something more than fleeting celebrity at work here. The intense reaction that Compay Segundo inspires among both Latin American and Anglo audiences suggests that the man has tapped a deeper human response.

To the public, perhaps he represents not only another Cuban traditionalist catapulted into the spotlight by *Buena Vista Social Club* but also an extraordinary link to nineteenth-century cultural values that have long since disappeared from modern life.

"I've always wanted to remain the old way, when people were more romantic and more loving," he says, characteristically using the language of the poet.

"Today, when young people dance, they make a lot of movement, a lot of sexual movement. They don't seem to want to dance cheek to cheek, they consider this old-fashioned. But for me it's lovely to feel the heat of a woman dancing, and maybe this is the romance that people hear in my music.

"It's something that they long for, although they may not even know it. But I can see it when I perform. The men and women, they come closer when they are listening to our concert."

Yet even the great Compay Segundo, who takes pride in noting that his grandmother lived to the age of 115, knows he cannot uphold glorious nineteenth-century cultural traditions forever. The question is whether this music can survive after he and his slightly younger peers no longer are romancing the world with their haunting Cuban nocturnes.

"I absolutely believe so," says his son, Salvador Repilado, a bassist who travels and records with Compay Segundo. "I think that is one of the reasons that my father and other musicians here in Cuba are working so hard and performing so much—so that the new generation will hear this music and value it."

Cuba's foremost singing nonagenarian concurs.

"I think this music is a lasting thing, the kids are being exposed to it in Cuba, and I hope that's going to develop a sense of continuation in them for the future," he says.

"In Cuba, you know, 'Chan Chan' is a big hit for kids, and all sorts of artists are doing their own versions of that song," he adds. "It is a good sign."

September 17, 2000

On September 18, 2000, Compay Segundo gave his first and last performance in Chicago, transforming a large auditorium into a tightly intimate space, complete with audience sing-along. "Even those familiar with the deep burnish of the man's vocals from his appearance in the Buena Vista Social Club *film and recording must have been struck by his improvisational prowess as instrumentalist," I noted in a review. "As if intent on reaffirming the immutable links among several Latin musical idioms, Compay Segundo touched on practically every genre he must have encountered in nearly a century's worth of listening. If 'Salud a Chango' ('Homage to Chango') pointed to the straightforward lyricism of Afro-Cuban son, 'Maria en la Playa' ('Maria on the Beach') captured the rhythmic exuberance of classic merengue. . . . But this evening reached back even further, to the emergence of Cuban trovadores of the late nineteenth century. So long as Compay Segundo is among us, that era lives." Compay Segundo died July 13, 2003, at age ninety-five, in his Havana home, at the pinnacle of his career and global recognition. Thousands accompanied his casket through the streets of Santiago de Cuba, his hometown, throwing flowers at his coffin. At his burial there, his fans sang "Chan Chan," the tune for which he was best known around the world. The subsequent deaths of vocalist Ibrahim Ferrer; singer Pio Leyva; bassists Israel "Cachao" Lopez (a progenitor of the mambo) and Orlando Cachaito Lopez (his nephew and the oft-described "heartbeat" of the* Buena Vista Social Club*); pianist Ruben Gonzalez (also celebrated in the* Buena Vista Social Club*); and conga virtuoso Tata Guines virtually silenced a generation of pre-Castro Cuban romantics. Their work echoes in the memories of those fortunate enough to have heard them.*

Back in the Swing: The Spotlight Is Finally Reaching an Early Master of Afro-Cuban Jazz

Just a few years ago, the enormously influential composer-bandleader Arturo "Chico" O'Farrill considered himself the forgotten man of a musical genre he helped invent, Afro-Cuban jazz.

Though admired by music historians and praised by the likes of Dizzy Gillespie and Tito Puente—both beneficiaries of O'Farrill's innovations—O'Farrill essentially had vanished from America's musical radar. The man who had been at the vanguard of merging Afro-Cuban rhythm with American jazz harmony and phrasing in late 1940s New York hadn't recorded an album under his own name for roughly thirty years. Worse, O'Farrill lacked a working band to perform his seminal compositions and to serve as a laboratory for new ones. So no one was more surprised than O'Farrill to find himself back in the swing in 1995. His majestic recording *Pure Emotion* not only restored the composer to public view but snared a Grammy nomination and spawned two follow-up discs: *Heart of a Legend* and a new CD to be released next month.

Whether or not *Heart of a Legend* wins a Latin Grammy at next month's awards ceremony in Los Angeles, the nomination affirms that O'Farrill is back, and with a vengeance. As he approaches his seventy-ninth birthday, he's savoring the kind of delayed recognition that often eludes jazz masters until long after they're gone.

"I was shocked," says O'Farrill, with characteristic forthrightness, in recalling his reaction to the popular and critical acclaim that has been so late in arriving.

"When we were making the *Pure Emotion* record I said to myself, 'Who's going to like this music today? It's not rock 'n' roll.'"

But in an era when American audiences increasingly have become attuned to various forms of world music, O'Farrill's Afro-Cuban repertoire was poised to rise again.

The sensational commercial success of the *Buena Vista Social Club* movie and disc surely didn't hurt, but the palpable nostalgia of the *Buena Vista* music stands at the opposite end of the Afro-Cuban spectrum.

If *Buena Vista* offered a luxuriant nostalgia trip into pre-Castro Cuban musical tradition, both *Heart of a Legend* and *Pure Emotion* attested to the contemporary tone, adventurous spirit, and complex instrumental textures of O'Farrill's best work.

Moreover, the man is a jazz musician to the core, preferring hard-charging orchestral charts ignited by brilliant horn solos to the genteel *danzon* and sweetly lyric *son* of his native Cuba. O'Farrill, in other words, didn't merely export Cuban song forms to New York when he moved there in 1948. Rather, he reenergized American big-band conventions with the ferociously syncopated clave rhythms he had heard since his youth in Cuba.

As if that weren't enough, he conceived his Cuban-tinged jazz compositions on an epic scale, proving that the merger of American jazz and ancient Cuban rhythms could yield works as vast and imposing as masterworks by Beethoven or Brahms.

The achievement, widely acknowledged by connoisseurs, should become more apparent to the general public when O'Farrill's newest disc is released. For the first time in decades, listeners will hear fresh recordings of O'Farrill's behemoths, his *Afro-Cuban Jazz Suite* and *Aztec Suite* of the 1950s. And the state-of-the-art recording technology, says O'Farrill, "lets you hear things that most people have never heard in recordings of this music."

But if O'Farrill ranks with such Afro-Cuban titans as composer-arranger Mario Bauza, bandleader Machito, and percussionist Chano Pozo, the riddle remains: why has broader public recognition come so late?

"A big part of it is because Chico was not really a bandleader—he was a composer first and foremost," says Arturo O'Farrill Jr., the composer's son, collaborator, and co-leader of Chico O'Farrill's Afro-Cuban Jazz Big Band.

"His main gig was at the writing desk, and that's why Chico never received the fame he deserved."

Indeed, since Chico O'Farrill didn't lead a famous band like Machito's, didn't attain the instrumental virtuosity of Pozo, and didn't develop a stage persona like Puente's or Gillespie's, he never really became an entertainment commodity in the United States. Instead, O'Farrill penned compositions and arrangements that enabled others to bask in the spotlight.

But viewed in toto, his life's work commands considerable stature.

For starters, O'Farrill helped codify the emerging Afro-Cuban jazz of the 1940s and '50s. Because he had been schooled in the art of classical composition (by Felix Guerrero in Cuba and Stefan Wolpe and Hall Overton in New York), he was equipped to capture an emerging art form on paper. And with the encouragement of jazz producer Norman Granz, by 1950 O'Farrill was writing vast jazz suites, accomplishing in Afro-Cuban idioms what Duke Ellington was doing in ambitious extended works such as *Black, Brown and Beige*, *Deep South Suite*, and *Liberian Suite*.

"To me, Chico's contribution is that he's the first real composer of Latin jazz," says Arturo O'Farrill. "Not just because he used larger forms, but because he thinks like a composer. He deals with themes, motifs, tonal centers—the same issues that Beethoven dealt with in writing a piano concerto."

But O'Farrill's journey to this level of achievement was neither easy nor predictable. Born in Havana to a family with ancestry in Ireland (hence the unlikely surname), O'Farrill got into so much mischief as a youth that his parents sent him to the Riverside Military Academy in Georgia in the late 1930s, hoping he might shape up. Instead, he was seduced by American jazz.

"They sent me to military school to get some discipline, and they made a big mistake," says O'Farrill with a laugh. "Because that was where I heard the big bands for the first time. I heard Benny Goodman, Glenn Miller, Tommy Dorsey, and I fell in love with that music.

"When I went back to Cuba, I was supposed to go to study law in Havana. No hope for that."

Uninspired by the older forms of Cuban music that dominated the island in his youth, O'Farrill moved to Manhattan in 1948 and immersed himself in the "Cubop" scene, collaborating with Machito, Pazo, Bauza, Gillespie, and others in nurturing an explosive merger of Cuban rhythm and American bebop. Two years later O'Farrill began penning monumental jazz works, including his *Afro-Cuban Jazz Suite* (1950), *Second Afro-Cuban Jazz Suite* (1952), *Manteca Suite* (1954), and *Aztec Suite* (1959).

But the rise of Elvis Presley and rock 'n' roll in the 1950s did not augur well for O'Farrill's brand of music-making, and his assignments dried up with astonishing speed. By 1960 he was leading a band in Mexico, and even when he returned to New York, in 1965, he slipped into the anonymity of writing charts for the Count Basie band and cranking out TV and radio jingles.

Some observers have criticized O'Farrill for going the commercial route, with saxophonist-bandleader Paquito D'Rivera recently telling the *Los Angeles Times,* "I think Chico could have been another Ernesto Lecuona," perhaps the preeminent Cuban composer of the twentieth century, "if he had decided to go that path. . . . But Chico spent too much time in the studios. I understand why he did it, because the money was very good, but he's one of the most original of our Cuban musicians."

O'Farrill's son disagrees, however, that O'Farrill made the wrong move.

"My father was very happy to make the money, because we had some very lean years, some real economic duress," says Arturo O'Farrill.

"Nobody wanted my father's art music, so he did the other. It's very hard to write without being asked to. But all the commercial music he wrote, it was all high quality."

Nevertheless, Chico O'Farrill was watching his career as a jazz composer crumble.

"Partially, I was sad about what was happening," he says. "But partially I told myself, 'Well, things change. Either you accept it and face it, or you do nothing.' "

At the very least, O'Farrill's commercial work kept his writing-arranging chops in working order, so that when producer Todd Barkan hit on the idea of a comeback album in 1995, O'Farrill was eager to start. His third such disc should cement O'Farrill's place back at the top of the jazz world.

Though the composer does not wax philosophical on the meaning of his reemergence, preferring to focus on the music, his return to the spotlight is bittersweet, says his son.

"It's a very emotional thing for him," explains Arturo O'Farrill. "A lot of the music that is being recorded now really for the first time in his life is music he wrote a long time ago. And he gets very melancholic to hear it, because it reminds him of a younger place in his life.

"Also, while my father would never admit it, I believe he felt a little anger and embarrassment that the larger jazz community didn't record him earlier.

"But, like everyone else, he's grateful to be appreciated—even if it's so late."

August 20, 2000

~

Arturo Chico O'Farrill died June 27, 2001, in New York Hospital, at age seventy-nine. In the last hours of his life, a recording of his work "Gold, Frankincense and Myrrh" played in his room in intensive care, as he had requested several days earlier. His son, Arturo O'Farrill Jr., remains the most fervent champion of his music, having created the Afro-Latin Jazz Orchestra for Jazz at Lincoln Center, in New York, in 2002. The group's debut album, Una Noche Inolvidable, *took a Grammy nomination in 2006 and was followed by the poetic* Song for Chico. *The band, which left Jazz at Lincoln Center in 2007, now is based at New York's Symphony Space and continues to perform around the world.*

Latin Evolution: The Remarkable Cachao Is the Real Mambo King

It inspired an international dance craze in the 1950s, a Pulitzer Prize–winning novel in the '80s, and a major Hollywood movie in the '90s.

But the lilting Cuban rhythm known as the mambo is much subtler and more profound than its many commercial spinoffs might suggest. Indeed, only in the past year or so have American audiences come to know the splendor of the mambo—and related dance forms—thanks to the late-breaking stardom of a septuagenarian Cuban musician known simply as Cachao (pronounced ka-CHOW).

Though Oscar Hijuelos's 1989 novel *The Mambo Kings Play Songs of Love* drew wide critical acclaim and inspired a 1992 film starring Armand Assante and Antonio Banderas, its protagonists—loosely based on Cuban musicians of the 1950s—were artistic descendants of the real mambo king, Cachao. Hijuelos eloquently chronicled the adventures of the Cuban virtuosos who arrived in New York in the 1950s, but Cachao's equally remarkable story dates at least a generation earlier.

What's more, it's a tale that would have been lost to the world were it not for a mesmerizing documentary film, *Cachao . . . Like His Rhythm, There Is No Other,* and a splendid recording, *Cachao: The Master Sessions, Vol. 1,* both released last year. With the newly issued video version of the film (on Epic) and a striking follow-up CD, *Master Sessions, Vol. 2* (Crescent Moon/Epic), Cachao once again finds himself thrust belatedly into the limelight.

"I certainly never expected anything like this," says Cachao, speaking through a translator from his rented apartment in Miami. "I am a musician. I never dreamed I would be in movies."

The film and the recordings that star Cachao, however, do more than point a spotlight on a deserving musician. More important, they detail Cachao's seminal role in the evolution of Latin music and document the grandeur of the music itself.

For Cachao, who was born Israel Lopez, the musical journey began in 1922, when, as a four-year-old in Havana, he took up the double bass. His interest was not surprising, considering that fully thirty-five members of his extended family played the instrument.

"I studied with my father, Pedro Lopez, and my [older] brother, Orestes Lopez, and when they couldn't teach me, my uncle, my aunt, my mother taught me," says Cachao, with a laugh.

"Everybody in the family taught me—I could not escape it."

By the time he was eight, Cachao was performing publicly in a Havana pop group ("The Band of the Beautiful Sea"), and at twelve he had advanced to no less than the Havana Philharmonic Orchestra. Though Cachao had to be perched on a soapbox to stand even with his colleagues in the bass section, he held his own in Havana's top classical orchestra for years to come.

With this kind of experience, and with his remarkable pedigree, perhaps it was no surprise that by age twenty-two, Cachao—joined by his brother Orestes—would conceive a composition that would set a new beat for popular Cuban music. They titled their work simply "Mambo."

"The word 'mambo' comes from the people of the Congo, from certain tribes in Africa," explains Cachao. "It was a little syncopated song that they would sing to the children to put them to sleep. . . . And every one of these little songs had a little different story, almost like a nursery rhyme, which African people knew since they were children.

"And that was the inspiration for our 'Mambo,' although what we created was very different from their mambos."

Indeed, if the ancient African form of the genre was rhythmically gentle and lilting, its Cuban counterpart bristled with syncopations and shifting musical accents. As Cachao says in the film, "The Cubans have an infinite amount of rhythms," and many of them inexorably worked their way into his "Mambo," first recorded in 1939.

"We thought it was going to be a big hit, but the dancers really hesitated, because it was too fast.

"At that time in Cuba, there was a lot of romanticism, the *danzon* was really strong, so we slowed down our 'Mambo,' and that is when it really took off."

In other words, the mambo that American audiences later would consume in the television appearances of Desi Arnaz and in the immensely popular recordings of Perez Prado and Xavier Cugat, among others, bore only a distant relation to the real thing. If the American mambo was fast, loud, and heavily accented, its more authentic forebear was intensely lyrical, romantic, rhythmically intricate, and never rushed.

That much is apparent from both volumes of Cachao's recent *Master Sessions* recordings, but especially from the first. Here, Cachao's original "Mambo" exudes a lyric sophistication as well as a gently undulating backbeat.

Even so, Cachao does not begrudge those such as Prado and Cugat who later would popularize the mambo and other Cuban dance idioms in somewhat corrupted form. On the contrary, Cachao thanks them.

"I love Perez Prado, and all Cuban musicians of any stature owe a lot to him," says Cachao. "They all respect him for his creativity and his ability, and, more important, for his marketing ability.

"He was the guy who, along with [singer] Benny More, was able to take the mambo and internationalize it, to get the attention of the whole world, and we are all eternally grateful to him for it. If he popularized it in a faster form, so what?

"And it wasn't like today, when you can get the word out instantly and promote it. At that time, things worked real slowly, but Perez Prado broke those doors down, and we all were able to jump on board."

Cachao, however, didn't jump on board. While such colleagues as Machito, Mario Bauza, Chano Pozo, and others went to New York in the 1940s and '50s and made great names for themselves, Cachao stayed behind in Havana, refining the traditions he had helped invent.

By 1957 he was creating yet a new sound, with his fabled recordings of the *Cuban Jam Sessions* or *Descargas*. Never before had anyone gathered Havana's top musicians in a recording studio for a freewheeling improv session. The musical results were revolutionary, merging Cuban musical idioms with the improvisatory techniques and rhythmic swing of African American jazz.

"When the *Descargas* started out, the idea wasn't anything more than to just get all the best musicians in the studio and just jam," says Cachao. "They all knew each other, and they were all pretty much doing straight [nonjazz] gigs.

"And what happened was that as people started coming in, everybody got inspired, and they started getting pretty serious about this, and we wound up having some pretty tremendous sessions. The sessions were so informal and so unstructured that the tapes actually sat around for a couple of years before someone came along, heard them, and decided to release them.

"And it turned out they were important, because here the Latin musicians [in Cuba] were able to show that they, too, were part of the tradition of improvisation and inspiration."

By 1962 Cachao had fled Cuba, working thereafter in Europe and the United States in relative obscurity, though revered by anyone who understood the legacy of Cuban music.

Among his admirers was actor Andy Garcia, who was born in Cuba and whose family was known to Cachao. With his Hollywood clout, Garcia arranged to film a 1992 Miami concert featuring Cachao in an updated *Jam Sessions* show, which resulted in the *Cachao* movie and the two recordings.

"It was all masterminded by Cachao," Garcia has said, referring to the weeklong recording sessions that produced both of the CDs. "It was a historical event. The music was like a live organism of sound . . . and he's the driving force of the rhythm."

In the film, Garcia asks Cachao about the future.

"I am an old man," says the maestro, who's now seventy-seven, "and the only thing I ask young people is that they maintain the tradition."

Certainly Cachao has done his part in establishing it.

December 17, 1995

Like pianist Bebo Valdes, Compay Segundo, and the Buena Vista Social Club, Israel "Cachao" Lopez enjoyed an unexpected career resurgence at the end of the twentieth century. In his case, it extended into the twenty-first, Cachao recording with Cuban pianist Bebo Valdes on the Grammy Award–winning album El Arte del Sabor, *receiving a star on the Hollywood Walk of Fame, and winning a National Heritage Fellowship from the National Endowment for the Arts. Cachao died March 22, 2008, in Coral Gables, Florida, at age eighty-nine.*

Sound Architect: *Buena Vista*'s Unsung Hero Brings His Band to Chicago

According to conventional wisdom, the sensational success of the *Buena Vista Social Club* CD and film—as well the general resurgence of interest in Cuban music—is to a large degree the handiwork of American guitarist Ry Cooder. The story goes that Cooder ventured to Havana in 1996, rounded up musicians who had been forgotten even by the Cuban public, and recorded them, thereby resuscitating careers and sparking renewed interest in Cuban musical culture in the United States and around the world.

Cooder indeed took part in the *Buena Vista Social Club* recording dates but, alas, a bit too much credit may have been showered upon him. For without the efforts of Juan de Marcos Gonzalez, a native Cuban musician who has been championing indigenous sounds at least since the 1970s, Cooder might still be in Havana trying to dig up phone numbers for such faded stars as nonagenarian singer-guitarist Compay Segundo and octogenarian pianist Ruben Gonzalez.

Though Cooder played an important role in establishing the link between Cuban artists and the American record industry, the musical architect of *Buena Vista Social Club* and several subsequent recordings was Gonzalez, a fact widely known within the world of Cuban music but barely acknowledged outside of it.

"Yes, it is a little sad that people don't always know what I did, but it's much more important that the music of our culture is heard," says Gonzalez, who will lead his Afro-Cuban All Stars in concert Thursday at the Chicago Theatre.

"For some people, maybe it's comfortable to think that someone from America came to Cuba and saved these musicians, and that is fine. But the idea to bring the old guys to life was mine."

Indeed, Gonzalez began his campaign in the late 1970s, when he created the legendary Sierra Maestra, a band that celebrated historic Afro-Cuban musical forms and by the '80s had emerged as one of the most important nonrock ensembles on the island. With its repertoire of exquisitely lyrical *son* and intricately conceived Afro-Cuban jazz, Sierra

Maestra foreshadowed the revival of interest in traditional musical forms among listeners in Cuba, the United States, and beyond.

"We created Sierra Maestra to bring to the youth the sound of the original Cuban music," explains Gonzalez, who's known across the island simply as Juan de Marcos.

"Basically, we tried to make a revolution in the taste of the youth. And we accomplished it, because Sierra Maestra became maybe the most important group in Cuba in the 1980s. Our main object was to show the youth that we in Cuba had a history, a very important history.

"It was important that young Cubans have the spirit of this music inside of them, to discover themselves through this music."

The remarkable artistic success Gonzalez achieved by bringing young and old musicians together in Sierra Maestra inspired him to follow the same approach when Cooder and the World Circuit/Nonesuch label came calling in Havana in 1996. But it was Gonzalez and his wife and artistic collaborator, Gliceria, who located the forgotten Cuban virtuosos and brought them to Havana's Egrem recording studio to cut the *Buena Vista Social Club* recording. The sessions went so well that they also yielded two more pivotal recordings: *Introducing Ruben Gonzalez* and the Afro-Cuban All Stars' *A Toda Cuba le Gusta.*

"The man who brought us back to the world and to the United States was Juan de Marcos, the passion was his," recalled Compay Segundo, speaking through an interpreter, during a conversation a year ago in Havana. "Juan de Marcos believed the world would embrace us once again, and he was right. For this he deserves tremendous credit."

To Gonzalez, however, it's a wonder that no one else had thought of bringing back to the international stage Cuba's genre-defining artists.

"For some of the musicians that my wife and I found, it was like a dream when we came to them and said we wanted to record them again," recalls Gonzalez. "Ibrahim Ferrer thought it was a joke, because nobody cared about him anymore. Ruben Gonzalez said, 'Thank you very much for believing in me,' which was very touching to us.

"But I always have believed in the mixing of generations, because the youth brings strength and energy to their performances, and the old guys bring the real Cuban history. Probably I'm a bit idealistic, but this is the way I think."

This distinctive blending of youthful exuberance and hard-won experience has given listeners a poignant view of one of the world's most vibrant musical cultures. Because slaves from various African tribes, as well as immigrants from Spain and the Caribbean, have long lived in Cuba, the island has always been a cauldron of exotic musical experimentation.

Gonzalez has captured at least a few of these strains in the recordings he has produced, and they have ranked among the most admired world-music CDs. Most recently, he and his Afro-Cuban All Stars have brought out *Distinto, diferente* (World Circuit/Nonesuch), which explores more contemporary facets of Cuban music.

For Americans, especially, these recordings have been invaluable, since the sounds of Cuba have been difficult to come by during the United States' long-running embargo of the island.

Moreover, the critical and commercial success of these albums has made Gonzalez a recognized force in the music business, which is why he plans to open his own London-based label within the next year. The new, still-to-be-named label will document ancient and modern Cuban music, from historic *charanga* to Cuban pop, with Gonzalez making his recordings on the island but distributing them via London.

Should Gonzalez's label take flight, the man might finally receive the wider recognition that he deserves. Even if he doesn't, however, at least the aficionados will know that he was the musician who produced the most important Cuban recording sessions of recent years (in addition to singing and playing *tres* and guitar on these discs).

But even a producer-musician as formidable as Gonzalez knows that the United States' infatuation with any passing fad—in this case, Cuban music—is temporary at best.

"Right now we are in the boom, but the boom is going to pass, of course," says Gonzalez, age forty-five. "What's going to remain is that Cuban music at least will be a valid option for audiences, just as it was before 1959," when the U.S. government began to isolate Cuba.

"Our music completely disappeared off the market then, but now we are back."

And the lion's share of the credit belongs to Gonzalez.

April 2, 2000

Juan de Marcos Gonzalez did create his record label, DM Ahora, based in Cuba, with administrative support in London. He continues to tour the globe with the Afro-Cuban All Stars, though now the name refers to a younger generation of musicians—expatriates who do not live on the island. The glamour and media attention have faded, just as Gonzalez predicted, but his campaign to disseminate the music has not.

IV

Musings on Satchmo

Behind the Famous Facade (in Two Parts)

In the last twenty-plus years of his life, Louis Armstrong documented his personal thoughts and observations on self-made, diary-like tape recordings. This is the first of two articles that reveal the content of Armstrong's private, reel-to-reel tapes.

Jazz Giant's Private Views Show Anger Behind Smile

Though many jazz musicians saw Louis Armstrong as a sellout, he personally seethed at the racism he endured.

FLUSHING, NEW YORK—To people around the world, he was the perpetually grinning black jazzman who brought comic relief to films such as *Hello, Dolly,* with Barbra Streisand, and *High Society,* with Bing Crosby and Frank Sinatra.

To many jazz musicians who admired his art but loathed his public persona, he was at best a "clown," as trumpeter Miles Davis once called him, and at worst a promoter of a "plantation image," in the words of bebop giant Dizzy Gillespie. But as the world prepares to celebrate the centennial of Louis Armstrong's birth on August 4, a new portrait of him is about to emerge, revealing that he privately seethed at the racism he endured throughout his life.

Armstrong—the first jazz icon, as well as the public face of the music to this day—often erupted into high-decibel rants at the injustices routinely accorded people of color in the United States. He threatened to walk off the set of movies in production, privately blasted entertainers who nurtured black stereotypes, became transfixed with TV coverage of the assassination of Reverend Martin Luther King Jr., and railed at the unrelenting prejudice he saw in sports, culture, and practically every other facet of American life.

These revelations, contained in hundreds of hours of previously undocumented tape recordings examined by the *Tribune,* fundamentally alter Armstrong's image in the great civil rights battles of the twentieth century and render at least partly obsolete more than a dozen biographies of the entertainer.

Created from the late 1940s until his death in 1971, Armstrong's homemade tapes for the first time document his private thoughts—in uncensored fashion—on the "shame" of racism in America, as he called it in the tapes.

"This punk is going to hand me . . . that [expletive]?" Armstrong shouts on one of the tapes, recalling how he blasted a white workman who insulted him. "You try to be a gentleman, they won't let you, that's all. I'm just showing you what we have to go through."

Considering Armstrong's lifelong public reticence on racial politics, as well as his perpetually optimistic stage manner, his often acidic comments on the tapes defy long-held assumptions about the man's supposed lack of interest in the plight of blacks in America. With the exception of a single, well-publicized incident—when in 1957 Armstrong publicly criticized President Dwight D. Eisenhower for failing to take swifter action to enforce school desegregation in Little Rock, Arkansas—Armstrong had long been deemed disturbingly mute on the subject of racism.

The tapes fill this void, though it will take years before scholars measure the full import of these recordings.

The tapes have been stored in a vault at the Louis Armstrong Archives at Queens College in Flushing, about a ten-minute drive from the home that Armstrong and his fourth wife, Lucille, shared in the nearby Corona neighborhood beginning in 1943. The trumpeter's taped discourses cover several subjects, yet no single ideology can sum up Armstrong's wide-ranging philosophies on the subject of race.

"Of course not, Louis is a very complicated person, a phenomenal artist, and we're not going to fully understand the complexities of a creator of his stature," said Albert Murray, an esteemed author on black culture and, at age eighty-five, a firsthand observer of the rise of Armstrong, Duke Ellington, Count Basie, and other American jazz masters.

"If Louis is going to talk about race, it's going to be deep stuff," added Murray, speaking from his Manhattan apartment. "This is not mere political etiquette. He is not going to have any ideology that he got from somebody else. He's going to make a decision and take responsibility for it."

And record it.

Fascinated by the reel-to-reel tape recorders that became commercially available in the United States after World War II, Armstrong took the machines with him on the road in a custom-made traveling case. He kept the tapes rolling while friends visited him in hotel rooms, often failing to inform guests that the conversations were being recorded and sometimes himself half-forgetting that his words were being preserved.

As a result, Armstrong can be heard uninhibitedly producing fiery soliloquies on racism, punctuated by the saltiest street language. But Armstrong also ripped civil rights champions such as Josephine Baker and Marcus Garvey, whom he explicitly condemned as exploiters, rather than healers, of racial woes. In addition, he is heard criticizing some black Americans in general and reciting jokes that demean a variety of races, including whites, blacks, and Asians.

The startling range of Armstrong's sentiments, from outrage at racism to indulgence in the worst racial slurs, indicate a man apparently torn and tormented by race in America—quite the contrary of the jovial image he consistently projected onstage, screen, and recordings.

"I'll tell you an incident that happened right at the Brown Derby [restaurant] since I've been here in Honolulu," Armstrong tells a friend on one of the recordings. "You remember that white boy, he's a sailor or something, on one of these battleships, on Pearl Harbor, and he caught my show, and I come to find out he has damn near every record I made from childbirth.

"He come up and shook my hand after the whole show was over . . . and he said, 'You know, I don't like Negroes.'

"Right to my [expletive] face, that [expletive] told me. And so I said, 'Well, I admire your [expletive] sincerity.'

"And he said, 'I don't like Negroes, but you're one [expletive] I'm crazy about. I've got every [expletive] record.'

"I've said it for years. You take the majority of white people," continued Armstrong, "they always got one [expletive] at least that they're just crazy about, [expletive]. Every white man in the world got one [expletive] at least that they just love his dirty drawers."

As a general philosophy, Armstrong believed that black Americans simply had to endure these blows, according to several statements on the tapes. Though espousing this point of view in words, he sometimes contradicted it in deeds.

Advising a friend who had witnessed an incident of blatant racism in collegiate football, Armstrong said, "You just have to live it down. You just have to go through it—it's a shame."

But then he immediately recalled reacting quite differently under similar circumstances.

"Like on the set there, when I'm making *Glory Alley*," added Armstrong, referring to a 1952 film in which he had a cameo role, alongside Leslie Caron, Ralph Meeker, and Gilbert Roland.

"This ofay," said Armstrong, using an antiquated, slightly pejorative term for a white person, "he wasn't nothing but a callboy. He'll come to the stars' dressing rooms and let them know when they want them for the camera. . . . He'll come up [and say], 'Mr. Gilbert Roland, Mr. Meeker, Miss Caron,' and everything.

"And then he'll come to my dressing room with a whole lot of [expletive]: 'Satchmo, you better come on out there. . . .'

"I said, 'Listen you [expletive]. . . . You tell MGM to shove that picture up their [expletive]. . . .

"I said, 'I ain't no movie star.' I said, 'Why are you on me with that [expletive]? 'Cause I'm colored?'. . .

"All the bigwigs were out there too," added Armstrong, referring to studio executives, to whom he threatened to quit if he weren't treated the same as everyone else on the set.

Armstrong held no more affection for black actors who showed a comparable lack of respect for their race. Stepin Fetchit, who earned millions portraying black Americans in stereotypical fashion, "is kind of playing catch-up," as Armstrong delicately put it on the tapes, referring to the out-of-date, minstrel-show nature of his act. "That's the worst thing in the world in show business."

Ultimately, Armstrong devised a strategy for dealing with racial discrimination that was as complex as any solo he ever played. For the most part, he avoided direct confrontation unless absolutely goaded into it. Meanwhile, he continued to portray himself onstage as the perpetually upbeat entertainer, a strategy that made him immensely popular among a broad, diverse audience but also drew attacks from socially conscious concertgoers of various races.

The criticism, which only increased during the turbulent 1950s and '60s, took its toll on Armstrong's reputation as an artist, with biographers such as Laurence Bergreen noting in *Louis Armstrong: An Extravagant Life* that Armstrong never could shake his "Uncle Tom reputation." But Bergreen did not know that after Martin Luther King Jr. was assassinated in 1968, Armstrong was mesmerized by the television coverage of the tragedy, taping hours of it for future reference.

"Even Armstrong's demeanor seemed suspect in a day when jazz musicians were doing everything they could to avoid the label of entertainer," wrote Gary Giddins in *Satchmo*. "Jazz musicians were demanding respect as artists, and Armstrong, who was paradoxically the most respected of all jazz musicians, seemed to undermine their cause. He had too much fun out there. It was embarrassing. Artists don't grin and mug and roll their eyes."

But Armstrong had a ready answer for such criticisms.

"Showmanship does not mean you're not serious," he said on the tapes. His jocular stage manner, he explained, simply represented a means of disarming a predominantly white and therefore potentially hostile audience.

To many jazz musicians who have followed in Armstrong's wake, the man had a point.

"Sometimes his artistry is not held in high regard because of his showmanship and his antics onstage," said New Orleans trumpeter Nicholas Payton, today's leading proponent of Armstrong's clarion trumpet style. "The way Armstrong acted was part of his genius, that he could bring such a high level of art into his performances, yet do it in a way that would appeal to the common, ordinary person. That's a great achievement.

"Plus, it's because of a Louis Armstrong that the doors of the music industry were opened to later people who then could take on certain attitudes, like Miles Davis."

Regardless, the tapes—which are being cataloged by the Louis Armstrong Archives—inevitably will give Armstrong a long-overdue opportunity to be heard more fully on the subject of race, an appropriate turn of events for a man who shattered racial barriers early in the century.

The tapes were acquired by the archives in 1987 but only recently sorted out from the rest of Armstrong's cache of memorabilia (including eighty-six self-made scrapbooks, hundreds of LPs, and thousands of pages of personal documents). They stand to put new generations more closely in touch with the real Armstrong.

"Our ultimate goal is to get some of these tapes out on sale around the world so that everyone can listen to them," said archives executive director Michael Cogswell.

When the tapes reach record stores, presumably several years down the road, they likely will startle listeners with Armstrong's frank discussions of artists who tried to "pass" as white and with his prescient observations on political correctness as applied to song lyrics.

The man may not have let on, but race never was far from his consciousness.

"He was not satisfied with the way things were, and many times he let the people who were harassing him know exactly how he felt," said Selma Heraldo, age seventy-eight, Armstrong's former next-door neighbor in Corona, who sometimes accompanied the Armstrongs on tour.

"He often expressed himself."

July 29, 2001

In the last twenty-plus years of his life, Louis Armstrong documented his personal thoughts and observations on self-made, diary-like tape recordings. This is the second of two articles that reveal the content of Armstrong's private, reel-to-reel tapes.

The Thoroughly Human Side of a Jazz Virtuoso

FLUSHING, NEW YORK—The raspy voice may be instantly recognizable, but the words come as a shock.

For Louis Armstrong—whose centennial is being celebrated around the world this weekend—was not supposed to be an angry, somewhat embittered man. Perpetually cast as eager-to-please in films such as *The Glenn Miller Story* and *The Five Pennies,* practically deified as the embodiment of American optimism in Ken Burns's TV documentary *Jazz* and seen smiling broadly even in recent soft-drink commercials, Armstrong generally has been portrayed as a one-dimensional, nearly angelic figure. But the torrent of words that the trumpeter unleashes in hundreds of hours of homemade tape recordings, examined by the *Tribune* at the Louis Armstrong Archives at Queens College in Flushing, suggests that there was much more to the man's personality and attitudes than biographers, filmmakers, and cultural historians have realized. Indeed, Armstrong proves thoroughly human on these recordings, nourishing grudges, cursing enemies, smarting over insults, and telling racial, ethnic, and sexual jokes that are cruder than crude.

Whether or not Armstrong intended the recordings to be heard publicly, thereby shattering the ever-smiling public image he helped create, is open to debate. Yet he bequeathed to his self-named foundation more than 650 reels of tape made from the late 1940s until his death, in 1971, so certainly he must have realized that someone eventually would listen in on the intimate conversations and soliloquies he recorded. Sooner or later, then, the world would hear how he really felt about everything from sex to music to money.

Apart from Armstrong's seething resentment over racism in America, the man stewed over plenty of other issues as well, starting with the shenanigans of Joe "King" Oliver, the New Orleans trumpeter whom Armstrong publicly credited as his chief inspiration. It was Oliver, after all, who had given the young Satchmo pointers on playing cornet back home in the Crescent City, and it was Oliver who summoned his protégé to Chicago in 1922, in effect launching Armstrong's professional career.

In private, however, Armstrong's comments on Oliver were not entirely enthusiastic, citing "all that . . . crap" that Oliver put him through. It was Armstrong's wife, Chicago pianist Lil Hardin, who pointed out to him the true nature of Oliver's feelings toward the gifted cornetist.

Oliver, says Armstrong on the tapes, "did make a statement to Lil, during a conversation, [when] he said: 'As long as little Louis is with me, he can't hurt me.'" In other words, so long as Oliver could keep Armstrong in his shadow, playing second trumpet in Oliver's band, the younger man could not supersede his mentor.

But Armstrong's wife wouldn't let Oliver get away with it.

"She'd say, 'As much as you idolize him, daddy, you must leave him immediately, because King Oliver and his ego and wounded vanity may hurt you,'" says Armstrong on the tapes. "'It's all indication that King Oliver is trying to hold you back.'

"I didn't say or mumble a word," adds Armstrong, shocked that "a thought like that [was] in King Oliver's mind.

"I didn't say one word, even after she told me, I didn't say nothing. I just split, that's all," says Armstrong, meaning that in 1924 he quit Oliver's band in Chicago, finally realizing that Oliver would see to it that Armstrong never got very far in Chicago.

Perhaps it was not so surprising that Oliver—or any soloist, for that matter—would feel threatened by the gloriously robust tone, flawless technique, and brilliant high Cs that the young Armstrong dispatched at will. Naively, Oliver did not realize that talent of this magnitude cannot be stopped.

Even so, it would take the great Satchmo a couple more years to assert his preeminence, for when Armstrong arrived in New York to join Fletcher Henderson's big band, in 1924, he encountered more abuse. The bandleader and his players, in fact, went out of their way to crush Armstrong's ambitions.

"Fletcher only let me play third cornet in his band, the whole time I was in his band—dig that [expletive]," says Armstrong on one of the tapes.

"He'd only give me sixteen bars the most to get off with. But he let me hit—oh, come on now, I got to tell it like it is, or like it was—he let me hit those high notes that . . . the prima-donna first chair men couldn't hit.

"Here's a funny thing. Every time he'd give me credit for hitting a note, he always had a little, you know, 'pep talk' for me. He'd say, 'Hey, that was wonderful. You know, you'd be very good if you'd go take some lessons.'

"I'd say, 'Yes sir,' and in my head, you know, to myself, I'm saying, 'Man, you go [expletive] yourself. . . . He didn't dig me, so to hell with it. . . ."

Henderson's put-downs, as well as the sloppy playing of the band, speeded up Armstrong's return to Chicago, in 1925, where his career finally took flight. But the treatment Armstrong endured at the hands of both Oliver and Henderson left a bad taste in Armstrong's mouth, and he could not forget it.

"You know, being an underdog in a band is a bad thing," Armstrong says on the tapes. "Of course, as always, [there are] pets, and [Henderson] had 'em, believe that. . . .

"But I knew I could blow my horn, and I proved it."

Armstrong's life had not been easy, from his birth, dirt-poor in New Orleans, to the years spent in the Colored Waif's Home, a kind of reform school for youngsters who had gotten into trouble (Armstrong had been caught shooting a pistol into the air one New Year's Eve).

But once Armstrong picked up a bugle, and then a cornet, at the Colored Waif's Home, he finally had the means with which to compete in the world. To Armstrong, the tapes show, the trumpet wasn't simply a tool with which to make glorious, indelible music—it was a way of getting a leg up on those who hadn't been born as disadvantaged as he.

As Armstrong's fame in Chicago grew, the number of people gunning for him only increased, but Armstrong reveled in the competition. When he played for Erskine Tate's Vendome Theater Orchestra in Chicago in 1925, his solos became the talk of the city—much to the chagrin of his rivals.

"After the overture, I'd go in there and beat out a jazz number before they'd go back into the picture—[expletive], you'd think the walls was coming in, cats lined up all around the block, man," remembers Armstrong.

"They'd keep one picture three days, cats would come three days to see if I'm going to miss that note," adds Armstrong, bursting into laughter. "Man, beautiful [expletive], man."

No one, however, inspired more contempt from Armstrong than the jazz critics, who tended to be tone deaf or musically illiterate, so far as Armstrong was concerned.

"When them ofay [white] writers and all them cats want to make money on the situation, they say, 'Didn't [trumpeter] Bunk Johnson teach you?'" says Armstrong. "I say, 'Bunk didn't teach me [expletive].'"

The tapes overflow with such frank commentary from a man who proves considerably more deep, complex, and flawed than his admirers have been willing to acknowledge. But Armstrong's candor on these tapes does more than simply show his human side—it sheds welcome light on the evolution of a great artist.

Armstrong says, for instance, that it wasn't until he came to Chicago that he "got good" as a trumpeter, considering his work earlier in New Orleans and on the Mississippi River boats he played as apprentice work.

He says that although he enjoyed traipsing across Europe for the first time, in 1934, he did not exactly admire the American jazz musicians who became expatriates.

"You stay over in Europe five years, and you come over here, [expletive], forget it, everything done changed, man," says Armstrong. "They get over [there] . . . and everything's fine, but they get lazy, they can get away with too much over there."

Eventually, the Louis Armstrong Archives hopes to release these tapes as CDs, which should alter long-held beliefs about the first great jazz soloist.

A century after his birth on August 4, 1901, the man is finally having his say.

August 5, 2001

~

Several important books have begun documenting the treasures first reported in this two-part series. In Louis Armstrong: The Offstage Story of Satchmo *(Collectors Press, 2003), Michael Cogswell—who still serves as director of the Louis Armstrong House and Archives—unveils hundreds of previously unseen photos, letters, and collages (which Armstrong had applied liberally to the slender cardboard boxes in which he stored his precious tapes). In* Satchmo: The Wonderful World and Art of Louis Armstrong *(Abrams, 2009), Steven Brower digs deeply into the visual elements of Armstrong's creativity, beautifully reproducing more than one hundred collages at life size. And Terry Teachout's* Pops: A Life of Louis Armstrong *(Houghton Mifflin Harcourt, 2009) synthesizes extant Armstrong scholarship with a study of the archives. Together, these books represent the fullest way to experience the Armstrong ephemera—short of visiting the collection.*

V

Crisis of Culture in New Orleans

The Aftermath of Hurricane Katrina (in Four Parts)

Battered by Katrina

Can the cradle of America's artistic identity recover its vitality?

NEW ORLEANS—Trumpeters still blow their horns past midnight at Donna's, a weather-beaten club at the edge of the French Quarter.

Zydeco bands still raise Cain at Rock 'n' Bowl, a rowdy bowling alley that doubles as a music joint in Mid-City; and slow-cooked mustard greens and duck and andouille etouffee still get heaped high on gleaming white china at the celebrated Upperline restaurant, near the Garden District.

At first glance, a semblance of cultural stability has returned to New Orleans, ten months after Hurricane Katrina shattered the city.

But you rarely see kids with bottle caps tacked to their heels anymore, dancing fast for loose change on Bourbon Street. And the brass bands that once shook the narrow byways of New Orleans neighborhoods on Sundays—inspiring folks to come out of their homes to join the pageant, white umbrellas raised against the scorching Louisiana sun—surface only sporadically.

Look past the glittering facade that a battered New Orleans presents to tourists, in other words, and this city is struggling so far as its native culture is concerned. As America prepares to celebrate Independence Day, the place that first gave this country a cultural identity of its own—in the form of nascent jazz and offshoots such as swing, gospel, and R & B—faces the greatest aesthetic crisis of its history.

Vast neighborhoods that produced the talent that staffed the marching bands and lit up the jazz clubs have been wiped off the map. Cultural traditions that had been passed orally from one generation to the next have been scattered across the nation, surviving mostly in the hearts and minds of New Orleanians who fled.

Cuisines that were nuanced from one street corner to the next, bars where folk musicians exchanged ideas, and front stoops where the songs of the city cried out on sweltering summer nights have been wrecked.

Though New Orleans devotees drew hope from Mardi Gras parades in February and Jazz and Heritage Festival performances in late April and early May, these were short-lived, tantalizing reminders of yore.

"It's a national treasure that's going down the toilet as we're speaking," said Jerry Goolsby, a professor of music-industry studies at Loyola University New Orleans. "It's on life support. If someone doesn't do something, they'll regret it."

Added David Torkanowsky, one of the city's most sharply spoken jazz pianists, "New Orleans has always been the singular place where the confluence of the European and African traditions basically gave birth to truly American art forms. But the African American neighborhoods—where the village elders lived—have been decimated."

"We've lost not only the griots [cultural storytellers] but the legacy that they represent—the legacy of Storyville," he said, referring to the notorious vice district of late nineteenth- and early twentieth-century New Orleans where jazz first emerged.

Said Jerome Smith, a community organizer for decades, "At this moment, we're really walking on quicksand.

"It's about inheritance, and there's no one here to inherit this culture."

Among the tragedies that Katrina heaped upon New Orleans, one seems particularly cruel, in cultural terms: the destruction of African American neighborhoods that had served as unofficial repositories—and standard-bearers—for ancient folkloric traditions.

The Lower Ninth Ward, historic stomping ground of musicians as famous as Fats Domino and as obscure as the neighborhood marching bands that convened spontaneously on its streets, looks like a war zone. Pianos teeter on their sides in abandoned homes; scraps of sheet music flutter in the wind through empty streets; silence grips block after block of neighborhoods that once roared with homegrown, self-styled music.

Treme, where poor children routinely banged on pots and pans as they joined the second-line parades that made the neighborhood an international cultural destination, looks like a ghost town. And large swaths of Mid-City, where craftsmen who built New Orleans by day doubled as musicians by night, are eerily devoid of life.

In essence, the African American and Creole populations of New Orleans—which in the nineteenth century transformed America's starched, European-derived culture into something more original, dynamic, and populist—have been disproportionately punished by Katrina, resulting in enormous cultural loss. The polyglot, multiracial city that produced Jelly Roll Morton and Louis Armstrong, Spanish colonial architecture and tiny but distinctive "shotgun" houses, has had much of its cultural DNA erased.

"We are fortunate that many of our historic neighborhoods, such as the French Quarter, are coming back to life, but the real indigenous culture—particularly the African American culture that came to the neighborhoods and founded our traditions—is devastated," said Don Marshall, executive director of the New Orleans Jazz and Heritage Festival and Foundation.

"These are neighborhoods where people lived forever, and now they're in different parts of the country."

Left behind are areas of the city—outside the tourist stops—that for decades fed New Orleans's rambunctious cultural scene.

"Every neighborhood had clubs and restaurants that had music, [and] all of that now is not up and running," said singer Charmaine Neville, a New Orleans stalwart who lost her home in the Lower Ninth Ward and now lives outside the city.

"But all the neighborhood stuff, it's going to be a long time before that's back, if—I hate to even say this—if ever," she added.

"You feel like a part of you is missing—your culture is missing."

Even those who promote New Orleans's hometown artists are hard-pressed to find them. After Katrina cast an international spotlight on New Orleans culture, interest in its best practitioners soared, but the global demand for Crescent City talent now is difficult to meet, said longtime promoter Scott Aiges.

"If somebody calls up and says, 'I need a brass band,' I really have to look around," said Aiges, who before the hurricane was the city's first director of music development and now heads a nonprofit marketing firm called the Louisiana Music Export Office. "Before, there were at least fifteen or twenty brass bands you could hire. Now, there's not even half that.

"The brass bands still function, in a way, but they have to fly in from different places because most of the members don't live in New Orleans.

"And the networks of communication are gone. You don't have the second-line parades every week anymore, so you don't know who's around."

The easily observed dearth of New Orleans talent is substantiated by a report from the Cultural Committee of Mayor C. Ray Nagin's Bring New Orleans Back Commission, issued this year and still the only comprehensive study of its kind.

The study found that after Katrina:

> A pool of more than 2,000 musicians had plummeted to fewer than 250.
>
> About 40 Mardi Gras Indian tribes, or clubs, had suffered $1.6 million in losses.
>
> Seventy social aid and pleasure clubs incurred $1.4 million worth of losses.
>
> Fewer than 250 of the city's 1,000-plus arts organizations had reopened.
>
> A cultural workforce of 15,000 had dropped to fewer than 5,000.

Though a systematic updating of the study has yet to be launched, the picture has not improved significantly, said one of its authors, Jay Weigel, director of New Orleans's Contemporary Arts Center.

"We said in the report that 10 percent of the musicians were back—maybe now it's 20 percent, or 25 percent, or 18 percent," Weigel said. "Staffs are still down, 50 to 80 percent."

In all, the report envisioned a price tag of six hundred million dollars to bring the city back culturally.

But that amount of money, even if it's forthcoming, won't necessarily reignite cultural New Orleans.

First, the exodus of the city's artists—both celebrated and obscure—has had an unintended consequence: the performers are flourishing in new places.

"I'm having the best year economically that I have had in probably eight or nine years," said legendary New Orleans pianist-singer Henry Butler, who now lives in Boulder, Colorado, and doubts he'll move back.

Like Butler, many noteworthy New Orleans figures have left, including singer Aaron Neville and the brilliant young trumpeter (and former Chicagoan) Maurice Brown.

"Even people who may not have been making a lot of money in New Orleans, even the brass bands, are making more money these days out of town," Butler said. "I think everybody is sort of realizing a renaissance by being in new environments."

The numbers support the anecdotes. Though the New Orleans metropolitan area's population dropped significantly after Katrina, from 1.29 million in July 2005 to 914,000 in January 2006, according to a Brookings Institution analysis of U.S. Census Bureau data, the most severe effects were felt in Orleans Parish—the region's cultural center. There, the population in the same period went from 437,000 to about 158,000.

The cultural implications of that exodus are profound.

"We're going into a second year in which young musicians are not being taught the music and their culture," said Bill Taylor, executive director of the Tipitina's Foundation. "I'm not a cultural anthropologist, and I don't know exactly how long it takes to lose a tradition when it's not passed down, but that's another major issue we're facing."

Should the New Orleans diaspora want to return, it will not be easy.

"All our affordable housing was destroyed—it was wiped out," said Missy Whittington, executive vice president of the New Orleans Metropolitan Association of Realtors.

Many of the artists who have defiantly returned, said singer Fredy Omar, find themselves sharing cramped quarters with strangers.

And if federal dollars eventually pour into the city, inspiring waves of new construction, something culturally vital will still be missing. The narrow streets where poor New Orleanians lived cheek by jowl, teaching each other age-old songs, were wrecked by Katrina.

Rebuild the old neighborhoods up high, so that the waters can't get them, and it won't be the same, observers said.

"You can't re-create cracked weatherboard, you can't re-create leaky roofs, you can't re-create ramshackle houses, nor would you want to," said Torkanowsky, the jazz pianist.

"But the conundrum is that that in fact is where a lot of the richness came from. The funk was in Bywater. The funk was in the Lower 9, which is gone. A lot of people had moved from Lower 9 to New Orleans East—all of that is gone.

"It's a stake to the heart of where a lot of the funk was."

Added Goolsby, the music industry professor, "What made New Orleans great, what made the music of New Orleans great, is a lot of stuff that you don't want back: economic poverty.

"Sometimes the music expresses great suffering. Do you really want to make a class of people in New Orleans miserable so they can start writing again? The economic segregation and the racism—do you really want that back?"

Still, there have been flickers of hope.

New restaurants, such as Alberta, on Magazine Street, have opened, and established ones, such as the aforementioned Upperline, have returned, even though epicures await the return of icons such as Dooky

Chase, a Creole landmark in Mid-City; Dunbar's Creole Cooking, in Uptown; Willie Mae's Scotch House in Treme; and Commander's Palace, an upscale restaurant in the Garden District. Venerable institutions such as the Historic New Orleans Collection, a leading repository of the region's cultural legacy, are up and running in the French Quarter. Performers are commuting into New Orleans from across the Southeast and Southwest, "holding on to their gigs with the hope that they'll get back here, though I don't know how long that's going to be able to last," said Tipitina's Foundation's Taylor.

Habitat for Humanity's Musicians Village, where struggling artists can get no-interest, no-down-payment loans for houses through "sweat equity," recently handed the keys to its first property owner, singer Omar.

Yet everyone knows that this summer could be crucial in determining the future of New Orleans's distinctive culture.

With only one major convention booked for the season (a gathering of the American Library Association, which ended last Wednesday), the popular Essence Music Festival having decamped to Houston, and visibly tiny audiences in the French Quarter for the typically slow summer months, a culture hangs in the balance.

One more hurricane could wipe away the remnants of the city's artistic life, residents said.

"If we get a hit this summer, then that's going to be very alarming because then [New Orleans artists] are going to be very leery of returning and making a real commitment to this town," said Jason Patterson, who books 361 nights of music each year for the jazz club Snug Harbor.

"Everybody is terrified," said Aiges, the Louisiana talent promoter.

"If we get clobbered over the head, the carpet will be pulled up over us."

July 2, 2006

Five years after Hurricane Katrina, the struggle to nurture the culture of New Orleans continues, with mixed results. The nonprofit organization Sweet Home New Orleans—which has given $2.5 million to more than 2,500 of New Orleans's cultural figures—released a comprehensive study of post-Katrina culture in 2009. "State of the New Orleans Music Community Report" pulled no punches in its summary: "The reduced size of audiences paying for live music in New Orleans is one of the largest challenges to our cultural economy," *the study reported. Job opportunities for musicians have not returned to where they were before Katrina, but the cost of living has risen. Paying audiences are smaller, and "as clubs are less able to guarantee performance fees, musicians are absorbing the financial risk." On the plus side, the study found that 80 percent of the city's musicians and other tradition bearers have returned to the New Orleans area, up 5 percent from 2008. Even in the devastated eighth and ninth wards, the figure rose 15 percent between 2008 and 2009. Second lines are now as frequent as they were before Katrina; and some social aid and pleasure clubs have grown beyond pre-Katrina levels. Though a decline in paying audiences has diminished musicians' incomes, New Orleans is the city that elevated whistling past the graveyard to an art form. Vast swaths of traditional culture have been devastated along with the physical destruction, but music has emerged as one of the more resilient forces in the city. The biggest auditoriums and the tiniest neighborhood clubs have been shuttered, yet the New Orleans Jazz and Heritage Festival and the Frenchmen Street music district are moving forward.*

The Long March Back

Once the greatest high school band in New Orleans, St. Augustine faces a daunting challenge.

NEW ORLEANS—Trombones and sousaphones bellowed hysterically. Saxophones brayed, badly out of tune. Drums rumbled behind or ahead of the beat.

Considering that the biggest game of their football season was five days away, prospects did not look good for the most revered marching band in New Orleans, the Purple Knights of St. Augustine High School.

And a great deal was at stake. For St. Augustine and for this shattered city, the band's halftime show would represent a small but symbolic resurgence of indigenous music in a city that has lost most of it. So in a blue-collar neighborhood where boarded-up houses still bore spray paint indicating how many corpses had been found inside, an inspired bandmaster and a group of high schoolers struggled to keep alive a New Orleans rite.

They knew that Saturday's show would be just the first challenge of many, culminating with the main event: parade season in January and Mardi Gras pageants the following month. That's when the eyes of all New Orleans—and of visitors from around the world—will be upon them.

If the band can't succeed during halftime, it will never survive Mardi Gras.

On that autumn day, the Marching 100—as the Purple Knights proudly call themselves—totaled merely sixty-four sweaty, exhausted, distracted musicians.

Most of the kids had never marched on a field before; many hadn't touched an instrument until a few weeks earlier. Worse, they were preparing to take on their archrivals, McDonogh 35 Senior High School, its football team long considered St. Augustine's biggest threat.

But for this second game of the season—and the first in which the band even had mustered sixty-four members—practice was going terribly, and bandmaster Virgil Tiller had had it up to here.

"Don't think you're going to get away with what you're doing today," Tiller shouted, "because you gotta face me tomorrow."

Before Katrina, the Marching 100 flourished as the greatest high school band in New Orleans, the incubator of jazz stars such as trumpeter Terence Blanchard and saxophonist Victor Goines, the training ground for generations of lesser-known but ubiquitous Crescent City musicians. The Purple Knights played for presidents in the Superdome, broke the color barrier in the Mardi Gras parades, and flourished for more than half a century as a symbol of black musical culture and achievement in New Orleans.

Then the flooding that followed Katrina washed away almost every trace of this band, including its state-of-the-art rehearsal room, gleaming brass instruments, and opulent purple-and-gold uniforms. With the school shuttered, the band ceased to exist for nearly a year, a glorious musical tradition suddenly silenced.

This summer the twenty-nine-year-old Tiller, an alumnus of both St. Aug and its Purple Knights, signed on as band director.

"Everybody says, 'We're going to understand if your band is not the same, [if] it's not up to par,'" said Tiller. "I don't even list that as being an option. The Marching 100 will be the Marching 100. . . . I'm not going to let fifty-five or fifty-six years of that legacy of being the best just go down because of a storm."

Filled for decades by some of the city's most promising young musicians, who competed by the hundreds for coveted spots in the band, the Marching 100's all-male ensemble played everything from New Orleans parade romps to jazz-tinged versions of the latest pop hits.

In 1967, the band made history by crossing a notorious color line. Founder-director Edwin Hampton accepted an invitation to march his band in Rex, the city's top Mardi Gras parade—which had excluded blacks since 1872. As the Marching 100 showed its colors, the kids, blowing their horns along swanky St. Charles Avenue, expected the worst, and got it.

"People flicked lit cigarettes on us," recalled Lawrence Winchester, age seventy, who played in St. Aug's first marching band before working as an assistant band director. "They were drinking, and, of course, they would spit on us."

Others remember ducking condoms filled with urine.

But the Marching 100 marched on, fighting back by refusing to rumble, instead playing their tunes and parading in sleek formation, undaunted.

Looking out into the crowd, "I saw a black lady go to her knees and thank God . . . that she lived to see this day," Hampton remembered.

In recent years, the band—devoted to a distinctly American beat—has won berths to the Rose Bowl Parade and Macy's Thanksgiving Day Parade, thriving as a nationally celebrated symbol of New Orleans culture. Until August 29, 2005, the day the music stopped.

When Tiller took over the band from Hampton in June, he was astonished by the extent of its wreckage. All the charts diagramming the band's ornate field choreography were destroyed. Many musical scores survived, but the band's two sets of instruments—one for the rigors of daily practices, the other a "dress set" (with golden skins on the drums) kept spotless for performances only—were ruined.

Even after the school raised funds to pay for repairs, the instruments performed terribly. Trumpet valves stuck, causing players to hit clinkers at random. Mouthpieces fit poorly, making it difficult to coax a decent sound from some horns, especially the enormous sousaphones.

Meanwhile, instruments kept falling apart, from overuse, and Tiller found himself working with mostly untried musicians, as only ten seniors and five juniors returned to St. Aug and the band after the storm.

But Tiller took on his formidable rebuilding task because he believes St. Aug saved him from the tough streets of the Lower Ninth Ward, where he grew up. And he saw hope in the faces of a few seasoned players.

To many of these musicians—who saw the storm bring death and devastation—the St. Aug band appears to be an island of order amid the chaos of life in post-Katrina New Orleans.

During rehearsals on St. Aug's blacktop, drum majors Montrell Givens and Kenneth Caldwell—who function as Tiller's de facto assistants—paced the field nervously, firing instructions at younger band members, ordering students to do push-ups as penance for goofing off.

Tiller, meanwhile, often applied a wooden paddle to his players' backsides, when the students made the same mistake twice.

In the days leading up to St. Aug's big game, the band improved, by degrees. The tunes at least became recognizable; geometric field patterns started to emerge.

Then, the afternoon before game day, something started to click. Pumped up by a pep rally in the school parking lot, the students returned to the blacktop and finally, belatedly, started to capture the soaring lines of Earth Wind and Fire's "And Love Goes On," the rhythmic kick of Gnarls Barkley's "Crazy," and the bittersweet chord changes of Rihanna's "Unfaithful."

The musicians pointed their horns skyward, pivoting on the balls of their feet to turn one way or another. They began to resemble a functioning band.

Still, Tiller was furious when the inevitable wrong notes rang out and missteps caused collisions. "You're not going to play this song unless you know it," he barked.

The setting sun glinted off the instruments as the band rushed into the stands of Hoss Memtsas Stadium, neutral ground between St. Aug and its public-school nemesis, McDonogh 35.

The drum majors, Givens and Caldwell, positioned themselves like two conductors preparing to rouse a mighty symphony orchestra. The two young men wore black T-shirts spray-painted on the back with three graffiti-style words: "After the Disaster." They raised their hands, then, with a flourish, signaled the band to start playing, the musicians unleashing the loudest, biggest, brawniest chord they had all week, launching an aptly named tune: "Confidence."

Across the field, McDonogh 35's band responded with "The Star-Spangled Banner" in a solid, credible, but not particularly robust rendition.

The battle had been joined.

Bandmaster Tiller, smelling blood, shouted "Sound off—Purple!" while the game commenced on the field. The St. Aug musicians instantly tore into the tune "Purple," sounding so loud, so brash, so combustive, you might have thought a microphone had been soldered to each musician's horn.

Unfortunately for St. Aug, its football team soon fumbled, giving McDonogh 35 a quick six-point lead, which turned into a 20–6 pummeling by halftime, when the Purple Knights' band ran onto the field for its show.

Adrenaline coursing through their veins, the Marching 64 took their tunes fast, rendering their crescendos bigger, stormier, and, alas, somewhat messier than in rehearsals. Surprisingly, though, their precision drill unfolded more elegantly than ever, with only a few minor mishaps and not a single train wreck.

And in a finale that had barely been rehearsed, a few of the youngest students ran long strands of gold fabric amid the columns of musicians, creating a stunning, billowing tableau on the field. Even the opposing crowd cheered the effect.

The St. Aug musicians looked ebullient when they returned to the stands, playing almost constantly throughout the second half of the game, never sitting down, muscling through their repertoire even as their classmates on the gridiron collapsed, losing 33–6.

On the late-night bus ride back to the school, everyone seemed convinced they had won the game—musically speaking—and that the St. Aug band could come home proud. Yet back at school, Tiller told them they still had a long way to go.

When the football season ended a few weeks ago, Tiller turned up the heat to prep the students for the punishing parade season ahead.

For hours on end, he marched them up and down the school's blacktop, trying to build the endurance they'll need for parades that can last for hours.

"The wear-and-tear on the lips and the legs is awful," said Lucien Peters III, who marched in the St. Aug band in the late 1950s.

Even so, the youngsters endured these rigors, many inspired to do so because they first had encountered the Marching 100 during Mardi Gras parades they witnessed as toddlers, longing to join the procession ever since.

"That's just part of our culture in New Orleans," said Blanchard, the virtuoso trumpeter and St. Aug alum.

Indeed, musical parades have been wending through the boulevards of the city since at least the turn of the last century, reflecting New Orleans's distinctly street-focused culture.

The question is whether the Purple Knights will hold their own at Mardi Gras—the band's first since the hurricane.

"We've got to be out there and looking and sounding good," said Tiller, who hopes he can get the band fully staffed by then.

"To have the band out in the street as the Marching 100, as Purple Knights, it says we're back in operation.

"And it says we're rebuilding this city."

November 23, 2006

Edwin Hampton, the visionary who founded the Marching 100 and led it to glory, died in his sleep on the morning of July 21, 2009, at age eighty-one. The young men of this great band—dressed in purple and gold, wearing white shoes and golden helmets—played exultantly outside Corpus Christi Catholic Church, where a Mass preceded his burial in Providence Memorial Park in

Metairie. Virgil Tiller led the musical farewell to his mentor and continues to coach, encourage, and excoriate his young musicians. A few months before Hampton's death, the Marching 100 drum line thundered at the New Orleans Jazz and Heritage Festival.

Treasures of Music Lovers Now Just So Much Debris

Even as the city rebuilds, "a whole universe" of jazz history is lost.

NEW ORLEANS—For more than a century, musicians and fans in this proudly musical city have hoarded mementos of their culture.

Self-styled collectors packed tiny attics with precious scores, filled ramshackle apartments with antique musical instruments, and stored irreplaceable photos of long-gone artists in cramped back rooms.

But as New Orleans struggles to rebuild after Hurricane Katrina, one of the great casualties of the storm is starting to emerge: the loss of the documents and ephemera that chronicled New Orleans's distinctive musical life.

Unlike most major American cities, where cultural riches tend to be officially designated and then stored in grand museums, everyday New Orleans citizens always have done much of this work themselves, out of sheer love for the music.

These deeply personal troves disintegrated in the flooding that followed Katrina. From the rare historic instruments that clarinet star Dr. Michael White stashed in his bedroom closet to the career memorabilia that Fats Domino stored throughout his home, the material floated away, forever beyond the reach of scholars and historians.

"There's a whole universe of material from people's collections that was lost," said Greg Lambousy, director of collections at the Louisiana State Museum.

The scope and toll of this cultural loss cannot be measured, though, because no one knows exactly what was stuffed into the attics and back rooms of homes in the Lower Ninth Ward, Bywater, New Orleans East, and other damaged neighborhoods. There was no master list of who owned collections, let alone inventories of particular items.

Collections at the Louisiana State Museum and Tulane University's Hogan Jazz Archive survived unscathed. But officials there still mourn the loss of material that would have added significantly to the world's understanding of jazz and New Orleans culture.

"The losses," said Bruce Raeburn, curator of the Hogan Archive, "are staggering."

White, a revered New Orleans jazz clarinetist and one of the world's leading experts in the city's music, will never forget the day he walked into his home in the Gentilly neighborhood after Katrina, in October 2005. Though he did not expect to find all of his fifty-plus rare clarinets, hundreds of priceless 78-rpm records, and thousands of photos dating to the Civil War era, he wasn't prepared for what he saw.

"When I first came into the house, it felt like I had been cut to pieces and my body was just scattered all over the house," said White, who recalled hearing records crunch under his feet as he stepped inside a home that had been engulfed for weeks.

White instantly realized he had lost it all—everything but a few nineteenth-century clarinets he had tossed into his car before escaping the city with Katrina approaching.

As White assessed the damage, he opened instrument cases that were caked in mold and mildew and sludge. "It felt like there were bodies in there," he said.

On a recent day, as White walked gingerly through his ruined home, he surveyed what remained: jagged pieces of broken clarinets, shards of old records, corners of musical scores ground into the floor, reduced nearly to pulp.

His four-bedroom, three-bath house in the Mirabeau Gardens area of Gentilly had overflowed with rare treasures of America's first Jazz Age: handwritten notes from his interviews with jazz musicians born at the start of the twentieth century; a gleaming white mouthpiece that New Orleans clarinet icon Sidney Bechet once owned; scores for old Baptist songs; delicately lettered hatbands from extinct New Orleans brass ensembles.

Like many of New Orleans's intrepid cultural collectors, White never really intended to amass such a library; he always considered himself a musician first, a collector second.

His obsession began nonchalantly, in the late 1970s, when White realized that the early jazzmen were starting to die off. Determined to preserve what they knew of the music's roots, White started interviewing them, scribbling their stories on scraps of paper.

The jazzmen generously shared their secrets.

New Orleans bassist Chester Zardis, who was born in 1900, told White what Louis Armstrong was like as a child still trying to play cornet, in the Colored Waif's Home. Trombonist Preston Jackson, who was born in New Orleans in 1903, told White how Bechet really sounded on the clarinet—live, not on record.

"I became sort of almost like an addict," recalled White, who scoured pawnshops in New Orleans and junk stores around the world for tokens of early jazz, his collection growing inexorably.

"A year before Katrina, the value of it was just starting to set in. It was overwhelming," said White, who had long planned to inventory the material but never found the time.

He realized that because New Orleans's London Avenue Canal bordered his backyard, his collection someday might be in danger. But moving it to a distant location or placing it in storage seemed to defeat the purpose of owning and perpetually referring to the material for his recordings, performances, lectures, and writings.

Because White had been forced to evacuate New Orleans just twice in his lifetime before Katrina, he did not imagine the worst.

If there was a private collection as valuable as White's, it belonged to Danny Barker, who was born in 1909 and would have been known merely as a fine, early-period guitar and banjo player were it not for his compulsion to document the first chapters of jazz history. Early in life Barker had befriended the first jazz composer, New Orleanian Jelly Roll Morton, when Morton was attempting to revive his career in New York, from 1938 to 1940. It was Barker who shot the best-known photographs of Morton in Harlem, and thereafter Barker collected every shred of paper, image, and recording of early jazz that he could find.

Until his death in 1994, at age eighty-five, Barker continually augmented the collection he jammed into a 17-by-20-foot room at the back of his New Orleans house, on Sere Street. Anyone who ever stepped into the single-story home had to be startled by the sheer volume of material packed into it, floor to ceiling.

"When he would come home at night, he would sit at the kitchen table and he would work on things, write a song lyric or work on a chapter for a book," recalled his daughter, Sylvia Barker.

"And when the housekeeper came in the morning, he'd say, 'Just take all my stuff and throw it all in a bag.'"

Hundreds, perhaps thousands of these little plastic bags filled the back room. They included unique material: questionnaires Barker distributed to New Orleans musicians as far back as the 1940s; unpublished manuscripts for first-person articles he was writing about early jazz; original black-and-white negatives documenting the musicians he had known for more than fifty years; and handwritten notes, artifacts, and music from uncounted sources.

Though representatives of the Hogan Jazz Archive at Tulane were able to rescue Baker's collection of commercial recordings from the front of the house, most of his treasures in back were floating in waterlogged plastic bags. Even material that the Barker family had put in safe-deposit boxes in a nearby bank, such as his literary manuscripts, succumbed. All but twenty boxes of material were lost—more than 80 percent of Barker's collection, according to Raeburn, the Hogan Archive's curator.

"Everything was gook," said Sylvia Barker.

The same outcome awaited Sybil Kein, who had spent twenty-six years traveling the world to find and reconstruct long-lost Louisiana Creole folk songs, a precursor of New Orleans jazz.

Louisiana Creoles—known as "free people of color" who had mixed European and African bloodlines—thrived in New Orleans in the nineteenth century, developing a middle-class society with its own cross-continental cuisine, distinctly French- and Spanish-tinged patois, and deeply autobiographical music. Blending elements of European harmony, African rhythms, and Caribbean-inspired melody, the earliest Creole folk songs survived in the twentieth century largely in the memories of those old enough to have heard them from their parents and grandparents.

Kein had traveled Louisiana, Europe, and the Caribbean to track down Creole descendants and listen to them sing these tunes to her. She transcribed the melodies and lyrics onto score paper, piecing together more than 150 of these songs and recording a fraction of them on CD.

"I'm told I had the largest collection in the world by some of the other guys who had collected a few" of the songs, said Kein.

But when she returned to her New Orleans home on Spain Street, in the Gentilly neighborhood, she realized that eight and a half feet of floodwater had destroyed her library of Creole songs, as well as 5,000-plus books, 1,000 baptismal records of slaves and free people of color, interviews with musicians, and other original research for books she was planning.

The material "fell apart in my hands," she said. "I'm sorry I'm not twenty years old and don't have a lifetime to give to this again. But I'm not."

Other collections also were destroyed.

Nearly everything in Fats Domino's home, in the Lower Ninth Ward, was waterlogged, said Lambousy, the Louisiana State Museum curator.

The same fate destroyed the personal collection of Michael J. Gourrier, who for decades amassed documents on antebellum orchestras in which many post–Civil War black musicians learned to read score—laying the groundwork for the emergence of jazz.

Some collectors have begun collecting again. In the past year, White has acquired several hundred CDs, storing some in his new apartment in Houston, some in his FEMA trailer in New Orleans.

But he despairs over what has slipped away.

"People say to me, 'Could you save anything?' " White said.

"How do you really explain?"

November 27, 2006

The evanescent treasures of Dr. Michael White, Danny Barker, Sybil Kein, and uncounted others obviously never will be retrieved. Kein has moved to Asheville, North Carolina, but her work—though interrupted—endures, in part, in books such as Gumbo People *(Margaret Media, 1999) and* Creole Journal *(Lotus Press, 1999) and in CDs such as* Creole Ballads and Zydeco *and* Maw-Maw's Creole Lullaby *(both on Margaret Media). White's work still is central to New Orleans music and scholarship, nowhere more than in the landmark album he released after the storm,* Blue Crescent *(Basin Street Records, 2008). The perfervid lyricism and swaying backbeats of this work, its spiritual undertow and early-jazz sensibility, express in music what White's collection attempted to preserve in documents and ephemera.*

The Struggle to Reclaim Threads of the Past

For 250 years, "Black Indians" brought this city sounds, ceremonies, and sights unlike any other. Post-Katrina, they fight to keep the tradition alive.

NEW ORLEANS—Though his fingertips throb and his shoulders ache, Big Chief Darryl Montana won't stop sewing.

He has been at it for months—sitting at a table in his compact apartment outside New Orleans, endlessly pulling thread through cloth, squinting through high-magnification lenses to stitch beads onto fabric, suffering so many cuts on his fingers that a couple of them look almost mangled.

He says he's making an Indian suit for February's Mardi Gras, but he knows he's doing much more: with needle and thread, he's trying to preserve a culture that is unraveling before his eyes.

For more than 250 years, the "Black Indians" of New Orleans have sung the ancient chants and donned the opulent costumes of a culture unique in the United States. Dubbed Mardi Gras Indians more than a century ago, they have nurtured the ancient rituals of Africa and the Caribbean in Louisiana, merging them with the rites of another marginalized people: Native Americans.

Post-Katrina, it has become commonplace to lament the decline of New Orleans's distinctive character. But nothing cuts closer to the soul of this city's culture—or the origins of American music—than the endangered art and ceremony of the Mardi Gras Indians.

Though little known to the public at large, because it operates mostly outside New Orleans's official culture, the traditions of Black Indians have helped shape the course of American music. Jazz musicians from Jelly Roll Morton to Wynton Marsalis have evoked their chants. New Orleans icons such as Dr. John and the Neville Brothers have performed and popularized their songs. Uncounted bands have covered their most famous melody, "Iko Iko."

"A large percentage of American popular music, and jazz music, has been influenced by this root culture," said Donald Harrison, a prominent New Orleans jazz saxophonist-bandleader and Big Chief of the Guardians of the Flame tribe. "It's the link for all the music that we hear, that takes us right back to what was going on in Africa."

The freely improvised singing and circle-dance rituals of the Black Indians predate jazz and, therefore, helped lay the groundwork for a new American sound. Thanks to the Mardi Gras Indians, as well as the city's brass bands and second-line parades, America developed a freewheeling, African-inspired music that differed radically from the straitlaced classical symphonies and high-flown operas of Europe.

But a Mardi Gras Indian culture that was always embattled has been shattered in the aftermath of Hurricane Katrina. Like other New Orleanians, the Black Indians have been scattered across the country. Yet the Indians face a particular challenge: reclaiming not only their homes but also their artistic heritage, which is diminishing by the day.

Montana, chief of the Yellow Pocahontas tribe, is among the few who have moved back after a post-Katrina exile, hoping to rescue a culture that has endured tremendous loss—from the ornate ceremonial suits stolen by the storm to ephemeral oral traditions dating to Louisiana's colonial past.

"If we don't pass it on, it surely will die off," Montana said.

His fears are echoed by virtually every Black Indian willing to discuss the subject. The tribes are famously reclusive, emerging just a few times a year to parade in the streets, then vanishing. They say they are struggling just to stay alive.

"You have to ask yourself: should I spend two dollars on beads or try to buy something to eat?" said Norman Cook, a member of Creole Wild West, New Orleans's oldest known tribe.

Such stark choices underscore the tenuous future of this culture.

"If we lose the Indians," said David Freedman, general manager of WWOZ-FM 90.7, New Orleans's leading indigenous-music radio station, "we go from being a living musical culture to a dead or embalmed musical culture.

"We lose the root."

~

A couple of hundred spectators gathered last February near the corner of Second and Dryades streets, a famous Mardi Gras Indian meeting place in Central City. But none of the Indians was to be seen on this first Mardi Gras since Katrina.

Then, out of nowhere, the brilliant plumage and enormous headdress of Big Chief Bo Dollis came into view. Wearing foot-high feathers on his head, vibrantly beaded patches on his chest, an intricately embroidered apron across his lap, and fantastically bejeweled boots on his feet, Dollis looked like a mystical figure, half man, half God, his face barely visible inside a costume that weighed more than one hundred pounds.

Dollis was surrounded by a half-dozen Indians in his Wild Magnolias tribe—all chanting, singing, dancing, striking drums, and shaking their arms.

These tribes have their own lexicon and hierarchy. At the front of the procession stood the Spy Boy, who looked to see if rival tribes—or police—lurked around the corner. Nearby marched the Wild Man, dramatically brandishing a spear, to ward off enemies. A bit farther back, the Gang Flag waved the colors of the tribe, meanwhile keeping a close eye on the chief, to protect him.

The February return of a few Indians drew cries of celebration from the crowd. Many had wondered whether the Indians would resurface, or if they simply had been washed away by the storm. Still, the afternoon's turnout of tribe members was far smaller than before the hurricane and positively picayune compared to majestic Indian ceremonies that shook the streets in the past.

Scholars cannot say exactly how or why a Black Indian culture arose in New Orleans. But a few historical facts shed some light on this improbably enduring society. As early as 1729, African slaves joined forces with Natchez Indians in a revolt against colonial French authorities. The interests of two persecuted peoples suddenly aligned. Thereafter, black slaves in New Orleans escaped their captors into the swamps and bayous, aided by Native Americans.

From the nexus of these two besieged peoples, experts believe, rose the Black Indian culture, which combined the chant, dance, and costume rituals of Native Americans and African American slaves. Caribbean émigrés who arrived in the nineteenth century added to the mix.

"It's African, Native American, and Caribbean cultures all coming together in one stream," said Joyce Marie Jackson, an ethnomusicology professor at Louisiana State University in Baton Rouge. "It's the whole history of New Orleans, really, expressed in the rituals of these people."

Because New Orleans—unlike much of the country—in the eighteenth century condoned interracial marriage, these cultures are merged in blood as well as custom. Many of the Black Indians are of Native American descent.

By 1885 the first documented Black Indian "gang," Creole Wild West, marched on Mardi Gras. And a uniquely New Orleans street tradition began to spread.

"They'd form a ring, and one would get in the center and he'd start his kind of a Indian dance," Jelly Roll Morton recalled in 1938, during his historic interviews with Alan Lomax. "And he'd be singing, throwing his head back and downward, and stooping kinda over and bending his knees, and doing a kind of a jug dance, I'd call it."

Occasionally, said Morton, fights would break out, "and I have known many cases where there have been killings in the city of New Orleans with the Indian bands."

The bloodshed indeed made the Black Indians notorious in New Orleans. But Allison "Tootie" Montana—Darryl Montana's father and the most celebrated Indian chief of the twentieth century—transformed the tradition decades ago. A metalworker by trade, Tootie Montana created enormous suits of sculptural dimensions, encouraging his Indian brethren to follow his model and compete, like him, not with weapons but with needle and thread.

Whoever had the "prettiest" suit, as Montana often said, would be deemed triumphant.

The fighting among the Black Indians indeed ended. But they have consistently complained of mistreatment at the hands of police. The harassment dissuaded youngsters from taking up the tradition, say many Indians, and changing tastes and times didn't help. In recent years, tribes that decades earlier had included two hundred members or more had dwindled to five or ten.

On March 19, 2005, the Indians began their annual St. Joseph's night parade, a tradition that follows Mardi Gras by a few weeks but ranks close to it in importance. Shortly after the pageant began, however, police dispersed the tribes, leading to a large protest in the City Council in June. With Indians gathered around him, Tootie Montana condemned the mistreatment, saying "I want this to stop." He then fell to the ground, dying of a heart attack at age eighty-two.

Two months later, Hurricane Katrina blew into New Orleans, and an already embattled culture faced its gravest threat.

~

The Indians emerge fleetingly—on Mardi Gras day, St. Joseph's night, and a couple of other occasions. They're virtually invisible in this city once they strip off their extraordinary suits and return to their mostly minimum-wage jobs as manual laborers, temporary day workers, and, in some instances, craftsmen.

Because of that, no one knows exactly how many tribes were still functioning in New Orleans when Katrina hit. The Black Indians have long operated underground, in impoverished neighborhoods, mostly outside the view of the city's power structure.

But longtime observers estimate that about twenty-five tribes, some with just two or three members, were functioning at the time of the storm, bringing the Mardi Gras Indian population to a few hundred, at best. For all the plush beauty of their suits, the allure of their rituals, and the poetry of their names—Flaming Arrows, Blackfoot Hunters, Wild Tchoupitoulas, Fi-Yi-Yi—they had become an endangered species.

Since the storm, most have not returned.

Creole Wild West is "scattered out everywhere," said Irving "Honey" Banister, Gang Flag of Creole Wild West, sitting in the mold-ridden New Orleans home of his mother, Littdell, the tribal queen. "I think I've got a contact with about six of them, but basically I couldn't even tell you" where everyone is.

For the past year, he has been working as a garbageman in Baton Rouge. His mother, who is seventy-one, has been sewing assiduously in preparation for this coming Mardi Gras, but she grieves for what Creole Wild West has lost. Flooding that breached the city's levees also ruined decades' worth of the tribe's suits, materials, and memorabilia that had been stored in the Lower Ninth Ward home of its chief, Little Walter Cook.

"You could sew for fifty years and never replace it," Littdell Banister said.

~

On a recent Sunday, Chief Darryl Montana and his wife, Sabrina, had been sewing for two days, pausing just twice to step out for cigarettes.

Come Monday morning, Sabrina would go to her job in city government, while Darryl would sew all day, joined again by Sabrina in the evening. Between now and Mardi Gras in February, they will sew virtually without interruption. They estimate that sewing one suit takes about 5,200 man-hours. (Several people often work on a single outfit.) And a new suit is required each Mardi Gras. To wear last year's suit is to invite derision.

Though organizations such as Tipitina's Foundation and the New Orleans Jazz and Heritage Festival gave feathers and money to many Indians for this past year's Mardi Gras, the gesture was slight compared to the costs of an entire suit. The cheapest run about $4,000 in materials; the more expensive top $14,000.

"Most Indians work in minimum-wage jobs," said Sabrina Montana. "If you're making $5.15 an hour, and you have a household to support, that's a big commitment."

Truly art for art's sake, the practice of the Mardi Gras Indians brings its participants scant income or fame. Though the Wild Magnolias and the Wild Tchoupitoulas play concert performances outside the city, most flaunt their freedom at great personal cost.

Their sacrifice earns them a few hours of cultural exultation, then a return to another year of painstaking work with needle in hand.

Yet without these rites, they are anguished.

"The ones who are away, outside of New Orleans, are suffering an identity crisis," said Jackson, the scholar of Mardi Gras Indian culture.

"In New Orleans, they were a Big Chief or a Gang Flag. In Atlanta or Houston, they're nobody."

Most of the Indians, though, do not have homes to come back to or enough money to lease an apartment in a city where rents have skyrocketed since Katrina.

And no one knows if an age-old New Orleans culture can survive long without them.

December 26, 2006

Perhaps not surprisingly, the Mardi Gras Indians—who always have faced financial stress and official resistance—continue to struggle. According to the "State of the New Orleans Music Community Report" of 2009, the Great Recession has decreased employment opportunities outside the music industry. Specifically, 40 percent of clients of Sweet Home New Orleans, which released the report, lost nonmusic work. But those day jobs provide the money Mardi Gras Indians need not just to support themselves but to finance their fantastically elaborate costumes. In this case, economic deprivation translates directly into cultural loss.

VI

Ellington's Legacy

Grasping an Enormous Oeuvre

Maestro's Mystique

The Duke Ellington "sound" remains an enigma in the year of his one hundredth birthday.

The message may have been sacred or carnal, cocky or cool, viscerally exciting or languorously relaxed. But somehow Duke Ellington's orchestra perpetually transformed itself to suit the score at hand. For more than five decades, despite continuous changes in personnel, musical tastes, and economic fortunes, Ellington's band endured as perhaps the most protean in jazz.

Yet even as we celebrate Edward Kennedy Ellington's hundredth birthday on April 29, it still remains something of a mystery precisely how he and partner Billy Strayhorn achieved this enormous expressive range. They guarded their techniques jealously and left very little clear, written evidence for subsequent generations to study.

As Leonard Feather complained in a 1962 *DownBeat* article, "Voicings were heard that no other writer has ever quite succeeded in duplicating. And because Ellington has refused to publish the band's arrangements, probably nobody ever will."

Though the Smithsonian Institution in Washington, D.C., overflows with thousands of pages of Ellington band manuscripts, much of it is in frayed condition and little of it is widely available to the public in authoritatively edited, pristinely published form. One hundred years after the composer's birth, listeners still lack fundamental information on how Ellington achieved his sometimes shimmering, sometimes crisp orchestral effects.

Performing musicians, meanwhile, remain at the mercy of transcribers who heroically attempt to decode sounds from old and often poorly mixed recordings. Worse, the myths that have sprung up to fill the information void have tended to diminish the importance of Ellington's achievements. Strip away these common misconceptions, however, and you'll find a composer who went to great lengths to create detailed, autobiographical sounds unlike those of any other large jazz ensemble, past or present.

"To this day, I still hear people say, 'Duke didn't really write all that music out,'" laments Clark Terry, the trumpeter who put the flugelhorn on the map in Ellington's band, beginning in 1957. "He wrote out everything except solos. There's no way in the world that eighteen musicians could get up there at once and harmonize and balance in the way that Duke wanted them to without the scores.

"People are just confused because the band knew that music by memory, and because over the years the scores were tattered or water-soaked or torn. That doesn't mean that Duke didn't know exactly what he wanted and didn't originally write it down."

In fact, Ellington did more than just pen the notes and the voicings he wanted to hear. From the beginning of his career as bandleader, in the late 1920s, he established a practice of hiring fiercely individualistic instrumentalists and writing specifically for their strengths. The surviving Ellington scores in his own hand show that the composer generally didn't list the name of the instrument alongside the staff but, instead, the name of the players (as in "Rabbit" for Johnny Hodges), a sure indication of how he built his orchestral sound.

Ellington, in other words, wasn't writing for saxophones in general but for Hodges, Paul Gonsalves, Harry Carney, and others in particular.

"He knew that [baritone saxophonist] Harry Carney had this unusually iconoclastic sound in the upper register that nobody else on earth would ever produce," adds Terry, imitating it by making a rumbling vocal sound roughly akin to a loudly buzzing bee. "It didn't sound like a lead alto, it didn't sound like a typical baritone, it didn't sound like nothin' but Harry Carney.

"Or take [trumpeter] Rex Stewart. Duke found out that Rex could use his third valve to produce a trumpet E, which is a concert D, that had this incredible, ringing sound. So almost anytime there was a concert D in Duke's music, Rex would get that note, because Duke so loved the sound of it. Duke studied his band and his personnel like we study our instruments."

In this way, Ellington formed an early band in which there was no mistaking Barney Bigard's fluid clarinet, Cootie Williams's plunger-muted trumpet, "Tricky" Sam Nanton's growling trombone, Juan Tizol's fleet valve trombone, or Hodges's ineffably expressive, bent-note alto saxophone.

Though the myth persists that Ellington's distinctive orchestral sound owed mostly to this collection of unusual musical characters, the casting was in fact merely the starting point for the composer's easily identifiable but virtually inimitable orchestral writing style.

For starters, Ellington savored peculiarities of voicing. In many instances, Carney is asked to play his baritone in its highest register, while Gonsalves must dip to the lowest notes of his tenor. Such part writing defies convention, often feels uncomfortable to the players, and tests any bandleader's ability to balance the ensemble, yet it also creates bracing new colors.

"'Mood Indigo' is a great example," says David Berger, whose elegant transcriptions have been used by Wynton Marsalis's Jazz at Lincoln Center Orchestra and William Russo's Chicago Jazz Ensemble, among other repertory bands. "In the original arrangement, Duke has the trumpet in his middle register, the trombone in his higher register, and the clarinet in his low register, and it all creates this magical sound that you just wouldn't expect.

"He loves using the extreme ranges of instruments," adds Berger. "For instance, there are some pieces that he wrote in the key of D, which some people might think is an unusual key to use for jazz. Why did he do it? Often the reason is simply that when he gets to the tonic, he wants to hear it on the lowest note of the clarinet.

"Probably the most interesting thing I've learned from transcribing his writing is that it's player-generated. Duke once even said in an interview, 'You know what I do? I make [musical] settings for these wonderful soloists.'"

But a band of soloists became a more formidable, cohesive, and ambitious ensemble in the 1930s, with expanded brass and reed sections.

And by 1940–42, a period featuring what many listeners consider Ellington's best band, the composer was working with a dramatically expanded tonal palette. In part, this owed to the recent addition of brawny tenor saxophonist Ben Webster, groundbreaking bassist Jimmy Blanton, versatile trumpeter-violinist-vocalist Ray Nance, and, above all, composer-arranger Strayhorn (who joined the band as lyricist in 1939 and began arranging a year later).

If Ellington brought to their partnership a deep jazz knowledge attained through long years on the road, Strayhorn offered expertise on classical forms and textures (an area that Ellington apparently had not studied in depth). The hand-in-glove collaboration, which former Ellington drummer Louie Bellson still calls "something that the Lord meant to be," gave rise not only to 1943's controversial *Black, Brown and Beige* but also to the extended orchestral suites of the 1950s and thereafter.

This fusion of jazz elements and quasi-symphonic colors radically altered the definition of the working jazz band and what it could achieve in sound. And this evolution could only have occurred as a result of the Ellington-Strayhorn partnership. Each composer learned from the other, and though listeners probably will argue for all time the importance of Ellington's contribution versus Strayhorn's, the two clearly enhanced what either might have achieved alone.

"They arrived at a lot of the same ideas through opposite means," says Berger, perhaps best summing up the strengths of the union.

Together, Ellington and Strayhorn redefined the band's sound, creating a prototype that would feature five saxophones, four trumpets, and Ellington's signature three trombones.

"Automatically, each section had to have a different sound," if only because of the differing sizes of each unit, says Berger. "Each would be automatically different in its texture.

"With five saxophones you get this sensual kind of sound. With four trumpets you get tremendous power. And with three trombones there's a great feeling of nobility, since Ellington can write basic triadic sounds for this section."

Equally remarkable is Ellington's audacious use of dissonance, with minor seconds and other seemingly harsh clashes of neighboring pitches producing startling harmonic effects. By placing seemingly errant pitches into otherwise familiar chords, and by shrewdly tucking them deep into the orchestra fabric, Ellington achieves a deep-blue exoticism that remains one of the most appealing facets of his orchestral sound.

"In an Ellington blues, you'll find a passage where three trumpets and a trombone are playing what's supposed to be a C7 chord in close, four-part harmony, and one of the trombones has an F," says Berger, pointing to a note that in no way figures into a C7 chord (which is built on C, E, G, and B-flat). "That F doesn't belong there, it's totally foreign, and yet there it is, plain as day. It's important to realize that these strange notes did not come out of nowhere. He knew harmony so well that he could do these unusual things.

"When Ellington was in his early twenties, [bandleader] Will Marion Cook told him, 'Find out the normal way of doing things, how everyone does it, then do it your way.' I think he took that advice."

Ellington, in other words, was perpetually seeking and inventing new expressive tools, often ignoring convention. In passages of the "Queen's Suite," the tenor and baritone saxes alternate the octave doubling of the melody; in certain blues passages, the bass line traces the standard, twelve-bar blues chord progression, but the chords above do not. In portions of the "Jungle Triangle" overture from the musical *My People,* chords frequently move in parallel fashion, though this violates one of the most basic rules of orchestration.

"He didn't routine-ize himself," says Russo, who has spent a lifetime studying and performing Ellington's works.

Or, as Berger puts it, "With Duke, we're dealing with such a broad palette that there's no way of making a formula of all this. With Ellington, every chart or two you hear a whole new world of sound, a whole new set of techniques that he has discovered for himself."

Virtually every major composition, in fact, has its own innovations. The multiple, antiphonal sections within the orchestra that play off one another in "Rockin' in Rhythm," the compositional techniques of Debussy and Ravel in "Anatomy of a Murder," and the provocative high-trumpet passage of Cat Anderson all stem from a composer intent on not repeating himself.

Strayhorn, for his part, nudged Ellington toward increasingly ambitious, classically tinged works that led, inexorably, to the oft-sublime, translucent orchestrations of the *Sacred Concerts* of the 1960s. Even in his senior years, Ellington obviously hadn't lost his appetite for new musical forms: he was pushing toward an abstract, creative concert music.

The band that had seduced the Cotton Club crowd in the late 1920s with its hot dance rhythms and wah-wah, jungle sound effects had gone on to become a formidable vehicle for documenting American swing and blues culture. Just as George Gershwin, Roy Harris, Aaron Copland, and others had expressed the American experience through the European symphony orchestra, Ellington had done so by transforming an American dance band into a profound concert ensemble.

You can hear as much in the buoyant street rhythms of the *New Orleans Suite,* the lush orchestral tone painting of the *Deep South Suite,* and the sheer scope and ambition of Ellington's other large-scaled works. Yet for all their sweep, these pieces have at their heart Ellington's propulsive rhythm section.

"Duke was a vital force—a lot of people forget that he was a great piano player, very percussive, very dynamic in the rhythm section," recalls Louie Bellson, who helped revitalize that rhythm section when he joined the band in 1951. "And boy, when he started playing, and the drummer and the bass jumped in, man, with that threesome, look out, it swung.

Duke had the right times, and the fire and the ability to really move that band."

If you doubt it, just listen to Ellington's solo introduction to Strayhorn's "Take the 'A' Train," a curtain-raiser that sets the orchestra flying practically from the first note. Berger goes so far as to call it "the best introduction in all of jazz."

Beyond Ellington's abilities as pianist, composer, and orchestrator, he had one more gift that helped produce a distinctive sound: his effect on the players themselves.

"Duke was always aware of the need for the player to pour himself into the music, and most players just don't do that," says Russo. "Even the best bands, black and white, are not noted for the attention to personal playing that Duke's was. He got the players to do things they might not have done otherwise."

Indeed, Bellson takes pride in noting that "there was no drum book at all, nothing. I had to feel my way through, and that's what Duke wanted.

"He said to me, 'I want you to keep your eyes and ears open, and you'll hear it,' and that's true, because sometimes a drummer can be too involved in reading a part and not using his ears enough. He allowed you plenty of time to think it out yourself."

Or, as Terry puts it, "Duke taught us who we were."

Yet for all the variety and fluidity of Ellington's orchestral music through the decades, it maintains surprising continuity. Instrumentation and players may change, but the ensemble always sounds, well, kinda Dukish.

"When you listen to 'Black and Tan Fantasy' [1927], and then you put on something from the 1960s, you're hearing different music that nevertheless is very closely allied music," says Orrin Keepnews, who with Steven Lasker has produced a 24-CD boxed set, *The Duke Ellington Centennial Edition: The Complete RCA Victor Recordings, 1927–1973*. "There's a clear consistency there."

Though the deaths of Strayhorn and Hodges, plus the departures of Jimmy Hamilton and others meant that the 1970s band never approached the virtuosity of earlier incarnations, Ellington's unit to the very end sounded like none other in the business.

"I was at this symposium for Ellington alumni at Lincoln Center recently, and one of the guys said something great," recalls Berger.

"He said, 'A lot of people can play this music, but they don't understand their notes. We loved our notes, so we made them sound right. Even though some people might say, that's a funny note or a wrong note, we believed in those notes.'"

April 1999, DownBeat

Significant advances in transcribing Ellington's scores have been made since the composer's centennial, with Jazz at Lincoln Center, especially, creating new scores and distributing them to high schools, colleges, and other outlets. Though the particular alchemy of Ellington and Strayhorn's instrumental voicings remains difficult to replicate, the Jazz at Lincoln Center Orchestra has come close. Then, again, the organization has been addressing the challenge for roughly two decades, since releasing its debut CD, Portraits by Ellington *(Columbia, 1991, and reissued 2002) and its follow-up,* Live in Swing City: Swingin' with the Duke *(Sony, 1999), both when the band was still called the Lincoln Center Jazz Orchestra.*

Fans Recover Ellington's Lost Musical

1963 show confronted issue of civil rights.

Thirty-five years ago—in the midst of the civil rights battles of the 1960s—Duke Ellington unveiled in Chicago his most radical statement on race relations, the stage musical *My People.*

Never before had Ellington, one of America's most significant composers, addressed the subject so unflinchingly, his show reflecting Dr. Martin Luther King Jr.'s social activism while King marched on Washington in 1963. Until a month ago, it appeared as if the work would never again see the light of day—Ellington's blues-drenched score, red-hot text, and multihued lighting and staging design presumably lost forever.

But thanks to some detective work, computer technology, and considerable sweat, a group of Ellington devotees has managed to retrieve a piece considered a milestone in the career of a composer better known for his jazzy pop tunes. *My People* takes on a much more ambitious challenge, looking at a century of black life in America through music, dance, and spoken word.

When the curtain goes up Friday at the New Regal Theater on east Seventy-ninth Street, fans and scholars from around the world will see more than just a historic re-creation of *My People.* They will discover how intensely Ellington felt about civil rights and how close he felt to King at a critical juncture in American history.

Nevertheless, "just last month, I was getting ready to bail," recalls David Baker, head of jazz studies at Indiana University and conductor of *My People.* The performance had been planned months ago as the headline event of the sixteenth annual Duke Ellington International Conference, meeting in Chicago through Sunday.

"The Ellington people had called me some time ago to conduct this, but I was working on the assumption that the score existed," Baker said. "So I began acting like a sleuth. I went to the Smithsonian Institution [in Washington, D.C., where Ellington's papers are housed], but most of *My People* was missing and in disarray, and there was nothing that could be used in its existing form."

With the clock ticking toward a scheduled performance just a few weeks away, Chicago conference organizer Josie Childs leaped into action. After working the phone, she discovered that veteran Los Angeles trumpeter Bill Berry Jr.—who had played in the original production—owned a reel-to-reel tape of *My People.*

"I don't remember where I got the tape or how I got the tape—it had been sitting among hundreds of my tapes for more than thirty years," Berry says. Apparently, he had obtained the pre-edited tape that Ellington had made in a Chicago recording studio during the run of *My People,* which was performed twice daily from August 16 to September 2, 1963.

Because there was too much music to fit on an LP, a great deal of material had been cut from the recording released in the 1960s. With most of the original band members deceased, Berry represented possibly the last chance to learn that a tape even existed.

Berry's tape included several musical pieces that had not surfaced previously ("Jungle Triangle," "Blues at Sundown," "Walkin' and Singin' the Blues"), but it was far from complete. Parts of the narration and all the stage, dance, and lighting directions did not exist.

By combining the scraps of information that Baker had found in the Smithsonian (such as song lyrics without music) with the memories of those who had appeared in *My People* (such as Barbara Wright-Pryor, a chorister who had saved her notes and vividly remembered the choreography and stage design), the Ellington aficionados were on their way.

Unfortunately, there still was nary a written note for the band and vocal soloists to perform.

"I didn't even hear about this project until April 10, and it wasn't until the next week that I got a call that there was nothing in hand that could be used to play the performance, so I was terrified," says Chicago jazz guitarist Charles Harrison, who specializes in transcribing recordings. "When I got a copy of Bill Berry's tape, it sounded like a copy of a copy of a copy—it was not the greatest fidelity, which makes it much tougher to transcribe. Fortunately I've got sound equipment that could boost the low end and cut the hiss of the recording."

In addition, Harrison's computer program—which can print musical notes as they are played on a keyboard—enabled him to complete a finished score in days. Without it, he says, "we would have needed an army of copyists working for months to produce this score."

Nevertheless, the task was difficult because many of Ellington's regular players, whose work Harrison easily could have identified and transcribed, weren't in the *My People* band. They were on the road with Ellington generating funds to help support *My People,* which was being presented on a tiny budget as part of the Century of Negro Progress Exposition in McCormick Place, marking the one hundredth anniversary of the Emancipation Proclamation.

But why can't you just buy a score of *My People,* just as you might buy music for Beethoven's Fifth?

"Because Duke, at least at that point in his life, wasn't that interested in documenting what he had written—he was interested in what's happening tomorrow or the next day," Baker says.

Indeed, "Ellington wrote so much that none of us realized how much, including himself," remembers Ellington veteran Louie Bellson, who played drums in *My People.* "Sometimes we'd say, 'Hey, Duke, why don't you play so-and-so'—a piece of his own—and he'd say, 'What's that?' "

Because Ellington was constantly tinkering with his pieces, the shape of a work typically changed from rehearsal to performance to recording, often with no surviving, definitive score. So even though Ellington had reworked some music from his *Black, Brown and Beige* for *My People,* details of instrumentation and voicing had to be determined.

Ellington never before or since wrote a work as confrontational on the subject of race. "King Fit the Battle of Alabam'," for instance, is loosely based on the spiritual "Joshua Fit the Battle of Jericho" and portrays King and his followers braving the billy clubs and attack dogs of Birmingham public safety commissioner Bull Connor. And in the work's title narration, Ellington himself proclaims: "The foundation of the United States rests on the sweat of my people."

"My grandfather never made absolutely direct statements like that; he usually implied or insinuated his view," says Mercedes Ellington, who has created dances loosely based on Barbara Wright-Pryor's recollections of Alvin Ailey's original choreography. "So *My People* is the strongest piece of its kind that he wrote."

That *My People* was running in Chicago just as King and two hundred thousand protesters were marching on Washington underscored Ellington's racial agenda.

"In May of 1963, Birmingham [demonstrations] had occurred," recalls Chicago cultural historian Timuel Black, "and Dr. King became international immediately. He came to Chicago [in August], I had the opportunity to take him around town, and we wound up at McCormick

Place. Ellington was coming out of the theater after rehearsal, and these two giants exchanged pleasantries."

King attended a rehearsal of *My People,* then led the march on Washington on August 28, which helped set the stage for passage of the Civil Rights Act of 1964 and the Voting Rights Act of 1965.

"My grandfather was very influenced by Dr. King and his efforts," Mercedes Ellington says, "and now perhaps people will realize just how deeply."

May 8, 1998

Silent for Thirty-Five Years, Ellington's Restored Musical Celebrates Black Culture, Composer's Genius

The history of jazz acquired a new chapter over the weekend, and it will forever change the way listeners perceive the music of Duke Ellington.

Until Friday night, Ellington's 1963 stage musical *My People* survived as a tantalizing fragment, with only part of its score preserved on a notoriously truncated recording. Until someone resurrected its missing musical numbers, complete narration, and original lighting and staging design, audiences would never know the full meaning and importance of Ellington's fabled civil rights show (which had its first and only performances in Chicago's Arie Crown Theater in 1963). Thanks to a persevering group of Ellington scholars and devotees, however, *My People* was heard again in complete form—for the first time in thirty-five years—Friday night in the New Regal Theater, on east Seventy-ninth Street in Chicago. The results were revelatory.

For starters, the production restored three musical numbers that flesh out an otherwise skeletal *My People*. The most striking is "Jungle Triangle," an orchestral curtain-raiser built on driving rhythms, fiercely dissonant chords, and a pervasive mood of incantation.

"Blues at Sundown" and "Walkin' and Singin' the Blues"—the other rediscovered numbers—significantly deepen our understanding of Ellington's art. Both show how adroitly the composer could adapt his signature jazz-blues language to contemporary musical idioms. "Blues at Sundown," for instance, could pass for a romantic pop ballad of the day, while "Walkin' and Singin' the Blues" carries the rhythmic swagger and gritty, declamatory vocal style of nascent 1960s R & B. Clearly, Ellington created *My People* not only to celebrate black cultural contributions of the past but also to speak to contemporary audiences on their own musical terms.

It's not just the restored music of this *My People,* however, that clarifies Ellington's purposes. Several passages of original narration underscore the ferocity of the man's commitment to civil rights.

The most significant, "Purple People—Green People," unfolds as a devastating, metaphorical commentary on the futility of war between the races. Written by Ellington in a wry, storybook manner, the piece laments a world in which people of differing skin colors bludgeon each other. Tragically, they learn on the battlefield that "all of the blood was red."

The central miracle of *My People,* though, is that the show can address issues such as racism and class warfare without becoming heavy-handed or depressing. In fact, Ellington obviously took pains to keep *My People* brisk and entertaining, the show developing not as a typical "book" musical (with storyline and characters) but as a revue in which one witty sketch quickly gives way to the next.

So *My People* now emerges as a key transitional work bridging the innovations of Ellington's *Black, Brown and Beige* (1943) with the mature statements of the *Sacred Concerts* (of 1965, 1968, and 1973). In other words, the expressions of faith that Ellington makes throughout *My People*—as in "Ain't but the One" and "David Danced"—would come to new prominence in the *Sacred Concerts.*

It's worth noting that this restoration of *My People* did not precisely duplicate the 1963 version. Mercedes Ellington's choreography, for instance, is only loosely inspired by the original; and the orchestra platform did not rise up from below stage level, as in the Arie Crown production.

Yet this *My People*—brilliantly conducted by David Baker and exceptionally well sung by Robert Sims, Lucius Bell Jr., Roberta Thomas, and Joya Sherrill—may be about as close to the original as we are likely to get.

For that reason, among others, the one-night-only performance ought to be restaged in a longer run so audiences everywhere can behold a critical, missing link in Ellington's evolution.

May 11, 1998

Unfortunately, My People *has remained a rarely performed fragment of Ellington's oeuvre, overshadowed even by minor works. The demands of presenting* My People *as a stage piece, as well as its historic subject matter, have contributed to its obscurity, notwithstanding the fine detective work that made possible this revival. For the foreseeable future,* My People *seems likely to surface only on anniversaries and, perhaps, in student productions, where at least Ellington devotees can discover the social message that few listeners have heard.*

Lost Classics

Duke Ellington, one of the giants of music, left little printed evidence of his genius.

Imagine the public outcry if thousands of pages of music by Beethoven or Mozart could not be performed, heard, or studied anywhere in the world.

The prospect of life without Beethoven's Fifth Symphony or Mozart's *Marriage of Figaro* would distress listeners from Chicago to Vienna. Yet that's the predicament of Duke Ellington's music on the hundredth anniversary of his birth.

Even as the cultural world on Thursday celebrates the occasion, many of Ellington's most imposing orchestral and stage scores are in too poor a condition to be performed publicly. And when bands do perform Ellington's instrumental masterworks, their scores rarely include every note, phrase, and musical detail as the composer originally penned them.

Moreover, though listeners will be hearing countless musicians riffing on "Satin Doll," "Sophisticated Lady," and other Ellington hit tunes throughout this centennial year, the tattered remains of the composer's exquisitely detailed manuscripts are years from being properly edited for public consumption.

So the Ellington centennial is proving bittersweet: although Ellington is as famous as ever, his painstakingly written scores are extremely difficult to come by a quarter-century after his death.

Thanks to Ellington's desire to keep his writing techniques secret as well as his scores unpublished, the man's written music was kept far from public view until he died in 1974. Ever since then, cultural and racial attitudes, as well as a morass of copyright conflicts, have prevented dozens of Ellington's works from being heard in live performance.

Instead, listeners must turn to scratchy old recordings that never did justice to the symphonic brilliance of such Ellington scores as *Afro-Eurasian Eclipse*, *The River*, or the stage work *Jump for Joy*.

Although some of the lost or destroyed scores have been re-created by arts groups in Chicago, Washington, and New York, and in addition the

Smithsonian Institution has cataloged approximately two hundred thousand pages of Ellington ephemera, most of the music is in no shape to be performed publicly.

"In most cases, the [complete] scores don't exist, and even when they do, you typically can't get them," said William Russo, conductor of the Chicago Jazz Ensemble and a music professor at Columbia College Chicago.

"And the real tragedy is that the scores are being re-created and transcribed [from recordings] by people all over the world. But there's no collective editing going on, no definitive version of all this music being made available," as there is in music of Bach, Beethoven, and Brahms, Russo said.

The loss is staggering, not only because of the sheer size of Ellington's catalog, which spans the 1920s to the 1970s, but because of its stature.

"We're talking about music by the greatest all-around musician this country has produced," said John Edward Hasse, curator of American music at the Smithsonian Institution in Washington, where the Ellington family donated the composer's archives in 1988.

"I know that's saying a lot, because the United States has produced many great composers, outstanding orchestrators, brilliant soloists, gifted band leaders and conductors, but no one who did all of those things so originally."

Yet much of the music that made Ellington's reputation is beyond public reach, in part because of the idiosyncratic working methods of Ellington and his band. Though the myth endures that Ellington sketched themes for his players to improvise upon, in fact he wrote his scores meticulously, marking specific passages for individual musicians.

Because Ellington band members typically stayed with the group for years, they played from memory, and the scores eventually decayed.

Why didn't Ellington preserve them?

"For one thing, he was secretive about his writing," said Russo, who as a composer worked with Ellington. "It's like the old New Orleans trumpet players who kept a handkerchief over the valves of their horns so other musicians wouldn't see their fingerings and steal them.

"Duke was concerned about the sources of income of his band, and he didn't want the secrets of his sound widely available."

Ellington was also a prolific artist, consumed with the present and the future, not the past.

"I think Ellington's attitude was that we create music because it's fun, and when we're tired of it, we move on to new pieces," said David Berger, whose authoritative transcriptions of Ellington scores have been played by Russo's band, Wynton Marsalis's Jazz at Lincoln Center Orchestra, and others.

"Once, some of the copyists in Duke's band prepared beautiful books of the scores for his *Liberian Suite* and all these great compositions at considerable cost and effort, and they presented it to him at a celebratory dinner. Duke graciously thanked them, never looked at the books, and left them at the restaurant where the dinner was held. That roughly summed up his attitude on the past."

Unfortunately, Ellington's scores have suffered general neglect, in part because American culture never regarded music in the black-jazz tradition as equal to its European symphonic counterpart. To this day, Ellington exists in the American imagination more as a pop entertainer than as a serious composer.

"And we have a long, long way to go to change that notion," Hasse said. "Most people think of Ellington as a leader of a dance band or a writer of popular song hits, but a very small number recognize him as one of the great instrumental composers of the twentieth century."

Yet there are glimmers of hope on the horizon. The Smithsonian, for instance, in addition to organizing his archives, has championed Ellington's instrumental music via concerts by its touring repertory band, the Smithsonian Jazz Masterworks Orchestra. And Jazz at Lincoln Center, in New York, during the last four years has transcribed and published twenty-eight Ellington compositions, distributing them for free to high schools participating in its annual Essentially Ellington competition.

In addition, the Jazz at Lincoln Center program is negotiating with publishers, lawyers, and copyright experts to win permission to disseminate roughly six hundred additional Ellington works that it has had transcribed during the last decade. Jazz at Lincoln Center hopes to begin publishing and releasing these scores in the next few years, said director of education Laura Johnson.

But bringing some of Ellington's most imposing pieces back to life is a formidable task, as a group of Chicago cultural activists discovered last year when offering the first performances of the musical *My People* since its premiere at McCormick Place in 1963. By unearthing surviving bits and pieces of the original score at the Smithsonian and scouring the country for a single reel-to-reel tape of the show, the group was able to stage the show for the first time in thirty-five years.

The performance of the reconstructed score, which will be donated to a musical archive, kicked off a year's worth of Ellington centennial activities. Still to come is Thursday's performance of Ellington's *Sacred Music* in Washington, D.C., his hometown; Saturday's Field Museum performance by Billy Taylor and others; Russo's Symphony Center tribute on May 7; and an all-Ellington evening during the Chicago Jazz Festival on September 5.

But the heroic task of re-creating *My People* will have to be repeated dozens of times if listeners are to hear all the music Ellington wrote the way he wrote it.

"It took Ellington approximately 50 years, 10 million miles of travel, 20,000 engagements, 10,000 recordings, and 800 musicians who passed through his band to accomplish what he did," said the Smithsonian's Hasse.

"We can't expect to absorb it in ten years. There's enough here to keep students, scholars, teachers, and musicians working for decades."

April 29, 1999

The Unknown Ellington

Jazz composer considered epic works among his best, but these longer pieces are still rarely played.

Ask almost anyone to name Duke Ellington's greatest works, and chances are you'll hear roughly the same litany: "Sophisticated Lady," "In a Sentimental Mood," "Don't Get Around Much Anymore," "It Don't Mean a Thing If It Ain't Got That Swing."

Each richly deserves its place in the classic American songbook. Yet none approaches the artistic reach of Ellington's *Such Sweet Thunder,* the exquisite orchestral detail of his *Deep South Suite,* or the lush harmonies and driving rhythms of his *New Orleans Suite.* These epic works, and others like them, meant a great deal to Ellington, who spent much of his career attempting to coax jazz beyond the loosely improvised, three-minute song form and into more ambitious realms of serious composition.

But as the music world prepares to celebrate Ellington's centennial, on April 29, the man's immense oeuvre stands at an odd juncture: the public adores his short pieces but barely knows his larger compositions exist.

"On some of those pieces, we sold maybe one copy a year, if that," says music publisher Joe Muccioli, whose King Brand Co. in New York has been the major provider of Ellington's large-form scores for jazz bands. "And I don't think we've ever sold one hundred copies of any of the larger pieces."

Why do substantial works by America's preeminent jazz composer languish on the shelf, while the familiar tunes are repeated ad infinitum? The reasons are as numerous as they are frustrating.

For starters, neither Ellington nor his staff went to the trouble of preserving the master's scores. Because Ellington's band members typically knew his work from memory, and because the prolific composer was more interested in writing new pieces than in documenting old ones, the band's repertory book was poorly maintained. To this day, thousands of tattered, virtually unedited pages of music are stored at the Smithsonian Institution in Washington, D.C.

To return a piece such as the *New Orleans Suite* or *Toot Suite* to the repertory, an extremely skilled musician has to transcribe the music from a recording, note by note, which is what King Brand Co. co-owner David Berger has done with a dozen or so scores.

But to date, as during Ellington's lifetime, jazz musicians have resisted these pieces.

"Mainly, that's because the music is above their heads; they don't understand it," says Berger, who does not mince words.

"And that goes for many critics, too," adds William Russo, whose Chicago Jazz Ensemble has been in the forefront of playing Ellington's large works.

"They don't necessarily understand music this sophisticated."

Thus Ellington's first grand opus, *Black, Brown and Beige* (1943), was savaged in the press.

"It is too long a piece," complained Robert Bagar in the *New York World-Telegram*. "A bit self-conscious, as these tone poems usually are," wrote Abel Green in *Variety*.

Bruised but not defeated, Ellington continued to unveil major works in a series of Carnegie Hall concerts during the 1940s, and elsewhere for the rest of his life. He believed that the Carnegie Hall concerts, especially, "had helped establish a music that was new in both its extended forms and its social significance," wrote Ellington in his memoir, *Music Is My Mistress*.

Yet the works never caught on with most critics or the public, and one reason is more disturbing than either the frayed state of the scores or the undeniable complexity of the music.

"There's a racist position at work here, among many people who dismiss this music," Russo says. "Their position is that jazz [essentially a black musical form] has to be entertaining and adorable.

"But this music isn't entertaining and adorable. It's profound music in the sense that Beethoven and Brahms wrote profound music. It's longer forms; it makes a bigger statement. Many people think jazz is not supposed to do that, which is unfortunate. The anti-intellectualism in jazz is staggering."

So long as Russo's Chicago Jazz Ensemble and Wynton Marsalis's Jazz at Lincoln Center Orchestra are up and running, so long as scholarly musicians such as Gunther Schuller, David Baker, and Berger are guest conducting jazz bands around the world, the music will be heard, albeit sporadically.

The sumptuousness of these scores, as well as their expressive range and orchestrational virtuosity, should persuade any serious listener who gets a chance to hear them.

"Count Basie is more easily understood, Glenn Miller is more popular, but I think ultimately Duke Ellington will win out," Berger says. "A lot of his richest material is in these suites, and, in the end, the music speaks for itself."

April 4, 1999

The prejudice against Ellington's most ambitious scores endures, with precious few ensembles equipped for or interested in taking them on, in toto (though excerpts, such as the "Second Line" movement from the New Orleans Suite, *turn up on concert programs more frequently). Outside of the aforementioned large groups based in New York, Chicago, and a few other places, Ellington and Strayhorn's achievements in large-scale composition are rarely shared with the jazz public, and then are often dismissed by observers who sadly prefer jazz to remain a short-form idiom forever more.*

VII

Sinatra Songs

Listening Anew to the Voice

A Bouquet for Sinatra

Honoring the first great balladeer of American song.

Without so much as an introduction over the PA system, Francis Albert Sinatra quietly steps onto the stage of Radio City Music Hall in New York—and the place goes nuts.

Shrieks of a kind more commonly reserved for heavy-metal bands pierce the night, and before the crowd can begin settling down, Sinatra is swinging with one of his countless signature tunes, "Come Fly with Me."

Even now, as he approaches his seventy-fifth birthday (on December 12), Sinatra sounds like a million bucks. The Voice—growling on the bottom, imploring on top, still remarkably warm and embracing in the center—belies both the passage of time and the rumors that perpetually swirl around the world's foremost interpreter of popular song.

Forget everything you've heard about how the years have caught up with Ol' Blue Eyes. On this night, the man who ennobled the popular song—or at least made it one of America's most universally admired and widely exported cultural forms—is swinging for the fences. Whether igniting rhythm numbers by the Gershwins, sensual vignettes by Cole Porter, blues ballads by Harold Arlen, or show tunes by Rodgers and Hart, Sinatra is teaching everyone in this house exactly how it's done. It's an art Sinatra has been defining since the mid-1930s, when he toiled as one-quarter of the Hoboken Four vocal group, shortly thereafter joining the bands of Harry James and then Tommy Dorsey.

More than half a century later, Sinatra still sells out theaters around the world, though Chicagoans can hear him Saturday evening at Poplar Creek.

"No, I've never studied [voice] and can't read sheet music very well," notes Sinatra, when asked how he managed to develop the apparently infallible sense of pitch and rhythm he still possesses.

"[But] I am very aware of enunciation," adds Sinatra, understating the case, just as he does when singing. (Sinatra rarely gives interviews but agreed to answer written questions.)

"What is the point of singing wonderful lyrics if the audience can't understand what is being said or heard? There must be a special relationship, a marriage, between lyric and music."

No one has consummated that marriage better than Sinatra, who stands at a unique juncture in the history of American music: by nearly any measure, he was America's first great balladeer, yet he also stands as one of the last. Having outlived and outsung nearly everyone else, he has come to represent virtually an entire tradition of American song, from the start to nearly the finish.

If you don't believe that Sinatra virtually started it all, consider that even though such diverse Sinatra predecessors as Bing Crosby, Russ Columbo, Al Jolson, and Louis Armstrong enjoyed immense popularity, none championed key American songwriters as specifically, as enduringly, or as singularly as Sinatra.

The proof lies in Sinatra's immense discography, which has been synonymous with impeccably crafted American popular song for fully five decades; and in Sinatra's vocal style, swing-based and jazz-driven, and as far removed from Bing's dreamy, laid-back vocals as a shot of gin is from a mug of warm milk.

No wonder his voice—with its inimitable mix of bel canto vocal embellishments and colloquial American rhythms—permeates popular culture, whether in contemporary film (Sinatra tunes pervade such movies as *Baby, It's You*) or modern dance (consider Twyla Tharp's *Nine Sinatra Songs*).

Perhaps Sinatra's greatest blessing, and ours, was that the skinny kid from Hoboken, New Jersey, happened on the scene at the peak of the big-band era, when gloriously swinging groups led by Harry James, Glenn Miller, Tommy Dorsey, Jimmy Dorsey, and the like still barnstormed the land.

For Sinatra, the journey began in earnest when he left Harry James's band, switching (in January 1940, at age twenty-four) to a group that showcased singers as none other did.

"It was heaven when I joined Tommy Dorsey's band," recalls Sinatra today. "I didn't think anything could ever be better. I had always admired his apparently seamless playing, and I wanted to capture that in my singing.

"Sitting on the stage between my numbers, I studied Tommy and over the months realized he took very small, subtle breaths out of the side of his mouth. Of course, he had the trombone and his hand to hide the movement.

"It was a revelation, and over time I was able to do the same thing Tommy did with the trombone to sneak in air to vary my phrasing.

"I also swam laps in hotel pools—and continue to do so—to build up lung capacity, which increases my ability to lengthen phrases.

"From the beginning, I was determined to find a different sound," adds Sinatra. "Bing was the crooner, and nobody could compare, but I could be different."

That he was.

"He practically invented the art of popular singing," says veteran songwriter Sammy Cahn, who penned lyrics for such Sinatra classics as "Come Fly with Me," "All the Way," "Only the Lonely," "Love and Marriage," "The Tender Trap," and a number particularly beloved in this corner of the world, "My Kind of Town (Chicago Is)."

"Sinatra learned how to do that legato [long-lined] singing, and it really had a romantic, almost sexual kind of connotation. It was very, very seductive, a fact well known to women, as well as to the men who took them to concerts. There simply had been nothing else like it before him."

With American boys fighting the good war in Europe and the Pacific (Sinatra was rejected from service because of a perforated eardrum incurred at birth), Sinatra became a kind of romantic Everyman, the voice of the American male at a time of intense national stress.

By the early 1940s he had emerged as a genuine phenomenon, the first teen idol, a guaranteed hit at palaces such as New York's Paramount Theater, where he would sell out the house six shows a day, performing more than a hundred songs in a few hours.

Had Sinatra been merely a beneficiary of lucky timing, the career nosedive he experienced in the postwar 1940s and early '50s would have continued. But saved by an Academy Award (in 1954) for his performance as the poor Italian kid Maggio in *From Here to Eternity*, Sinatra—and his songs—were airborne again.

More important, the recordings he began turning out for Capitol Records in the 1950s, as well as his sellout concert engagements around the world, proved that he was still redefining the art of the American popular singer.

"He was giving pop singing something it never had before—style," says Jule Styne, who composed such Sinatra standards as "Time After Time" and "As Long as There's Music" (with lyrics by Cahn).

"Before Sinatra's great rise in the late 1950s, songs were just sung—straight and without much panache. Crosby had a little sense of style, but Sinatra was the one who went the whole way.

"He was phrasing the lyric, not just the music, which is the right way. He was finding the right tempo, the right kick for the music.

"Just as important, he is the one—and no one else—who made a songwriter somebody. Before Sinatra, the songwriter had been virtually negated by Hollywood especially—the songwriter was nothing. They [Hollywood studios] just paid you off, and they thought they owned you.

"So along comes Sinatra, who actually works with the songwriters to see what they're after! Can you imagine the shock of that?"

Or, in the words of veteran songwriter Cy Coleman (who composed Sinatra's "Witchcraft," as well as the new, Tony-winning musical *City of Angels*): "Sinatra can justly take responsibility for a whole generation of songwriters. He encouraged people like me right down the line, getting us to write the most complex kind of popular songs.

"Today, songs have a lesser importance. It's the visuals that matter nowdays."

As a singer Sinatra is profoundly persuasive, whether he is expressing quiet romantic despair ("Only the Lonely," "Angel Eyes," and "One for My Baby"), the high life ("Come Dance with Me," "My Kind of Town"), erotic love ("I've Got You Under My Skin," "Strangers in the Night," "Satisfy Me One More Time") or defiant proclamations ("My Way," "All the Way").

Perhaps that's because Sinatra's ability to understand and project a song is as much intuitive—beneath the surface of his consciousness—as it is cerebral.

"When Sammy [Cahn] and I would present a song to Sinatra, he didn't seem to really analyze it at all," recalls Jule Styne. "He reads a song, hears it, and starts breathing the song. And then he falls in love with that song."

Or, as Sinatra once said in a *Playboy* interview, "I get an audience involved, personally involved in a song—because I'm involved myself. It's not something I do deliberately. I can't help myself."

Songwriter Mitchell Parish—who has written such Sinatra favorites as "Star Dust," "Moonlight Serenade," and many more—sums it up: "Sinatra is the third dimension in songwriting; there's the composer, the lyricist, and then there's Sinatra."

No doubt Sinatra's voice has evolved over the years. As Cahn says, "He went from the violin sound to the viola sound to the cello sound, which is where he is now. It's the most natural progression in the world."

But there's more to it than that. If anything, Sinatra's style is more economical, more dramatically cunning than ever. In short, he's reaping the artistic rewards of a career devoted to discovering and nurturing the American songbook.

"We have a library of probably thousands of songs and dip into that from time to time for additions to concerts," says Sinatra on the eve of his Chicago performance, when asked how he chooses the repertoire he performs.

"But audiences love to hear the standards, and I enjoy singing them. We have a ballad portion of the show and usually change these numbers. These are my favorites—they're saloon songs.

"There are [just] so many great songs to choose from. I didn't do [Paul Anka's] 'My Way' for a long time, but it was requested at every show, so we've added it again."

Surely the aching question among Sinatra fans is: will there ever be another album?

"I'd like to record," says Sinatra, "but it is difficult to find the time. And, quite frankly, I haven't seen many new songs I want to record. We do songs by the Beatles ['Something'] and Stevie Wonder ['Just the Way You Are'] in the show, and they're beautiful, but it's hard to beat the classics."

As to which of Sinatra's recordings have meant the most to him, he'll only allow that "every song I've ever recorded has meant the most to me at the time it is being recorded."

Yet in that brief statement lies the essence of Sinatra's art—the ability to become totally involved in a song, to make it sum up a lifetime's experience.

Along the way, Sinatra has drawn inspiration from a short and elite list of singers who can be considered peers.

Among them, "I absolutely adore Ella Fitzgerald," says Sinatra, who hastens to add that "Mabel Mercer and Lady Day [Billie Holiday] made every song their own."

To many listeners, Sinatra represents the high point—the final step in the evolution of American popular singing.

"There's almost no one left," says Styne. "I see the art of male singing deteriorating now.

"We're all still hanging on to Tony Bennett. After that, there are no new male singers coming up. Most of the rock singers you hear today belt out loud high notes and that's it. So what does that have to do with interpreting a song?"

Sinatra himself, however, remains more optimistic. The man who helped create the genre insists its future is relatively bright.

"I don't think anything can affect the great American classics," says Sinatra, when queried on how the rise of rock 'n' roll affected the decidedly more soft-spoken and literate American popular song. "They are timeless and immune to changing fashion.

"And I am delighted that young people are coming to our concerts to listen to those wonderful lyrics and the big-band sounds.

"I hope those songs will endure and always be around in records, and there are young singers who do standards as well as write their own music.

"Billy Joel has written some beautiful words," says Sinatra. "Anita Baker does wonderful things with lyrics and music.

"You can't keep good music down."

August 26, 1990

Sinatra launched his final tour in 1994 and played his last Chicago concert on October 22 of that year, at the United Center, the home of the Chicago Bulls. The singer seemed to sense that the end was near. At the finish of the concert, he held the microphone close to his lips and told the screaming crowd, "Think about me once in a while," the last words he said to a Chicago audience that had followed him fervently since the mid-1930s. A few months after, Sinatra slipped into an unannounced retirement, unable to participate in the grand, eightieth birthday celebration that was being planned. His managers had envisioned a series of concerts in Carnegie Hall—perhaps a week's worth—with each evening's performance exploring a different chapter of his musical career. Sinatra died of a heart attack on May 14, 1998, at age eighty-two, the news prompting blanket coverage on TV, commemorative sections in newspapers, and countless tributes around the world.

Frank Sinatra: The Virtuoso

Strip away the Hollywood glamour, the lady-killer reputation, the ring-a-ding-ding shenanigans, and you'll find something far more important at the heart of Frank Sinatra's turbulent life: the work of a virtuoso musician.

In other words, though it's easy enough to lump Sinatra in with various high-living, high-rolling singers of his day—from fellow Rat Packers Dean Martin and Sammy Davis Jr. to Vegas denizens Wayne Newton and Vic Damone—Sinatra's music prevails, and not simply because of the man's notoriety. Rather, it was Sinatra's natural gifts and hard-won achievements as a musician that made possible all the rest.

From his first recordings in 1939 to his last in 1994, Sinatra used a good, though not necessarily great, instrument to achieve profound artistic results. It took more than an adept vocalist to achieve so many stylistic innovations (in swing, ballads, bossa nova, and other idioms), and only a restlessly inventive and deeply accomplished musician could have done it.

Admittedly, Sinatra from the start was a skilled crooner, able to meet Bing Crosby on his own dulcet-voiced terms. As early as the 1939 recordings, there's no doubt that Young Blue Eyes had the accuracy of pitch and felicitous way with a phrase to stand among the top singers of the pre–World War II era.

"When I was a kid, and Sinatra was singing with Tommy Dorsey, I loved him then," says Ray Charles, whom Sinatra once dubbed "the only genius in this business."

"All the teeny boppers just loved Sinatra, but I was always listening to the way he controlled his voice, the way he controlled notes. You could tell that this guy was into what he was doing. I wasn't looking at him like the teenagers; I was looking at him like a musician, so I was paying attention to what he did and how he did it. I tried to pick him apart, especially from a musical point of view, but there was nothing you could find wrong with what he was doing. Nothing."

But Sinatra himself found something wrong with what he was doing, at least stylistically. Though he often conceded that Crosby was his early hero, the fiercely competitive younger singer also yearned to step far beyond Crosby's shadow, to "find a different sound," Sinatra said in a 1990 *Chicago Tribune* article.

Furthermore, Sinatra—though unable to read music—instinctively knew that he needed to develop the physical side of his instrument in order to accomplish artistic breakthroughs he had not yet conceived. By relentlessly swimming laps, he built his ability to draw long, deep breaths and, therefore, to better sustain and control a phrase. By analyzing Tommy Dorsey's trombone technique, he learned that it was possible to steal small bits of air out of the side of his mouth, in order to extend a melodic line.

Sinatra was already laying the technical groundwork for the ballad innovations of the 1950s, unveiled in recordings such as *In the Wee Small Hours* (1955) and *(Frank Sinatra Sings for) Only the Lonely* (1958). If the incomparably long lines that he unspooled in these and subsequent recordings brought an operatic intensity to his singing, he nevertheless sounded nothing like the European-tinged crooners of an earlier day.

In part, that was due to Sinatra's distinctly American approach to rhythm. "He came from the big-band era, and Dorsey and most of the bands leaned on the backbeat—on two and four," says Bill Miller, Sinatra's pianist for most of the last four decades of the singer's career. "And that's what they instilled in him over the years. To the very end, he preferred that slight accent on two and four, and it worked."

Indeed, "if Frank Sinatra belonged to one section of the orchestra, it was the rhythm section," says Gregg Field, who played drums for Sinatra briefly in 1981 and from 1991 to the end of the singer's performing career, in 1995. "That's where he lived, even on the ballads. There was such a sense of pulse within his ballads. And he needed the rhythm section to continue the rhythmic spark and momentum even when he was singing a ballad. The momentum didn't let down at all."

Beyond rhythm, Sinatra pushed past Crosby's manner by declining to use very much vibrato until the final moments of a note. The technique represented the antithesis of the crooner's art, and it defined Sinatra's ballad singing through the end of his career.

"That was his thing—no vibrato until the end of the phrase, that was real important to him," says Mike Smith, who played winds in Sinatra's bands from 1988 to the end. "I consider him the originator of that style. It reminds me of Miles [Davis], who would also carry a melody across the bar lines, just like Frank always did." Indeed, Davis, in his memoirs, credited Sinatra as a key influence in matters of phrasing.

To the sublime legato technique and irrepressible swing rhythm, Sinatra added a keen sense of pitch.

"Sinatra didn't just sing in tune, he had perfect pitch," says Harry "Sweets" Edison, whose Harmon-muted trumpet adds shimmering color to many of Sinatra's studio recordings, beginning with *In the Wee Small Hours.* "He didn't have to hear the [first] note that he would sing. He could just start off and hit it, bam, just like that."

Obviously, perfect pitch is not essential to great musicianship—well-developed relative pitch serves most musicians just fine. But Sinatra's mastery of pitch sheds light on his ability to achieve exceptional results in the recording studio. Regardless of how dense or harmonically complex the orchestrations might have been, Sinatra's pitch was unwaveringly accurate, an impressive accomplishment considering that he insisted on recording with the band roaring behind him (not via headphones in the recording booth) and that he loathed multiple takes.

Thanks to his control of pitch and line, in other words, Sinatra could cut a definitive version of a tune in the first or second take, thereby preserving the freshness and spontaneity upon which his art always thrived.

"Working with Sinatra in the recording studio was like nothing I've ever seen," remembers Field, who played drums on *Duets* and *Duets II.* "The first night, Frank showed up and left—he didn't sing a note. The second night, he came in and claimed that his voice was giving him some problems. My personal feeling is that he hadn't been in the studio in about ten years and was probably a little nervous. The third night he came in, he did something I've never seen: he recorded nine songs in three hours. It was incredible.

"He usually would do one take, maybe two, and he would not ask for a playback unless he thought he had it. He wouldn't say, 'Let me hear that back,' and then say, 'No, I don't like that, let me do it over.' It was a big shock, because the first thing that I recorded with him was 'Come Fly with Me,' and we did one take on it. I'm expecting to do another take, and suddenly I hear on the [head]phones, 'Next.' "

Above all, though, Sinatra distinguished himself as a musician through his uncanny talent for redefining himself to suit the musical occasion. The singer crooned in the 1930s, learned to swing in the '40s, created profound balladry in the '50s, and produced exquisitely understated and thoroughly authentic bossa nova singing in the '60s. Sinatra, in other words, perpetually adapted to the setting.

"When Sinatra sang with different bands and players, his feelings took shape with the musicians around him," says Joe Lovano, who tipped his fedora to the singer with his recording *Celebrating Sinatra* (Blue Note). "That's the essence of jazz as far as I'm concerned. The way he sang within the [arranger] Neal Hefti sound, for instance, was different than the way he sounded when there were strings accompanying him. That's why most of the singers who try to copy him, they can maybe try to imitate a style, but they couldn't capture that feeling, that mood he could create."

It was a mood Sinatra invented on the spot, reacting to the players, the arrangements, the audience, the emotional temperature of the setting and of the singer himself. The familiar repertoire and the lack of melodic embellishment may have led some listeners to believe Sinatra's performances essentially were set in stone, but, in fact, no two performances were alike. Sinatra improvised freely—at least when it came to phrasing, rhythm, tempo, color, and attack.

"In rehearsal, he would sing all the way through a song, he would get into it and let the orchestra know, say, to pull back here—he's going to sing this part real slow," remembers Smith. "But then during the performance, it could be totally different. The rubato section that he had pulled way, way back during rehearsal, he might rush through during performance. So you had to watch, to be really on your toes. He sang just for the moment."

Or, as Field puts it, "He allowed himself to react. He operated on instinct. There were certain things I could almost count on him always doing, but for the most part it was a very spontaneous thing that we created onstage. You listened to where Frank sang, where he heard the rhythm of the song, and then you reacted to it. In other words, if we heard him put beat one in a particular location, that told us where we needed to lay beat two. It took a conductor that really knew what he was doing to be able to follow the old man. And though Frank [Sinatra] Jr. got the job because he was Frank Jr., he kept the job because he was a very good conductor, and nobody knew Frank Sinatra's music as well as Frank Jr."

As anyone who attended Sinatra's concerts at the end of his career knows, they often were bittersweet affairs, with the great singer often struggling to perform despite somewhat diminished vocal resources. Yet on a good night, such as Sinatra's stunning farewell performance to Chicago at the United Center in October 1994, the man could muster the sonic force, rhythmic fury, and interpretive power of old.

"He was really on top of the game in that concert, complete command," remembers Smith, who played that night. "He was like a prizefighter who suddenly has his strength back. But even on nights when his instrument wasn't up to par, he had so much style and timing and musicianship that it still sounded great. In fact, I think he still could have kept performing, but it got harder for him when his hearing started to get a little shaky. Those are the things, in fact, that made him retire. His [failing] hearing was bothering him, and I know it because he used to tell us it was bothering him, just not being able to hear as well as he wanted to."

No longer able to nail a pitch dead-on every time, often clipping phrases short when he couldn't sustain a note, Sinatra was witnessing the diminishment of his fabled skills. Perhaps it was no surprise, then, that he would stop performing in 1995, after a final, private performance in Palm Springs, California.

"On his last performance, unbelievably, he did seven or eight songs, and sang them all perfectly, exactly as they were supposed to be sung," remembers pianist Miller. "And everybody [in the band] kind of looked at each other like, 'Wow, maybe he's OK, maybe he's got it back.' "

Sinatra never again would sing in public, but to those who performed and recorded with him, the man's musicianship will not be forgotten.

"He was a total musician, a total natural," says Smith. "There wasn't any formal training there, but he knew exactly what he wanted."

And he knew how to get it.

August 1998, DownBeat

The Memory of All That . . .

The high-living, lady-killing rebel is gone, but the music—no, they can't take that away from us.

He started out as a scrawny crooner from down-in-the-dumps New Jersey, but before it was all over, Francis Albert Sinatra would make millions, conquer Hollywood, reinvent the art of singing several times over, seduce more starlets than he could remember, and grab enough glory to satisfy even his own outsized ego.

He could be poetic or profane, a sublime balladeer who would break your heart or a tyrannical friend who would explode into violence in a flash. He bloodied journalists and gamblers, nourished vendettas long after the objects of his rage were dead, smoked, drank, and womanized as if every night were the last of his life.

He also sang so exquisitely as to render archrival Bing Crosby irrelevant, danced before the cameras alongside no less than Gene Kelly, turned in dramatic performances worthy of more Oscars than he received, and kept America—and the rest of the world—humming his tunes for several decades.

To the celebrity worshipers and gossip hounds, Frank Sinatra, who died Thursday night at age eighty-two, was all about high living and hard drinking.

To others, Sinatra was simply that ancient crooner from the 1930s, a perpetually graying Hollywood eminence who—inexplicably—sold out arenas around the world bellowing "New York, New York," "My Kind of Town," "My Way," "It Was a Very Good Year," and other tired pop anthems.

In truth, however, neither of those images has much to do with Sinatra's greatness or staying power as an artist through six decades—a feat unprecedented and unapproached in American popular music.

The rebel image that latter-day rock stars (such as U2's Bono) claimed to admire, the lady-killer reputation that preceded Sinatra into some of the world's most celebrated boudoirs, the mob ties and Rat Pack carousing and White House shenanigans all brought Sinatra ample notoriety. Yet they had no more impact on Sinatra's artistic life than did the few overly familiar tunes audiences beseeched him to sing until long past the time he must have grown weary of them.

The public Sinatra, in other words, was not necessarily the towering artist who reshaped American popular music on several occasions. Rather, it was a more private Sinatra—the revolutionary singer working in the isolation of the recording booth, the dictatorial artist demanding superhuman virtuosity of his studio bands, the outlandish big spender lavishing fortunes on state-of-the-art recordings and brilliant new orchestrations—that was the Sinatra who mattered most, at least so far as the art of music was concerned.

Certainly it was Sinatra-as-innovator who bewitched the cognoscenti—and four years later the rest of the world—with his haunting recording of "All or Nothing at All," in 1939. This was, after all, the era of Bing Crosby, whose unruffled tones and mellifluous baritone defined American pop music at the time and represented a sunny optimism against the coming dark clouds of World War II.

With "All or Nothing at All" (backed by trumpeter Harry James's fledgling band) and "I'll Never Smile Again" (the singer's first No. 1 single, in 1940), Sinatra threw down the gauntlet to Crosby, singing with a fervor not only unmatched in Crosby's repertoire but unheard of in pop singing to that time. That Sinatra, not yet twenty-five years old, dispatched this music with flawless pitch, disarming tenderness, and a sensitivity to the song lyric that suggested the work of a dramatic actor rather than a mere "crooner," surely signaled the beginning of the end of Crosby's reign.

Sinatra's "All or Nothing at All" was no hit—at least not initially—but it caught the ear of Tommy Dorsey, who by 1940 signed Sinatra as his lead "boy singer." In most of the dozens of recordings that the young Sinatra made with the band and its vocal group, the Pied Pipers, Sinatra seconded Dorsey's sublimely expressive trombone, which opened and closed most cuts.

Even so, Sinatra achieved remarkable musical transformations. Never had a lead vocalist spun the kinds of silken legato lines that young Sinatra brought to "Star Dust" (1940), nor had anyone expressed the intense melancholy Sinatra found in "Everything Happens to Me" (1941). The sweet, bel canto grace notes with which Sinatra embellished "Let's Get Away from It All" (1941) similarly reimagined American popular music.

No wonder that teenage girls squealed when the skinny singer with the angelic baritone stepped up to the microphone. By now, their boyfriends or fathers were fighting the Good War, and Sinatra—with his melting vocals and caressing way with a phrase—became the natural recipient of their affection.

All of the adulation convinced Sinatra that he didn't need the Dorsey band and would fare better as a star in his own right, so, after some arm-twisting, Dorsey freed Sinatra to pursue his destiny. By 1942 Columbia Records, recognizing the meteoric rise of the young singer, reissued the 1939 "All or Nothing at All" and watched it become one of the first bona fide hits of a career that eventually would rack up dozens.

With all the fame and fortune that ensued, a lesser artist might have been content simply to cling to the tried-and-true formula, but Sinatra instead continued to experiment.

Exactly how he hit on the radical idea of singing two distinct phrases with the same long breath—thereby achieving in songs such as "Stella by Starlight" (1947) an urgency of expression that even the songwriters had not imagined—is anyone's guess. Perhaps, as Sinatra said at the time, he truly had been inspired by violinist Jascha Heifetz's recordings, applying the master's unrivaled way of arching a long, lyric phrase to the realm of popular singing.

No one ever had taken the art of pop singing quite that seriously before, though Sinatra certainly stumbled occasionally as he reached for the stars. The decorously swooning phrasing he brought to his first recording of "How Deep Is the Ocean?" (1946), the quaint whistling passage with which he closed his inferior, first recording of "One for My Baby" (1947), and the ineffective slow tempo he chose on his first recording of "Night and Day" (1947) point to an artist still struggling to establish a musical and interpretive vocabulary of his own.

By the late 1940s, Sinatra had embarked on a volatile and ultimately doomed relationship with Ava Gardner (they were married from 1951 to 1957), an experience that shattered his legendary self-confidence and, by most accounts, brought him new depths of sorrow. But if Sinatra was experiencing emotional pain as he never had before, he also was singing with a profundity he barely had hinted at just a few years earlier.

Listen to his harrowing recording of "I'm a Fool to Want You" (1951)—with its excruciatingly slow tempo and deeply imploring phrases—and there's little doubt that an innately gifted singer is on the verge of becoming a great one.

The nosedive his career took in the early 1950s—when the screaming, fickle bobby-soxers shifted their allegiance to the lesser Eddie

Fisher—surely gave Sinatra some of the darkest moments he ever had known. At the same time, however, Sinatra's fall helped turn a pretty-boy vocalist into something far more substantial.

If the Academy Award he won in 1954 for his performance as Maggio in *From Here to Eternity* put his career back on track, he now had profound new things to say in music as well. That much was obvious from albums such as *In the Wee Small Hours* (1955), with its hushed title dirge; and *Where Are You?* (1958), defined by mournful songs such as "Lonely Town" and "The Night We Called It a Day," all bathed in Gordon Jenkins's lush string arrangements.

These were all "concept" albums, a new genre of recording that Sinatra essentially invented. Liberated from the constraints of the comparatively short 78-rpm recordings on which he had made his name, Sinatra used the new long-play format to string together several songs on a particular dramatic theme or idea.

No one had done it before him, no one else had the box-office clout to make it happen, but Sinatra proved it could be done.

None of his concept recordings, however, matched the depth, sorrow, or dramatic intensity of *(Frank Sinatra Sings for) Only the Lonely* (1958). An audacious, expressionistic statement that makes zero concessions to commercial considerations, *Only the Lonely* to this day stands as Sinatra's most daring and profoundly satisfying album. In romantic elegies such as "What's New," "Willow Weep for Me," "Goodbye," "Ebb Tide," and others, Sinatra merges expressions of pain, sexual desire, and romantic longing more persuasively than any popular singer had done before (or since).

Like Judy Garland, another great tragedian of American popular music, Sinatra was taking listeners to dark places they never had dared to go before.

The marvel, though, is that at the same moment, Sinatra was reinventing himself as a swing singer, creating such high-flying theme albums as *Swing Easy* (1953), *Songs for Swingin' Lovers* (1956) and *A Swingin' Affair* (1957). With their glistening Nelson Riddle orchestrations and propulsive rhythmic backdrops, these albums expressed a kind of romantic euphoria and hedonism that represented precisely the flip side of Sinatra's brooding ballad albums.

Sinatra often quipped that he was "a 24-karat manic depressive," and the startling juxtapositions of his airborne swing albums and bleak torch recordings seem to prove it.

And yet, remarkably, there were still many more Sinatras yet to come. The soul-tinged crooner who belted the funk-tinged tunes of *That's Life* (1966); the coolly understated bossa nova artist who sang at barely above a whisper on *Francis Albert Sinatra and Antonio Carlos Jobim* (1967); the poetic interpreter who redefined hits by Jimmy Webb on *Cycles* (1968) and Rod McKuen on *A Man Alone* (1969); the profoundly introspective artist who dared to record a song cycle inspired by Schubert's *Winterreise* on *Watertown* (1969)—each of these represented new and utterly unexpected facets of Sinatra's art. The man simply never stopped finding new ways of addressing a pop song, along the way taking the art form in unforeseen directions.

Through the decades, Sinatra's lustrous baritone of the 1950s inevitably became deeper, darker, and more grainy. To some observers, the Sinatra of the late 1960s, '70s, and '80s was not the singer he once had been. They longed for the creamy tones and cushioned phrases of old.

For this listener, though, the changes in Sinatra's instrument rendered his art more intriguing, not less so. Certainly one wouldn't want to hear such world-weary songs as "There Used to Be a Ballpark" (1973) and "Send In the Clowns" (1976) from the same sweet voice that had caressed "Star Dust" and "Let's Get Away from It All" nearly half a century earlier.

And there was something distinctly moving about hearing Sinatra rerecord "The Song Is You" (1979), one of his earliest standards, so late in life. The once-silken voice had turned rough, the exquisitely smooth phrasings had become punchier and more angular.

Like all of us, Sinatra had changed through the years, life's bruises and disillusionments inexorably altering the color, texture, and tone of his work. Yet if his voice had lost its warmth, he never gave up the fervor and pugnaciousness of old.

Along the way, Sinatra certainly made his share of musical mistakes, none more glaring than the final installment of his *Trilogy* series (1979), its futuristic subject matter and simplistic musical score showing just how far out on a limb Sinatra was willing to go—and how far he was capable of falling. Apart from Sinatra's *Duets* and *Duets II* CDs (1993 and 1994), which seemed more concerned with commerce than art, listeners probably will debate forever the way the great singer chose to end his career. To some, *Sinatra 80th: Live in Concert* (1995) depicts an artist whose voice was shot literally decades ago.

To others, *Sinatra 80th* represents a haunting portrait of a great artist at the end of his incredible journey. The voice may be dry and less supple than before, the phrases clipped and economical, but the fiery spirit rages on.

Listen to the deep swing rhythms of "What Now My Love," the bottomless sorrow of "Angel Eyes," the mystery of "Where or When," and it seems apparent that—with the exception of the first several years of his career—Sinatra's art never really was about the Voice. It was what he did with the Voice.

Now, in the final days of his career, he still could melt your resistance with the way he lingered on a phrase, or quicken your pulse with the way he surged ahead of the orchestral accompaniment roaring behind him.

It takes a lifetime to learn to do so much with so little, and only one singer lived long enough and sang long enough to pull it off.

May 17, 1998

VIII

"The Sound of Surprise"

Unexpected Developments in Jazz

Let Freedom Swing

In selecting a jazz composition, the Pulitzers finally honor a distinctly American form of music.

From coast to coast, newspapers trumpeted the same remarkable tune: a jazz artist had won a prestigious award hitherto given only to classical musicians.

"Marsalis swings a Pulitzer," noted *USA Today,* evoking the jazz idiom with its choice of verb. "Wynton Marsalis captures music honors; first jazz artist to do so," said the *Los Angeles Times.*

But the real significance of Marsalis's award, presented for his epic vocal-orchestral suite *Blood on the Fields,* runs deeper than that. By awarding the prize to jazz trumpeter-bandleader Marsalis, the Pulitzer board gave the distinctly American art of jazz improvisation a degree of recognition and honor it had never before received.

From 1943 (when William Schuman won for his *Secular Cantata No. 2, A Free Song*) to 1996 (when George Walker won for *Lilacs*), the Pulitzer Prize in Music had gone to works in which every note had been put on paper by the composer, in the tradition of most European classical music.

Look at the score to *Blood on the Fields,* however, and you will see vast stretches of white space in which the three vocalists, instrumental soloists, and jazz orchestra riff freely on Marsalis's musical themes. That feature distinguished *Blood on the Fields* from virtually all the entries jurors heard when they met secretly last month in New York to pick three finalists from eighty-plus contestants (the Pulitzer board chooses the winner, typically taking into account the jury's recommendation).

By inviting two listeners associated with jazz (Modern Jazz Quartet pianist-composer John Lewis and this writer) to sit on the jury, the Pulitzer board clearly showed some interest in expanding the range of music to be considered for the award. The other jurors were three winners of music Pulitzers: John Harbison, Joseph Schwantner, and jury chairman Robert Ward.

From the outset, it was clear that *Blood on the Fields* raised two critical questions about the nature of American music: what is the value of improvisation, and can it yield genuine masterworks?

To a jazz devotee, the answer to those questions would seem obvious. Louis Armstrong's sublime trumpet solos in "West End Blues" and "Weather Bird," the Benny Goodman Orchestra's stunning "head arrangement" (unwritten) of "Sing, Sing, Sing," Miles Davis's haunting album *Kind of Blue*—all were conceived with the barest bones of a score. More important, Armstrong's glorious melodic flights, Goodman's thrilling ensemble passages, and Davis's hushed poetry were created specifically through the art of improvisation. No composer sitting in his garret could have dreamed up such inspired final products.

Improvisation also has played a role in classical music. But although baroque composers leading up to J. S. Bach typically improvised solo and ensemble pieces, and although pieces by Chopin and Liszt suggest the improvisations they routinely played at the piano in European salons, the art of improvisation has all but dried up in twentieth-century classical music. With the exception of church musicians, who still improvise organ preludes and the like on Sunday mornings, classical music has become a composer's art.

The issue is crucial, because roughly three decades ago a furor erupted when the Pulitzer board declined to give Duke Ellington a special citation recommended by the jury in 1965. When the full Pulitzer committee turned down their recommendation, wrote Ellington in his memoir, *Music Is My Mistress,* jurors Winthrop Sargeant and Ronald Eyer resigned.

"Since I am not too chronically masochistic, I found no pleasure in all the suffering that was being endured," Ellington continued. "I realized that it could have been most distressing and distracting as I tried to qualify my first reaction: 'Fate is being very kind to me; Fate doesn't want me to be too famous too young.'" Ellington was sixty-six at the time.

If any doubt remained that such comments dripped with irony, it was erased by the composer's remarks to writer Nat Hentoff, recorded in a 1965 *New York Times Magazine* article titled "This Cat Needs No Pulitzer Prize":

"'What else could I have said?' the Duke asked rhetorically. 'I'm hardly surprised that my kind of music is still without, let us say, official honor at home. Most Americans still take it for granted that European music—classical music, if you will—is the only really respectable kind. I remember, for example, that when Franklin Roosevelt died, practically no American music was played on the air in tribute to him . . . by and large, then as now, jazz was like the kind of man you wouldn't want your daughter to associate with."

The anger over the committee's rebuke simmered for years.

"The Pulitzer rejection of Ellington," wrote John Edward Hasse in his biography *Beyond Category: The Life and Genius of Duke Ellington*, "was, as cultural critic Jonathan Yardley has observed, 'a confession, however unwitting, of the cultural establishment's hostility to the new and the different and the unsanctioned. . . . [Ellington] put on a brave front, but he more than anyone else knew the true value of his music and he badly, if not desperately, wanted it accepted for what it was: the great American music, the true voice of his country, a total body of work that was neither jazz nor classical but something that drew strength from both and emerged, triumphantly, sui generis.'"

In Marsalis's *Blood on the Fields*, the 1997 jury heard a work that similarly drew on both jazz and classical traditions and therefore represented a broad spectrum of American musical tradition. By alternating exuberant improvised passages with meticulously composed sections, by juxtaposing high-flying instrumental and vocal solos with brilliantly conceived orchestral writing, Marsalis in effect picked up where Ellington had left off (with references along the way to the music of Charles Mingus).

To hear (via tape) Marsalis's radiant trumpet lines, Cassandra Wilson's throaty vocal solos, Jon Hendricks's nimble scat passages, the Jazz at Lincoln Center Orchestra's resplendent chords, and the rhythm section's pervasive swing backbeat was to savor a major composition that could not have been created without improvisation. Further, *Blood on the Fields* evoked many sprawling jazz pieces that Marsalis and his sidemen have invented over the last decade, from the hypnotic *The Majesty of the Blues* (1989) to the three-CD *Soul Gestures in Southern Blue* (1991) to the evocative *In This House/On This Morning* (1994).

Perhaps it was not so surprising, then, that *Blood on the Fields* emerged as the jury's top choice for the Pulitzer, with John Musto's lyric *Dove Sta Amore* and Stanislaw Skrowaczewski's *Passacaglia Immaginaria* following.

In honoring Marsalis's *Blood on the Fields*, the Pulitzer board for the first time had swung the gates open to jazz and the improvised, oral tradition it implies. If *Blood on the Fields* could win, then why not a scoreless jazz recording on the order of Davis's *Kind of Blue*, or a thoroughly improvised work, or a sublime group of American popular songs?

The Pulitzer board, in fact, took the gesture a step further, changing the definition and entry requirements for next year's awards. While the previous definition awards the prize "for distinguished musical composition by an American in any of the larger forms including chamber, orchestra, choral, opera, song, dance, or other forms of musical theater," the new text obliterates genre lines, instead giving the award simply "for distinguished musical composition of significant dimension."

And while the previous instructions required that "all entries should include . . . a score or manuscript and a recording of the work," the new instructions ask simply for "a score of the nonimprovisational elements of the work and a recording of the entire work." Explicitly, improvisation is now an accepted part of the Pulitzers.

Whatever happens from here, it would seem there's no turning back. By giving *Blood on the Fields* a prize widely considered "America's most prestigious musical honor," as Hasse termed it, the Pulitzer board has begun to acknowledge an entire world of music outside the realm of the symphony hall.

As the twentieth century approaches its end, the development comes not a moment too soon.

April 11, 1997

It took a while, but after Marsalis's win the Pulitzer Prize board increasingly began conferring the award on other musicians outside the narrow confines of classical music. The 2006 Pulitzer Prize in Music went to "free jazz" visionary Ornette Coleman for his Sound Grammar, *the first time the honor was given on the basis of a recording rather than a written score and live performance. Thelonious Monk received a Special Citation from the Pulitzer board the same year, as did John Coltrane in 2007 and Bob Dylan in 2008. Jazz composer Don Byron was a finalist in 2009, for his "7 Etudes for Solo Piano," suggesting that mind-sets are changing when it comes to the Pulitzers. Better late than never.*

The Measure of *Jazz*

A new mega-documentary doesn't tell the whole story.

Even if Ken Burns's TV documentary *Jazz* were not marred by errors, distortions, and omissions, it would shortchange the music it attempts to explore.

For *Jazz,* a nineteen-hour film that feels about twice that long, lumbers, laboriously, from one leaden biographical portrait to the next, from one creaky cliché to a thousand more yet to come. Its chesty-voiced narrator doesn't so much trace the evolution of jazz as issue ironclad pronouncements. The magisterial, unseen speaker declares some musicians immortal, others beneath contempt. Period. Thus spake Burns.

Perhaps the omniscient tone and stentorian delivery would have been appropriate for a film about Wagner's *Ring* cycle of operas, or perhaps the technological workings of Hoover Dam.

But jazz? How was it possible to suck the very life out of Louis Armstrong's trumpet or Charlie Parker's blazing alto saxophone or the sweet thunder of Duke Ellington's orchestra?

This was no easy task. In fact, it took Burns and friends six years and more than three million dollars to achieve it. Yet they made one of the more exciting and unpredictable genres in American music seem ponderous, pretentious, and dull. If the art of jazz truly were as stultifying as this film, it never would have survived its first decade, let alone its first century.

Those who admire earlier Burns documentaries, such as *The Civil War* and *Baseball,* might not object to the talking-head format that gives *Jazz* much of its droning quality. But anyone looking for an intellectually honest, factually accurate history of the music that also captures its spontaneity, freedom, and fearlessness will not find it in *Jazz*.

Instead, Burns has fashioned a dilettantish, ten-episode lecture in which hyperbole overwhelms fact and omission destroys credibility. If principles of truth-in-advertising had been applied here, the film would not be called *Jazz* but "Some Colorful and Eccentric Jazz Celebrities, 1900–1950." At least under that name, viewers would be alerted that vast swaths of jazz history, stylistic development, and critical perspective had been intentionally skipped in favor of lively, lightweight anecdotes.

Unfortunately, *Jazz* may lead some viewers to believe that Burns's tunnel-vision view of the music tells the whole story. It does not come close.

Essentially, Burns has laid out the film as the saga of a few central characters, with other, supposedly lesser, artists toiling in their shadow. This tack proves fundamentally flawed, since most musical forms—and certainly jazz—stem from vast social movements as well as individual achievements.

We are told by one of the film's talking heads, critic Gary Giddins, that "Armstrong invented what for lack of a more specific phrase we call swing." In truth, no single individual invented swing—an entire African American culture did. Moreover, the genesis of twentieth-century swing dates back to at least 1906, when Armstrong was five years old and Jelly Roll Morton wrote "King Porter Stomp," a linchpin in the emergence and evolution of swing rhythm.

We are informed by another effusive speaker, entrepreneur George Wein, that Ellington "created the whole history of American music prior to 1956." Considering that Buddy Bolden, Bunk Johnson, Freddie Keppard, George Baquet, Lorenzo Tio, Johnny Dodds, Sidney Bechet, Tony Jackson, Alphonse Picou, Johnny St. Cyr, and dozens more were thriving before Ellington played his first note in public, Wein's assessment strains credulity.

We are also instructed by the film's narrator that Parker "discovered a new way to create a compelling solo based not on the melody of a tune but on the chords underlying it." In fact, musicians had been building solos on chord changes since the dawn of jazz.

Ken Burns's *Jazz* overflows with such mistakes, misjudgments, and misleading information, including these gems:

> The film describes the famous 1924 Aeolian Hall concert in which George Gershwin first played *Rhapsody in Blue* as "four hours of elegant and orchestrated music, without a hint of improvisation." In fact, Gershwin's piano solos were not written down and were totally improvised.
>
> After discussing the early jazz trumpeter Buddy Bolden, the film features the sound of a lone trumpet. Viewers naturally assume that Bolden's horn is being heard on a recording, but no Bolden recording is known to exist.

> The film portrays the world premiere of Duke Ellington's *Black, Brown and Beige* as an unabashed success but fails to mention the devastating reviews it received and the toll they took on the composer.

At times, the film's speakers inflate their assertions so broadly as to push biography into orgiastic hagiography. One talking head proclaims: "I don't believe that Louis Armstrong was a real human being. I believe, I still believe that God sent him to this earth to be a special messenger, to make people happy." The sentiment might suit a Hallmark greeting card but not a serious documentary.

Unfortunately, the exaggerations extend well beyond Burns's portraits of individuals. For *Jazz* consistently overdramatizes or oversimplifies its analysis of jazz history, style, and form.

Swing music, the film contends, "had grown up in the dance halls of Harlem." Really? What about the dance halls of Chicago and Kansas City and Los Angeles and hundreds of small towns dotting the full breadth of the United States?

The blues, the film claims, are "built on just three chords, most often arranged in a twelve-bar sequence called choruses." In reality, the blues require no chords at all—a lone voice singing in a field can articulate the blues, as can a modern big band playing hundreds of chords.

By the 1940s, the film asserts, "the living heart of jazz had already moved to a single block of old brownstones on the West Side [of New York], Fifty-second Street, between Fifth and Sixth Avenues." The living heart of jazz contained on a single city block? What about the mighty blocks of south State Street and South Park Way in Chicago, or the hard-swinging blocks of Central Avenue and Jefferson Boulevard in Los Angeles?

This simpleton's view of jazz history may make for punchy cinema, but it belies the breadth and fabric of this music, which has flourished wherever African Americans congregated and others followed. As for the film's omissions, they are as plentiful as they are egregious. How is it possible to film a sprawling history of jazz but not interview nonagenarian Benny Carter, the first great alto saxophonist and a witness to pivotal early chapters in jazz evolution? Of what worth is a jazz documentary that omits Ahmad Jamal, a revolutionary pianist who influenced several generations of musicians, not least Miles Davis? And what happened to Nat "King" Cole, a piano innovator; Dinah Washington, a powerhouse vocalist; and Stan Kenton, a towering big-band composer?

Also left on the cutting-room floor: the entire sweep of Latin jazz, which profoundly influenced the music at its start and does so to this day. Ditto for the entire West Coast of the United States, which Burns doesn't address until the eighth of his ten episodes! Worse, when one of the film's speakers, critic Nat Hentoff, finally discusses West Coast jazz, he dismisses it as "pretty bland."

But Burns's most narrow-minded posture concerns the jazz avant-garde, which he quickly dispatches in a final episode that—incredibly—compresses the last forty years of jazz history into less than two hours of footage. The information that Burns provides, meanwhile, often proves specious. In cursorily discussing the groundbreaking Art Ensemble of Chicago, the film notes that the band "once found itself playing to just three people in its own hometown, and it attracted its largest following among white college students—in France." The film fails to acknowledge, however, that after the Art Ensemble's historic tour of Europe, in 1970, it played to packed houses across the Continent, throughout the United States, and, yes, even its hometown. More important, the Art Ensemble helped revivify an art form that otherwise appeared to have reached a creative dead end.

Yet the very gesture of judging jazz music by the size of its following, rather than the depth and complexity of its content, points to another significant flaw in Burns's project: the film applies inappropriate, commercial criteria to a sophisticated art form.

Repeatedly we are told of the supposed commercial shortcomings of modern and avant-garde jazz. Dizzy Gillespie, the narrator intones, "failed to attract a wide audience." Black avant-garde ensembles, the narrator notes ominously, could not "win back a black audience." Other, more mainstream performers, however, are applauded for achieving hit records.

But by gauging the art of jazz by record and ticket sales, Burns applies the criteria of modern-day pop and rock to an art form with very different goals. This is akin to saluting Rush Limbaugh for making the top of the best-seller lists while demeaning Eudora Welty for failing to rack up sales. One could fill a book documenting the missteps of *Jazz,* but at least one more cries out to be acknowledged: missing primary sources. The film rhapsodizes on John Coltrane's landmark recording *A Love Supreme* but fails to interview the surviving musicians who helped create it, pianist McCoy Tyner and drummer Elvin Jones. The film gushes about Sonny Rollins and Ornette Coleman, yet neither appears to have a word to say to Burns.

One is left with the troubling conclusion that Burns chose to feature only those musicians and commentators who would give him the exaggeration he clearly prefers. Ultimately, the distortions and omissions of *Jazz* render it almost useless, which is a pity, for it contains some interesting footage.

The best jazz documentaries, such as Jean Bach's *A Great Day in Harlem,* choose a manageable subject and examine it in depth.

Jazz, on the other hand, presumes to take on a seemingly infinite topic and treats it capriciously. What a waste.

January 7, 2001

Completely Hot: *Live at the Plugged Nickel*

A Miles Davis classic emerges in full—thirty years later.

For three inspired nights in Chicago in 1965, trumpeter Miles Davis presided over some of the most sublime music-making of his career.

It was a few days before Christmas, and Davis, who was born in East St. Louis, Illinois, and maintained deep ties to friends and family in Chicago, was playing his annual holiday engagement in town, at a Wells Street club called the Plugged Nickel. The place, which had all of ten tables and could hold a standing-room-only crowd of one hundred, tops, folded years ago, but Davis's Plugged Nickel performances have achieved the stature of myth ever since that winter of 1965.

To those who heard the sets, the trumpeter's work with his incendiary quintet of the period was as daring as it was profound, the players stretching beyond recognition many long-honored rules and rites of jazz improvisation.

Fortunately, Columbia Records taped the last two nights of Davis's engagement in their entirety. But the label waited until 1982 to release a fragment of the material in the United States; five years later, fifty-seven more minutes' worth was released on a *Cookin' at the Plugged Nickel* reissue.

Now, thirty years after the historic gigs, four years after Davis's death, at age sixty-five, and one year after Columbia discovered dozens of long-forgotten Plugged Nickel master tapes in an East Coast warehouse, the world finally is about to hear what really happened on those fabled Chicago nights. Later this month, Columbia will issue *The Complete Live at the Plugged Nickel, 1965,* an eight-CD set that contains every note that Davis and friends played on December 22 and 23, 1965, or at least as much of it as is known to exist. (In addition, Mosaic Records, which specializes in historic jazz reissues, will later this year release the same material on ten LPs.)

An advanced hearing of the complete recordings suggests that the music that Davis's band created at the Plugged Nickel justifies the legend that has accrued around it, even if the recordings also reveal the flaws and frailties of Davis's trumpetry. What's more, the recordings put into new perspective the importance of this chapter in the musical career of the chameleon-like Davis.

The trumpeter himself always treasured the memory of the Plugged Nickel dates, as he indicated in his memoirs, *Miles: The Autobiography* (with Quincy Troupe, Simon and Schuster). Having spent much of 1965 recuperating from two painful hip operations, he was eager to get back onstage.

"It was a great comeback and the people received the music real well," wrote Davis, referring to his November 1965 date at the Village Vanguard, in New York.

"After that, I went on the road in December to Philly and Chicago, where we played the Plugged Nickel. . . . Everybody played like we hadn't been separated at all. Like I said, I have always believed not playing with each other for a while is good for a band. . . .

"It just makes the music fresher, and that's what happened at the Plugged Nickel, even though we were playing the same book we had always played."

And therein lies the sweet irony of the Plugged Nickel dates.

Though Davis had begun forming his second great quintet in 1963 (with tenor saxophonist Wayne Shorter, pianist Herbie Hancock, bassist Ron Carter, and drummer Tony Williams), and though the band had created a sensation with its complex, original compositions on such Davis studio albums as *E.S.P.* and *Miles Smiles,* the quintet turned to Davis's old book of standards for the Plugged Nickel shows.

Davis, according to his memoirs, simply felt that audiences were coming in specifically to hear tunes such as "'Round Midnight" and "My Funny Valentine," which had graced his popular earlier studio albums and live recordings alike. So even if Davis's mid-1960s quintet was developing its radical musical ideas in the recording studio with newer, fresher compositions, Davis stuck to standards at the Plugged Nickel.

As a result, we hear his quintet applying its oft-eccentric, unorthodox methods to vintage tunes. The irony, then, is that there could be no better way to perceive, savor, and measure precisely the innovations that Davis and friends were formulating at the time than to hear these innovations applied to songs from an earlier era.

Or, as Davis put it in his memoirs, "We found ways to make the old music sound as new as the new music we were recording."

Listen closely to the eight CDs on the *Complete* set and you will hear a new musical language as it is being created and refined. Though Davis clearly was following Ornette Coleman's lead in pushing past traditional chordal vocabularies, he and his band were doing so with an elegance and a sonic beauty all their own.

That the quintet is recorded in three sets one night and four sets the next makes matters even more interesting, for the listener can hear Davis and friends addressing many of the same tunes repeatedly, each time differently than the last.

The sessions open boldly, with Davis brazenly bending pitches and fracturing traditional phrasings in "If I Were a Bell" and "Stella by Starlight." The smudged tones, wavering notes, splintered lines, and chromatic meanderings of Davis's solos stretch the limited musical vocabulary of these chestnuts to the breaking point. These harmonically traditional tunes were not written to slip into one key and out another with every bar. The long melody lines were not designed to be broken down into so many brief and sighing phrases.

Yet Davis does precisely that, coaxing the repertoire into a more modern realm.

For all the muted poetry and whispering lyricism of Davis's playing, however, the trumpeter's work is not the most arresting feature of these tracks or those that follow. Rather, it's the ensemble playing—with its textural transparency and palpable sense of wide-open space—that consistently commands attention.

To hear Davis's ineffably tender lines reflected in Hancock's crystalline pianism on "Walkin'," Shorter's elliptical and haunting phrases on "I Fall in Love Too Easily," Williams's soft but propulsive brushwork, and Carter's fleet and lithe bass playing throughout is to understand why many listeners consider this band superior to Davis's first great quintet (with tenor saxophonist John Coltrane, pianist Red Garland, bassist Paul Chambers, and drummer Philly Joe Jones).

The delicate sound that the Plugged Nickel quintet could achieve, the driving energy that the rhythm section could produce without disturbing the band's dynamics, the revolutions in structure and form that these players wrought throughout the 1965 sessions underscore the importance of this band, as it is now heard on the *Complete* recordings.

The solo passages, too, distinguish this ensemble and underscore the historic importance of the Plugged Nickel dates.

Indeed, though Davis deserves full credit for having had the vision to put together this quintet and for giving his players plenty of room in which to explore new ideas, the trumpeter does not stand as the foremost soloist in the band.

Rather, it's Shorter—with his consistently gleaming tone, technical virtuosity, unpredictable starts and stops, and utter defiance of predictable harmonic turns—who towers over the rest. The restless and volatile lines he plays on "Agitation" (in the second set of December 22) and the ease with which he turns from hard bop to modal to "free" idioms on "No Blues" (the third set of December 22) are still breathtaking to behold.

For his part, Davis proves capable of both haunting lyric statements and startlingly wrong notes, of flashes of improvisational virtuosity followed by passages of less than clean and controlled playing. Yet Davis was shrewd enough to share the microphone generously, placing more attention on his ensemble than on himself, perhaps knowing that it was as leader and visionary that he was at his strongest.

That much seems apparent from the many hours of bristling ensemble improvisation that the Plugged Nickel set contains, most unheard until now. For this, Davis fans can thank Columbia executive Steve Berkowitz, who halted the reissue process last year when he was led to believe that extra reels of the Plugged Nickel dates were lurking somewhere in the Manhattan storage space of Sony (which owns Columbia).

"[The librarian] called me and said, 'Hey, Steve, there are 25 boxes on this shelf of half-inch multitrack recordings of "Live at the Plugged Nickel," and these boxes look very old,'" recalled Berkowitz in a recent *Billboard* magazine interview. By sifting through those boxes, Berkowitz "found a lot of things that had been previously edited out, or things that were not known to have existed before."

Thus, what was to have been a seven-CD set was pushed up to eight. Though there's no diminishing the import of Davis's innovations on recordings such as *Birth of the Cool* (Capitol), his orchestral collaborations with Gil Evans on *Porgy and Bess* and *Sketches of Spain* (Columbia), and so on, perhaps it's fair to say that Davis put together his most accomplished band with the second quintet.

Certainly it's not difficult to make that statement with the ethereal and revolutionary sound of the *Plugged Nickel* set still lingering in the ear.

June 18, 1995

Maturity Isn't the Right Key in Today's Jazz

The suicide of Susannah McCorkle.

You can find them in any major city in America, singing in half-empty piano bars, peddling compact discs they had to produce and finance themselves. At some point in their lives, decades earlier, they believed they were following in the wake of Frank Sinatra and Judy Garland, destined to bring their music to millions. But somewhere along the way they made a terrible mistake.

They grew old.

Today more than ever, the performer who's graying at the temples or developing deep lines in her face need not harbor illusions of ever attaining fame or fortune. Neither record-company executives nor talent agents will be knocking at her door, for the music industry prefers its stars young, photogenic, and malleable.

That message rang out clearly again last month, when Susannah McCorkle, one of the country's most intelligent and accomplished jazz cabaret singers, committed suicide at her Manhattan home at age fifty-five. Though McCorkle had been fighting depression for years, the last seven months of her life had been particularly painful, for she had been discarded by the same music industry that had supported her in her youth.

Dropped by her record label and erased from the lineup at the Algonquin Hotel in New York, where she had played annually for years, McCorkle hadn't worked for seven months. And no prospects were on the horizon.

Considering that she had recorded seventeen albums and worked with such top-flight musicians as pianist Dave Frishberg, trumpeter Randy Sandke, and saxophonist Chris Potter, she must have wondered what had gone wrong. How could a career more than two decades in the making suddenly have come apart?

To find out, all McCorkle or her admirers had to do was scan the *Billboard* jazz charts, where singers of considerably less talent and fewer years were riding high. None could sing and speak fluently in five languages, write erudite magazine articles on the art of songwriting, or command a repertoire of literally thousands of songs, as did McCorkle.

Yet the youthful appeal and movie-star good looks of Diana Krall, Jane Monheit, Harry Connick Jr., John Pizzarelli, and the like have made them bona fide stars, largely thanks to the relentless support and promotion of the major record labels. Knowing a saleable commodity when they lay eyes on one, the record execs have spent fortunes marketing singers of slight artistic achievement, sending them touring around the world backed by the best sidemen that money can buy.

It wasn't always like this, at least in the realms of jazz, swing, and classic pop.

Though virtually every artist runs into a dry spell now and then, sublime interpreters such as Sarah Vaughan, Betty Carter, Carmen McRae, Joe Williams, Mel Torme, and others recorded and toured prolifically in the mature stages of their careers.

But a remarkable shift has taken place in the last decade or so with the rise of the MTV and VH1 cable television music channels. In an era when music is marketed heavily on the tube and in glossy magazines, youth and beauty have become high virtues, with vocal skill and interpretive insight barely entered into the equation.

Thus singers with pint-size pipes—from the breathy pop diva Toni Braxton to the unprepossessing jazz singer Nnenna Freelon—bask in the spotlight, while major talents such as Ann Hampton Callaway in New York, Frank D'Rone in Chicago, Everett Greene in Indianapolis, Barbara Morrison in Los Angeles, and dozens more work on the periphery of the record industry.

Callaway last year went so far as to reinvent herself as a Broadway actress, while D'Rone plays mostly private parties, Greene picks up gigs where he can find them, and Morrison plays mostly for Angelenos. Each has a better chance of winning a multistate lotto than landing a major-label record contract, as well as the promotional muscle that goes with it.

Meanwhile, fledgling performers bask in the glow of a spotlight created by shrewdly spent marketing dollars, with overreaching copywriters daring to compare Krall with the great Peggy Lee, Monheit with the incomparable Ella Fitzgerald, and so forth.

So why should we care?

If audiences want to listen to near-novices fumbling their way through indelible jazz and pop standards, what's the difference?

Plenty, for the mysteries of timeless songs by Gershwin, Porter, Berlin, and Kern tend to elude even the most talented youngsters. These great songwriters, and others in the Tin Pan Alley tradition, knew how to pack multiple layers of meaning and subtext into 32-bar vignettes. And only interpreters of comparable gifts—as well as the seasoning of the years—can hope to express all that a great song has to say.

After all, Sinatra didn't begin to create his best work until he had felt the bruises that one acquires during the course of life. Torn apart by his tempestuous, on-again, off-again romance with Ava Gardner, in the mid-1950s he finally was emotionally equipped to create such profound albums as *In the Wee Small Hours* (1955) and *Only the Lonely* (1958).

Billie Holiday, though a distinctive singer from her earliest days fronting dance bands, didn't reach her creative apex until the last years of her life. Though one cringes at the pain she suffered at the hands of brutish police, junkies, and pushers, she transformed her anguish into such recordings as her searing "Come Rain or Come Shine" (1955), her tersely phrased "Lover Man" (1958), and her vocally rough and unflinchingly honest rerecording of "God Bless the Child" (1956).

The same can be said of Garland's *Judy at Carnegie Hall* double album (1961), and even Sinatra's *Duets* (1993) and *Duets II* (1994) CDs from the end of his career. Though his voice was too craggy, grainy, and weathered to match the honeyed tones of the early Columbia years of the 1940s, the sound of the old man swinging like crazy said more about life—and the fighting spirit—than all the sweet crooning he did half a century earlier.

Sinatra and Holiday are, by definition, irreplaceable, but other grizzled veterans are still out there, belting them out five nights a week in dingy saloons where only the diehards really listen.

What a pity they're ignored by just about everyone else.

If given half a chance, they would drive the novices back into the practice rooms and show audiences across America what real singing is all about.

June 24, 2001

Landmark Blues Opera *De Organizer* Powerfully Reborn

DETROIT—More than sixty years ago, two pivotal figures of the Harlem Renaissance—poet Langston Hughes and jazz composer James P. Johnson—collaborated on a blues opera that received one performance in Carnegie Hall, then vanished.

Ever since that premiere, on May 31, 1940, scholars have assumed that although Hughes's text to *De Organizer* survived, Johnson's score was irretrievably lost. That assumption was shattered Tuesday night when eight vocal soloists, a forty-five-piece orchestra, and a forty-voice mixed choir performed a groundbreaking reconstruction of *De Organizer* in this city's Orchestra Hall. The work proved so powerful in its melodic content and so poetic in its choral writing that it's easy to imagine the piece might have attained broad popularity—had it survived beyond its one-night-only engagement.

An overflow crowd turned out for the reemergence of *De Organizer,* not surprising considering the stature of its creators.

Though not as famous as he should be today, Johnson towers as one of the most influential jazz pianists of the 1920s and '30s, his lightning-quick "stride" piano style inspiring Fats Waller and generations to come. But Johnson was more than just a keyboard wizard who penned such three-minute classics as "Harlem Strut" and "Steeplechase Rag." He also blossomed as a composer of large works, his rhapsody *Yamekraw* (1927) and *Harlem Symphony* (1932) reminding listeners that black jazz and blues could be applied eloquently to vast forms once reserved for classical music.

In Hughes, Johnson found a collaborator of comparable genius whose lyric poems, such as "The Negro Speaks of Rivers" (1921) and "The Weary Blues" (1926), tapped the mysticism, tragedy, and hope of black life in America.

What little background information on *De Organizer* survives suggests that Hughes and Johnson were proud of the work and championed it after the Carnegie Hall performance (which had been organized by the International Ladies Garment Workers Union).

"Both Hughes and Johnson tried to have the piece performed," jazz scholar James Dapogny told the crowd in his introductory remarks. Dapogny, a University of Michigan music professor, unearthed the vocal score for the thirty-five-minute work in 1997.

"But they were told by CBS Radio, for example, that this was just too controversial a piece."

Indeed, as its title suggests, *De Organizer* addresses the American labor movement in heroic terms, often equating it with black liberation. At one point, the choir thunders: "If you want to be free, organize." At another, the title character snarls that when "we got a big strong union, folks, a union of black and white, there'll be more difference in this old South than there is 'twixt day and night."

In 1940, these themes of racial oppression and labor exploitation—built into a simple story about a union man organizing sharecroppers—were deemed too hot to handle by mainstream concert presenters, and *De Organizer* disappeared.

Had it not been for Dapogny, a noted jazz musicologist who has published an indispensable volume of Jelly Roll Morton's *Collected Piano Music*, *De Organizer* still would be silent, its text preserved in Hughes's anthologies but never brought to life onstage. Dapogny found the music almost by serendipity, having noticed the fifty-one-page vocal score amid papers donated by choral director Eva Jessye to the University of Michigan, where Dapogny has taught since 1966.

Jessye had rehearsed the chorus for George Gershwin's *Porgy and Bess* and Johnson's *De Organizer*, but her working score contained only the vocal lines, not the instrumental support that goes with it.

Using Jessye's score as his starting point, Dapogny launched a hunt for every scrap of paper related to *De Organizer*, eventually locating piano-vocal sketches and Johnson's instructions on instrumentation (found amid the composer's papers). Armed with all of this material, Dapogny began his attempt at reconstructing the score, deciding that the project was feasible because the most important portions of the music—the vocal solo and choral passages—had survived. They were the heart and soul of the piece, and Dapogny needed only to provide the instrumental support.

"If the vocal score indicated that one song was followed by six bars of instrumental music linking to the next song, I would write those six bars," said Dapogny in an interview last week.

"I had to write in Johnson's style. But because you already know the material in the two songs that you're linking, it's not necessarily so difficult to determine the melodic themes that Johnson might have used to make the transition."

Moreover, in a score stretching 1,004 measures, only 80 measures of instrumental music were missing. The concert performance affirmed that Dapogny's handiwork blended seamlessly with Johnson's. Like any top-notch restorer of musical theater, Dapogny subsumed his own voice to the style of the composer at hand, ensuring that one piece flowed elegantly into the next.

Though Johnson and Hughes subtitled their work "a blues opera," in fact the piece also embraces jazz, swing, and Broadway idioms, switching easily among these styles. Listen to the resuscitated *De Organizer,* and it's not difficult to detect the influence of Gershwin's *Porgy and Bess* and *Blue Monday,* Jerome Kern's *Show Boat,* Eubie Blake's *Shuffle Along,* and, possibly, Scott Joplin's *Treemonisha.*

Considering that Johnson penned the score in 1939–40, when he already was a mature composer, it's a bit of a surprise how much of *De Organizer* recalls the ragtime music of Johnson's youth. Though bebop music already was coming on strong when the opera premiered, and though Johnson reigned as the father of stride piano, the composer reached back to the turn of the century to find inspiration for many of the rhythms that drive *De Organizer.*

Yet *De Organizer* also dips into sublime blues expression in a segment of music that reiterates the line "Where Is That Man?"; folklike song forms in "There's Gonna Be Some Organizin' Here"; rousing anthem writing in "(My Man Is Like) John Henry"; and exquisitely polished vocal writing in a duet written for *De Organizer* after the 1940 premiere, "Glad to See You Again."

Any one of these tunes surely held the potential to become hits. Together, they represent a work of sustained melodic inspiration that, on further hearing, may persuade some listeners to reassess Johnson's position in the jazz pantheon. For if Johnson already is admired as a top-flight virtuoso who wrote such classics as the finger-breaking "Carolina Shout," *De Organizer* shows that he ranks among the finest melodists to have worked in jazz-influenced musical drama.

Perhaps not surprisingly, this first performance of Dapogny's restoration—by the University of Michigan's Symphony Orchestra and Chorus—had its ups and downs. Most distracting was the tendency of the orchestral forces to obscure the vocal soloists, while listeners surely would have benefited from a program that included all of the lyrics and song titles.

Nevertheless, *De Organizer* emerged as an instantly attractive work steeped in the black vernacular of the first half of the twentieth century. It deserves to be heard across the country and, ultimately, to be documented on a recording.

"All I can say is that it's really nice music that people will be interested in hearing," said Dapogny, whose assessment may be too modest.

De Organizer is so beautifully crafted by Johnson and so adroitly restored by Dapogny that it may yet earn a place among key dramatic works in the jazz-blues repertory.

At least it should.

December 6, 2002

Lady Has Her Say

A new CD set redefines Billie Holiday's life and music.

It has taken more than three decades, but finally the myths about Billie Holiday are being shattered, one by one.

Until now, history books have tended to cast Holiday—who died in 1959 at age forty-four—as the ultimate victim, a frail and wounded singer who succumbed to drugs, alcohol, rape, violence, police brutality, and commercial exploitation.

To those who grew up listening to Holiday, she tended to represent the inspired artist who somehow sang divinely even amid hellish circumstances. Despite a minimum of formal musical training, she seemed to possess a natural way with a song that couldn't help but seduce her generation and those succeeding.

Though that scenario holds a great deal of romance, it turns out to have had precious little to do with the reality of Holiday's tough life and intellectually brilliant muse. More in control of her world, her music, and her instrument than either casual listeners or musical scholars have acknowledged, Holiday turns out to have been an artist very much of her own making. In other words, she sounded precisely as she wanted to sound, and she was more aware of the personal and artistic obstacles she faced—and of precisely how she would overcome them—than anyone knew.

The proof is in a remarkable new, ten-compact disc package, *The Complete Billie Holiday on Verve, 1945–1959* (Verve), which documents, and redefines, the final chapters of her life and her music. Here are the songs and the conversations that puncture the myths.

Chief among them is the still widely accepted belief that her greatest work came in the 1930s, when her voice was young, her body not yet ravaged by drugs and pain. Listen to those early recordings, mostly on Columbia, and it's difficult not to be charmed by the sunny voice, the bright tone, the predominantly up-tempo dance arrangements, and the buoyant phrasing of everything Holiday sings.

But by the mid-1940s, Holiday's life and music had taken dramatic turns. While trying to survive drug addictions, brutalizing men, and horrifying prison stints, Holiday began reaching interpretive depths hitherto unachieved in American song. The long and mellifluous melodic lines of the early days were replaced by halting, introspective phrases that suggested a harsh new reality. The danceable tempos were set aside for ballads slower than anyone else had imagined possible.

Alas, the new sound and direction of the last ten to fifteen years of Holiday's life were almost universally disparaged, with critics considering them merely the unfortunate side effects of a life ruined by drugs and other indulgences.

"By the time she entered the Fifties," wrote critic John S. Wilson, shortly before Holiday's death, "her private life was becoming increasingly difficult, her voice would no longer respond as readily as it once had and, like the aging fastball pitcher who has lost his stuff, she was depending more and more on craft and guile to put across her songs."

To Wilson, and a generation of listeners, her late recordings evoked "a performer who is more diseuse than jazz singer, who is depending largely on mannerisms to carry her through tempos which are often killingly slow for a limited voice. . . . She seems reduced to a ragged, wavering ghost of the inspired singer she once was, straining for the remembered effects that she can no longer achieve."

To this day, you'll hear similar comments made of everyone from Ella Fitzgerald to Rosemary Clooney to Billy Eckstine to Frank Sinatra, though, in these instances, their "decline" is attributed to age rather than vice.

The Complete Billie Holiday on Verve compellingly sets the record straight and offers listeners a different and decidedly more enlightened way to hear this music. Has anyone else, after all, conjured up quite the sorrow or pain that Holiday yields in "One for My Baby"? Has anyone else summoned tones that cry as openly as Holiday's long-held notes on "Body and Soul" (both from 1957)?

Listen to her trade soft, sighing phrases with Harry "Sweets" Edison's muted trumpet on "Willow Weep for Me" (1957), or suspend the meter—and all sense of time—in "My Man" (1952), and you are hearing an artist in complete control of her idiom and her instrument.

More to the point, Holiday was keenly aware of what she was doing musically and why, a message that comes through clearly on discs 4 and 6 of this set. Here we hear Holiday in rehearsal with her sidemen, trying out tempos, cursing difficult passages, bemoaning the artistic rejection she is facing in her late years.

To hear Holiday working and reworking the music, all the while commenting on the scores at hand, is to understand just how sophisticated a musician she was.

"They run me out of Chicago," she says during one rehearsal. "The Grand Terrace in Chicago. . . . Aw man, they say, 'I don't dig her, she's a drag.' They just didn't like my singing. 'She sounds like she's asleep. She sounds like she's tired.' They didn't dig me, and I wouldn't change. I wouldn't change. [Manager] Joe Glaser had me about seven, eight years and he say, 'You got to sing pop songs, you gotta speed up the tempo.'

"I gonna sing like I wanna sing. This is my way of doing it and Mr. Glaser, I'm sorry. And when I get mad I say, 'Look you [expletive], you sing it. I gonna sing my way, you sing your way. . . .

"I've been with some pretty big shots during the time [recent years], and man, they don't dig me no kind of way, you know. They don't understand me, and I don't understand them—so we get no work."

Amid her stream of anecdotes and salty language, Holiday tells her sidemen precisely what they are to do. It is she who selects the tunes, snaps her fingers to set the tempos, shapes the interpretation, decides who should play an obliggato here and there.

Only a musician as accomplished as Holiday could get away with laying down the law to the likes of "Sweets" Edison, Charlie Shavers, Buck Clayton, Oscar Peterson, and others of their stature. They form the backdrop for Holiday's late years, their deference to her work saying more about her musical accomplishment than all the myths could.

And though it's true that Holiday enjoyed little in the way of formal musical training, in jazz, it's who you work with and what you learn from them that counts most. On that score, too, Holiday's résumé destroys the myth of her "natural" genius. On the contrary, she developed her art by listening to the great artists who were drawn to her.

Only through painstaking trial and error did she evolve from the comparative simplicity of the 1930s to the profundities of the '50s, as this package attests.

By the last two or three years of her life, it's true that little remained of Holiday's instrument, though her artistry was undiminished. Vocally, her whispered phrases and slightly quivering vibrato in late 1950s tracks such as "There'll Be Some Changes Made" and "All of You" suggest a small, flickering flame about to be extinguished.

Through sheer will alone, she manages to sustain a line, to shape a phrase, to carry an audaciously slow tempo. That she can make something lyrically profound of a tune as slight as "Day In, Day Out," even in the waning days of her turbulent life, shows how fearless an artist and a spirit Holiday was.

This boxed set—which includes a scholarly, 220-page program book—proves the point through Holiday's own words, spoken and sung. More important than the lavish packaging of the set, with its numerous photos and essays, is the sweet fact that it presents Billie Holiday as seen by Billie Holiday, a feat not even accomplished by her ghostwritten autobiography, *Lady Sings the Blues.*

Finally, Holiday herself can tell the truth of what really happened.

November 15, 1992

IX

Gershwin Reconsidered

Assessing America's Quintessential Composer, a Century Later

Bittersweet Rhapsody

George Gershwin's centennial reminds us not only of all that went unwritten, but also how underappreciated he remains.

NEW YORK—As she sits in the drawing room of her elegant Manhattan apartment, George Gershwin's last surviving sibling recalls the whirlwind that was her brother's life in music.

Although it has been sixty-one years since the great composer died, Frances Gershwin Godowsky never has gotten over it. His unexpected death, of a brain tumor at thirty-eight, still stings, and nowhere more than in this room, where George's presence seems nearly palpable. In the corner stands the family grand piano, the same instrument on which her older brother often serenaded relatives and friends, playing the signature tunes that turned a poor New York song plugger into America's most famous composer. On the walls are vintage paintings and drawings by Alexander Calder, Marc Chagall, and Gershwin himself, all reminders of an era that stirs mixed feelings in Frankie, as everyone calls her.

So perhaps she can be excused for feeling ambivalent that next Saturday all the world will mark the hundredth anniversary of her brother's birth.

"This is the centennial year—I'm afraid I have to think about it, but I don't like to," she says, strong of voice and cogent of thought at age ninety-one.

"George died so full of ideas, he really thought that he could do so many things, and it makes me very sad to think that he had to give it up. It was such a loss to the world, he was so anxious to do bigger things."

The centennial likely will evoke bittersweet feelings in anyone who loves a Gershwin melody, and not only because of the music left unwritten. For Gershwin remains today, as he was throughout his lifetime, greatly beloved but not widely respected.

How can a man whose music not only continues to earn millions but epitomizes American musical culture around the world possibly be considered underappreciated? Don't all the centennial commemorations signify widespread respect?

Not really, considering that most of the Gershwin tributes, though plentiful, focus essentially on the same repertoire (*An American in Paris,* a handful of hit songs), overlook less-familiar fare (*Second Rhapsody,* "I Got Rhythm" Variations), and neglect the lost material discovered in a Secaucus, New Jersey, warehouse in 1982 (most of which has not yet reached listeners).

Worse, the crown jewel of the Gershwin repertory, the innovative folk opera *Porgy and Bess* (of 1935), is receiving no fully staged performance anywhere in the United States in this centennial year. Lyric Opera of Chicago never has staged the piece, and the Metropolitan Opera House in New York didn't do so until 1985—nearly half a century after the composer's death.

Meanwhile, the performances of Gershwin's instrumental music tend to be of remarkably low quality, such as last month's sloppy but all too typical reading of the Concerto in F in Grant Park. Pianist Christopher O'Riley, essentially faking the difficult passages and playing wrong notes galore, obviously hadn't mastered the work but performed it anyway; surely he never would have dared to treat a Beethoven concerto in the same manner.

Classical performers, alas, tend to regard Gershwin as a mere tunesmith whose work does not bear serious rehearsal. Jazz performers, meanwhile, offer fascinating improvisations on Gershwin's music but rarely play it as written.

On recordings, Gershwin's instrumental scores have been treated poorly more often than not, whether in Leonard Bernstein's gaudy rhythmic distortions of the *Rhapsody in Blue* or Katia and Marielle Labeque's bludgeoning of his sparkling two-piano scores. In 1994, player-piano enthusiast Ardis Wodehouse did a tremendous disservice to Gershwin's piano-roll performances by rerecording them on a Yamaha Disklavier, a kind of modern-day player piano souped up with digital technology. The result was a heavy-handed, lumbering sound that in no way resembled Gershwin's pianism.

So why is America's quintessential twentieth-century composer treated so badly a century after his birth?

The reasons are many, starting perhaps with the man's decidedly humble beginnings as the second of four Gershovitz (the original family name) children, Russian immigrants living in the tenements of New

York's Lower East Side. Musically late-blooming and largely self-taught as a teenage piano player, Jacob Gershwine (his birth name) dropped out of high school and did not seem destined for success in music or, for that matter, anything else.

Neither the sensational reception of his first hit tune, "Swanee" (written in 1919 with Irving Caesar), nor the unprecedented phenomenon of his jazz-meets-the-classics *Rhapsody in Blue* (which made him a star at age twenty-five) persuaded even his family that he was anything more than a mildly talented kid who got lucky.

"I didn't appreciate him, I didn't realize what he was, I didn't appreciate his great talent," says Frankie. "I wasn't aware, and neither were our parents. . . ."

But Gershwin in his early twenties already was achieving something in music that no composer had accomplished before him: he was bringing to popular and concert music the unmistakable sound and tempo of modern American life. Specifically, the blue notes of black jazz, the syncopated melodies of American ragtime, the aggressive rhythms of the Harlem stride pianists, and other American influences all helped shape Gershwin's music and made possible the innovations of *Rhapsody in Blue.*

Still, he never received the respect that was his due.

"I think there always was and there still is a snobbism about Gershwin," says Michael Feinstein, one of the most erudite interpreters of Gershwin's music as singer and pianist.

"That's evidenced by these pianists who think that they can play Gershwin, it's evidenced by [opera star] Kiri Te Kanawa making a Gershwin album and just walking in [to the recording studio] reading the music and thinking that she can interpret it.

"It's that same kind of attitude that keeps Gershwin from being taken more seriously."

And there may be another, darker reason why Gershwin was never accepted as a "serious" composer: anti-Semitism, which was in full cry during his ascent.

"These academicians at the universities, they felt the very idea that this songwriter—even though successful—would dare to write art music was outrageous," says conductor Mitch Miller, who played oboe in Gershwin's *Porgy and Bess* in 1935. "Their attitude was: how dare he!

"And, of course, what they were covering up was their anti-Semitism. Never mind that some of Gershwin songs are every bit as good as Schubert's. He was a Jewish songwriter, and that was enough for some."

Yet Gershwin pushed ahead, refusing to confine himself to the 32-bar song form that he had mastered with indelible tunes such as "Somebody Loves Me," "Fascinating Rhythm," "Lady Be Good," "That Certain Feeling," "Clap Yo' Hands," "Someone to Watch Over Me," "'S Wonderful," "My One and Only," "How Long Has This Been Going On?" and other classics of the Roaring Twenties.

All the while, Gershwin rapidly was maturing as symphonic composer, by 1928 completing the evocative orchestral tone poem *An American in Paris.*

Those who believed that Gershwin had gotten lucky with *Rhapsody,* those who dismissed his masterful songs as mere populist fare, could not persuasively deny the achievements of *An American in Paris.* The glitter of Gershwin's orchestration, the intricacy of his rhythmic devices, and the ingenuity of his use of car horns to re-create the hustle and bustle of Parisian streets attested to the man's expanding realm as a composer.

The artistic success surely helped Gershwin summon the courage to take on *Porgy and Bess,* an epic work so boldly conceived and brilliantly executed that even Gershwin was surprised by its power.

"I tell you, after listening to the rehearsal today," he said to director Rouben Mamoulian, "I think the music is so marvelous—I really don't believe I wrote it."

Nevertheless, Gershwin's rising musical ambition faced increasing hostility. After a successful tryout in Boston, *Porgy* opened in New York in 1935, and the critics had their knives ready.

"Gershwin does not even know what an opera is," snorted critic-composer Virgil Thomson in *Modern Music* magazine. Samuel Chotzinoff in the *New York Post* dismissed *Porgy* as "a hybrid," while Paul Rosenfeld slammed it as "an aggrandized musical show." The attacks put *Porgy* and Gershwin on the defensive, prompting the composer to take to the pages of the *New York Times* in hopes of explaining to critics and other cynics the worthiness of his venture.

"It was my idea that opera should be entertaining—that it should contain all the elements of entertainment," wrote Gershwin in 1935.

"It is true that I have written 'songs' for 'Porgy and Bess,'" added Gershwin, apologizing for using the "song" form that had made him a major name on Broadway. "I am not ashamed of writing songs at any time so long as they are good songs. . . .

"But songs are entirely in the operatic tradition. Many of the most successful operas of the past have had songs. Nearly all of Verdi's operas contain what are known as 'song hits.' 'Carmen' is almost a collection of song hits."

It was all to little avail, with *Porgy* closing after only 124 performances. The blow to Gershwin was considerable.

"He was hurt, because he had worked on *Porgy* so hard, he had done it entirely by himself and was thrilled about that," remembers Frankie. "He even had a special desk built for writing that opera, it meant so much to him."

The last two years of the composer's life were not pleasant, and only partly because of the initial commercial failure of *Porgy.* His doctors could not explain the periodic memory losses and overpowering headaches that sometimes brought Gershwin to his knees, crying out in pain.

After the composer died following brain surgery, writer John O'Hara famously said, "I don't have to believe it if I don't want to."

"It was shock all over the world," remembers Frankie. "I was in Vienna at the time, and [brother] Ira sent me a wire saying, 'Everything possible was done,' but it was pure disbelief."

Though Gershwin's admirers lament the works he might have written in the decades to come, the tragedy ran deeper than that, for the composer already had sketched—in his head—themes for a Hebraic opera and a string quartet.

"The string quartet was something that George played on the piano for friends, and everybody was crushed when they found that he had not written it down," says Feinstein. "He also had planned to write a symphony.

"He had so many ideas, so many discussions with people. He had intended one day to reorchestrate *Rhapsody in Blue,* to do his own orchestration, because it bothered him that it wasn't his arrangement." (Ferde Grofe had penned the original orchestration under Gershwin's supervision because the composer had only three weeks to write the piece.)

"Ira always stressed that George definitely would have continued working in musical theater and film, that he never would have given up one for the other," adds Feinstein, who served as Ira Gershwin's secretary beginning in the late 1970s.

"He also was experimenting with a Hammond organ right before he died, because he was so interested in the modern technology. He once sat down and played it for Ira for about two hours, and Ira said that if he could have had a recording of any moment in George's life—anything—that's what he would choose."

Gershwin's early death, in other words, represented an incalculable loss to American music. Though Gershwin devotees applauded the special Pulitzer Prize he was awarded posthumously this year, they bemoan the "snobbism," as Feinstein put it, that still defines performances and recordings of his music.

A century after Gershwin's birth, "I think George would have been thrilled to think that his music is still popular, that it's held on," says Frankie.

He probably wouldn't have been surprised, however, to find that the world of music has yet to treat it with proper regard.

September 20, 1998

Gershwin at One Hundred

Though virtually everyone in show business will be singing George Gershwin's praises come September 26, the one hundredth birthday of America's most revered composer, perhaps the most deeply felt tributes of all will come from the world of jazz. Gershwin's great Broadway musicals, after all, now belong mostly to the history books, while his singular opera, *Porgy and Bess,* rarely receives a fully staged performance (in fact, no major American revival has been scheduled this centennial year).

But jazz musicians—who have made Gershwin's music their lifeblood since at least the early 1920s—will be delving en masse into the man's immense songbook. By reinvestigating exactly why his music still sounds so fresh and so rich in improvisation possibilities, they'll be performing a vital service: keeping Gershwin's music contemporary, as jazz musicians always have done, and in the process reaffirming its value a century after his birth.

"Gershwin's music never goes out of fashion, it's as alive today as it was when it first came out," says singer Tony Bennett, who will offer his own tip of the top hat to Gershwin in January. That's when Bennett will release a still-to-be-titled retrospective of his Gershwin recordings, culled from more than four decades worth of LPs and CDs.

"When I go around the world and sing 'They Can't Take That Away from Me,' 'Nice Work If You Can Get It,' 'A Foggy Day'—everybody knows the songs, they all cheer them. I've been to Japan ten times, and audiences know the music there. This is international now." Bennett credits this to jazz virtuosos who have proven that Gershwin's music can be perpetually reworked to express new ideas.

If Broadway occasionally has succeeded in reviving a vintage Gershwin musical, if symphony orchestras have made Gershwin showpieces such as *An American in Paris* and the Piano Concerto in F staples of their pops programs, jazz musicians have proven that Gershwin's music constantly rejuvenates itself, continually spawning new creativity.

"There's just so much great music that has come out of Gershwin," says Bennett. "There was Art Tatum, Charlie Parker, [longtime Bennett accompanist] Ralph Sharon—everybody did Gershwin. . . . It's the best music there is. It's like [lyricist] Yip Harburg used to say: the music hits you emotionally, and the words hit you intellectually.

"When you get the two together, you have a great song on your hands. Plus, the Gershwins' music is so well crafted. The [brothers George and Ira] knew everything. They knew never to ask a singer to hold a note with a bad sound on top—if it's a high note, they always have a nice 'ahhh' sound, or an 'ohhh' sound. As for Gershwin's melodies, that's a gift of god. That's inspired, that's spiritual."

Though one can debate endlessly whether or not Bennett technically qualifies as a jazz singer, the jazz-influenced nature of his swing singing and ballad reading established his prominence as a prime Gershwin interpreter. If one associates Frank Sinatra with the erotically charged love songs of Cole Porter (especially with Nelson Riddle's glistening orchestral arrangements), Bennett surely stands as a leading interpreter of tunes by Gershwin (typically accompanied by Sharon's jazz trio).

"I think Tony always has had a tremendous affinity with Gershwin," says Sharon. "It has something to do with being a fellow New Yorker, being born in New York [as Gershwin was], and Tony enjoys the ambience of Gershwin, even apart from the music. When Tony discusses Gershwin, he talks about what a great life Gershwin had," though it ended tragically early, with Gershwin's death of a brain tumor in 1937, at age thirty-eight. "Tony also does well with Gershwin because he [Bennett] generally hits his groove at a nice, easy, medium tempo, not so much the fast stuff. Sometimes he'll sing a Gershwin tune at an even slower tempo. For instance, he's been singing 'They Can't Take That Away from Me' for many years as a sort of slow swing thing. What he brings to Gershwin tunes is the knowledge that they can be played and sung at different tempos, with completely different moods."

Therein lies a great deal of the appeal and durability of Gershwin's music: play it fast or slow, loud or soft, straight or improvised, swung or straitlaced, it always survives sounding unmistakably like Gershwin. As veteran conductor Mitch Miller—who played oboe in a tour of Gershwin's orchestral works in 1934 and in the 1935 premiere performances of *Porgy and Bess*—puts it, "Gershwin's music is indestructible. Even performed badly, you can't kill it."

How can a music that's so instantly identifiable also prove so utterly malleable, thereby making it ideal for the jazz musician's art?

"In part, it's because he picks certain melodies and chords to make sure that you can mix ideas on top of them—he did that all the time," says pianist Marcus Roberts, whose *Portraits in Blue* (Sony Classical) includes a radical *Rhapsody in Blue* in which both soloist and accompanists improvise on portions of Gershwin's original. "I think Gershwin was just somebody who understood that flexibility needed to be a part of the sound of his music.

"You don't go messing with Stravinsky. The premise of Stravinsky's music is: 'I really don't want this messed with, so I'm going to hook it up now, and all I really want you all to do is to play the hell out of it.'

"With Gershwin, I get the sense that he wanted to mess with it himself. And I think without even thinking about it or projecting that as a mission, it was in his music, and a lot of musicians—Louis Armstrong and Ella Fitzgerald and all these folks—would hear that and realize that it just lent itself to what they were doing."

No doubt Gershwin was an accomplished improviser, famously entertaining friends at Manhattan parties with his keyboard variations on his own tunes. But there's something even more fundamental to the definition of Gershwin's music that makes it so adaptable to various musical needs: more than any American composer of his day, he brought multiple musical cultures to bear in virtually everything he wrote.

"If you look at the premise of his music, it has a very heavy proposition," says Roberts. "He wanted to put together the artistic principles of Europe and America. That he even thought to do that puts him in a category by himself."

Gershwin, in other words, melded several disparate elements: traditional European harmony, Jewish cantorial melody, distinctly American rhythm, passing blue notes, and at least the flavor of black jazz improvisation. "What we did with the *Rhapsody*," adds Roberts, "was just to impose the conception of jazz on the piece, which hadn't been done yet—it always had been performed from a classical [European] perspective.

"I wanted to see what would happen if you put a New Orleans groove over certain sections of it, without interrupting what was written. And that experiment just kind of pulled the *Rhapsody* over to the other side—the American side.

"That you could do something like that probably makes *Rhapsody* one of the most important pieces written in this century, because it's one of the few works that can maintain its integrity from either a European perspective or from an American perspective."

Considering the 1920s and '30s era in which Gershwin was working, such a notion was positively revolutionary. Yet it quickly inspired cross-cultural imitations from Aaron Copland, whose Piano Concerto of 1927 followed Gershwin's 1925 opus and mirrored its jazz-meets-the-classics spirit (if not its vast structure); Maurice Ravel, whose Piano Concerto in G (1932) merged Gershwin-like, blues-tinged melody with the techniques of French impressionism; and Stravinsky's Ebony Concerto for Clarinet and Swing Band (1946), which applied Gershwinesque syncopations to Stravinsky's brittle, neoclassical musical vocabulary.

It took an unusually innovative composer to take on such a task, as well as one who declined to condescend to populist musical forms. "I think Gershwin was unbiased about musical mediums," says pianist Oscar Peterson, whose recordings of *The Gershwin Songbooks* (Verve) stand among the finest keyboard traversals of the man's music. "I think Gershwin was very interested—and I know this from his brother Ira—in the jazz medium, and I think that showed in his music, and in the kinds of tunes that he wrote, because it was so easy for all of the people in jazz to play.

"He also opened up a lot of harmonic areas to us that other composers haven't," Peterson adds, "and that, too, owes to the breadth of Gershwin's musical vision."

Yet it's critical to remember that Gershwin was not born into a vacuum. He was smitten with the stride pianism of James P. Johnson and Luckey Roberts, the vocal sounds of the black church, and various musical traditions of Gullah Negroes who lived outside Charleston, South Carolina (and whose influences he absorbed into *Porgy and Bess*).

Thus, when pianist Herbie Hancock was working on his forthcoming *Gershwin's World* recording, to be released in the fall on Deutsche Grammophon/Verve, he decided not to include only the usual standards.

"We decided that we would give really the wrong impression, that it would be a disservice if we gave credit to George Gershwin without giving credit to the music that made Gershwin Gershwin, which is jazz," says Hancock, whose recording will include Johnson's "Blueberry Rhyme," W. C. Handy's "St. Louis Blues" and other music of the period. "We didn't want to do what they used to do with Paul Whiteman, calling him the King of Jazz, while all the black people who created the music and died for it get nothing."

But Hancock hastens to add that Gershwin's achievement in bringing the spirit of jazz improvisation, blues scales, and black church music to the concert hall and the opera house represents an enormous musical contribution. "There are only two basic forms in jazz: one of them is the blues, which was not written by any particular person but is a part of black culture, and the other one is 'Rhythm' changes, and those were written by George Gershwin," says Hancock, referring to the quick-change chord progression on Gershwin's "I Got Rhythm." That tune, in fact, launched uncounted alternate versions, including Ellington's "Cottontail," which also will appear on Hancock's Gershwin disc. "'Rhythm' changes are fundamental to the way jazz is improvised, and it's really interesting that they were created by a single individual," says Hancock.

"And this was at the height of an era that was a kind of fairy tale, when Fred Astaire was wearing top hat and tails in his movies, which were about posh supper clubs with big orchestras and guys wearing tuxedoes and white ties," Hancock says. "All of that elegance was, I guess, the dream, or the fantasy of the American people at the time [during the Great Depression].

"And in the height of that, Gershwin writes *Porgy and Bess,* which is about a crippled black guy who falls in love with this beautiful black woman, and about their humanity and what they have inside. Now that was totally contrary to what was being sold, and it's incredible that Gershwin had the courage to do that."

Yet the music of *Porgy and Bess,* adds Hancock, "was deeper than just the black experience, and that's why people all over the world can relate to it—it's really about the human spirit."

Like most observers, pianist-arranger Dick Hyman considers *Porgy* Gershwin at his greatest, and not only because of its profound social message. Musically, too, it's a tour de force. "All the harmonies and countermelodies and rhythms that are in his more commonplace pieces are expressed even more intensely in *Porgy and Bess,*" he says. "It's so complex and advanced that there's really very little you can do to improve on it."

Not that jazz musicians haven't at least tried to offer a personal view of the piece. The Miles Davis–Gil Evans *Porgy* may be the most famous, as well as one of the most evocative, versions, but Joe Henderson's *Porgy and Bess* (Verve) showed that the work still casts its spell on major jazz figures.

"I just happened to be watching part of *Porgy and Bess* on cable TV the other day, and just hearing it again opened up a whole new sound vista in my brain," says Henderson. "I've been inspired by Gershwin. He sometimes used these nine-bar phrases where you would normally expect an eight-bar structure, like in 'My Man's Gone Now,'" from *Porgy.*

"That's what started me thinking about other ways to write—you don't have to fit inside an already existing structure," Henderson says. "You can figure out what the structure will be after [you write a theme], rather than before. I think that the world is a better place in so many ways because we had Gershwin around writing about this 'foggy day in

London town.' I mean, these are things that get the love juices going at a certain point in your life."

What's more, Gershwin's music shows no sign of losing its importance or vitality.

"I'll never forget, I was playing a club in Beverly Hills a while ago, and there were all youngsters in the audience, really, really young kids," recalls Bennett. "And when I got to 'They Can't Take That Away from Me,' all the young people sang the song with me. I felt like Mitch Miller.

"Now that's against everything that the marketing people say, that the kids don't know these songs. Everybody forgets that we're all watching AMC [American Movie Classics cable service], and the kids love watching Astaire dance and listening to a Gershwin song.

"That music will always be around—it's what American culture is all about."

September 1998, DownBeat

Porgy and Bess

Glyndebourne produces a definitive Gershwin classic, long after the composer's death.

Who could have guessed it would take fifty-four years before we would hear a definitive recording of George Gershwin's *Porgy and Bess*? Or that the recording itself would be conceived by two Brits who had never so much as set foot on the South Carolina soil from which America's most beloved opera sprang?

Yet more than half a century after Gershwin completed *Porgy* in 1935, the new, complete recording—by a cast that won international acclaim at the Glyndebourne (England) Festival Opera three years ago—proves that only now are performers and audiences perceiving *Porgy* in all its dimensions.

Despite many endearing earlier recordings, *Porgy* now fully emerges as the genuine "folk opera" Gershwin always insisted it was. Though most previous recordings (as well as many stage productions) erred with too much operatic stiffness or too many jazz transformations, the new *Porgy* achieves a remarkable balance of the two. "It wasn't terribly easy," says Simon Rattle, the gifted young British conductor who teamed with director Trevor Nunn to stage *Porgy* at Glyndebourne and led the three-disc recording for EMI.

"In fact, it was a struggle all the way. It's hard for any orchestra and any cast of singers to get the style of this music, to get the rhythms to come naturally.

"The performers are faced with music that is harder to play than *Wozzeck* [Alban Berg's torturously difficult opera], and yet to do so from fairly skimpily written-out jazz materials.

"The music, in other words, is notated rather straight, yet the performers must learn to swing.

"That's hard for any orchestra, but particularly for an English one.

"However, at least in England, the musicians don't have the slight feeling at the back of the mind, as they often do in America, that: 'Oh, yes, this is merely pops music.'

"So although it takes much longer for the British musicians to learn to swing, they at least take the music on face value and believe in it.

"And I believe that we all came into the Glyndebourne production, as well as this recording, loving and respecting the piece, and believing it to be a masterpiece. All we wanted to do was make a performance as truthfully as possible."

Beyond that, however, Rattle and company (the London Philharmonic and a cast of American vocal soloists) have come up with a *Porgy* that simply sounds different than the way we're used to hearing it.

For one, the tempos veer radically from convention. In lullabies such as "Summertime" and dirges such as "My Man's Gone Now" Rattle takes daringly slow tempos, stretching out melodic lines nearly to the breaking point. In up-tempo sections, such as the piano/orchestral introduction and various transitional passages, he pushes the orchestra to a furious pace.

As a result, the instrumentalists combine the feel of a hot jazz band with the sonic power of a modern symphony orchestra.

"It all got so intense that, for all of us, it felt as if *Porgy* had become a chunk out of our lives, rather than just a production," says Rattle (who adds that the planned film of the Glyndebourne production has been scrubbed because the backers "felt there would be no public for it, which is one of the silliest things I've ever heard").

"I've talked to a number of the soloists recently, and we've all had the same, odd experience, which is that we actually can't listen to the recording.

"We listen for five or ten minutes, and then it becomes difficult for us to hear—that's about as much as any of us can take at a time.

"I think the Glyndebourne production was successful because it felt as though there were seventy people on the stage who were all real. Everybody knew everybody, they had worked extensively in improvisation together with Trevor Nunn.

"Beyond that, I had been conducting the opera in concert for about ten years prior, with Willard [White, who portrays Porgy], and it simply had grown into our skin.

"So there was a feeling that this wasn't, for instance, just an opera chorus onstage; this was seventy individuals with seventy lives. It's hard to describe without turning very pretentious, but this was real theater."

At first glance, it may seem strange that it has taken more than half a century to arrive at this particular alchemy, but it's not as surprising when one considers the hurdles and tragedies that afflicted *Porgy* nearly from the beginning.

Though brothers George and Ira Gershwin worked on the opera for roughly two years with southern poet-author DuBose Heyward (who wrote the source novel and play *Porgy*), the trio never truly saw their dreams materialize onstage.

At the start of the collaboration, in 1933, the prospects looked good. George Gershwin had gone so far as to travel with Heyward to the small islands near Charleston, South Carolina, to absorb regional black culture.

"The Negro [there] prides himself on what he calls 'shouting,'" said Heyward at the time. "This is a complicated rhythmic pattern beaten out by feet and hands as an accompaniment to the spirituals and is indubitably an African survival.

"I shall never forget the night when, at a Negro meeting on a remote sea-island, George started 'shouting' with them. And eventually to their huge delight stole the show from their champion 'shouter.' I think that he is probably the only white man in America who could have done it."

Thus Gershwin imbued *Porgy* with a kind of music that had never been heard on the American musical stage. The style of shouts, chants, and contrapuntal spirituals that he heard eventually bloomed in *Porgy*, though the music was entirely Gershwin's.

After auditioning dozens of singers to play the critical title role, Gershwin phoned a Washington, D.C., music professor on the recommendation of critic Olin Downes.

"I started to sing 'Lungi dal caro bene,' by the Italian composer Secchi, and only got as far as a few bars," recalls Todd Duncan, the original Porgy, who's eighty-six today.

"George played [the piano] for me, and he asked me to sing the same bars [again] and look straight at him while I sang it.

"And he looked up at me at the end of about eight or nine bars and said, 'Will you be my Porgy?' It was rather simple."

The rehearsals, however, were not.

"I had to learn how to sing in every position—kneeling, lying, crawling around the floor like a snake," recalls Duncan of the vicissitudes of playing the crippled Porgy. "I practiced and I practiced, just like a baby learning how to crawl.

"But, still, those rehearsals were beautiful, and a great revelation to me, a great inspiration.

"George would come every day, but he would just say little things—he was not very meddlesome, not very intrusive at all."

When the show opened in Boston on September 30, 1935, it took nearly four hours to perform, running till nearly one o'clock in the morning. The audience—as well as the critics—were overwhelmed.

Gershwin had "traveled a long way from Tin Pan Alley," wrote Moses Smith in the *Boston Evening Transcript*. "He must now be accepted as a serious composer."

But it was straight downhill after that.

New York's Theatre Guild, which was producing the opera (its first), worried that the show was too long and too expensive (though the full cost of its run was less than fifty thousand dollars) and demanded cuts. Immediately after the Boston opening, the producers ordered that nearly an hour's worth of music be cut—including the opening "Jazzbo Brown" piano music, the deeply spiritual "Six Prayers," the caustic "I Hates Yo' Struttin' Style," the Buzzard Song, and more.

"They emasculated it," recalls conductor Mitch Miller, who played oboe in the original *Porgy* orchestra.

"The opera starts with the crap game, and they took it out! This was in an era when producers were afraid to start a show quietly and let it build. They wanted a big bang."

When the truncated *Porgy* opened at the Alvin Theatre in New York on October 10, 1935, the critics massacred it.

Virgil Thomson wrote, condescendingly, in *Modern Music* magazine that "Gershwin does not even know what an opera is." Samuel Chotzinoff intoned in the *New York Post* that *Porgy* was "a hybrid," while critic Paul Rosenfeld called it "an aggrandized musical show."

Yet, by all accounts, audiences that heard even the chopped-up *Porgy* loved it. Kay Swift, a longtime Gershwin devotee, remembered that "during the intermission, we went out into the alley on the side of the Alvin, and I remember Libby Holman saying, 'Oh, George, it's so great I haven't stopped crying,' and she was sobbing right then. Everybody was. It was so moving."

Why did the New York press slice it up?

"The main reason was that they thought: 'How dare a popular Jewish songwriter write an opera? How dare he write serious works?'" says Miller.

"The critics did the same thing with George's *American in Paris* and the Concerto in F.

"They went out of their way to destroy George—they had a field day. All the musicians in the orchestra were very depressed, because here was a guy who tried to say something differently, and no one was ready to listen."

There were grimmer reasons, as well, for rejecting *Porgy*.

"The fact that the show had an all-black cast was part of it," says Duncan. "Remember, that was fifty-four years ago—a time when Negroes weren't allowed into this theater or that, into this church or that restaurant. It was a sick time, but I still don't think that was the only reason.

"George Gershwin was a great success—he had never had a failure, but he had been Tin Pan Alley, he had been Broadway, and now he was coming out with something that he insisted was opera, and many of the erudites simply said: 'George can't do that.'

"They thought: 'This cannot be opera. George thinks it is, but it isn't,' and so they went about proving it.

"That, plus the fact that you've got a double problem going there—a Jewish composer and Negro themes—and that's a lot of ammunition."

Gershwin was devastated by the reception accorded his "labor of love," which ran for merely 124 performances (two months) and never regained its investment. Two years later, he was dead of a brain tumor, "and I'm sure the failure of *Porgy* only hurried his demise," says Miller.

Yet the critics and the naysayers were wrong, for *Porgy* has survived. Though it was performed in truncated versions in the 1940s and '50s; though the Hollywood version (starring Sidney Poitier as Porgy) is no longer in circulation; though more complete versions did not begin to appear onstage until the 1960s and '70s, *Porgy* has perpetually attracted new generations of listeners. Tunes such as "Summertime," "I Got Plenty o' Nuttin'," and others quickly became American standards.

"The first time I heard George play *Porgy* for me," recalls Duncan, "I did not realize it was a masterpiece. I only knew that it was a medium and an idiom that I had never heard before, and I knew it was something that touched my soul; I knew it reached a part of me that all great music does, and I didn't need any critic or any musicologist to tell me that. I simply never doubted it.

"Since then, I've seen too many *Porgy* productions that try to out-Gershwin Gershwin—they don't obey what the composer wrote, they try to improve on it," adds Duncan, who hasn't heard the new recording.

"I attended the [first] Metropolitan Opera production in 1985, which was quite well done, though the Met was many years late doing what it should have done long ago.

"But for me, as well as others in the cast, *Porgy* was a springboard.

"It opened doors that never would have been opened for a black singer. And in that way, it changed the face of music in America."

August 20, 1989

~

Rattle's recording of Porgy and Bess *has not been matched, much less surpassed, nor is it likely to be any time soon. This was the first—and perhaps last—recording of the complete* Porgy and Bess, *with Rattle having gone to great lengths to obtain permission from the Gershwin estate to restore every measure the composer wrote. These rights had never been given before, but they belatedly enabled listeners to hear* Porgy and Bess *in full for the first time. Fortunately, too, a DVD of the Glyndebourne production has been released, giving* Porgy *devotees around the world a chance to at least get a sense of how the complete opera played on the stage. At full length, it's a deeper, more profound and complex work than even devotees could have realized without the benefit of the Rattle version.*

X

Race Music

Crossing the Color Line—in Sound

"It Took Our Minds off of the Bad Things"

Japanese internment camp survivors remember the swing music that helped them endure.

They are old men now, decades removed from the nightmare that was World War II. Yet when they think of that time, they don't linger on the suffering and the indignities they endured.

Instead, they hear music—the tunes of Glenn Miller and Duke Ellington and Artie Shaw—that they played in the internment camps for Japanese Americans, where the United States government locked them up during the war. Today, the story of the young Japanese American swing musicians who helped make life tolerable in the detention yards is practically unknown, even to jazz aficionados. But thanks to a photo exhibition on view at the Museum of Contemporary Art and an accompanying book, the jazz and swing culture that thrived behind barbed wire is belatedly coming to public attention.

"The music got our minds off the war and what was happening to us," recalls Chicagoan Art Hayashi, a seventy-nine-year-old former singer-bandleader and one of the last living survivors of the internment camp bands.

"We would try to convert almost all of our arrangements to the Glenn Miller sound, which was so beautiful. We would be in there, in the camp, working up these [musical] scores, then we'd test them out during our rehearsals.

"And because we were so concerned about the music, it took our minds off of the bad things," adds Hayashi, who led the Harmonaires, named for Camp Harmony, the housing area of the detention camp at Washington State Fair Grounds in Puyallup, Washington.

"I'm sure prisoners of all kinds do this kind of thing—find some way to take your mind off of your misery.

"Otherwise, you'd go crazy."

The impulse to make music under dire circumstances proved universal, with swing bands sprouting in all the internment camps. Some were sleek swing machines, such as the Harmonaires, staffed by technically proficient young musicians who had played big-band music long before the onset of World War II. Other ensembles were frequently out of tune, their personnel barely able to play horns they only recently had begun to study.

"I must admit our band sounded very meek," remembers Chicagoan Todd Yamamoto, who formed the Music Makers at the Gila River Butte Detention Camp in Arizona. "The kids in the band weren't professionals. They weren't even musicians. If they happened to own a saxophone, they played a saxophone, so it was pretty hard on the ears.

"You had to have patience to listen to this band," adds Yamamoto, one of only two bona fide musicians in the Music Makers, having earned his union card as a teenager.

"But there's a lot of time in camp—what is there to do, besides playing ball? So I started the band to get some people involved in doing something, just anything."

Yet there would appear to be an unspoken but inescapable irony here: the Japanese American families that were rounded up and detained as "enemy aliens" on American soil were playing and dancing to the music of the very culture that imprisoned them. Was this evidence of some kind of masochistic self-loathing or simply a way to earn favor with the captors?

"Neither one," says Hayashi, who was born in Seattle. "We're Americans. Why shouldn't we love American music? Glenn Miller was our idol."

Indeed, though most of the elders in the internment camps were émigrés from Japan, their children generally were American born, attended English-speaking schools, and listened to American radio.

"You have to remember that we had American-style dance bands in the Japanese community in the United States as early as 1926," explains George Yoshida, age seventy-nine, who lives near Berkeley, California, and was incarcerated with his family in Poston Detention Camp No. 1 in Arizona.

"We literally grew up with this music, we absorbed the American culture very quickly. We certainly did not dig the Japanese music that our parents brought over with them."

Or, as Yamamoto puts it, "We were brought up in the American style, for everything. We might eat some Japanese food, but we still liked American food, American movies, American music, American everything.

"What people forgot was that we were Americans, and we are Americans."

But on December 7, 1941, with the bombing of Pearl Harbor, Japanese Americans discovered that they were a different kind of American—at least so far as white America was concerned. Before that infamous day, Hayashi could lead his Mikados of Swing band in a tour of the entire state of California, during the summer of 1941.

"The thing that's amazing is that the night before December 7, 1941, my band, the Mikados of Swing, played at a dance hall in Seattle, and our orchestra sounded great, and I was very happy," remembers Hayashi.

"I went to bed that night at around two o'clock in the morning, and I always kept the radio on at night, in those days. Next thing you know, I hear someone screaming on the radio: 'There are planes over Honolulu, they're dropping bombs, and it looks like they're Japanese planes.'

"And I remember thinking to myself, 'I hope it's not Japanese,' but it was.

"I ran downstairs to tell my father, but he knew already, and he told me that some of his friends already were being picked up by the FBI, and he might be going soon."

Within weeks, Japanese Americans along the entire stretch of the West Coast were rounded up, dispatched first to temporary camps, then sent by train to larger, more permanent facilities in remote, scorching parts of the Southwest.

"When you got to camp, they asked you questions," Hayashi says. "The first one was: 'Do you consider yourself an American citizen?' I said, 'Yes.'

"The next one was: 'Would you volunteer for the U.S. Army to prove it?'

"And I said, 'Why should I? I haven't done anything wrong. Draft me. Treat me like any American citizen.'"

For the elders in the camp, this turn of events was a tragedy, for many lost the property they had owned in civilian life and feared for their lives. But for the teenagers who played in the swing bands, life was more carefree, perhaps because many did not grasp the gravity of their situation, turning to music as a pleasant distraction from boredom.

"The youngsters like us were basically happy," recalls Yoshiko Yamamoto, Todd Yamamoto's wife, who danced to his band in camp.

"We were all teenagers, and I think it's our parents who were kind of down or depressed. We didn't fully understand, and we just had a good time dancing to the music.

"I don't even know if the music was good or bad. It was just fun to dance to."

Soon enough, however, even the youngsters would learn that the years in the internment camps held profound implications for the rest of their lives. Hayashi, for instance, forfeited a scholarship to Oberlin, the esteemed liberal arts college, when he was interned. After the war, he never got to Oberlin, facing the more pressing task of supporting himself.

Yamamoto and Yoshida, meanwhile, harbored dreams of becoming great jazz musicians, "but there was no future for a Japanese American jazz musician in the United States," Yoshida says. "It was hard enough to be a black jazz musician in the U.S."

As the war ended, each of these survivors headed to the same city to start over: Chicago.

"What happened was that a year or so after we were put in the camps, the government decided that we were law-abiding," Yoshida says. "So if you could line up a job or go to school, you could leave the camp [before the war ended].

"You could not go to the West Coast, however, because the government did not want us there. So we came to Chicago, thousands upon thousands of us. Chicago was the mecca.

"There was a big labor shortage during the war, and we were able to find jobs in Chicago. In fact, we were flooding into Chicago at the same time as blacks from the South.

"We even set up another jazz band in Chicago, because people loved this music here."

Indeed, hotels in the Loop were swinging hard during and immediately after the war. So even though musicians such as Yoshida, Yamamoto, and Hayashi needed day jobs to help make ends meet, the swing music they played in the internment camps helped set the tempo for their lives afterward. Each has maintained some contact with swing music ever since, whether it's singing weekly in a karaoke bar, as Hayashi does, or playing in swing bands, as Yamamoto and Yoshida regularly do.

Yet for all they've been through, none of these survivors seems particularly bitter.

"The Japanese are not an angry people," Hayashi says. "We have this attitude that we call '*shikata ga nai*,' which means, 'you can't help it.'

"In other words, what can you do? In a war, you can't change much, so you have to learn to get along."

Not surprisingly, each of the survivors notes parallels between their experience and that of Muslims in the United States today. Though internment camps have not been established in the wake of last month's terrorist attacks, "you know that Muslims are taking a lot of heat these days," Yamamoto says.

And that's why Yoshida spent years documenting the swing-band experience of the internment camps in his book *Reminiscing in Swingtime: Japanese Americans in American Popular Music, 1925–1960* (National Japanese American Historical Society).

"We were put into camp mainly because the mainstream didn't know who we were," says Yoshida, who for years belonged to the black musicians' union in San Francisco because its white counterpart would not admit him.

"It's still happening too. There's a lot of ignorance about who the Asians are, because we look different.

"What the American mainstream didn't realize was that we were very much like everyone else, which was why we were so attracted to the swing music.

"If people just listened to us play, they would know that we're as American as anyone else."

October 10, 2001

Coming to America

A new generation of immigrant musicians is rejuvenating jazz.

They come from urban Japan and war-torn Yugoslavia, from cosmopolitan Warsaw and impoverished Havana. They are fleeing age-old hostilities between India and Pakistan, between Israelis and Palestinians, yet they find refuge in the same place: America. By coming here, these musicians are dramatically changing the sound of America's most autobiographical music, jazz.

Though jazz always has welcomed external influences, from French Creoles and descendants of African slaves in the 1890s to Cuban expatriates in the late 1940s and '50s, the transformation this time has been more radical, more sweeping, more complex.

Indeed, the most dynamic innovations in jazz during the past few years have emanated from a new wave of young, hard-working, and prodigiously gifted immigrants. Trained in music of their own cultures but also surprisingly accomplished in the techniques of American jazz, these immigrants have helped alter the course of jazz.

If the 1970s marked the heyday of jazz-rock fusion and the '80s saw a resurgence of back-to-basics swing and blues, the mid-1990s and the new millennium have seen jazz develop along unmistakably international lines. Thanks to visionaries such as Panamanian pianist Danilo Perez, Puerto Rican tenor saxophonist David Sanchez, Palestinian oud player Simon Shaheen, Israeli bassist-pianist Avishai Cohen, Chilean vocalist Claudia Acuna, and Brazilian vocalist Luciana Souza, the improvisatory spirit and deep-swing rhythms of jazz have taken on exotic new hues.

Better still, the immigrant musicians have mingled the sounds of their own countries with ours so adroitly as to seduce an American public long wary of foreign cultural influences. And though they often balk at being called "world music" players rather than bona fide jazz musicians, in truth they are redefining both genres. Indeed, they are blurring the lines between the two, along the way attracting a growing audience that pays scant attention to how music is labeled.

"For a lot of younger people, it's just not so far-fetched anymore to be listening to jazz from a foreign country, or at least inspired by a foreign country," says Michael Orlove, who at thirty is a leading force in presenting foreign-born jazz artists in Chicago and across the country. As a programmer for the Chicago World Music Festival and Chicago Cultural Center, Orlove has aggressively championed Perez, Souza, Shaheen, Cohen, and dozens more.

"People are becoming a lot more adventurous and a lot more curious about each other today, probably because of the Internet and all the fast, global communication we have now," adds Orlove. "So hearing contributions of great young jazz talents from other countries is becoming almost normal."

In the small and often insular world of jazz, such explicit mixing of foreign cultures has not always been the norm. Though American artists long have understood the musical influences of distant countries, with Jelly Roll Morton embracing the habanera and tango rhythms that he dubbed the "Spanish tinge," the jazz mainstream generally has been defined by certain American-made signatures. Straight-ahead swing rhythm, blue-note melodies, English lyrics, and a freewheeling spirit of improvisation have long been the basic building blocks of American jazz and constants in music by Morton, Louis Armstrong, Duke Ellington, and other pioneers.

But as early as the 1930s, a subtle shift began to occur. Japanese American big bands with colorfully cross-cultural names such as the Mikados of Swing started to flourish on the West Coast, and a decade later trumpeter-bandleader Dizzy Gillespie broke new ground by collaborating with Cuban giants such as writer-arranger Mario Bauza and percussionist Chano Pozo. These partnerships yielded Latin jazz masterworks such as "Tin Tin Deo," "Manteca," and "Cubana Be, Cabana Bop."

Fast-forward to the early 1990s, when a small group of foreign-born, twenty-something musicians came to the United States and decided to try something more radical than even Gillespie had envisioned. Rather than simply apply jazz style to Latin tunes or Middle Eastern riffs, they invented a new, unabashedly personal music. It was a sound built—from the ground up—not only on the intricate rhythms and indigenous scales of their homelands but also on the swing backbeats and blues spirit of classic American jazz.

But these young musicians quickly discovered that America was not exactly interested.

"When David [Sanchez] and I played our music from *The Journey*, very few people wanted to hear it, almost nobody was around," recalls Perez, a Panamanian who lives near Boston. Indeed, he played to mostly empty clubs when he toured the music from this CD, in 1994.

"Even the record industry people told me that the music was a little bit too mixed, that it had too many influences."

Adds Sanchez, who is Puerto Rican and now lives in New York: "People would say to us, 'This is Latin, but it is not real jazz.' They put labels on us. It seemed like they didn't really want to understand."

Yet artists such as Sanchez and Perez—who had grown up hearing American jazz on the radio and on record—persevered. Equally smitten with their native folk music and with jazz imported from the States, they went about incorporating the two in everything they played. Indeed, rather than make distinctions between *plena* rhythms and American swing, between Caribbean song forms and American twelve-bar blues, they simply found ways of making the two cohere.

For the immigrant musicians, this was the most natural thing to do.

"I was listening to jazz and absorbing jazz even before I knew that it was called jazz," explains Chilean singer Claudia Acuna, who was born in Santiago and for six years has been based in New York.

"I just knew that I liked this music that I was hearing on the radio, and I sang it. It wasn't until I was fourteen years old that a married couple who loved jazz informed me that I was a jazz singer.

"From that moment I wanted to come to the United States. Because for jazz, America is the mecca."

Acuna and immigrants like her did more than just absorb the music around them. By refusing to let go of the sounds they heard back home, they created new forms of composition and improvisation that have yet to be named.

The Palestinian oud player, bandleader, and composer Simon Shaheen, for instance, dared to intertwine exuberant swing backbeats with Middle Eastern instrumentation and even classical-influenced violin playing. No one—not even Shaheen himself—yet knows what to call this music, but there's no question that it could not exist if jazz and European symphonic music and Palestinian folk songs had not preceded it, for Shaheen borrows liberally from each, combining them in idiosyncratic ways.

When Shaheen and his genre-bending Qantara band played Orchestra Hall last year, listeners cheered after bravura solos as if they were in a jazz club, yet the crowd also listened raptly while Shaheen unfurled

Brahmsian violin cadenzas as if he were playing with the Chicago Symphony Orchestra.

But for Shaheen, like the other jazz immigrants, the journey to this level of acceptance has been arduous and sometimes painful.

"When I first came to the United States, in 1980, and I heard some of the earliest experiments in fusing jazz with other cultures, I was disappointed, it hurt me," says Shaheen, who lives in Brooklyn. "It was so superficial. It was like a Hollywood composer trying to give the impression of Arabic music but just using the most obvious clichés. There was very little integrity to it, and this caused me sadness. It was a mishmash.

"But now we have truly great musicians who are taking the trouble to really understand world music and to make it work with jazz in the most fundamental ways."

Instead of playing American jazz standards, artists such as Shaheen and Perez and Sanchez increasingly have drawn upon the folk repertoires of their homelands, transforming them via jazz technique. The result has been innovative, extended works such as "Suite for the Americas" on Perez's *Motherland* CD (2000) and "Rhythm in Blue Suite" on his *Central Avenue* recording (1998). Sanchez produced similarly up-tempo, unusually lush jazz explorations of the music of Cuba, Brazil, and Puerto Rico on his *Obsesión* CD (1998).

These works, among others, stand as original creations, neither all folk nor all jazz but a profound synthesis of the two. In these major pieces, the young jazz immigrants affirmed that they were pointing the music in bold new directions.

But it wasn't just the audiences who were enthralled by these sounds. The musicians themselves also were startled by the artistic discoveries. Though they had been drawn to America by its deep jazz traditions, the immigrants came to understand the music in ways they had not anticipated.

"When I moved to Oakland [California] several years ago, I almost could not believe what I was hearing," recalls Cuban pianist-bandleader Omar Sosa, who now divides his time between homes in the San Francisco Bay area and in Barcelona, Spain.

"This was when I realized that the United States was really home to the African diaspora. I met the black jazz musicians, I met the black rappers, I met the black blues players, and suddenly I realized that I am really hearing the African roots of American music.

"I had moved to the States because in Cuba we saw jazz as born in the U.S.A. But after a few years in Oakland, I realized that, in a way, jazz actually was born in Africa."

This concept inspired Sosa to expand his vision of the music in grand ways. At the moment, for instance, he's holed up in Barcelona composing a symphony that embraces American jazz improvisation, Afro-Cuban percussion, religious music of Gnawa, as well as sounds of Mozambique, Senegal, and the European symphony orchestra. The new work, commissioned by the Oakland Symphony and scheduled to be premiered in 2003, may be the most ambitious venture yet in transforming jazz through sounds from foreign shores.

In the past few years, even the major jazz labels—which are slowest to respond to course changes in the music—have documented a remarkably broad range of music by jazz immigrants. In fact, it's not an exaggeration to note that the best major-label recordings of the 1990s were authored by foreign-born artists.

Surely Columbia Records has released few records of the stature of Sanchez's *Melaza* (2000) and *Travesia* (2001), while RCA and GRP/Impulse have distinguished themselves with discs such as Perez's *The Journey* (1994) and *Motherland.*

Chicagoans, in particular, have been blessed by various forces promoting the music, with institutions such as the World Music Festival, HotHouse, and the Old Town School of Folk Music providing critically important venues for immigrant musicians. Another important player has been WBEZ-FM 91.5, which has championed world music on its long-running program *Passport.*

The trend toward immigrant jazz has become so pervasive, in fact, that young musicians today can hardly avoid it.

"To tell you the truth, I never even intended to have a band like this," says Israeli bassist Cohen, who lives in New York and heads the aptly named International Vamp Band.

"I just wanted to put together an ensemble where I could provide an environment for experimentation. And suddenly I looked at my band and said to myself, 'Wow, there are four different countries represented here,'" adds Cohen, referring to band members from Israel, Mexico, Argentina, and Cuba.

Or, as Shaheen puts it, "You cannot be in a city like Boston or New York or Chicago or Washington without being exposed to music from all over the world.

"And this clash of civilizations, as I like to call it, definitely results in new projects, new genres, new combinations. Some of it is bad, some of it is mediocre, some of it is great, but it happens on a bigger scale in America than anywhere else."

If Chicagoan Tatsu Aoki's work merging Japanese and American musical cultures represents a new high point in jazz cross-breeding, it was the product of a thriving local scene that teems with foreign influences. The music of Chicago artists such as Polish singer Grazyna Auguscik, Chilean-Pakistani guitarist Fareed Haque, and the Yugoslavian guitarist Goran Ivanovic attests to the range of cultures that are rejuvenating jazz in this city and beyond. Haque and Ivanovic have been increasingly in demand as a duo.

It's worth noting, however, that the great immigrant experiment is closer to its start than its finish, with some obstacles still looming.

For one, though many record stores have vastly expanded the space they devote to "world music," everything from Egyptian prayer music to the Dutch jazz avant-garde is dumped into these bins helter-skelter, as if this were one cohesive genre, which it is not.

Similarly, the music of jazz immigrants is encountered only sporadically on the radio, with instrumentalists bemoaning that their work turns up haphazardly on everything from NPR to smooth jazz to foreign-language stations, but not with any regularity on any of them.

Yet the situation is a far cry from just a few years ago, when artists who brought music of their own cultures to bear on American jazz were practically ignored.

"Look at what has happened in just seven years or so," says Perez. "At one point, we were called 'too diverse' and 'too different' and 'too much.' Now we're called 'the new thing in jazz.'

"And I believe it's just the beginning."

January 13, 2002

Indeed, the impact of immigrants who redefined jazz in the late twentieth and early twenty-first centuries has only intensified. In 2007 Sanchez released the eighth and most ambitious recording of his career, Cultural Survival, *its cornerstone a twenty-minute suite titled "La Leyenda del Canaveral" exploring the slave trade and its effects on jazz. In 2008 Puerto Rican jazz saxophonist*

Miguel Zenon won a coveted MacArthur Foundation Fellowship, or "genius grant," which gives him five hundred thousand dollars—over the course of five years—to do with as he wishes. His first release since winning the MacArthur, Esta Plena, *shows Zenon burrowing more deeply than ever into the ancient* plena *music of Puerto Rico, yet transforming it through jazz syntax. The MacArthur Fellowship brought new prestige to the immigrant influence in jazz, which continues to grow. In 2009 the Chilean-born singer Claudia Acuna released* En Este Momento *(Marsalis Music), her first CD in five years, its tracks almost entirely in Spanish. Brazilian singer Luciana Souza, at the same time, released* Tide *(Verve), which segues freely among Brazilian, jazz, and pop idioms. Meanwhile, pianist Vijay Iyer has brilliantly applied Indian musical techniques to jazz (and vice versa), as in his CDs* Historicity *(Act, 2009) and* Tragicomic *(Sunnyside, 2008). So has his frequent partner, saxophonist Rudresh Mahanthappa, on recordings such as* Apti *(Innova, 2008),* Kinsmen *(Pi, 2008), and* Codebook *(2006). Similarly, the free-ranging guitarist Fareed Haque has dramatically expanded the color palette and technical resources of jazz by drawing upon his South Asian heritage, with thrilling East-meets-West recordings such as his evocatively titled* Flat Planet *(Owl Studios, 2009), featuring his Flat Earth Ensemble. So far as jazz is concerned, the earth is getting flatter all the time.*

Anniversary Tune

A pioneering avant-garde organization finds itself at a crossroads, still struggling to catch America's ear.

Three decades ago, when audiences across America seemed to be turning their backs on jazz, a dramatic and unexpected turn of events on the South Side of Chicago helped give the music a future.

Unable to find decent paying jazz gigs and uninterested in playing the pop tunes of the day, a group of Chicago's more daring jazz virtuosos decided to go into business for themselves. If no one was going to hire them to play jazz, they would hire each other, put on their own concerts, develop their own audiences, and—most important—invent new ways of creating music. By forging novel sounds and techniques, they reasoned, they might revivify the language of jazz and, perhaps, win a few new listeners in the bargain.

Thus was born the Association for the Advancement of Creative Musicians, a pioneering South Side organization that now is known around the world simply as the AACM. When several AACM alumni from all corners of the globe converge on Chicago next weekend to celebrate the thirtieth anniversary in concert, their emotions likely will be mixed.

"We have survived the odds," says Mwata Bowden, chairman of the AACM since 1989. "We've had hard times, families have broken up, love affairs have fallen apart, but we have persevered, we have continued to look forward, we have moved the music all the way around the world."

No doubt the past three decades have brought equal measures of triumph and heartbreak, with each artistic advance seemingly counterbalanced by a financial setback, each musical breakthrough tinged with its own personal cost. Yet not even the radicals who conceived the organization in 1965 could have imagined the ways in which the AACM would change the world.

"Muhal Richard Abrams and I sort of dreamed up the idea one night at some West Side bar," tenor saxophonist and AACM founding father Fred Anderson recalled in a 1990 *Tribune* interview.

"It was really tough at first. Anytime you're breaking new ground and playing original music, you can expect resistance. But that was no problem, because the Chicago guys were used to that."

As early as 1962 several up-and-coming Chicago musicians began tinkering with new sounds in the aptly named Experimental Band. Here were musicians daring to build on the then-outlandish musical ideas of Ornette Coleman, John Coltrane, and Sun Ra.

Harmonic structures that transcended or ignored traditional Western rules, rhythms that defied conventional meter, solos that sometimes screamed in hysterical tones—these were just some of the tools that were forged on the South Side. The players (including such now-celebrated artists as Anderson, Joseph Jarman, Roscoe Mitchell, Jack DeJohnette, and Muhal Richard Abrams) would teach themselves how to improvise collectively, how to use ancient instruments and how to invent new ones.

By the time the AACM officially came into existence, in 1965, the concept had inspired six distinct bands: Phil Cohran's Artistic Heritage Ensemble, Jodie Christian's quintet, and ensembles led by Abrams, Jarman, Mitchell, and altoist Troy Robinson. A year later, Anthony Braxton, Lester Bowie, Phillip Wilson, and others had joined the fray.

All were formidable instrumentalists, yet the going was not easy.

"In the early days, we had maybe four people sitting in the audience," recalls singer-bandleader Rita Warford. "And then, when the music would start, two of those people would get up and run out of there, because they thought it sounded so bad."

If American ears weren't yet ready for the kinds of incendiary solos and startling dissonances at which the AACM bands excelled, Europeans were. In 1969 the Art Ensemble of Chicago (with Jarman, Mitchell, Bowie, and Malachi Favors) created a sensation among European listeners and came home as conquering heroes. Braxton's trio (with Leroy Jenkins and Leo Smith) followed shortly thereafter, with similar results.

"I remember when the Art Ensemble came back from Europe and the guys started to become real, real successful," remembers Warford. "And I told them, 'I'd like to be successful, like you.'

"To this day I remember what Joseph Jarman said to me: 'Success is being successful in the moment, with what you're doing right now, what you're practicing, what you're studying, what you're performing in front of an audience right now.'

"That's the kind of integrity those guys had."

And therein lies the essence of the AACM, and one of the reasons it has commanded the respect of musicians and jazz listeners around the world. This was an organization that did not merely produce its own concerts but did so with a set of inviolable principles, all under the motto "Great Black Music, Ancient to Future."

By largely avoiding raucous clubs in favor of better listening rooms, for instance, the musicians were demanding that jazz musicians be taken as seriously as their classical counterparts. By wearing ceremonial African garb and borrowing improvisational techniques from ancient Africa, they were paying homage to their heritage.

"When I was a teenager, just seeing people like the AACM founders was inspiring," says Kahil El'Zabar, today a well-known Chicago percussionist-bandleader in his own right. "Watching them and listening to them, you could tell it wasn't about monetary gain, it was about human potential."

Combine this ennobling way of presenting art with the visionary nature of the music itself, and you had the makings of a revolution. Thus the Far Eastern experiments of Henry Threadgill, the unusual instrumentation of Roscoe Mitchell, the heaven-storming solos of Anderson, and the theatrics of Lester Bowie helped rewrite the rules for improvising jazz. In time all of these players, and others, would become stars of the international avant-garde.

If the success of the AACM meant that some of its key players eventually would move on (Threadgill now lives in India, Abrams in New York, Mitchell in Wisconsin), the organization never lost its fire. A second generation of Chicagoans took up the torch, with virtuosos such as percussionist El'Zabar, tenor saxophonist Edward Wilkerson Jr., alto saxophonist Ernest Dawkins, multireed player Bowden, and others starting remarkable bands of their own.

Certainly El'Zabar's Ritual Trio and Ethnic Heritage Ensemble, Wilkerson's 8 Bold Souls and Shadow Vignettes, Bowden's Sound Spectrum, and Dawkins's New Horizons Ensemble today stand at the forefront of new music in America.

Equally important, these groups have left an indelible imprint on bands coast to coast and beyond. When the German avant-garde bands in the FMP Festival played Chicago's HotHouse last weekend, for instance, their debt to the pioneers of the AACM was evident in every phrase they played. Even mainstream musicians today often use once-radical techniques created and developed by the AACM.

For all the triumphs, though, there have been unrelenting hardships. Financing for the not-for-profit organization always has been hand to mouth, with ticket sales and an occasional foundation grant paying the bills (barely).

And the South Side building where the AACM had its headquarters and school was destroyed four years ago when a chimney caved in through the roof. To this day, the AACM lacks a single full-time administrator, with the musicians themselves still doubling up to book concerts, plan tours, write grant proposals, and sell tickets.

"In the early days, we could throw on a concert practically anywhere—churches, schools, wherever there was a good open space," says Wilkerson. "We'd put up a few posters, and people would come.

"Today that won't do anymore. You need media attention, advertising, grants, foundation support; you need to network with different organizations to have a success.

"So we're at a crossroads now. We've got to move to the next level."

Even in this regard, however, the AACM seems to be pressing ahead with ingenuity. By creating a home page on the Internet earlier this year, Wilkerson, Bowden, and friends have been able to inform fans around the world about their upcoming festival.

More important, new blood has been flowing into the organization, in the form of young, creative artists such as drummer Reggie Nicholson, guitarist Jeff Parker, bassists Thaddeus Expose and Gerald Lindsey, singer Maia, and the Samana ensemble.

"The public ear is becoming accustomed to our music, you can tell from all the people who come to our concerts now," says Bowden. "Yet we're still strapped for cash. In Europe, they consider us the music of today, not tomorrow. In America, we value our artists only after they're dead.

"Still, we do not give up."

November 26, 1995

As the AACM prepares to celebrate its forty-fifth anniversary in 2010, the organization's durability is overshadowed only by its productivity. Money may be scarce and performance opportunities mostly self-generated, but the AACM continues to create new generations of jazz iconoclasts. Yesterday's revolutionaries have become today's elders, among them multi-instrumentalists Roscoe Mitchell and Douglas Ewart; percussionists Kahil El'Zabar and Hamid Ddrake; reedists Mwata Bowden, Edward Wilkerson Jr., and Ernest Dawkins; and trombonist George Lewis, author of the definitive history, A Power Stronger Than Itself *(University of Chicago Press, 2008). Each relentlessly tours the globe, building new constituencies for AACM aesthetics. These seasoned musicians, in turn, have nurtured a new wave of potentially major figures, such as flutist Nicole Mitchell and guitarist Jeff Parker, as well as rising musicians in their twenties and early thirties, such as trumpeter Corey Wilkes, saxophonists Greg Ward and Kevin Nabors, pianist Justin Dillard, bassist Junius Paul, and cellist Tomeka Reid. The experiment continues.*

"Strange Fruit": The Song Too Painful to Sing

Billie Holiday's classic has all but vanished from concert halls—yet it haunts our culture.

More than sixty years since Billie Holiday first performed the most incendiary song in her repertoire, its lyrics still burn. So much, in fact, that audiences usually don't know how to react when a performer sings of "strange fruit hanging from the poplar trees," as searing an indictment of the horrors of racism as any in song. At the end of the piece, the crowd typically responds with stunned silence, then, after what seems an eternity, erupts into nearly deafening applause.

Not even the prospect of noisy ovations, however, can persuade today's preeminent jazz divas to perform "Strange Fruit" in concert. Though the song has gained new prominence thanks to several recent recordings and a book-length study of its impact, "Strange Fruit" has had a haunting effect on those who record it: they admire the song, but they won't perform it anymore.

Though the piece dates from a distant era, its cry against brutal racism still shatters those who attempt to sing it in public.

The reason may be tragically apparent: this stark chronicle of a lynching resonates as urgently today as in 1939, when Holiday first shocked audiences with it.

"I would not do it today; I would refuse if anyone asked me to," says Dee Dee Bridgewater, the American expatriate singer who has lived near Paris for more than a decade.

Distraught over the way black artists in general, and jazz musicians in particular, were treated in the United States, Bridgewater immigrated to Europe in 1986 (she recently began living part time in the States).

"I couldn't handle singing that song again," adds Bridgewater, who recorded "Strange Fruit" for her 1991 live album, *In Montreux*, but hasn't sung it since.

"I think it's bad enough that we've got all these race problems going on as it is. I would not subject an audience to that. This is a very delicate moment in America."

To say the least. Although the lynchings of the Jim Crow era may be consigned to the past, racial violence is chillingly contemporary.

Two years ago, three Texans dragged James Byrd Jr. to his death with a truck. Last month, seventeen-year-old Raynard Johnson was found hanging from a pecan tree in front of his family's Mississippi home; though a pathologist deemed this a suicide, Johnson's family considers it a lynching. And racially motivated beatings such as the Lenard Clark case have roiled Chicago and several other cities in recent years.

So when Billie Holiday's musical heirs attempt to sing "Strange Fruit," they see much more than a fable of a lynching in the Old South. They see America today.

"I used to sing that song often in Atlanta, whenever I was there," recalls Cassandra Wilson, who recorded "Strange Fruit" on her *New Moon Daughter* album of 1995 but dropped the tune from her repertoire not long after.

"That song is about today. I don't think we've gone anywhere since Billie sang it. I think we have the illusion of moving away from that time and place, but we still have pretty much the same attitudes when it comes to race—they're just perhaps not as open, not as vociferous as they were in the past.

"But when you look at all the events that have happened to blacks in the past few years, it's very close to the way it used to be when 'Strange Fruit' was new.

"It's a difficult time."

Perhaps that's why the song won't go away, even if the artists who have recorded it most persuasively no longer can bring themselves to sing it. Beyond the searing recordings by Wilson and Bridgewater, "Strange Fruit" has been revisited by Duane Wiggins of Tony! Toni! Toné! (earlier this year), by the Sounds of Blackness (1994), and by rockers such as Sting (1986) and Tori Amos (1994).

The song has even inspired a slender but worthy book, released earlier this year by *Vanity Fair* writer David Margolick and entitled *Strange Fruit: Billie Holiday, Cafe Society and an Early Cry for Civil Rights.*

In truth, however, cries for civil rights have resonated in American musical culture for centuries, first through the Negro spirituals that pleaded for deliverance, and later in blues laments and jazz dirges. By comparison, "Strange Fruit" is not so much an early cry as an especially painful and potent one.

Yet it was Holiday, more than anyone, who gave the song its identity with several stark, emotionally wrenching recordings of a tune she never tired of reinterpreting.

To hear Holiday unfurl the dramatically charged lyrics with such profound understatement—her gritty, grainy alto every bit as honest as the subject demanded—was to feel the power of her message. No Ella Fitzgerald–type scat singing or Sarah Vaughan–style melodic adornments were called for, and none was sung. The slightly bent notes, the running-out-of-breath phrase endings, and the occasional crack in the voice told the story.

Bridgewater, who sang the piece nightly during the 1980s when she was portraying Holiday in the play *Lady Day* in Europe, will never forget the song's hold on her.

"It puts you in a very strange place," says Bridgewater. "It brings up all the bad racial incidents that I saw and that I knew happened to other people, it brings up this feeling that won't go away.

"When I did that show, I kind of walked around with a cloud over my head."

And when she began singing the song again in Europe in the early 1990s, in support of her *In Montreux* album, Bridgewater found herself breaking down in tears by the end of it. After about seven performances, she says, she realized she couldn't sing it anymore.

Even while she was performing "Strange Fruit," she never considered singing it in the United States.

It might come as a surprise to listeners that such a gripping piece was written by a white schoolteacher, but not those familiar with the unconventional life of Abel Meeropol. Writing under the pseudonym Lewis Allen, Meeropol also penned the famous lyric to "The House I Live In," a plea for racial peace sung by Frank Sinatra in the 1945 short film of the same name. And it was Meeropol and his wife who adopted the orphaned sons of Ethel and Julius Rosenberg after the political activists were executed for spying. The man clearly nourished a passion for the disenfranchised.

Holiday often claimed to have written the tune, but at least the lyrics are purely Meeropol's (some observers have claimed that arranger Danny Mendelsohn had a hand in reshaping Meeropol's melody).

Yet it was Holiday who gave "Strange Fruit" to the world, not only by introducing it but by making it indelibly her own through several harrowing recordings and uncounted club performances. Each time she sang it, she recalled, it tore her up.

"Another time, on Fifty-second Street, I finished a set with 'Strange Fruit' and headed, as usual, for the bathroom," she wrote in her memoirs, *Lady Sings the Blues* (with William Dufty).

"I always do. When I sing it, it affects me so much I get sick. It takes all the strength out of me."

But it wasn't just the general sentiment of the song that ate at Holiday. Her father, guitarist Clarence Holiday, died tragically in 1937 while playing in Texas with Don Redman's band. Catching a cold on tour is business as usual for most musicians, but Holiday's lungs had been damaged by gas poisoning in World War I.

Wary of what might happen to a black man wandering into an unfamiliar hospital in Texas, Holiday put off the visit until he found a veterans hospital, where he arrived too late.

"It wasn't the pneumonia that killed him, it was Dallas, Texas," wrote his daughter, who added that "Strange Fruit" "seemed to spell out all the things that had killed Pop."

For singers taking on the song today, "Strange Fruit" similarly recalls not just a distant era but grim personal experience.

"You always run a risk when you try to speak for someone else, but I would imagine that these singers may have experienced some personal [racial] flare-ups," says Rachelle Ferrell, an exceptional vocalist who never has performed the tune and says she probably never will.

"When you sing a song like 'Strange Fruit,' it can validate your experience; it's something you can identify with. And why try to write something brand-new when a particular song speaks to your experience so beautifully?"

Yet Ferrell chooses not to sing "Strange Fruit" for different reasons from Bridgewater's and Wilson's. To Ferrell, there's a danger in repeating Holiday's lament.

"For me, it's important not to get stuck where Billie was when she sang that song," says Ferrell. "That was a very real experience for many people for a very long time, and it was valid to bring attention to it, so that it can be healed. . . . But we also can get stuck in some deep trenches."

Regardless of how singers choose to address or avoid "Strange Fruit," the piece clearly has not lost one whit of its communicative power. And that says a great deal about the tenor of our times.

"What's really haunting about that tune is that the man who wrote it couldn't possibly have realized that it would be so true fifty or sixty years later," says Bridgewater.

"But why should the song go away if the disease that inspired it never has?"

July 30, 2000

XI

Chicago Radicals

The Alluring Eccentrics of Chicago Jazz

Ragtime Blues: Reginald Robinson

Though he wowed critics with his fresh interpretation of a century-old genre, Reginald Robinson toiled for years in musical obscurity. Good thing somebody knew a genius when they heard one.

It's standing-room-only on a late February afternoon at tony Occidental College in Los Angeles, where some two hundred students are about to learn that genius can come in unexpected forms.

The guest lecturer is from the very un-tony West Side of Chicago. He seats himself at the piano, gently places his fingers on the keyboard, and proceeds to reel off ragtime tunes of astonishing complexity. In just a few beats his hands become a blur, the instrument begins to shake, and the kids find themselves swaying in their seats.

Between numbers, each of which draws a clamorous ovation, the pianist weaves a lecture. His subject is ragtime, and he traces the music's evolution from the classic works of Scott Joplin to the ferociously difficult and ornate original rags that he is unfurling on this balmy California day.

Seldom, if ever, have the students at Occidental, where tuition and lodging hover at forty thousand dollars a year, received tutoring of this sort. The visiting professor, after all, dropped out of high school and taught himself his art before going on to compose a stack of certifiable, state-of-the-art ragtime masterpieces.

"How much did you get for the MacArthur 'genius' award?" one of the students inevitably asks, referring to the MacArthur Foundation Fellowship that the pianist received last fall.

"Half a million dollars," replies thirty-two-year-old Reginald R. Robinson, with a demure grin. "And that's half a million more than I ever had before."

Indeed, just before Robinson learned last September that he had won one of the most lucrative and prestigious awards in the country, the gas in his West Side apartment was cut off and overdue notices from the electric company were piling up.

He was so broke and despondent that he'd given up practicing piano, ceased composing new music, and very nearly stopped believing that he could make a living in ragtime—an art form that had been dead for roughly eighty years until Robinson came along and decided to try to breathe life back into it.

That a young man whose childhood was punctuated with shootings and other inner-city horrors—a kid who failed seventh grade before eventually bailing on the Chicago public schools—should emerge as the leading hope of a long-lost art form would seem remarkable enough. But that he taught himself practically everything he knows about music, spending years decoding notes and chords, only underscores the magnitude of his achievement.

Yet on this day, as on most others, his focus is not on his arduous journey but on its goal, the music.

"A lot of people think ragtime is hokey," concedes Robinson, who stands about five feet eight inches but produces the colossal sound of a much larger man. "But in my mind, it's deeper than that. . . . You can hear every emotion; all of life is in it."

Certainly all of Robinson's life is.

~

Above all else, Reginald Robinson remembers two things about his turbulent childhood—the gang-bangers who repeatedly broke into his family's third-floor apartment in the Henry Horner Homes, and the ice-cream truck that chimed a lilting, syncopated melody as it rolled slowly along west Lake Street in the crushing summer heat.

If the violence scarred Robinson, the ice-cream truck's mechanical jingle may have saved him.

Robinson recalls jumping every time he heard gunshots fired in the streets. "I mean, almost anything you can imagine was going on over there. One time, some guy was trying to break in while we were at home! We were looking at him, and he was looking at us."

Another time, the Robinson family—two parents and six children—returned home from a movie to find their apartment being ransacked. "These guys had everything all over the place," says Robinson. "The front door had melted. I guess they used some kind of heating apparatus or something to get in."

Amid the chaos, Robinson sought refuge in music wherever he encountered it—on the radio, on the LPs that his folks played at home, ranging from Bach to Basie. And even from that ice-cream truck, with its twinkly little tune that was written by ragtime legend Scott Joplin—though back then Robinson had no idea who wrote it, nor had he ever heard of Joplin.

In fact, Robinson never thought about that song—Joplin's indelible "The Entertainer"—until one Friday afternoon during his second tour of seventh grade in 1986. A group of Chicago jazz musicians from the Urban Gateways program was playing at Robert Emmet School, in the Austin neighborhood, where Robinson's family had moved a few years earlier.

To Robinson's amazement, one of the musicians began playing the ice-cream truck song. The music evoked pleasant memories that stood out against an unsettling childhood, and awakened in him an overwhelming desire to capture those sounds, to make them on his own.

"Something really was pulling me into that music," says Robinson. "It's strange to me; I'm still trying to figure that out."

Though he may never determine exactly why Joplin's melody changed him, he knows that he had never felt anything like it before or since. In that beguiling little tune, he found a purpose for his young life, a way to bring some order out of the anarchy surrounding him.

"It just did something to him, it excited him so much," says his mother, Janet. "He came back home and told me all about it."

The thirteen-year-old Robinson immediately began rifling through dictionaries and other books at home, searching for any reference to "ragtime" but finding none. So he wrote the word down on a piece of paper to ensure that he wouldn't forget it before Monday, when he was able to look it up at school.

Every day after that he wandered to the back of the classroom to thumb through the pages of a dictionary until he arrived at "ragtime," reading the definition over and over, writing it down, memorizing it, absorbing it. The text cited Joplin as "the king of ragtime," and soon other books pointed Robinson to the Oscar-winning 1973 film *The Sting,* which used Joplin's music as a backdrop and sparked a brief revival of interest in ragtime in the 1970s. Robinson found a videotape of the film and played it repeatedly to study its score. Then he moved on to Charlie Chaplin and Buster Keaton silent films, which similarly featured high-spirited ragtime piano music as accompaniments.

Each day, his obsession deepened. "I was on a hunt," says Robinson. He begged his parents for a piano and eventually got a small electric keyboard, which he hammered constantly. His playing was crude, as the tapes he made of himself show, the fledgling pianist inventing snippets of melodies akin to nursery-school songs.

Meanwhile, the violence of the neighborhood constantly bumped up against Robinson's life. The house that the family bought in 1987 on the South Side had more space than anything they had before, but the new neighborhood didn't seem to be any less dangerous than the ones they left behind. Drug deals and armed violence remained fixtures of everyday life.

It got so bad that Robinson's mother decided she had to walk her kids to the front door of their schools and pick them up in the afternoon to ensure their safety. Even when Robinson was a teenager, his mother accompanied him to the steps of Tilden High School.

"The young people that went to that school began to carry guns," she recalls. "Reginald saw several of his classmates get shot, and it made him not want to go back."

He dropped out during his freshman year and retreated into his bedroom, teaching himself piano on an old Jensen spinet his mother had acquired from a neighbor. Someone had put stickers on each key with the name of every note, so that Robinson was able to read the long runway of otherwise inscrutable black and white keys.

From morning until night he struggled at the piano, trying to find chords where the unskilled hand strikes only dissonance, working to pick out melodies from a seemingly infinite range of possibilities. When he wasn't hitting the keys, he was listening to recordings by Joplin, Louis Chauvin, Tom Turpin, and others, trying to re-create on his piano the intoxicating sounds they had invented a century earlier.

For three years, Robinson rarely left his bedroom. And through the sheer intensity of his focus and the depth of his gifts, he began to play ragtime.

"He played continuously, over and over and over, until one day it turned into music," says his mother.

Adds elder brother Marlando Robinson, "I couldn't believe what he was accomplishing. One day he put on a tape of something for me, and I said, 'Was that Joplin, Handy, or Chauvin?'

"And he said, 'No, that's me.'"

A skeptical Marlando marched Reginald over to the piano, insisting that he demonstrate this feat live.

"His hands flew so fast, you couldn't even see them," recalls Marlando, still somewhat incredulous.

In those three years—a blink of an eye in the course of most musicians' training—Robinson had remade himself from a kid who didn't even know the word "ragtime" into a creator of original tunes.

Though at age sixteen he still had a lot to learn about writing a first-class composition—how to create multiple themes, how to switch from one key to another, how to replicate and even extend the formal structures of Joplin and other ragtime greats—Robinson surely had found his voice.

Yet he was dissatisfied that he still stumbled at reading music, that he couldn't accurately put his compositions to paper, that almost everything about the nuts and bolts of ragtime music eluded him—except how to create it and how to play it. So he got a job at a silkscreen shop in the neighborhood to pay for a few music lessons at the now-defunct American Conservatory of Music, in the Loop. At his first session, his instructor was as skeptical as his brother Marlando had been.

"He played a number of his pieces for me, and I just couldn't believe he had created them, because he hadn't had any lessons," remembers his instructor at the conservatory, Ted Bargmann. "For a teacher, it was hard to believe. But then I realized it was true—he showed me the music. The stems on the notes were going in the wrong direction, some of the rhythm notations weren't correct, but these were basically the notes he played. It was some kind of miracle."

But Robinson was just getting started. Deciding that neither Bargmann nor anyone else could teach him how to create ragtime any better than he was already doing, he again holed up in the bedroom of his parents' house. In a burst of creativity, he wrote nearly a dozen compositions of unusual complexity and harmonic sophistication, even though he didn't know the names of the chords he was creating or understand the musical devices his ear was leading him to.

He saved up enough money to buy another used piano and added that to the other one in his bedroom, placing his bed between the pair of instruments. Night and day the young man literally was surrounded by music.

To help him connect with the spirit of the ragtime age, he pulled the red velvet curtains down from his parents' living room and hung them in his bedroom, conjuring the ambience of the old-time brothels where ragtime music emerged. Sometimes he took the shade off a lamp and placed the fixture on the floor so that it cast moody shadows across his room, the play of light and half-light helping him imagine that he was living in the gaslight era.

"It was like mentally transporting myself out of where we are now and into another zone," says Robinson. "Like I'm no longer in the present—I'm in 1907."

The result of these efforts was groundbreaking, even though almost no one outside the Robinson home knew it. The surging rhythms of "The Strongman" (composed in 1990), the poetic phrases of "Troubador Serenade" (1990), the Sturm und Drang of "Nile River Ripples" (1991), and the rhythmic swagger and bawdy chords of "Poker Face Blues" (1992) heralded the arrival of a new kind of ragtime, an art form that had essentially atrophied after Joplin's death in 1917.

Even the titles of Robinson's pieces reflected his fertile imagination. "Boogie Man Creep," "The Hustler's Two-Step," and "Ebony Venus" evoked exotic worlds of sound and image.

Though pianists such as Dick Hyman, Max Morath, and others long had played the old tunes nobly, and a couple dozen latter-day ragtimers wrote retro music of their own, no one was crafting compositions as intricate and original as Robinson's.

Perhaps because he was never taught the rules of harmony and theory, he was not constrained by them, building his oft-fanciful compositions on unanticipated chord changes, unusual bursts of dissonance, unorthodox turns of phrase, and unexpected clashes of traditional and contemporary techniques.

Feeling ready by the early 1990s to bring his ragtime creations into the world, he began seeking out other Chicago musicians, finally lucking out in 1992 when he met the brilliant pianist Jon Weber, who long has ruled over the lounge of the Four Seasons Hotel. Though commanding an encyclopedic knowledge of jazz history, Weber was stunned at the freshness of Robinson's art.

"'Where'd you study?'" Weber recalls asking. "And Reginald said, 'I didn't.'

"He was nineteen years old then, and these scores, they were so precise and so fastidious, I could hear exactly how they sounded by looking at them. And I'm thinking, 'I can't believe this humble man has produced all this.' It was almost like he was living in another time; he was living, breathing, dreaming that bygone period."

Weber soon realized that Robinson had perfect pitch, a gift that surely had enabled him to learn music and master composition without benefit of a teacher. Weber became his first and most ardent champion, paying for studio time so that Robinson could record his bulging satchel of original works.

The elder pianist brought dozens of cassette tapes of the studio sessions to sell at Robinson's low-key, Sunday-afternoon debut at Uptown's Green Mill Jazz Club in September 1992. The tapes practically flew out of Robinson's hands, inspiring him to bring a copy to Bob Koester, owner of the respected, Chicago-based Delmark Records.

"What he was playing sounded totally original," says Koester, who immediately signed Robinson to a recording contract.

"He wasn't just playing ragtime like most of these guys play it," a reference to the buttoned-down, note-perfect, often-anemic renderings of many players a generation or two older than Robinson.

Perhaps because he had learned ragtime as its original creators had—on his own, without formal training, note by grueling note—Robinson's music sounded all the more authentic, credible, and true. Not surprisingly, Robinson's recording debut in 1993, *The Strongman,* earned lavish praise from critics, musicians, and scholars.

Dick Hyman, for decades one of the country's top interpreters of ragtime and other early American styles, remembers being caught off guard by the quality and depth of Robinson's original works. "Reginald had so absorbed all the classic rags that he could write them as well as the old masters could."

And play them. His version of Joplin's "Maple Leaf Rag," which opens *The Strongman,* became something of an instant classic. "I don't think there's anyone in the world that plays a piece like 'Maple Leaf Rag' who comes as close to Scott Joplin's piano roll as Reginald does," says Trebor Tichenor, one of the leading scholars of the genre.

Within months, Robinson was taping Marian McPartland's *Piano Jazz* radio show and broadcasting live, nationally, during a New Year's Eve double bill with Weber at the Green Mill.

But just as Robinson's career was taking flight, he began to realize how marginal ragtime was in the spectrum of musical tastes at the turn of the twenty-first century. He was paid a one-thousand-dollar advance from Delmark for *The Strongman,* and got only two thousand dollars up front for its follow-up, *Sounds in Silhouette* (1994)—not exactly a big-time payday for work he had spent years creating, even including modest royalties. And though various ragtime festivals booked him when he was a novelty on the scene in the early 1990s, Robinson's engagement calendar never filled out.

"I simply had no money," he recalls of what he terms his first great "slump," in 1995. "I was at a really low state, where I was just trying to look for a [day] job, and ended up going from door to door in the Loop, trying to put in job applications. I was borrowing money from my mother just to try to live."

He began working as a day laborer for a packaging company in Elgin, serving food at a Loop restaurant, washing autos at a car-rental place downtown—anything to support himself and his music.

The three-thousand-dollar advance he received for his third and most ambitious Delmark CD, *Euphonic Sounds*—which made history by including a fragment of a Scott Joplin tune Robinson discovered while scrutinizing an old photograph—did not pull him out of debt. The bills only mounted after he moved out of his parents' house in 1999 to live with a girlfriend in Uptown.

Why couldn't a pianist of such distinction and achievement earn even the barest subsistence wage with his music?

"You've got to remember that 98 percent of any jazz musician's life is worrying about how to make the rent or a car payment," says Weber, a veteran of the financial squeeze. Robinson's position was all the more precarious because he had chosen to work in one of the most arcane subsets of jazz.

"He was in a strange spot. He should have been playing all the ragtime festivals, but there's a lot of latent racism there," says Koester, describing an insular milieu that features white performers playing for mostly white audiences. Robinson, with his urban-looking cornrows and ragtime iconoclasm, couldn't crack this nostalgia-based circuit.

"He should have been playing the jazz festivals, too," adds Koester, "but [they] generally turn their backs on traditional jazz."

There was another, deeper reason why Robinson was overlooked by the very music world that is starved for talent of his caliber, and that's the stigma of ragtime itself. Born in the postslavery era when blacks were suffering profoundly, ragtime was used as the backdrop for minstrel shows and other demeaning entertainments.

"Even when ragtime was popular, there definitely was a 50–50 split about it in the black community," notes Tichenor, the music scholar. "Eubie Blake said his mother told him to 'take that ragtime out of my house,' knowing where ragtime came from." In other words, the sporting houses and streets. Jelly Roll Morton, who started out as a ragtime piano player in the brothels of New Orleans's Storyville vice district, was kicked out of his family's home as a teenager and left to fend for himself when his grandmother found out he was playing the illicit music.

Associations of this sort, of course, have nothing to do with the inherent value of the music, as Robinson has proved, but the aura lingers. Many audiences and musicians, including a number of African Americans, "would rather put that part of the past behind them, and who could blame them?" says Hyman. "That's why what Reginald has done is such a brave act of individuality, to go against this attitude the way he has."

As the twentieth century slipped into the twenty-first, Robinson spent the hours away from his temporary day jobs composing tunes for his next—and still unreleased—album. Aptly titled *Man Out of Time,* the homemade CD contains one ornate ragtime opus after another, each a world of pitch and rhythm unto itself.

The recording, a milestone in the maturation of his art, culminates in "The 19th Galaxy," a ragtime tour de force that reaffirms Robinson's position at the front lines of the art form.

Reluctant to take the recording to Delmark, where he had received so little money for his previous efforts, he shopped the CD elsewhere but could find no takers. He moved out of his girlfriend's place in 2003 and into affordable housing for artists on the West Side, but he still found himself slipping into financial ruin. Only a cash gift from a friend made it possible for him to take his piano with him. The future looked bleak.

"Man, here I am again," he told himself. He looked for janitorial jobs, stockroom gigs, anything that could provide steady money. Even menial jobs were hard to find. Meanwhile, he felt himself losing his will to write music and practice the piano. "It was just not fun anymore," he says.

Out of desperation, he took his *Man Out of Time* CD to Delmark last year. Koester offered him a two-thousand-dollar advance, which Robinson urgently needed but ultimately declined to accept, saying it would amount to "signing my soul away" for a pittance.

On the day the MacArthur Foundation telephoned, Robinson was lying in bed, chilled to the bone because the gas had been cut off, wondering what he would do when the electricity went next. When Daniel J. Socolow, director of the MacArthur Fellows program, told Robinson that he was a winner and would receive one hundred thousand dollars annually for the next five years, he wasn't sure he hadn't dreamed it. For hours afterward, he kept checking his caller ID to make sure it really was the MacArthur Foundation that had phoned.

He went to the bathroom to splash his face with the icy cold water coming from both faucets, then spent the next couple of days chewing over what had happened before telling anyone else. Finally, he went to his mother's house on the South Side and asked her to come for a drive with him. They had traveled all the way to the suburbs before he pulled over and said, "Don't jump out of your skin, but I just won the MacArthur Award."

Janet Robinson was familiar with the prize and its mysterious ways—the foundation secretly seeks out and researches potential candidates before selecting winners whose lives will be changed.

On hearing the news, Robinson's mother couldn't catch her breath.

"I was surprised, I was ecstatic," she recalls. "Oh, man, tears just came to my eyes."

Suddenly, Reginald Robinson, ragtime pianist, was back in business, a development that posed interesting problems of its own.

For starters, the years in which he hadn't composed any music and the months in which he hadn't touched a piano meant that a great deal of his art had escaped his fingertips. To this day, he says, he struggles to recapture the pieces he once tossed off with ease, to relearn his virtuoso technique.

"The MacArthur thing kind of caught me off guard," says Robinson. "I'm getting engagements now where there used to be nothing, and so I'm being pushed to get my music up. That music on *Man Out of Time,* I have to learn it again."

~

After the lecture at Occidental College, students swarm around Robinson, asking to buy the CDs he brought and imploring him to autograph them.

Later that day he ventures to Hollywood, which he has never seen, and asks a journalist to photograph him with a disposable camera Robinson just bought. The setting is the famous corner of Hollywood and Vine, along the Hollywood Walk of Fame, where the beehive tower of Capitol Records looms nearby. Then on to other celebrated sites.

On practically every block, Robinson wants another picture to prove to his family—and perhaps himself—that he really was here, a kid from some of the toughest parts of Chicago, who literally played his way out of there.

Even so, Robinson is quick to point out that he's "still half literate" as far as music is concerned. "I still do not know simple things—simple terms in music, I still don't understand."

He goes to a Los Angeles video store to see if he can pick up any of the science-fiction films he devours in his spare time. Like ragtime, he says, these films take him to other places, far away from his everyday life.

For the most part, though, he spends his waking hours consumed with music—reading books about it, listening to recordings, practicing the piano, honing his compositions. Most of his life, in fact, plays out in his apartment, his never-ending immersion in ragtime music interrupted periodically with trips to the concert stage or visits to his family's South Side home.

Though he hasn't decided exactly what he's going to do with the MacArthur money, he knows what he wants to accomplish: "I want this ragtime music to be accepted, to be back in the mainstream," he says.

There's one more thing Robinson wants, and has wanted since he heard the ice-cream truck music played by real musicians in the seventh grade: he wants to compose the ragtime masterpieces that are still left unwritten—the music that he says wafts quietly through the ether, waiting for someone to capture it.

"I always had this thought in my mind that these melodies, if I listen long enough in silence, that I'll hear this music that's not yet written down—I mean that," he insists. "I think that there are things Scott Joplin never got a chance to write down, and things that many other ragtime musicians never got a chance to write down.

"And I can catch that—if I listen."

May 1, 2005

Robinson continued to struggle, and to persevere, since winning the MacArthur Fellowship. The funds enabled him to buy a small house—the first place he owned in his life—in a safe, working-class Chicago neighborhood. But engagements were difficult to come by, the pianist hired just a few times a year to play his solo ragtime masterpieces. So he spent his days essentially as he always had, since discovering the piano. He toiled at the keyboard, writing compositions most of the world didn't care to hear. Many are captured on the landmark CD he self-released in 2006, Man Out of Time *(88 PM). Ten years in the making—and, in effect, funded by the MacArthur grant—*Man Out of Time *represented a new high point in the antiquated art of ragtime. Robinson's "The 19th Galaxy," the tour de force of the recording, showed* *a copiousness of ideas and an ingenuity of keyboard techniques previously unknown in the history of ragtime. In addition, he began work on a self-made film documentary on ragtime, traveling the country to interview the last living individuals who knew, or heard, the original ragtime masters. And he waits for the phone to ring. In 2010, the MacArthur payments ended, and Robinson sold his home, moved into an apartment, and got rid of his piano. He also released a three-disc set,* Reflections *(88 PM), featuring brilliant new works and fresh recordings of his old ones. He still waits for the phone to ring.*

Patricia Barber Has Built Her Career Defying Conventions

Now the jazz world is knocking on her door. Even so, she remains an independent thinker.

In the small hours of Monday morning, when the streets are nearly deserted and most of Chicago has turned in for the night, a veteran singer-songwriter slips behind the baby grand of an Uptown jazz club. The audience—everyone from Gen Xers to hard-hats—huddles around the bar, barely stirring. Even the barkeep stops pouring drinks, instead relishing every phrase that Patricia Barber whispers into the microphone, accompanied by a lone, stand-up bass. For a few hours, at least, the normally rowdy Green Mill Jazz Club sounds almost as hushed as a highbrow concert hall, though admittedly one for insomniacs who want a last drink or another tune before heading into the night. The question is whether this extraordinary, intimate scene can play out much longer now that Patricia Barber, one of Chicago's most innovative jazz musicians, is about to step—gingerly—into the music industry's fastest lane.

"Should I do it? Should I take the tour?" she asks a visitor a couple days later in her North Side apartment. "There's a fax right there in the other room, East Coast tour, the whole shot. But should I do it?"

To the typical jazz musician, if there is such a thing, the answer is obvious. When you're being wooed by the Jazz Tree, a New York talent agency that has launched such stars as Diana Krall and Joshua Redman, you leap at the opportunity. Fame and riches await.

Barber, however, is anything but typical. During nearly two decades in Chicago, in fact, she has defied virtually every rule and expectation that the jazz music industry has set.

When Verve/Polygram, the most successful jazz label in the world, courted her a few years ago, she declined. Instead, she chose to record for a tiny Chicago independent label, Premonition, that operated out of its owner's kitchen.

When Paris-based Dreyfus Records flew her to France a few months ago to offer her a lucrative deal, she shot them down—though thanking them for a grand, all-expenses-paid week in Paree.

And when any number of Chicago club owners have told her how to dress, act, sing, bat her eyes, and otherwise help sell romance and booze, she has ignored them—sometimes getting canned in the process. Economic pressures notwithstanding, Barber simply has ignored the ancient archetype of the "girl singer" by refusing to coo to her audience (she prefers to make eye contact with her musicians) or to wear glittering evening gowns and spiked heels (slacks, blouse, and flats will do fine, thank you).

Incredibly, though, the iconoclastic artist appears to be enjoying the last laugh, for she's about to embark on high-profile tours of East Coast clubs next month and Europe's leading jazz festivals this summer. This is happening precisely when the rest of the mainstream jazz industry is imploding.

While major jazz record labels such as Verve/Polygram and Atlantic have slashed their artist rosters and watched their sales figures head south, Barber's new disc, *Modern Cool*, cracked the *Billboard* and Gavin charts shortly after its release last summer.

While other artists aggressively tour the country trying to generate favorable press, record sales, and the ever-elusive "buzz," Barber has achieved all three playing—of all things—the late, late show Sundays and Mondays at the Green Mill.

Clearly, something is awry in the province of jazz.

"Jazz is in trouble, big trouble," Barber says, speaking from the spacious apartment she shares with Valerie Booth, her partner of ten years.

"The major labels decided years ago that the phenomenon of the 'young lions' would sell records best, so they excluded so many other artists and so many other voices that the music became predictable and people lost their taste for it very, very quickly. So now you have a dire situation.

"I saw it coming five to seven years ago," adds Barber. "The record companies want to put out one record that sells 500,000 copies rather than 10 that sell 50,000. It's cheaper that way."

Barber's assessment may explain why Atlantic Records has dropped such artists as pianist Henry Butler and saxophonist Wess Anderson, instead putting most of its chips on young saxophone star du jour James Carter. The "young lions" theory also applies to Columbia Jazz Records, which was the king of the hill among major jazz labels in the 1980s but has made few noteworthy signings in recent years.

Though live jazz flourishes in major cultural centers such as Chicago and New York, jazz record sales have been in a steady slide. In 1989 jazz recordings commanded 5.7 percent of industry sales, but now it's 2.8 percent, according to the Recording Industry Association of America, which tracks the figures.

Recording executives have cited other reasons for the decline, including a saturated marketplace and a lack of new technology to excite buyers (as the new compact disc did in the mid-1980s).

Barber believes that the major labels, which have been trying to sign her for years, have deeper problems.

"They're interested in me because of *Modern Cool,* which has new material and is fresh and individual," she says. "So they get me in the office, and they say, 'Can we give you a lot of money?' And, of course, I say, 'Sure.'

"And then it begins: 'We're going to put you with this producer who did this kind of work with that particular artist,'" she adds, pointing to the record industry's instinctive tendency to try to clone previous hits, rather than invent new ones.

"And I'm thinking: 'You aren't getting it, you still don't get it.'"

Or perhaps the major labels simply need larger sales to support their huge, corporate structures.

"Basically, the majors, in the past several years, have approached jazz in the same way as pop," says Chris Heim, music director at WBEZ-FM 91.5, a Chicago jazz station.

"Their attitude has been: 'What's hot this month—young guys in suits? Let's record fifty of them.' That approach doesn't work in jazz."

Barber's success with an indie label points to another route, and it has caught the industry's attention.

"When *Modern Cool* started to appear on *Billboard,* a lot of people in offices in New York started wondering what was going on here," says Michael Friedman, president of Premonition Records, the minuscule label that Barber has put on the jazz map. "I talked to the president of a major label who said to me, 'Everybody's talking about your record.'"

What the major labels don't seem to realize, however, is that *Modern Cool*—which garnered the kind of critical acclaim and radio airplay that makes press agents weep with joy—did not emerge out of thin air. Quite the contrary, the record that brought the Jazz Tree to Barber's doorstep and won sobriquets from the *Los Angeles Times, San Francisco Chronicle,* and a coveted five-star review from *DownBeat* is the culmination of enormous and often painful efforts by Barber against seemingly overwhelming odds.

In fact, it has taken her nearly twenty years as a working musician and three earlier recordings to reach the high point that *Modern Cool* represents. The daughter of a Chicago jazz saxophonist who died when Barber was nine, the emerging artist decided early on that "becoming a jazz musician was a stupid thing for a smart woman to do," she once said. Yet as a classical music major at the University of Iowa, she finally gave in to the lure of jazz, which had appealed to her since the days when she used to put her hand in the bell of Floyd "Shim" Barber's saxophone to feel the vibrations of sound.

Like many generations of Midwesterners before her, Barber knew exactly where she needed to go to become a jazz artist: Chicago.

"When we started out, Patty did not have the respect of the jazz community," says Michael Arnapol, who has been her bassist and musical alter ego since 1980. "She frankly was struggling with piano and learning to play jazz, but eventually she just developed her own sound."

Indeed, though Barber long has cited superior vocalists such as Betty Carter and Sheila Jordan as influences, it's difficult to detect any direct link to these artists in her music. Barber's voice is simply too distinctive—with a luscious, wide-open sound and sleek, nearly vibratoless tone—to suggest anyone but Barber.

In addition, Barber was not content to work strictly as a singer. Through sheer force of will, she made herself into an exceptional jazz pianist whose solos can be as rhythmically volcanic or seductively minimalistic as the music demands.

The first great blossoming of Barber's talent took place in the since-shuttered Gold Star Sardine Bar, where she launched an eleven-year run in 1984. Her debut record, *Split* (1989), recorded on her own Floyd label, may have sounded a bit breathless—she tried a tad too hard to dazzle listeners with the voluptuousness of her voice and the fleetness of her keyboard technique. But it was strong enough to earn her a record deal with Antilles, a prestigious subsidiary of Verve/Polygram.

The resulting disc, *A Distortion of Love* (1992), signaled the arrival of a distinct new voice in jazz. Unfortunately, the experience of supporting a major label record—with its relentless schedule of touring, promoting, and performing—nearly ruined Barber's health and drove her from music.

"I was so burned out on this business after the Antilles record, I quit," says Barber, who has had asthma all her life and fell ill while on tour in Europe.

"Music is such magic for me, and I was always hoping it would be somehow isolated from all the nastiness, and then I found out that not only is it not isolated, you're just right in the heart of it."

When Barber was well enough to return to the United States from London in 1993, she holed up in her Humboldt Park apartment for nearly a year. Though surprised when the president of Verve/Polygram called to try to sign her, she was dismayed when he immediately outlined what she would record for her next album.

Nobody seemed to be listening, so she curled up on her couch and tried to determine her next move.

"I went through ten thousand dollars—my life's savings—until [Green Mill owner] Dave Jemilo called and said, 'Why don't you just come over and work one night a week?' " she says.

For her first set at the Mill, Barber "was kind of nervous," says Jemilo. "But I tell you, after a month, I just fell in love with her, I think she's a genius. A lot of it has to do with giving her space. If you just let her feel comfortable, she can be brilliant, and she is going to pull stuff out that you'd never ever imagine."

Restored to music and rejuvenated artistically, Barber began making remarkable aesthetic strides at the Green Mill. If she had been mostly a singer of jazz standards at the Gold Star Sardine Bar, now she was emerging as a bona fide songwriter. Her music caught the ear of Premonition president Friedman, who found the perfect way to obtain her services: sign a contract giving her complete artistic control, something no major label would have considered doing.

Recalls Barber, "I finally had permission to sit down and use my imagination to come up with music that I wanted to record, and we went from there."

The result, *Cafe Blue* (1994), was an artistic breakthrough. Deeply influenced by the minimalist school exemplified by Philip Glass and Terry Riley, *Cafe Blue* was leaner and more austere than Barber's earlier recordings and more personal as well, if only because it contained so many of her own songs.

Though Barber had not yet fully mastered the art of matching lyrics with melody, she had begun the process in earnest, a step that few young jazz artists are daring enough to take.

"When Charlie Parker and John Coltrane and Miles Davis were coming up, one of their main focuses was to do something new," says Friedman, whose success with *Modern Cool* has made it possible for him to move his business out of his kitchen and into an office.

"Their goal was to get their own sound. But today there's more conformity. Patricia wasn't about that, which is why I thought she'd be perfect for us to record."

Not that the journey has been easy. While record companies such as Columbia and Warner Brothers have literally hundreds of sales reps across the country, the indie distributor that peddles Premonition's wares, City Hall Records in California, has all of thirteen.

Yet by working the phones and otherwise spreading the gospel of *Modern Cool,* Friedman saw a homegrown record edge out major-label competitors to win berths on the record charts.

The news quickly made its way to Manhattan, where Jazz Tree founder Mary Ann Topper jumped on a plane to hear Barber live in August at the Green Mill.

"I was amazed, actually astounded," says Topper, who has booked several East Coast dates for Barber next month. She is also planning Barber appearances at North American and European summer jazz festivals.

"I remember being at the Green Mill and taking voluminous notes on each tune because each one was such a different story. So my immediate reaction to Patricia was, 'Well, here's a true independent.' I call her a passionate intellectual.

"I was interested in her because I believe, as she does, that we are in a creative crisis in jazz. We have a hole out there, a void to fill, and she is what I call a breakthrough artist, someone like [clarinetist-bandleader] Don Byron, artists who are really searching for something new."

Exactly how a musician of Barber's originality and conviction will fare as she tours "the big bad world," as she calls it, remains to be seen, though undoubtedly there will be battles ahead.

"I will be going into this with my eyes wide open," says Barber. "I think by now I'm old enough and strong enough and I have turned down enough money that I have a solid core."

Considering all that she has been through, Barber surely can survive anything at this point.

But can the jazz record industry?

January 31, 1999

~

Artistically, Barber has blossomed in every way during the past decade. Virtually each of her subsequent recordings has shown an expansion of her concept as pianist, vocalist, and, most important, composer. In the breakthrough recording Verse *(Blue Note, 2002) she offered a collection of original songs (with a nod to the poet Verlaine in "Dansons La Gigue"), pairing melody line and lyrics with an economy and wit reminiscent of Cole Porter. Unlike him, however, Barber was not writing for the stage in the heyday of the Broadway musical, so her songs are more treasured by cognoscenti than known by the wider listening public. Still, her radical reinventions of jazz standards (plus inclusion of a few beguiling originals) on* Live: A Fortnight in France *(Blue Note, 2004) documented the seductive power of her work before an appreciative live audience. In* Mythologies *(Blue Note, 2006) Barber took her greatest risk yet as composer, a Guggenheim Fellowship having allowed her to compose a quasi-Schubertian song cycle inspired by, of all things, Ovid's* Metamorphoses. *The result was a free-ranging opus that encompassed jazz, classical, pop, choral, and hip-hop idioms to surprisingly cohesive effect. Who knows what surprises Barber has in store?*

Jazzman: Kurt Elling

Can the talented Chicago singer heed his better angels?

The club, a Chicago jazz landmark, is packed to overflowing, the noise level almost at a roar. All at once the band lets loose with a couple of combustive swing tunes, and then, as if out of nowhere, the trumpeter steps up to the microphone and launches into a terse soliloquy.

"As you know, we're the JazzMasters, but tonight we've got a little surprise for you," says Chicago jazz veteran Paul Serrano. "We've discovered an amazing young cat who truly can sing. So we thought we ought to present him to you while we still could afford him."

And with that, the young, hungry, unknown young man takes the mike from Serrano and, as if with the flick of a switch, lets loose a torrent of sound, hitting his unsuspecting listeners directly between the eyes—and ears. The weird sound effects, ferocious scat singing, hysterical tempos, bizarre facial expressions, comical one-liners, and other forms of verbal and visual mugging may be way over the top, but they jolt the crowd.

It has been a long time since anyone under thirty walked in and electrified Joe Segal's Jazz Showcase, a storied club that over the last half century has presented such jazz deities as Charlie Parker, Dizzy Gillespie, Art Blakey, McCoy Tyner . . . the list goes on.

So on this night, everyone in the house is thinking the same thing: who is this kid, and what planet did he come from?

~

Just three years after that astonishing set, which took place on a frigid January night in 1994, Chicagoan Kurt Elling—not yet thirty years old—has become the most buzzed-about young jazz singer in America. And trumpeter Serrano's crack about presenting him "while we still could afford him" may well have been the most prophetic comment the trumpeter ever made.

Six months after the Showcase debut, the ferociously ambitious singer was signed by Blue Note Records, arguably the most prestigious label in jazz. In short order, Elling was nominated for a Grammy Award (Lena Horne aced him) and embraced by critics coast to coast (the *Los Angeles Times* raved about his "gleaming instrument," the *Washington Post* his "venturesome spirit," the *Boston Globe* his consistent "boldness").

With all this fuss, *CBS Sunday Morning* hustled to Chicago last year to film him crooning at his favorite haunt, the rambunctious Green Mill Jazz Club in Uptown; *DownBeat* honored him with coveted berths in its Readers Polls (Elling ranked ninth last year for Record of the Year, seventh for Best Male Singer); and Hollywood film producers began eyeballing him, clearly seduced by the young man's chiseled good looks and his ravenous appetite for success.

Not bad for a divinity school dropout whose academic career at the University of Chicago went up in flames in 1992, whereupon Elling redirected his studies in some of the South Side's smokier jazz clubs.

How a burned-out divinity student became America's most accomplished and promising young male jazz singer—and what that early blush of success has done to him—might someday make an intriguing motion picture, something like *The Jazz Singer* meets *What Makes Sammy Run?*

~

If Elling had succeeded at the University of Chicago Divinity School, where he had enrolled as a master's degree student in 1989, he probably would be preaching from a church pulpit or a university lectern right now, rather than from a bandstand. Surely his father's career as a Lutheran church organist in Rockford, where the Chicago-born singer grew up, and his paternal grandfather's work as a circuit-riding missionary in Canada, gave young Elling an abiding respect for theology.

But to his regret, Elling did not win standing ovations from his professors at the University of Chicago.

"About two-thirds of the way through I started to see the train pull out of the station and leave me behind," Elling recalls today. "I was white-knuckled all the time, because you've got about forty books per class in every ten-week quarter, and you never catch up, you're never on top of it, unless you're one of those people who's peculiarly gifted to do that.

"It was a real slam to me at the time. It was a real surprise, because I had spiritually devoted myself to what I thought was my calling, and I was still foolish enough to think that because I had devoted myself to the thing and had prayed about it and had tried to make it right, that it would be given to me to do this.

"And it wasn't given to me to do. So when I left, I was really disheartened and really angry."

Unlike many angry young men, however, Elling had a release. In fact, during the entire time that he was drowning in divinity school, he was learning to swim in a decidedly less devout setting: Chicago's jazz joints. The first week he arrived in town, Elling dropped in at Milt Trenier's Lounge, a past-its-prime, Vegas-style watering hole that reportedly held jam sessions for aspiring performers.

"The 'session' comprised a piano player and three other people in the room—one of them a call girl, one of them a low-life gangster, and the other one me," Elling remembers, with a chuckle.

"After I sang that first night, the first thing out of the owner's mouth was, 'I'm going to give this kid a job.'

"And I stupidly said: 'I'll work for free.' "

For the next year and a half, Elling rarely took home more than seven dollars in tips on any given night, but he came away with crucial information about the vocalist's art.

Even then "he was one of the most accurate singers that I have worked with," says Karl Johnson, still the house piano player at Trenier's (which, in another era, was the legendary Chez Paree, a mob-run joint where Frank Sinatra, an Elling hero, often worked his magic).

"Kurt's pitch, his rhythm, his concept of the music he was doing were really accurate," adds Johnson. "He was in the very basic root of his own style, so we just rehearsed and rehearsed a lot."

So much, apparently, that by the time Elling bolted from the University of Chicago ("in the middle of the night," he says, "because I had to break a lease"), he was ready to take on the South Side jazz joints, where the (mostly black) audiences know their jazz top to bottom.

"I think the first time I met Kurt was at Alexander's," says Serrano, referring to a steak joint on east Seventy-ninth Street, where the JazzMasters offer up down-home jazz every Thursday night. That's really a black-vibe joint, and most of those people have a history of growing up with jazz, and going to bebop dances when people like Lester Young and Billie Holiday were playing the Sutherland Lounge.

"The amazing thing was those folks at Alexander's just ate him up. He showed them that he was comfortable onstage with black jazz, and he seemed to have a direct 'in' to the music. He wasn't making it artificial, and it was amazing that he could scat like that, that he could be so exuberant and do just about anything [vocally] that he wanted to.

"Very few singers can really scat, you know, and with Kurt, even back then, it was just shoop-a-doo-be-doo."

~

Elling didn't come by his mercurial vocal technique quite so easily as it might have seemed. On the contrary, he had been singing in church as far back as he could remember, training his instrument all the way through Lutheran elementary and high schools in Rockford, as well.

By the time he reached Gustavus Adolphus College, a small liberal arts school in St. Peter, Minnesota, Elling was accomplished enough to tour Europe with the Gustavus choir, soloing in everything from Ralph Vaughan Williams to J. S. Bach.

Combine that lifelong classical training with the plush texture and amber color of his baritone, add a nascent interest in jazz (which Elling discovered at Gustavus Adolphus), and you had the makings of a fine young swing singer. The world, however, overflows with fine—and utterly indistinguishable—young singers.

But Elling had much, much more. For one thing, he had spent his college years (including an eight-month stint at the University of Edinburgh) studying Kierkegaard, Rilke, Hegel, Proust, Kenneth Rexroth, and similarly weighty thinkers, and he began bringing their texts and ideas to his jazz tunes.

Thus in a number such as "These Clouds Are Heavy, You Dig?" Elling dared to offer a hipster's account of Rilke's deeply metaphorical story "How the Thimble Came to Be God."

Bolder still, while most jazz singers invent melody lines and vocal effects, Elling began to improvise his lyrics as well—"ranting," as he calls it, or creating "poetry on the fly."

In the midst of a performance of the old chestnut "Everything Happens to Me," for instance, he might burst into singing a laundry list of mishaps that had befallen him yesterday or twenty years ago. At the climax of "Delores Dream," he might head-trip his way through a recollection of lost loves and crumbled romances, singing all the while.

It was a bizarre, unexpected, stream-of-consciousness form of singing that sprang naturally from Elling's theological background and took audiences utterly by surprise.

"There's this Charlie Mingus tune called 'Sue's Changes,' and during his solo, Kurt started getting into one of his made-up song stories," remembers Laurence Hobgood, who first heard Elling sitting in on saxophonist Ed Petersen's Monday night sessions at the Green Mill in 1991. Hobgood was the pianist, the music was outrageously avant-garde, and Elling fit in perfectly.

"The amazing thing was that Kurt wasn't speaking this story that he was making up—he truly was singing it," adds Hobgood. "Now you might assume that 'Sue's Changes' refers to chord changes. But in Kurt's made-up song, it turns out Sue was a baby and the changes referred to Sue's diapers.

"It wasn't so much funny as it was beautiful, and by the time Kurt got to the end of it, there were people in that crowd literally crying, it was so beautiful."

Though Elling was living in what Hobgood calls a "one-room hovel" in Hyde Park for $150 a month and feeding himself—barely—by moving furniture and working as a bartender, he also was writing profound lyrics and forging exquisite songs with Hobgood. By wedding his texts to Hobgood's tunes or writing lyrics to fit famous instrumental solos (an art form known as vocalese), Elling was creating a music at once fresh and familiar, distinctly personal yet deeply reminiscent of pioneering vocal work by Mark Murphy, Jon Hendricks, Eddie Jefferson, and King Pleasure.

Equally important, by collaborating with such brilliant young Chicago players as Hobgood and drummer Paul Wertico (guitarist Pat Metheny's percussionist for more than a decade) as well as such esteemed veterans as South Side saxophonists Von Freeman and Eddie Johnson, Elling was crafting a sound unique to this town. Its aggressive swing rhythms and lusty ensemble blasts, its full-bodied tone and rip-roaring sense of experimentation somehow caught the rough and rambunctious spirit of 1990s Chicago jazz on the fly.

A less ambitious artist might have been content to refine and perfect that formula over the next few years, but Elling was chomping at the bit.

"He kept saying, 'We've got to do a demo tape, we've got to do a demo tape,'" recalls Hobgood. "And I kept saying, 'Wait a minute, now hold on a minute.' I just didn't think he was ready."

Finally, in mid-1993, Hobgood agreed to produce the demo for the still green young singer, and the race was on. Elling had persuaded a friend to part with several thousand dollars to fund the tape. Then he managed to find a friend who knew a West Coast jazz manager.

The manager listened to the tape and passed it to Blue Note president Bruce Lundvall, who could hardly believe his ears.

"I was about to drive to my dentist's office," Lundvall recalled in 1995. "I grabbed my bag of tapes, and I spotted one that just had arrived from this same Kurt Elling [whom Lundvall had just read about in the *Chicago Tribune*], which was kind of a wild coincidence.

"So I put the tape on while I was driving, and while Kurt was singing 'Close Your Eyes,' I was thinking: 'This is really nice. He can sing.' Right after that came 'Delores' [with Elling's searing lyrics to a Wayne Shorter tune], and now I was getting very interested.

"And as the tape went on, with all these new and strange ideas, I started thinking: 'This guy is unbelievable, very fresh. He's coming out of an early tradition, but doing something very modern with it. He's got a voice that's terrific.' "

Four days later, Lundvall had jetted to Chicago to catch Elling at the Mill and, after hearing one explosive set, announced that he was going to sign the young man. From that moment forth, Elling's career was airborne, and no one seemed less surprised than Elling himself.

"The field was wide open," says Elling, who indeed announced himself at a moment when the jazz world was sorely lacking in charismatic young male vocalists.

"I mean, Frank [Sinatra] already was an older cat, Joe Williams was an older cat, Mel Torme was an older cat, and you had all these cats who had really had their time," adds Elling, clearly smitten with the jazz patois of the 1950s.

"And as you looked around the jazz world, there were a lot of great young women, but in terms of men, there's just a very small number."

How strange, though, that in the age of Wynton Marsalis—when the CD bins are crowded with work by young male trumpeters (Nicholas Payton, Marcus Printup), saxophonists (David Sanchez, Joshua Redman), pianists (Marcus Roberts, Eric Reed), and so on—the scene is almost devoid of emerging male vocalists.

"I think it has to do with the fact that for young boys, it's OK to be, say, a drummer," says Elling.

"You can be a drummer and be a man. In second grade, you can be a trumpet player and be a man. You can even be a saxophone player, and be a man.

"But singing isn't valued very much in American society as something that men do. At least not jazz singing."

When Elling's debut album, *Close Your Eyes,* came out in 1995, he quickly found himself playing stages from Montreux to Montreal, from Paris to San Francisco. The jazz world hungered for a fresh male voice, and the kid from Chicago was wowing them with his instrument, his technique, his versatility, his looks, his swagger, and, above all, his attitude.

"I remember we were opening for Michael Brecker in Malta," says Hobgood, "and the president of the country—the president of Malta!—is sitting out in the front row.

"We finish the song, and Kurt goes to the microphone, and he says, 'All right. Wow, this is really beautiful. I guess your president is with us tonight, and that's beautiful.'

"And then he looks over at the president, and he says: 'You have one very happening country on your hands here, my friend.'

"That's a direct quote. And I'm sitting here thinking, 'Oh my God, he just ticked off the president of Malta.'

"But the president gets up, puts his hands up in the air like a boxer, and the place goes wild.

"That's Kurt. That's pure Kurt."

Part comedian, part crooner, part hipster, part beatnik for the 1990s, Elling surely was one of a kind, a breath of fresh air in a world awash with clones of Sinatra (Harry Connick Jr.), Nat Cole (John Pizzarelli), Joe Williams (Kevin Mahogany), and on and on.

So Elling, an utterly unknown quantity in 1994, was heading for stardom just a year later.

The experience could turn the head of any young performer, and though Elling coped with the attention as well as one might expect, changes were afoot. Soon Chicago club managers were reporting that the singer no longer was returning their phone calls; tales of Elling's control-freak tendencies in the recording studio seeped out.

And though Elling was developing his technique and his art with astonishing speed, he also started to bring a palpable narcissism to the stage. The way he posed beneath the spotlight, gesturing grandiosely and perpetually running his fingers through his hair, suggested the antics of a preening rock star more than a serious jazz musician.

The *LA Weekly* observed as much earlier this year, noting after an Elling show in Hollywood's notorious Viper Room (where River Phoenix died of a drug overdose): "The man must have spent 20 of his 28 years in front of a mirror. This kind of chilled ham is palatable only when offered on a platter clearly marked 'outrageous kitsch,' but Elling shows no signs of conscious camp."

And though Elling early on won favorable press notices in most major American cities, his repeated forays into New York have generated indifference at best, unalloyed hostility at worst. Perhaps it's no surprise that a performer as increasingly cocky as Elling would fare so poorly in the capital of cockiness.

"Once when he came to New York, I invited all these people who had never heard of him," remembers a veteran of New York's jazz industry. "I told them, 'You're going to like this guy, he's different; he's an acquired taste.'

"And Kurt comes onstage with his usual bravura, and they were a little taken aback. I had one particularly famous musician in the house, and he was angry that I even got him down there."

When Elling played Carnegie Hall, on a triple bill with Dianne Reeves and Rachelle Farrell, *New York Post* writer Chip Deffaa chastised his "occasionally clumsy attempts at humor" and declared that "Elling hasn't been blessed with a great voice—in terms of tonal richness, strength or flexibility" (though he allowed that Elling "uses it honestly").

Even veteran Mark Murphy, Elling's idol as a singer, remarked in a radio interview that "there's a kid in Chicago who's stealing my gig," referring, no doubt, to Elling's artistic debt to the older singer.

And Will Friedwald in the *Village Voice* lamented that Elling offers "ideas so esoteric even repeated listenings don't clear them up."

In part, the press barbs may be credited to East Coast chauvinism. Even the aforementioned insider acknowledged that "you can't come in here cocky and say, 'Look at this, man—I'm hot stuff.' That's not going to work for a New Yorker.

"You have to really prove yourself.

"When a new artist comes in and does a great job, the [New York] critics will put the knock on him the first time and then, maybe, praise him the second time. It's a New York thing."

~

Yet Elling, who has dreamed of wooing a mass audience "beyond jazz" ever since he was signed by Blue Note, absolutely lusts for the approval of the New York press, the very contingent that has given him the cold shoulder.

"I'm confident that as soon as we have New York, we have the rest of the world," says Elling. "So I think that as soon as we make it there, we're going to have a lot of work, and I'm going to have to really be on top of it for the duration, or at least the next wave is going to be a lot more massive."

In his pursuit of that recognition, Elling will spend approximately a month blitzing New York clubs in May, a campaign similar to the one he conducted last year in Los Angeles.

"I think that it's only right that there be somewhere in the world where I haven't made it yet," says Elling, who may overestimate his success.

"New York has the most intense fraternity; membership is difficult to obtain there."

This time, though, "we're going to be there long enough that [the critics] are going to have to come out and deal with us, because we're going to have a lot of people, and people are going to be talking about us, and they're going to be digging it, and they're going to get the word on the streets, and the people will do what the critics haven't done yet."

What Elling, in his youth, doesn't yet understand is that in music enduring reputations are earned slowly, over time, and with artistic achievement, not swiftly, via shrewdly orchestrated media blitzes. The faster he tries to dance for the approval of others, the less likely his work will carry meaning for those who already admire it. And the wider an audience he seeks to seduce, the thinner his music is likely to become.

"When I walked into Kurt's one-room apartment in Chicago a couple of years ago, I saw that this was Kurt the artist," says Richard Elvee, chaplain of Gustavus College and an Elling mentor. "But if things work out, I imagine he might finally end up looking at Lake Michigan from some expensive high-rise.

"But when you're in that high-rise, is the artist still there? Does the muse still sing?"

That's the question Elling faces, as he chases success. Having been married since October to Jennifer Carney, a dancer who toured the country for three years in Andrew Lloyd Webber's *Phantom of the Opera*, Elling must decide how much of his personal happiness and artistic self-esteem he's willing to link to critical approval and media adulation.

For the moment, though, Elling—who turns thirty on November 2—is still a very hungry man, and it shows every time he prowls the stage.

"I'm going to be happy thirty years from now when there's a kinder, gentler Kurt onstage," he says. "I won't have any problems with the fact that I will have mellowed.

"But right now, I'm just a really aggressive cat."

March 23, 1997

Two starkly different Ellings have emerged since these early days of his career. One performs fearlessly, redefining the art of jazz singing. The other dilutes his work with dully conservative singing, nearly begging for broad commercial recognition that has not been forthcoming. The tremendous promise of Elling's debut release, Close Your Eyes *(Blue Note, 1995), seemed on its way to being fulfilled with* The Messenger *(Blue Note, 1997), a rip-roaring vocal tour de force that nonetheless left room for contemplative balladry. So, too,* Live in Chicago *(Blue Note, 2000) alternated gutsy vocals with tender introspection. But then Elling began releasing saccharine, sentimental fare such as* Flirting with Twilight *(Blue Note, 2001),* Nightmoves *(Concord, 2007), and, the blandest of them all,* Dedicated to You: Kurt Elling Sings the Music of Coltrane and Hartman *(Concord, 2009). In 2010 that disc won a Grammy Award for best jazz vocal album.*

Jazz Lovers Are Beating a Path to Fred Anderson and His Velvet Lounge

Admittedly, it's not a glamorous sight: a weather-beaten front door "protected" by badly rusted burglar bars.

There's a small barbecued chicken joint on one side, a tiny currency exchange on the other, and—sandwiched between them at 2128½ S. Indiana Avenue—a storefront bar that looks like something out of a particularly seedy Nelson Algren novel.

It's what happens inside the Velvet Lounge, on the Near South Side of Chicago, however, that draws music lovers from across the city and beyond.

Put your ear up to the bolted door, and you'll hear some of the most glorious music to come from the horn of a Chicago jazz musician. It's a huge, dark, rumbling sound rising up from the lowest reaches of the tenor saxophone, and it could belong to only one musician on Earth.

"I was just trying to get some practice in," says saxophonist-saloon owner Fred Anderson, admitting a visitor on a recent weekday afternoon.

"This is a never-ending process, you know," adds Anderson, who has been playing tenor for more than half a century. "The more I play, the more I realize that you've got to keep pushing ahead, finding new sounds, or you'll lose ground."

That has been Anderson's philosophy since the beginning, but perhaps not even he could have expected that, at this late stage of the game, his legend and his club both would be riding high.

Though Anderson has never been able to make enough money to work full-time as a musician, though he has never had a manager, agent, record contract, publicist, or any of the other trappings of success, he has become something of an icon to several generations of Chicago musicians.

More tangibly, the man who has been content to live his life well outside the margins of the music industry now has—incredibly—at least half a dozen independent records on the market, each a testament to his originality as tenor virtuoso and jazz improviser.

What's more, the Velvet Lounge, which used to present live music just twice a month, in recent years has emerged as an epicenter of musical experimentation on the South Side. From Thursday through Sunday evenings, some of the most accomplished virtuosos of the Chicago avant-garde converge there for rambunctious jam sessions.

And this year, after each night of the Chicago Jazz Festival in Grant Park, listeners will be heading to the Velvet Lounge for after-fest sessions.

"I don't know exactly why all this is happening right now," says Anderson, who surely never planned it. "I've been here all the time, but now I've got all these records out and all these people are listening to them.

"Maybe it's because people began to realize that I'm playing some basic stuff that they need to hear. I'm not trying to set the world on fire. I'm just trying to stay as close to the basics as possible and still try to be Fred Anderson."

That's saying quite a lot, considering that Anderson, who was born in Monroe, Louisiana, nearly sixty-nine years ago, always has been one of the most individualistic of musicians.

"You know how Fred Anderson sounds today?" Chicago tenor saxophonist Von Freeman once said. "Well, that's how he always was playing, right from the beginning, right from the 1960s.

"It's just taken thirty-odd years for the rest of the world to catch up with him."

For Anderson, the journey has not been easy. Having come to Chicago with his mother at age eight (his father had abandoned them in Louisiana), he picked up a tenor saxophone that belonged to a cousin and quickly found his life's calling. A couple months of lessons and music theory was all the formal training he received, his real education coming from records by professors named Bird (Charlie Parker) and Prez (Lester Young).

"Hearing those recordings of Bird blew my mind," remembers Anderson, who first listened to the bebop titan in 1947.

"I knew I never could play that swift and precise way that he did, but I thought maybe at least I could learn to understand what he was doing. That's when I got serious."

Yet from the time he first heard those Parker recordings until the early 1960s, Anderson played mostly for an audience of one: himself. Performing for adoring listeners and winning acclaim wasn't important to a musician who preferred to devote his energies to finding a musical voice, a harmonic language, and an instrumental technique of his own.

By the time Anderson considered himself ready to appear in public, in the early 1960s, the South Side of Chicago was rising again as a cauldron of musical innovation. Neighborhood jazz clubs may have been folding in the wake of rock 'n' roll, but musicians such as Anderson, saxophonist Joseph Jarman, keyboardist Muhal Richard Abrams, reedist Roscoe Mitchell, and others were forging new musical sounds and putting on concerts in churches, school auditoriums, and anywhere else they could find.

Recordings from the period, such as Jarman's *Song For* (on Delmark), not only documented free-ranging improvisations by Jarman and Anderson but suggested the emergence of a new musical movement. By 1965 it would be consolidated as the Association for the Advancement of Creative Musicians (AACM), a collective of South Side performers, composers, and ensembles who would show the world that there was more to playing jazz than reeling off endless variations of "I Got Rhythm."

The music of the AACM was harmonically audacious, rhythmically volatile, and technically innovative, all the while bringing ancient rituals of African music into the mix. "Great Black Music, Ancient to Future" was the group's motto, and Anderson found himself at the heart of the movement.

"Fred meant so much to me and the other guys going all the way back to the early AACM days," recalls Jarman today.

"He would always be showing me things about the saxophone—how to get certain sounds, how to express certain ideas.

"His own music was very strange and beautiful, like nothing else, really. That's why so many musicians hung around Fred. They wanted to figure out what it was he was doing and how they could learn from it."

Listen to tapes of Anderson during this period and you are hearing a thoroughly idiosyncratic approach to the tenor saxophone. Whether he was playing duets with Jarman or improvising in larger ensemble settings with trumpeter Billy Brimfield and drummer Steve McCall, Anderson was creating lines that leaped freely from one key to the next at a moment's notice.

"Even in those days, everyone said I was playing far out, but I never could see it," says Anderson. "I was just trying to play some good, serious music, trying to have my own sound.

"I don't just hear music in one key. I hear all these twelve tones together, they all relate, and you've got to deal with all their possibilities.

"And, anyway, no matter what they say about how far out the AACM music was, it was really all about blues, when you came down to it. It was playing blues in new ways."

Though other AACM artists such as Anthony Braxton and the Art Ensemble of Chicago headed to Europe in the late 1960s and eventually returned as stars, Anderson didn't get there until a decade later. But if his family obligations kept him hustling as a waiter by day and a musician by night, his art was maturing all the while.

That much is apparent from the recent reissue of recordings such as *The Missing Link* (Nessa) and *Fred Anderson and Steve McCall: Vintage Duets* (Okka Disk), which show a saxophonist delicately balancing tradition and innovation, euphony and dissonance.

"For me, Fred was the link between [traditional] saxophonists like Illinois Jacquet and a newer, more modern sound," says Edward Wilkerson Jr., a formidable Chicago tenorist who considers Anderson a major inspiration.

"His playing was also unusual because he was all over the instrument. Some players, you know, vary in sound from the top to the bottom of their horns, but Fred always was incredibly even in sound and tone everywhere on the instrument.

"And he always had this open attitude. He would allow young kids, like myself, to come up and play with him. He was a lot like Von [Freeman] in that way: the feeling was that music is for everyone, come and share in it."

In 1982 Anderson hung up his waiter's apron and bought the Velvet Lounge in what was then a down-and-out part of town. The South Side, after all, had fallen on hard times economically, and Anderson remembers his first decade of running the lounge as "weathering a storm."

But as the years passed, small record labels went out of their way to record Anderson's saxophone soliloquies. Records such as *Dark Day* (Message) and *Another Place* (Moers Music) point to the emergence of a tenor giant. Anderson, an artistically restless soul, never stopped evolving musically.

On recordings such as *Fred Anderson/DKV Trio* (Okka Disk) and *Fred* (Southport), the legendary musician can be heard pointing the way for younger avant-gardesmen such as reedists Ken Vandermark and Dave Rempis.

Meanwhile, the Near South Side neighborhood in which Anderson set up shop fifteen years ago also appears to be showing new signs of life.

Lofts, banks, condos, and the like are going up everywhere near the new McCormick Place South Building (a couple of blocks southeast of the Velvet Lounge).

The South Side as a whole, in fact, has been reawakening as a focal point for music, with audiences supporting performances at the refurbished Sutherland (Forty-seventh Street and Drexel Boulevard), DuSable Museum of African-American History (on east Fifty-sixth Place), and the South Shore Cultural Center (at Seventy-first Street and the lakefront), among other venues.

"Things are definitely picking up, which is good for the bar," says Anderson, who still divides his time between playing music and running a neighborhood saloon.

"I'm glad I stayed in Chicago. That's where most of the great jazz musicians come from, anyway.

"The city's been good to me, and it looks like things are getting even better."

August 28, 1997

Anderson lost the lease to his Velvet Lounge in 2005 and was forced out the following year, which might have been the sad end of the story. But the musician commands so much respect among those he has mentored that a groundswell of support materialized seemingly out of nowhere. Scores of Chicago's most respected musicians—many from the AACM—held benefit concerts across the city for more than a year. The money they raised, in tandem with Anderson's personal funds, underwrote the Velvet Lounge's $100,000-plus move to new quarters, at 67 E. Cermak Road (a few blocks from the original). Granted, the place lacks the run-down charm of the original, but it's a sleek, clean, acoustically alert room that remains an incubator for new ideas in music. Equally important, the turn of the century saw a once infrequently recorded artist documented as never before. Anderson's magisterial solos—which draw equally from bebop and "free jazz" vocabularies—course through releases such as On the Run: Live at the Velvet Lounge *(Delmark, 2001), with bassist Tasu Aoki and drummer Hamid Drake;* Back Together Again *(Thrill Jockey, 2004), a landmark duet session with Drake; and* From the River to the Ocean *(Thrill Jockey, 2007), with Drake, guitarist Jeff Parker, bassist Josh Abrams, and multi-instrumentalist Harrison Bankhead.*

Chicago celebrated Anderson's eightieth birthday in 2009, with musicians from across the country converging for a weeklong festival at the new Velvet Lounge and an epic concert at Millennium Park, downtown, which attracted an estimated ten thousand listeners. In addition, Fred Anderson: 21st Century Chase *(Delmark, 2009) documented the eightieth birthday festivities at the Velvet, the honoree performing with saxophonist Kidd Jordan, bassist Harrison Bankhead, guitarist Jeff Parker, and drummer Chad Taylor. Remarkably, Anderson has become something of a civic icon, a rare occurrence among avant-garde jazz musicians, even in Chicago.*

Chicago Jazzman Among "Genius Grant" Winners: Ken Vandermark

What will Ken Vandermark do with $265,000?
Motel rooms on tour would be nice.

Considering that he plays in at least a dozen bands and on more than forty recordings, Chicago avant-garde musician Ken Vandermark was bound to be in transit when he received the news: he had won a 1999 MacArthur "genius grant" worth $265,000.

Even so, the windfall in dollars and prestige, announced late Tuesday, carries unmistakable poignance, since Vandermark is in the midst of a characteristically low-budget, zero-frills tour—sixteen cities in sixteen nights, by car, with Vandermark and his band sleeping on the floors of friends' apartments. The man's relentless, guerrilla-style approach to playing unabashedly radical music has made him one of the most talked-about jazz musicians to emerge in Chicago during the last decade. *DownBeat,* the prominent jazz magazine, in January aptly referred to Vandermark as "a bright, articulate, unflinchingly committed tenor saxophonist, clarinetist, composer and bandleader whose presence has been a major defibrillator for the city since he set up shop here in 1989."

And though Vandermark can't say precisely how many ensembles count him as a member or exactly how many CDs he has cut—"It must be a few dozen by now," he guesses—the thirty-four-year-old artist clearly has thrived as an outsider.

But with his MacArthur Fellowship, Vandermark, one of thirty-two individuals honored this year, finds himself in an unexpected position. He's a lifelong iconoclast suddenly embraced by the cultural establishment, or at least by one of its best-funded outposts, the John D. and Catherine T. MacArthur Foundation in Chicago.

Having flourished artistically, if not financially, as a revolutionary out to obliterate the stylistic boundaries that separate jazz, alternative rock, avant-garde classical, and other genres, Vandermark now stands among several regal jazz figures who have won the same award. The honor roll includes such long-established artists as bebop drummer Max Roach, free-jazz pioneer Ornette Coleman, piano virtuoso Cecil Taylor, and heavyweight composer-improviser Anthony Braxton.

Suddenly, Vandermark may no longer be on the outside looking in.

"To be honest, I'm kind of afraid," says Vandermark, speaking by phone from his parents' house, outside Boston, where he stopped briefly during an east-of-the-Mississippi tour. "When I look at the other winners who work in similar music, like Max Roach and Cecil Taylor and the rest of them, those are people I'm in awe of, and I'm really overwhelmed by even being put in the same sentence as those people.

"So I'm really floored by this news. These guys, by the time they were my age, they were changing the face of the music. I feel like I'm still really a student."

Though it will take years to know for certain if Vandermark's often brazenly dissonant sounds also have redirected the course of jazz and related musical languages, there's no question he has energized the improvised music scene in Chicago more than any other single figure of the 1990s.

"Ken has been a force in spearheading this music, that's for sure," says Chicago tenor saxophonist Fred Anderson, an elder statesman of the avant-garde who collaborated with Vandermark on the recording *DKV Trio* (Okka Disk).

Adds Chicago drummer Hamid Drake, a longtime Vandermark partner on disc and onstage, "Just the amount of projects he works on has had a huge effect on music in Chicago, and even as far away as Europe, where he has played a lot."

Anyone who frequents such Chicago clubs as Anderson's Velvet Lounge on south Indiana Avenue or the Empty Bottle on north Western Avenue (where Vandermark regularly performs and helps curate a Wednesday night new-music series) will have heard his eruptions on tenor saxophone and clarinet. Moreover, a small but devoted group of record buyers know Vandermark from the decidedly unorthodox music-making of bands such as the Vandermark 5 (currently the focal point of his work), the Aaly Trio (with saxophonist Mats Gustafsson), the DKV Trio (with Chicagoans Kent Kessler on bass and Drake on drums), the Crown Royals (a funk-tinged outfit), Cinghiale (a duo with fellow reed madman Mars Williams), and others.

Yet Vandermark is the first to acknowledge that his artistic ascent in Chicago owes at least as much to the city's burgeoning new-music scene as it does to his own drive and talent. In that regard, his MacArthur award could be considered an acknowledgment of the vibrancy of new music in Chicago at the turn of the century.

"I don't have a good answer for why all this is happening in Chicago right now, but for some reason there's this incredible confluence of a lot of different elements going on," says Vandermark, who closes his current tour Friday night at the Empty Bottle. The performance will celebrate the release of the newest CD from the Vandermark 5, *Simpatico* (on Atavistic).

"You have a pool of musicians in roughly the same age group [their thirties] who have been working hard and communicating with each other," continues Vandermark. "You have labels like Okka Disk and Atavistic documenting the work, you have radio stations like WNUR-FM 89.3 and WHPK-FM 88.5 playing the music, and, most important of all, you have people coming out to hear the music.

"All that activity has brought a lot of national and international musicians to Chicago to play and record, so there's this influx of outside information feeding the local scene."

But it's important to remember that Chicago wasn't always so welcoming to Vandermark, who arrived here in 1989, disenchanted with life in Boston.

"In the beginning, he couldn't find anyone to play with, he couldn't find many gigs, paid or unpaid, so for the first few years he just practiced like crazy and wrote music nonstop, because there wasn't much else for him to do," says Ellen Major, Vandermark's wife since 1996 and a pediatrician at Children's Memorial Hospital.

"I remember going to his occasional shows in these horrible dives, and no one would be in the audience but me and my friends."

By spring of 1992, Vandermark was ready to move back to Boston in defeat. But Chicago musicians Kent Kessler and Michael Zerang persuaded him to stay, their partnership eventually forming the core of what would become the Vandermark Quartet.

Equally important, composer Braxton, another MacArthur winner, encouraged him to keep up the fight.

"I played Braxton a cassette of a trio, and he was incredibly complimentary about what we were doing," Vandermark says. "Braxton has had a major impact on me, and to hear him say, 'I think you're doing something interesting' gave me license to think, OK, I'm not crazy, maybe there's some merit here."

Though it's difficult for any musician to establish roots in a new city, Vandermark's difficulties in part may have been because of the still-nascent quality of his music-making. Granted, there was no denying the sheer size of his sound and the bravura of his technique during shows he played with Hal Russell's NRG Ensemble. But the relentlessly loud, rhythmically repetitive nature of Vandermark's work at the time pointed to a musician hungry to make a splash but seemingly less interested in developing a variety of ideas in sound. It wasn't until the mid-1990s that Vandermark began to show a more substantial expressive range.

"The early quartet material was interesting, but it didn't have a fullness or depth I was looking for," says Bruno Johnson, owner of the Okka Disk label, which has released several Vandermark recordings. "That first started to come through with [Vandermark] groups like Caffeine [in 1994]. That's when he started getting a sense of voicing for other instruments.

"Actually, the same thing happened with [past tenor saxophonists] Coleman Hawkins and Ben Webster, who realized, as they got older, that there's beauty in playing ballads and other things with less energy and display."

By 1996, a show Vandermark played at the Empty Bottle with such profound South Side musicians as tenor player Ari Brown, drummer Avreeayl Ra, and bassist Harrison Bankhead affirmed the young musician was beginning to find a lyric voice to counterbalance the manic energy for which he was best known. In 1997 his writing for the Brotzmann Tentet proved at once idiosyncratic and masterful, and last month, during the Empty Bottle Festival of Jazz and Improvised Music, Vandermark's playing opposite Gustafsson in the Aaly Trio established them as the most dynamic and musically versatile tenor pairing in cutting-edge jazz.

Nevertheless, financial concerns never have been far off for Vandermark, who didn't leave his day job at the School of the Art Institute's Video Data Bank until last year. Says Johnson: "I've seen Ken play five hours for ten dollars."

Yet Vandermark has steered clear of more lucrative jobs closer to the commercial mainstream, instead reveling in experimental jazz, alternative rock, avant-funk, and beyond.

"When I was growing up, music constantly was being played on the stereo at home all the time, and the attitude was wide open," says Vandermark. "My parents would play Stravinsky, Duke Ellington, Sly and the Family Stone, whatever.

"And their attitude wasn't: 'Stravinsky is great European music, Ellington is a great American composer,' and so on. Their approach basically was: 'This is music, and there's no separation at all among different kinds of music.'"

Vandermark nonetheless found himself drawn most intensely to his parents' jazz recordings. He took up trumpet in fourth grade and "played it terribly until eleventh grade," when he switched to tenor sax and began writing original works.

As a film major at McGill University, in Montreal, Vandermark relished analyzing cinema, but his fascination with music inexorably took over. By the time he graduated in 1986, he was ready to plunge into the Boston music scene but three years later decamped for Chicago.

After ten years, this city still holds a spell on him. In interviews with out-of-town media he consistently talks up the virtues of working in a town where minds are open, rent is cheaper than on the coasts, and audiences thrive on new ideas.

Though he hasn't yet decided what he's going to do with more than a quarter-million dollars, a number of possibilities leap to mind.

"I'd like to do a tour with [multi-instrumentalist] Joe McPhee and Kent Kessler, I'd like to do an outing with [drummer] Paul Lovens, and I'd like to do a U.S. tour with the Brotzmann Tentet," says Vandermark, who also hopes to help Johnson release recordings that are lingering in the can at tiny Okka Disk.

"And I'd like to be able to pay all these musicians to at least stay in a motel. That would be great. These guys have to put up with extreme conditions to work with me—this is not a commercial music, and it doesn't generate a lot of money.

"But it really would be nice to give them what they deserve."

June 23, 1999

The hardest-working man in show business (avant-garde division) won his MacArthur Fellowship a few years before the amount was upped to $500,000. Even so, Vandermark made his $265,000 go far, pouring his bonanza into music, in part to convene select musicians from across Europe and the United States for concerts and recordings by his newly christened Territory Band. Staffed by artists such as German trumpeter Axel Dorner and percussionist

Paul Lytton, the music for various incarnations of his Territory Bands shattered previous conceptions (and misconceptions) about Vandermark's art. The high-decibel, high-energy, nearly chaotic music of Vandermark's early career, in other words, gave way to more carefully measured, elegantly voiced work for large ensembles. In Territory Band recordings such as Transatlantic Bridge *(Okka Disk, 2001) and* Atlas *(Okka Disk, 2002), Vandermark presided over compositions and improvisations of considerable subtlety of color, line, and texture. At the same time, he has continued to perform and record prolifically with the Vandermark 5 and uncounted other ensembles. He'll tell anyone who will listen, however, that with the MacArthur money spent, the prospect of making a living performing experimental music remains a difficult quest. If anyone deserves a second MacArthur grant, it's Vandermark.*

XII

Profiles in Jazz

Major Voices Speak

Herbie's Blues

Chicago's giant of the piano comes home in April for a triumphant week of performances. But he strikes a mournful note in discussing the future of jazz.

After a grueling two months playing one-nighters around the world, Herbie Hancock ought to be exhausted, yet he can't wait to get his hands on a piano. So he seats himself at the nine-foot concert grand that dominates the living room of his Los Angeles home, and his fingers immediately—almost instinctively—begin wandering the keys.

With his right hand slowly caressing the quiet notes up high and the left hand answering softly down below, he's not so much playing a tune as communing with himself, in harmony and rhythm. Lost in thought, he articulates no discernible melody or recognizable chord changes, yet the sound is pure Herbie: mysterious, lyrical, seductive.

For more than forty years, Hancock, who has scheduled a week of Chicago performances next month at Orchestra Hall and other venues, has been beguiling audiences with precisely this disarming brand of piano jazz, a self-styled idiom that can veer from sublime sophistication to danceable accessibility at the drop of a sixteenth note. His knack for careering between complexity and simplicity, between art and entertainment, has won him nine Grammys, three gold and two platinum records, one Oscar, and enough plaques to cover several walls of his home, a short stroll from the Sunset Strip.

Yet on this typically golden California day—the midday sun is flooding in through his picture window and glinting off the top of his ebony piano—Hancock despairs for the very jazz world that catapulted a talented kid from a tough Chicago neighborhood to unanticipated stardom. He realizes that practically every institution that enabled his talent to blossom—nightclubs, record labels, radio stations, concert halls, schools—has been diminished, at least so far as jazz is concerned, during the long arc of his triumph. Somewhere along the way, jazz, the music that made him famous at age twenty-three and revered around the world ever since, got shoved into the margins of American culture.

All that remains is the afterglow of what once was the jazz industry in America, and Hancock grieves for the next talented youngster who might not transcend a rough-and-tumble childhood the way he did.

"It's all about money now, how the radio stations and the record companies and everyone else can make money putting out the hits as fast as they can," says Hancock, after stepping away from the piano and leading a visitor to his upstairs studio. "When one company owns 65 percent of radio, when 'smooth jazz' is pushing out the core music, when musicians have to write tunes to fit the formats of the radio stations to get anyone to listen to them, that's backward, and that's dangerous. It's bad for the artists, it's bad for the listeners, it's bad for humanity."

Not the sentiments one might expect from an artist whose oft-joyous music—despite its famously kaleidoscopic changes in style and direction—always has been optimistic and life-affirming at its center.

But Hancock, who turns sixty-four next month, has not given up on jazz or even on its chances of surviving into its second century. He simply rages against the forces he sees as conspiring against the music that gave him everything and hopes that someone, somewhere, will hit upon a way to keep it alive in America.

~

Herbie Hancock does not need a bar graph to understand the way the music business in America is edging jazz into a kind of oblivion.

Outside of long-standing jazz capitals such as Chicago, New York, New Orleans, and San Francisco, bona fide jazz clubs are scarce in the United States, and musicians who can make a living playing this intricate but profoundly American music are an endangered species, at best.

Among the major record labels, only one—Blue Note—can be said to maintain a thriving roster of jazz recording artists. Even mighty Columbia Records, once the home of Miles Davis and Dave Brubeck, has pared its roster of jazz musicians, with no less a figure than Wynton Marsalis recently ending a two-decade career there and switching to Blue Note. The vast majority of jazz musicians record for tiny independent labels that consider CD sales of three thousand copies a hit and six thousand copies a blockbuster.

Jazz record sales in America hover around 2 to 3 percent of total album sales, according to the Recording Industry Association of America, and the increasingly popular phenomenon of computer downloading stands to diminish even that.

The consolidation of radio station ownership into a few conglomerates, with Clear Channel Radio dominating the market, has long favored easily digested, mass-appeal music, relegating jazz to the ghetto of public radio stations on FM and dreadful-sounding outlets on AM, both with slender audiences. Even in Chicago, revered around the world as a jazz nexus since at least the Roaring Twenties, not a single radio station offers the music around the clock, though WBEZ 91.5 FM and WDCB 90.9 FM program jazz during parts of the broadcast day.

In purely artistic terms jazz remains remarkably robust, with gifted younger players such as reedist Ken Vandermark in Chicago, trumpeter Maurice Brown in New Orleans, and pianist Matthew Shipp in New York fearlessly redefining the music on their own terms. Yet the newcomers have succeeded in building audiences in spite of the crumbling jazz industry, not because of it.

"Some months, our business is half of what it used to be," says Bob Koester, owner of the Jazz Record Mart, billed as the largest such store in the world, and Delmark Records, one of the most respected and enduring independent labels in the country. "At Delmark, we're deleting titles we'd rather not, simply because people aren't buying them.

"In some record stores, they're giving jazz half the space they once did, which makes it harder to sell our recordings. And our sales on new product are terrible. Most of our recent releases sold between 656 and 2,148 copies."

To get by, many jazz musicians sell their discs from the bandstand, play gigs for comparatively low fees, and painstakingly book their own tours. They can make a living in music but enjoy nothing close to the rewards and vast audience that Hancock accrued after just a few years in the business.

Born in Chicago on April 12, 1940, Herbert Jeffrey Hancock grew up in various apartments between Forty-fifth Street and Sixty-second Street on the South Side, showing an interest in the piano at age six and receiving a $5 wreck of an instrument for his seventh birthday.

He began formal lessons a few months later, after his parents had saved up enough money to afford them, and his progress was so swift that by age eleven he had won a piano competition to play the first movement of a Mozart Piano Concerto in B-Flat Major with the Chicago Symphony Orchestra (CSO). When CSO managers informed him that they didn't want him to perform that concerto, the young pianist simply spent a few weeks mastering Mozart's "Coronation" Concerto in D Major, playing it in a pair of short pants in his Orchestra Hall debut.

For all of Hancock's talents, however, growing up in a South Side tenement was not easy. Though his father, who never finished high school, worked practically without pause, his income as owner of a small grocery store and later as a government meat inspector was not sufficient to make ends meet without taking in roomers. So Hancock's parents, Wayman and Winnie, vied for space in a small apartment with their three kids—Wayman Jr., Herbie, and Jean—and a recurrent population of boarders.

"It wasn't exactly the projects, but it was just barely a cut above that," recalls Hancock, who witnessed stabbings in his neighborhood and routinely saw gang members, drug pushers, and numbers peddlers working the block. At age six, he was robbed at gunpoint on his newspaper-delivery route.

But he found escape in music, announcing in an article in a neighborhood newspaper, at the time of his CSO debut, that he intended to become a concert pianist.

"He practiced piano so much I used to tell him, 'Please, Herbie, let the damn piano alone—go out and play with somebody,'" his father recalled in a 1997 *Tribune* interview. (Wayman Hancock died in 2001, at age ninety, and his widow, Winnie, lives in a Chicago-area nursing home.)

With Count Basie, Duke Ellington, and Fats Waller blasting on the record player at home, nightclubs such as the Checkerboard Lounge and Theresa's Lounge swinging along the Forty-third Street corridor nearby, and jazz giants such as Miles Davis and John Coltrane playing the Regal Theater down the block, Hancock discovered a music quite apart from Mozart's concertos. But to Hancock the new sounds proved as mysterious as they were alluring, for he could not understand how these jazz geniuses invented so much glorious art—on the spot—without a note of music in front of them.

For a youngster who had been trained in Bach, Beethoven, and Brahms, the thought of improvising an entire performance seemed incomprehensible at best, unachievable at worst. Yet once Hancock heard kids his age playing jazz at Hyde Park High School, which counted among its musical alumni the legendary Mel Torme, he leapt right in. Doubly blessed with a keen ear and an ability to learn at phenomenal speed, Hancock began imitating the recordings of pianist George Shearing, which he played over and over on the phonograph at home until he knew the solos note for note.

"It didn't take long before he was known as the top musician in the school," recalls his older brother, Wayman Hancock Jr., a retired salesman of computer supplies who lives in the Chicago area (their younger sister, Jean, died in the 1985 crash of Delta flight 191 in Dallas).

"Herbie wrote music, he played all these different instruments, he formed a doo-wop group," marvels Wayman, "and with all that, he still graduated school two years ahead of time."

By age sixteen, the precocious teenager was majoring in electrical engineering at Grinnell College, a small liberal arts school in Iowa, but he couldn't kid himself much longer: he was no more going to be an electrical engineer than he was going to ride a spaceship to the moon.

"The straw that broke the camel's back was in 1957, my second year at Grinnell, when I decided to put together a big band," says Hancock, smiling at the memory. "Now this is at Grinnell, where I had these sixteen musicians who didn't really know how to play jazz. So I had to rehearse all the sections of the band myself and teach them how to phrase. And that was after I had to listen to all these Count Basie records and copy the parts to write up the charts.

"It trained my ear like crazy, but I never went to classes, so I was getting a D in one class and everything else I was flunking—the handwriting was on the wall," he continues. "I saw what was driving me, what was pulling me like a magnet, where my real heart was, and as much as I liked science, jazz was the thing."

After graduating from Grinnell as a music major in 1960, Hancock returned to his old summer job at the Chicago Post Office, but quickly launched one of the most stunning ascents in modern jazz history. By October he was hired to accompany the regal tenor saxophonist Coleman Hawkins, one of the pioneers of that instrument in jazz, in a Chicago nightclub. And that December, when the famed New York trumpeter Donald Byrd came to town and suddenly needed a sub for a pianist who had ducked out on him, Byrd decided to give Hancock an audition.

"I completely freaked out when I heard this kid," remembers Byrd, age seventy-one, speaking from his New Jersey home. "He was already trying to get into new things, new sounds, new chords. I was amazed by how precocious he was, how much intelligence he had, how much integrity.

"In fact, when my original pianist, Duke Pearson, finally showed up for the gig, I said to him, 'You left me, you abandoned the band—and I'm so happy that you did that I'm giving you a first-class airplane ticket back to New York. Now get the hell out of here.' So Pearson went to New York and Herbie joined me on the road."

Byrd was so smitten with Hancock's talent that he invited the twenty-year-old to live in his New York apartment, and by 1962 had set about getting Hancock a date to cut his own record on one of the most artistically dynamic labels in jazz, Blue Note. Knowing that Blue Note would be reluctant to record an unknown artist, Byrd called Alfred Lion, the founder of the record label, and told him that Hancock had been drafted and wanted to make a record before going into the army.

"That was the scheme," laughs Hancock now. "And Lion said OK."

Hancock's aptly named debut, *Takin' Off,* made history, and not only because Lion allowed Hancock to build the entire recording on original tunes, a strategy virtually unknown in a music business that typically tries to introduce young artists with well-worn hits. Equally important, the recording opened with Hancock's "Watermelon Man," which soon would become one of the biggest hits of the decade and an enduring jazz classic.

With its funk-tinged rhythms, coyly lilting melody, and unpretentious, down-home sensibility, the tune ascended the charts in the summer of 1962. The following year, when bandleader Mongo Santamaria recorded an Afro-Cuban version, "Watermelon Man" became nearly inescapable in urban America, cracking *Billboard*'s Top 10. Eventually, more than two hundred artists recorded it.

"I was walking down the street, and all I would hear coming out of people's windows was 'Watermelon Man,'" remembers Hancock. "What a feeling—I was twenty-three years old."

He says that when he wrote the song, he thought of his South Side neighborhood and a particular gentleman who would come by his building at Forty-fifth Street and South Park Way (now south King Drive).

"He'd sing, 'Wateh-meh-LONE, wateh-meh-LONE,'" Hancock says. "And the melody came from the women calling out from the porches: 'Hey, watermelon man,' and from the watermelon man's song.

"Now this is before James Brown sang, 'I'm black and I'm proud,' before the whole pride thing. So watermelon was one of those things that we were ashamed of. I didn't know if I should call the tune 'Watermelon Man,' but I couldn't be that kind of a coward. So I just said to myself, 'There's nothing wrong with a watermelon man,' and I stood by it."

To a lesser artist, "Watermelon Man" might have afforded a quickly fleeting fifteen minutes of fame, but to Hancock it was just the first step in what would be an extraordinary, decades-long artistic evolution. His potential rings out from every track of *Takin' Off*, but specifically in the exquisite warmth of his tone, born of years of classical training, the easy fluidity of his technique, and the harmonic invention that drives his still youthful pianism.

Moreover, he was able to hold his own against the top-notch Blue Note artists who had agreed to join him for his debut as leader, including the veteran tenor saxophonist Dexter Gordon and the phenomenal young trumpeter Freddie Hubbard. With Billy Higgins playing drums and Butch Warren on bass, Hancock was forging a diverse range of musical talent into a genuinely cohesive unit, signaling his development from prodigy to artist.

Though conventional wisdom has given much of the credit for the freshness of Hancock's early playing to Chris Anderson, a pianist with whom Hancock briefly had studied in Chicago during the summer of 1961, Anderson knows better. "He already sounded like that when he came to me," says Anderson, seventy-eight, a visionary musician who played with Charlie Parker and long has lived in obscurity in New York.

"Herbie had his own style developing for a long time, before he even recorded for Blue Note. I heard him early in Chicago, and I don't think you can give anyone else credit for that. In fact, when he first came to me, I was surprised at how much alike we both sounded. And he had studied music a lot more than I had."

Like Anderson, Hancock had been developing an impressively sophisticated harmonic language that flowered at Blue Note. The ingenuity of his arrangements on *Inventions and Dimensions* (1963), the lyric beauty of tunes such as "Oliloqui Valley" and "Cantaloupe Island" on the masterpiece *Empyrean Isles* (1964), and the utter originality of compositions such as "The Eye of the Hurricane" and the title track on the great *Maiden Voyage* (1965) established Hancock as one of the most promising young pianist-composers of the era.

But for all the breakthroughs of Hancock's Blue Note albums, the greater revolution came with his work in Miles Davis's second great quintet. Davis, who throughout his career had shown an uncanny ability to hire players on the precipice of greatness, brought Hancock on board in 1963. With bassist Ron Carter and the prodigious drummer Tony Williams powering what would become the most honored rhythm section of the decade, and with the innovative reedist-composer Wayne Shorter joining Davis on the front line, the band opened up previously unimagined possibilities for jazz improvisation.

During their five and a half years of recording and performing together, they also brought extraordinary vitality to a jazz world already reeling from the emerging effects of rock 'n' roll. Though a music as sophisticated and rhythmically unpredictable as these Davis sets never was going to challenge the Beatles for record sales or celebrity, it proved that there was still plenty of invention and potential left in an art form born at the dawn of the twentieth century—eons ago, by the standards of perpetually changing American popular taste.

Nowhere is the explosive character of this band more palpable than in live sessions recorded at Chicago's pint-sized, long-deceased Plugged Nickel jazz club, at 1321 N. Wells Street, on December 22 and 23, 1965. A truncated recording of these fabled Plugged Nickel dates didn't come out until 1982, and the complete sessions were not released until 1995. But in retrospect this music shows Davis and friends torching the long-accepted rules for jazz improvisation.

No longer were the players observing 32-bar choruses or politely waiting for one another to solo, nor were they even observing the melodic contours and harmonic underpinnings of the standards they were performing. In fact, they were veering so far from the template of tunes such as "My Funny Valentine" and "If I Were a Bell" that the originals often were rendered unrecognizable, the sheer fluidity of the group improvisation and the freedom of the instrumental dialogues far upstaging the tunes themselves.

If this music stunned audiences, it forever changed Hancock, upending everything he thought he knew about jazz.

"What happened was that, by 1965, everyone in Miles's band got so comfortable playing together that we knew all the signals, we knew what to expect from each other, we knew that when a certain guy did this, he would follow it with that, and it became boring," says Hancock. "Well, not really boring, but almost boring. But at least we knew that we had to do something to break out of that."

He recalls that it was drummer Williams who came up with an idea. "He said, 'Look, on this next gig at the Plugged Nickel, I'm not going to play the things that you expect. I ain't going to do that.' And I said, 'I'm going to do the same thing. I'm not going to play anything that leads to what you expect it to lead to.' And we decided to call it 'anti-music.'

"Miles was cool with that, so we walk into the Plugged Nickel the first day, and what do we see? A bunch of tape recorders. And Tony looked at everyone and said, 'Oh, no, it's the worst time.' Because we knew that these people, this audience, were just going to be guinea pigs for a rebirth, a painful rebirth of this band. And they were going to have to suffer through that, for the good of all."

There was more pleasure than pain to be had, however, for the "Plugged Nickel" sessions not only opened up a new era in ensemble improvisation but proved to Hancock that he could adjust—on the spot—to practically any musical ideas swirling around him.

Davis, in particular, was in awe of Hancock's development during these years, noting in his memoirs: "Herbie was the step after Bud Powell and Thelonious Monk."

The band thrived because "there was no jousting over who's got the power," says Shorter from his Florida home, taking a brief pause from a still intense schedule of international touring. "It was not that kind of competition going on.

"We never entertained any fear of risk. We didn't worry about whether we went a little too far. We felt we never went far enough."

By the time the group disbanded in 1968—because, according to Davis's memoirs, most of the players wanted to go in different musical directions—Hancock had been transformed.

"I used to have this kind of tunnel vision about jazz, but Miles totally opened me up," says Hancock. "When we'd be hanging, I'd notice that Miles would have all these albums strewn about the room and lying on his bed. He'd have James Brown and Jimi Hendrix and flamenco guitarists and the classical pianist Arturo Benedetti Michelangeli. So when I saw that Miles, who to me was the epitome of cool, was open to all that different music, I realized that it was cool for me to be open to it too."

The rush of new ideas inexorably led to Hancock's fundamental rethinking of his art, and when he released his breakthrough electric album *Head Hunters* in 1972, he instantly became one of the biggest pop stars of the day, his fame rivaling that of Davis himself. The LP took its place as the biggest-selling album by a jazz artist up to that date, and though it still makes some purists scoff, its nearly symphonic tapestry of electric keyboards and synthesizers, electric bass, and arsenal of ancient and modern percussion instruments made it one of the defining funk releases of the 1970s.

Though critics began blasting away at Hancock's "selling out" of the jazz tradition, he tuned out the din, anchored by his embrace of Buddhism and what he considers his constant need to search for new sounds.

"I was being open, when the critics were being closed," asserts Hancock. "I believed in what I was doing, I was still improvising, I was still challenging myself, and I was still learning. So that's their problem, not mine.

"I mean, if they didn't like what I was doing, that's one thing. But what I picked up most of the time was that they didn't like the fact that I was doing it. Now who are they to tell me what I was supposed to be doing? I'm the one who decides that, not [critic] Leonard Feather.

"Some articles would say, 'Well, he's doing it because he wants to sell records.' That wasn't why I was doing it. I was doing it because it was a part of me that I wanted to explore.

"Look—it's black music, it's part of my background, give me a break. I'm black. This is our stuff."

In truth, the tension between Hancock and the self-appointed guardians of jazz convention said more about the plight of the music during the fusion-driven 1970s than it did about Hancock's art or his journey. For although much, if not most, of the jazz-pop ventures of the period have justly been forgotten, Hancock's efforts generally were a cut above.

By this time, the business of jazz was in serious trouble. All around them, jazz devotees saw clubs folding, record labels dropping jazz artists, and radio stations changing their formats to youth-oriented rock. The situation became so dire that jazz players across the country began presenting their music in churches, school auditoriums, lofts, and anyplace else that would have them. They formed organizations such as the Association for the Advancement of Creative Musicians in Chicago and the Black Artists' Group in St. Louis, which attempted to pick up where the clubs and the record companies left off.

Still, the demise of such beloved Chicago rooms as the Blue Note and the London House in the Loop, the Crown Propeller Lounge and Rhumboogie Club on the South Side, and the Plugged Nickel and High Note on the North Side took its toll. As their world faded from the marketplace, jazz lovers found themselves powerless to do a great deal about it.

But Hancock continued to invent, bringing turntable-scratching and synthesized, techno-blast rhythms into the mix with his *Future Shock* album (1983) and its hit dance single, "Rockit"; combining electric keyboards with Foday Musa Suso's vocal chants and an Afro-Cuban rhythm section on *Jazz Africa* (1986); and returning to acoustic work with recordings such as his sublime—though decidedly unconventional—duets with Shorter on *1+1* (1997).

Along the way there were disappointments as well, most notoriously the disco-driven *Feets, Don't Fail Me Now* (1979), with its relentlessly hammering backbeats and strangely lugubrious vocals. But even Hancock's critics had to acknowledge that the man was willing to try anything once, and his small role playing a jazz pianist in Bertrand Tavernier's 1986 film *'Round Midnight* won him not only another measure of visibility but an Oscar for his haunting, elegiac score.

Looking back on it, the critical and popular success of *'Round Midnight,* probably the greatest jazz feature film ever made, raised the curtain on what seemed a promising new era in acoustic jazz. It was in the mid-1980s, after all, that trumpeter Wynton Marsalis burst onto the scene, getting a running start by playing in Hancock's V.S.O.P. band.

Marsalis's massive success helped launch a bevy of similarly gifted artists, among them trumpeter Nicholas Payton, pianist Marcus Roberts, drummer Herlin Riley, and saxophonist Wess Anderson.

But the jazz bubble of the 1990s was to burst right along with the stock market. Although a new generation of players began attracting young people back to the music, most eventually lost their major-label recording contracts when the big record companies slashed their jazz departments to cut costs. If the new millennium has demonstrated anything about the business of music, it has been the lionization of increasingly bland, retro performers such as Norah Jones and Diana Krall, whose unadventurous warblings pull down huge profits, leaving the real jazz musicians virtually locked out of the cultural mainstream in America.

"To me, jazz, in order to be jazz, it must evolve," says Hancock. "It's part of its nature. And when you don't have the evolution of music, then it's not going to have the spirit of jazz anymore. Those people in the past played the music that they created. At best, we can only be second best at trying to emulate what they did. And I don't see young people being encouraged to find their own voice."

He says he's also disappointed in what has happened in radio: "[It's] not broadcasting anymore—it's narrow-casting. I see people getting their music from the Internet, which means that people can go directly to what they want to hear. So how do they get exposed to music they don't know they want to hear, the way you used to on radio?

"[It] keeps people confined within their own little worlds. It's like being in jail."

~

As night falls in Los Angeles, Hancock is still riffing on music in America, bemoaning the demise of a jazz culture that once enabled charismatic players such as Davis to reach a wide audience without necessarily diluting their art. Yet Hancock's own travels in music proceed apace, as the perpetually ringing phone attests.

The celebrated producer Phil Ramone is calling to see if Hancock can participate in a tribute concert to Sting; a TV producer wants to make an appointment to talk about a new TV animation program featuring Hancock's voice-overs; and all manner of agents, bookers, and managers are pleading for a bit of his time.

Meanwhile, Hancock's longtime assistant, Melinda Murphy, and his daughter, Jessica Hancock, work the phones, while his wife of thirty-five years, Gigi, pops into his studio occasionally to remind him that guests will be arriving soon.

No matter how the business of jazz develops—or recedes—in coming years, there's no question that Hancock will be out there swinging.

"I don't think you're going to see Herbie becoming a victim of the status quo," says Shorter. "You won't see him dwelling on the past or being unable to let go of something from before."

Indeed, Hancock, who says he has been approached to write his memoirs, has declined because "I've got a few more pages to turn before I do that.

"You know, when I perform, I see all these young people in the audience," says Hancock, who exudes a sense of youthfulness not uncommon among the most enduring jazz musicians. "And I'm not talking about 20 percent of them that are young—I'm talking about half or more that are young people.

"So if they're coming to hear music from a sixty-four-year-old guy, that tells me there's an audience out there, but they're clearly not being served by radio or the recording scene or the rest of it.

"After the old guys like me are gone, who's going to play for the kids next?"

March 21, 2004

~

What happens after "old guys" like Hancock aren't around remains to be heard, but Hancock himself has continued to flourish, artistically and otherwise. He made music history, of sorts, when in February 2008 his recording River: The Joni Letters *won the Grammy Award for Album of the Year (for 2007). Though this was widely touted either as the first time a jazz album had taken the top prize in the entire history of the Grammys or the first time it had done so since Tony Bennett won the 1994 Album of the Year for* MTV Unplugged, *these assertions do not hold up. Neither Hancock's* River *(essentially a tuneful duets album featuring Joni Mitchell, Norah Jones, Tina Turner, Leonard Cohen, and others) nor Bennett's* Unplugged *(not one of the most sophisticated recordings of his astonishingly productive career) can be considered a jazz album, even in the broadest meaning of the term. Nor were they intended to be; each pushed beyond the narrow jazz niche to reach a wider audience and succeeded. Yet there's no denying the glow that the top Grammy prize brought to both artists. In Hancock's case, it reaffirmed his stature as a protean musician and underscored his ability to finesse conventional borders in music and marketing. Far more impressive—at least artistically speaking—was an international tour that Hancock undertook in 2009 with the classical piano phenomenon Lang Lang (with whom Hancock had played a truncated version of George Gershwin's* Rhapsody in Blue *on the same Grammy Awards telecast at which Hancock took the top prize). On tour, Hancock played more than just the complete* Rhapsody *(with Lang): he plunged deeply into the classical repertory, performing alongside Lang in the four-hand piano version of Ravel's* "Mother Goose" Suite *and in Ralph Vaughan Williams's monumental* Concerto for Two Pianos and Orchestra. *In addition, Hancock offered solo jazz improvisations of his own. You probably could count on the fingers of one hand the number of jazz pianists of major reputation who could have pulled off this feat, let alone do it at the high technical and expressive level Hancock achieved (at least in performance with the Chicago Symphony Orchestra at the Ravinia Festival, outside Chicago). In this historic concert, Hancock illuminated why he has been able to thrive in jazz, classical, pop, fusion, and other realms: he knows how to play them all.*

Nobody Knows the Trouble She's Seen: Dee Dee Bridgewater

The hard times and bittersweet success of an expatriate jazz singer.

No sooner does the great singer slip into a booth in a crowded Chicago restaurant than a young waiter hustles over, armed with pen, paper, and a broad, enthusiastic smile.

"Could I have your autograph, please?" he says in a rush, catching her a bit off guard, though she's clearly flattered. Yet when Dee Dee Bridgewater—who has been living in artistic exile near Paris for more than a decade—happily signs her name with a flourish, the young man with the buzz cut looks positively crestfallen.

"Aren't you Me'Shell?" he says, referring to a twenty-seven-year-old pop star whose latest video has been saturating the airwaves via MTV.

"I'm afraid not, but you can keep the autograph anyway," says Bridgewater, a bit crestfallen herself. Once again she is reminded, as if she needed reminding, that no matter how big a name she has become in Europe, no matter how many French TV appearances she has made, no matter how many American Grammy nominations she has earned (three) while toiling several thousand miles away, she remains nearly invisible when she comes home. Worse, she is mistaken for a flavor-of-the-month pop star created by the same record industry that helped drive Bridgewater from the United States roughly thirteen years ago. Perhaps Bridgewater endures this latest slight without protest because she knows that finally, after more years of pain and frustration than she cares to contemplate, after encounters with artistic paralysis and near self-destruction, she is on the verge of conquering America once and for all.

On Sunday Bridgewater will appear on national television, headlining a twenty-fifth anniversary tribute to the Kennedy Center in Washington, D.C.

And less than two weeks later, on August 30, she will star on opening night of the eighteenth annual Chicago Jazz Festival, singing before tens of thousands of listeners in a Grant Park concert to be broadcast coast to coast on National Public Radio.

It is the biggest date she will have played in the States since gingerly launching her American comeback a little more than a year ago, and it will bring her full circle, back home to Illinois, where she began her professional career in Champaign-Urbana.

Bridgewater may have fled the United States for many good reasons—sexual harassment from individuals within the entertainment industry; beatings from a jealous husband; emotional pain from her crumbling self-esteem as a woman, a black, and an artist—but she is healed, she says, and she is back. With a vengeance.

~

Early on, before the disappointments, the betrayals, and the abuse, Bridgewater's future seemed rich with promise. Born Denise Eileen Garrett forty-six years ago in Memphis and raised in Flint, Michigan, she was crooning tunes before she could talk and reveling in her gift not long after.

"I used to lock myself up in the bathroom to sing," recalls Bridgewater. "I picked the bathroom because there was a huge, full-length mirror on one side of the room, a countertop mirror across from it, and if you looked into one mirror you could see infinite reflections of yourself singing.

"And I'd be wailing in there, and my mother would be yelling, 'Can't you just shut up?' "

No doubt about it, "she was always the entertainer," remembers her only sibling, Rhonda Whiters, now of Rochester, New York.

"She was like [a born] performer—she hungered for the stage," says the singer's father, Matthew Garrett, a former musician who had played trumpet for Dinah Washington and taught music at a high school in Memphis. By the time the extroverted girl everyone called Dee Dee was a teenager, she had formed a Supremes-like vocal group she dubbed the Iridescents and had won local talent contests as a soloist.

Her tumultuous journey didn't fully take flight, however, until 1969, when she played a collegiate jazz festival at the University of Illinois at Urbana-Champaign to pick up some spare cash.

"At that time, she sounded almost like Sarah," recalls Chicago saxophonist Andy Goodrich, referring to the divine Miss Vaughan. "I played that University of Illinois date with her, and she floored everyone with that singing of hers."

Indeed, no less than John Garvey—the feared, revered, and autocratic czar of the University of Illinois jazz band—on the spot invited the teenager to leave Michigan State University in East Lansing to enroll at the University of Illinois and join the ensemble's upcoming tour of Russia.

"I've had only two or three singers sing with my band over the years, and she was one of them," says Garvey, who does not praise easily or often. "She was already a very good singer. She sang with us on that tour, and she sang very well."

She also met University of Illinois grad student and trumpeter Cecil Bridgewater on that tour; the two of them had married and lived in New York by the time she was twenty.

"Dee Dee already was a terrific singer—she sounded a lot like Nancy Wilson, who was one of her idols," remembers Cecil Bridgewater.

Perhaps it was inevitable, though, that a young singer who was earning comparisons to Vaughan and Wilson would hit an artistic dead end playing "the wife, just tagging along" with her husband on tour (even if she had begun making a name for herself with the Thad Jones–Mel Lewis Orchestra).

The Bridgewaters separated not long after their daughter, Tulani, was born in 1972, and Dee Dee's career took off like a rocket.

By 1974 she had landed a supporting role in a daring new stage musical, *The Wiz*—a black version of the film musical *The Wizard of Oz*—though she had minimal acting experience.

"It was exciting, because 20th Century Fox was the [stage show's] producer, so there was big money in it," remembers Bridgewater, who originated the role of Glinda, the Good Witch.

"There were gorgeous costumes and a highly respected director [Gilbert Moses], so it felt like it was going to be something big—and it was."

Indeed, after the show premiered off-Broadway, the critics singled out Bridgewater, with Clive Barnes in the *New York Times* calling her voice "big and beautiful," Walter Kerr in the same paper dubbing her "persuasively sinuous."

And then, as she recalls it, the trouble began.

"One of the producers from 20th Century Fox kept hounding me to sleep with him," says Bridgewater. "And I kept saying, 'I'm not going to sleep with you. I don't do that.'

"So he says, 'Then I'm going to fire the director [Moses], because I know you're sleeping with him.'"

Bridgewater wouldn't relent, and Moses, with whom she indeed was involved, was fired; Bridgewater's role thereafter was cut by more than half before the show arrived on Broadway. Even so, she took a Tony nomination for best supporting actress in a musical, a turn of events that, alas, brought only more misery.

"When I got the Tony nomination, and Stephanie Mills [the fifteen-year-old star of the show] didn't get nominated for best actress, the black community just beat me up," says Bridgewater. "There were articles in the [black press] saying that I had slept around to get my nomination.

"And then when I won the Tony, it was like, 'Oh, my God, oh, my God.'

"People [in the cast] were not speaking to me. All these other actresses who had been in musicals before, they had studied and were trained, and here I am, this jazz singer, and I'm getting the Tony?"

As Bridgewater was discovering, success can have its perils, but that wasn't even the worst of it.

Moses, says Bridgewater, was jealous of her triumph in a musical that had been taken away from him, and he became emotionally, verbally, and, finally, physically abusive. The pressures she faced at home [she was living with Moses by then] and in the theater quickly proved too much to bear.

"I don't want to blame Gilbert [Moses] for everything, because he's dead now and can't defend himself," says Bridgewater of the actor-director, who died last year, at age fifty-two. Nevertheless, most of Bridgewater's memories of her years with Moses are bleak.

"He had undermined my self-confidence to the point that I just didn't think that I had any talent; I didn't think I was worth much as a person, as a human being.

"So I tried to commit suicide [via pills] and the only thing that saved it from getting into the papers was that when I went into the hospital it was with my maiden name.

"They had to pump my stomach, which was horrible.

"And I'll never forget this nurse who was pumping this [stuff] out of me just screaming: 'You're not going to die. Wake up. Wake up.'

"And I was crying, 'I want to die, I want to die.' "

Somehow, even against her deepest wishes, she lived. Perhaps she was tougher than she realized, or perhaps the unnamed and long-forgotten nurse just wouldn't allow her to slip away. To this day, Bridgewater doesn't know or understand precisely why she survived, but when she got back on her feet, she was reborn, ready to fight anew.

She quit *The Wiz,* packed her bags, took her daughter and fled to Los Angeles, hoping to leave New York and its ghastly memories behind. Moses, however, pursued her. And like many battered women, Bridgewater found it difficult to escape his grip and, in fact, agreed to let him move in with her and Tulani in Los Angeles. They were married in 1976.

"When we got back together, I started keeping a huge butcher knife under my pillow," she remembers, "and every night I went to sleep with this big thing under my head.

"Gilbert was a macho guy; he would never make a bed, so he'd never know. He had no clue that I had a blade with me that was this thick. But I told him, 'If you ever raise a hand to me again, I'll kill you. And if you ever touch Tulani, I will definitely kill you,' and I meant it."

At first, life with Moses among the Los Angeles show-business elite proved seductive, with "a lot of serious visitors, like Sidney Poitier and Harry Belafonte and all of these famous black celebrities coming to see me" when Bridgewater played in the Los Angeles cast of *The Wiz*.

"I was just totally awestruck by the film industry and the fact that you could go out to restaurants and see these celebrities. I'm from a small city in the Midwest, and this was exciting."

The battles between Moses and his wife, however, were far from over. Even before the birth of their daughter, China Moses, in 1978, Bridgewater had been looking for movie and TV work in Hollywood, and she thought she at last had succeeded when she seemed to have won the role of Mathilda in the 1977 TV miniseries *Roots*.

Before shooting, however, Bridgewater had to have her tonsils out, and Moses, not surprisingly to his wife, leaped into action.

"He went to the producer and the three directors that I was going to be working with [on *Roots*] and told them all that I had just had my tonsils out, and that if I worked, I would ruin my voice," says Bridgewater, with a sigh.

"And he did such a convincing job that even when my surgeon, my throat doctor, my speech therapist, and everybody else said that it would be OK, that it wouldn't be a problem, they decided not to give me the role.

"And then Gilbert turned up getting a job as the director—so we were doomed from the beginning.

"Everything I got, he undid.

"Later on, I had signed a contract to be a regular on *Hill Street Blues*," adds Bridgewater, "and Gilbert said, 'If you take this role, I'll leave.'

"So there I was. My agent said: 'Dee Dee, you've already signed the contract. They've got your costumes, you've got rehearsals in two days, you start shooting in a week. You're going to be blacklisted; you won't be able to work in Hollywood at all. He's not going to leave you. He's just jealous. I've seen it before. Don't do it.'"

But Bridgewater did, she says, and thereafter she watched both her marriage and her acting career unravel.

"Dee Dee suffered terrible things from Moses at that time," says Cecil Bridgewater, her first husband. "Because we have a daughter together, Tulani, I still was pretty aware of what was happening in Dee Dee's life.

"Moses, probably because he was a director, wanted to be in on all of the things that Dee Dee was involved with, and he wanted to be a step ahead of her, too. It became a very competitive thing for him, unfortunately.

"The beatings were so awful that at one point she was living in a hotel under some kind of guard."

Her recording career wasn't faring well either, because Atlantic Records lost interest in her, she says, when she refused to lie down for one of its executives.

"My album [*Dee Dee Bridgewater*] was just coming out on Atlantic in 1976 when I got a call, and this man said: 'We just found out that you said no to so-and-so, and we think you should reconsider, if you want your album to work.'

"And I said, 'Well, I'm sorry, but no, I won't.'

"And the man says, 'If you don't, then we'll have to shelve your album. That's really too bad for you.'

"And he hung up, and they pulled my album, which was getting great reviews."

The three pop-fusion albums Bridgewater did for Elektra from 1978 to 1980 did not exactly set the world ablaze, and by the start of the new decade Bridgewater seemed to have come to the end. Finished in Hollywood, tossed aside by the pop record industry, no longer working anywhere as a jazz singer, she was a has-been in a town ever searching for the next big thing, the starlet.

With her divorce from Moses painfully wending its way through the courts, she wanted nothing more than to get out of town.

"I was completely disillusioned, completely lost as a person," she says. "L.A. was just 'lost souls land.' [In Los Angeles] you get so caught up in trying to be somebody that you just lose sight of what it is you want to do."

So in 1983, Bridgewater bought a one-way ticket out of town, accepting an offer to join the international touring production of the musical revue *Sophisticated Ladies,* which took her to France later that year.

She didn't speak a word of French; she knew almost nothing of the culture or the country; her audiences were utterly unaware of who she was, what she did, and, most assuredly, what she had been through. Yet suddenly and inexplicably, at one of the lowest points in her career, Dee Dee Bridgewater found herself a star. The French press wrote reams about her. French TV pursued her. French audiences flocked to the show.

"By the end of the four-month run, I had become this starlet," she remembers, still a bit incredulous. "I was always out at all the discos and all the best private parties, constantly getting in the papers and doing TV shows.

"So I stayed on after the show closed and lived this glamorous night-life. I started doing jazz concerts in theaters! It was incredible."

Indeed, nothing like it had happened to Bridgewater before. Though she owned a Tony, though she had appeared numerous times on Johnny Carson's *Tonight Show* in the 1970s, she never really had triumphed in the role she had envisioned since childhood, when she still was crooning in front of bathroom mirrors: jazz singer.

Now Paris was hanging on her every note.

After a brief stint back in Flint, to help her ailing mother recover from a bout with lung cancer, Bridgewater returned to Paris in 1986 to star in *Lady Day,* based on the life of another tormented American jazz singer, Billie Holiday. Because Bridgewater didn't speak French, she learned—and performed—the script phonetically.

Again, France went wild, prompting *Lady Day* to extend its run for months.

By now divorced from Moses and living with her two children in Paris, Bridgewater began to realize that she had found something that had eluded her back home in the States. Call it acceptance, popularity, respect, honor, whatever, it felt more embracing than anything she had experienced in Manhattan or Hollywood or any point between.

"I found out that I had started to feel completely stunted artistically in the States," says Bridgewater today. "In the entertainment business, I had spent all my time listening to people telling me what I needed to do if I wanted to have that hit, if I wanted to have that success. I forgot who I was.

"In fact, I don't think I even would have come back to jazz singing if I hadn't gone to France. There, people actually wanted me to do jazz concerts.

"I couldn't believe it."

Practically from the moment Bridgewater set foot on French soil, in 1983, she had led a charmed life, and the romance between the American jazz singer and the Parisian public matured like a great love affair. Before long, she was hosting her own TV show (*52nd Street,* a jazz interview program), performing on national variety programs, appearing in made-for-TV movies with French star Charles Aznavour, performing as a black Sally Bowles in an African American version of *Cabaret,* and signing autographs as she strolled down the Champs-Élysées.

In France, she soon became known simply as "eclectic Dee Dee" or, better still, "Josephine Baker of the '90s," to quote two French reviews that point to her stature in her adopted home.

In a way, of course, Bridgewater simply was retracing the steps that so many gifted but neglected American jazz musicians had made before her. From New Orleans saxophone virtuoso Sidney Bechet in the 1920s to Chicago tenor giant Johnny Griffin in the '60s, black American jazz artists have found in France the honor and respect they deserved, but rarely received, at home.

But for Bridgewater, the seduction of France extended well beyond music. "We all felt free there," says Bridgewater, referring to her daughters, who implored her to let the family take root in France.

"My eight-year-old was taking the subway to school by herself; we could go out at night and not feel afraid.

"And the daily living was so much better, this whole idea of walking everywhere and buying your food on a daily basis and keeping just a little refrigerator, rather than freezing everything in advance, as we do in America. We ate better, because everything was fresh. We lived better."

Not long after Bridgewater had arrived in France to do *Lady Day,* she met Jean Marie Durand, a jazz club manager who would become her husband in 1991 and father of their son, Gabriel Morgan Durand-Garrett, in 1992.

A year later, Bridgewater released the most stunning recording of her career, *Keeping Tradition* (Verve), which all at once reminded the jazz world outside of France that one of its most promising talents had blossomed into a master. The brilliant scat vocalizing she produced on this recording was of a caliber no female singer under fifty had achieved since the heyday of Ella Fitzgerald and Sarah Vaughan.

More important, the maturity of Bridgewater's singing, the depth of her interpretations, the funk-tinged flavor of her rhythms announced the arrival of a major figure. It would only be a matter of time before the jazz world caught up with her.

~

"I kept reading in the French jazz magazines about this supposedly glorious American singer who could make it only in France, and I must admit I was suspicious," recalls Andre Menard, codirector (with Alain Simard) of the world's biggest jazz festival, the Festival International de Jazz de Montreal.

"I read about how eccentric she was, and I thought it was a bit of a put-on.

"But then my partner, Alain, and I were both stranded in Cannes one evening, and so I said, 'Well, why don't we go see Dee Dee Bridgewater—there are a few good guests on her show.'

"And when we saw her, I was totally floored. Her delivery, obviously, is pretty brash, and this pleases [non-Anglo] peoples. But at the same time, she could sing.

"You know how we always say, 'Too bad, the great singers are all gone. There's no more Ella, no Sarah'?

"When I heard her, I thought, 'Well, she fits in there somewhere among the greats.' "

Putting their money where their tastes were, Menard and Simard booked Bridgewater as an opening act for American singer-guitarist John Pizzarelli in 1993; Montreal reacted much as Paris had done a few years earlier. Critic Alain Brunet of *La Presse* called her "the jazz singer." Manon Guilbert of *Journal de Montreal* wrote that "Madame Bridgewater has a sublime voice" that "disguises itself as an instrument."

"I went to that performance, and it just blew me away," remembers Rhonda Whiters, Bridgewater's sister, who hadn't seen her perform since *The Wiz*, in the mid-1970s.

"I think what happened to Dee Dee is that France just allowed her to go through a natural growth process that probably had stopped when she was still in the United States.

"To be a great performer, I think you really have to come to terms with yourself, to be relaxed enough to be your best. And that's what happened to Dee Dee in France. She figured out exactly who she was, apart from husbands and record companies and all the rest."

In 1994 Bridgewater headlined her own Montreal show at the festival's midsized Theatre Maisonneuve to similar raves, with critic Claude Cote writing in *Voir* that she was "passionate to the tips of her long fingers." Critic Patrick Gauthier noted in *Journal de Montreal* that "this singer is a veritable dynamo . . . a very great singer."

And last year, when Bridgewater headlined at the festival's biggest auditorium, in Montreal's Place des Arts, she earned screaming, standing ovations for her tribute to the music of Horace Silver. The composer, who was to have accompanied Bridgewater, didn't show up, but Bridgewater sang tunes such as "Filthy McNasty," "Opus de Funk," and "Sister Sadie" with a vigor and naturalness that established her as the definitive vocal interpreter of Silver's music today.

The sellout concert was aired nationally on the Canadian Broadcast Corporation a few days later, and shortly after that Bridgewater's all-Silver *Love and Peace* CD was nominated for a Grammy in the States (she lost out this year to Lena Horne).

Having conquered Montreal, Bridgewater obviously would be heading south of the border next, but as soon as she began appearing here, she says, "I was scared. I found out from doing just the first few gigs that I'm psychologically still very fragile about performing in America.

"Just the places you play, the way you're treated is so different here.

"I just played a club in Fort Lauderdale that should not even be allowed as a building. It's a dump. And it gets depressing after a while. You say to yourself, 'If this is what jazz is in the United States, do I need this?'

"Musicians are treated so well in France; to have to come back and be reduced to staying in funky motels where you're scared to walk barefoot is just sad. I don't get it."

But with Bridgewater's star ascending in the States, perhaps it won't be long before American promoters begin booking four-star hotel accommodations for her. Her growing roster of dates and her scheduled appearance next year as a presenter during the Grammy Awards suggests that her moment finally may have come.

Nevertheless, Bridgewater probably will always come back to America as a tourist, nothing more.

"Dee Dee often has told me that ever since she got to Paris, she has been treated as an individual, and it didn't matter if she was black or blue or brown or man or woman," says Matthew Garrett, her father.

"She is quite the celebrity over there in Europe. I'm sure that she'll never come home."

August 18, 1996

In fact, Bridgewater did come home—to Nevada, to take care of her ailing mother. Based back in the United States, she enjoyed heightened visibility here, though nowhere near the adulation she's still accorded in Europe. Even so, the United States has slowly been recognizing her importance as a jazz artist, Bridgewater receiving a 1997 Grammy Award for Best Jazz Vocal Performance for Dear Ella *(Verve, 1997), an Ella Fitzgerald tribute that proved, once more, that Bridgewater ranks among the few female vocalists equipped to attempt Fitzgerald-like flights of scat-singing virtuosity. A decade later, Bridgewater created a bona fide masterpiece with the CD* Red Earth *(Universal/DDB Records/Emarcy, 2007), a profound exploration of the African roots of her ancestry and her art. Recorded in Mali, the recording evoked musical antiquity, as Bridgewater partners with various African griots. Yet, at the same time, she incorporated the modern-jazz techniques that have long defined her art. Dispatching with equal authority Malian songs and the music of Nina Simone and Oscar Brown Jr., Bridgewater practically summed up the breadth of her career in this recording, while also expanding into new realms. It was an astonishing achievement, though one unacknowledged by the Grammys. Her latest CD,* Eleanora Fagan (1915–1959): To Billie with Love from Dee Dee, *explores the legacy of Billie Holiday.*

Ornette Coleman Still Blazing a Musical Trail

Critics praise or skewer his musical theories.

NEW YORK—He has been called a charlatan and a genius, a musical illiterate and a fearless visionary, a destroyer of noble traditions and a builder of enthralling new idioms.

He has been skewered by listeners who yearn for the days when jazz was sweet and easy on the ear. He has been showered with some of the most prestigious prizes in American culture.

Along the way he has also been falsely arrested, attacked by muggers, beaten, bludgeoned, and left for dead.

Yet on this warm September morning, Ornette Coleman—his name to this day sparks fierce debate among listeners around the world—looks and sounds the picture of tranquility and peace, a soft-spoken, septuagenarian gentleman if ever there were one.

As the saxophonist-composer welcomes a visitor into the lobby of his Manhattan loft building, one might suspect that Coleman had never seen a day of strife in a career that, in truth, has generated more than its share of distress.

"Oh, man, I've had some really terrible things done to me," says Coleman, arguably the most influential jazz composer, theorist, and free-thinker of the past half century.

Nevertheless, "at a certain point in my life, I just decided that I would never fight any kind of class, any kind of race, and if someone said, 'I don't like you,' I wouldn't try to defend myself," continues Coleman, who plays a rare Chicago performance Friday night at Symphony Center.

"I'm not trying to control, change, dominate, kill, or be against anyone, or put somebody above another," adds Coleman, speaking at a hush in a spartan loft dotted by African-inspired sculpture and vividly abstract paintings. The accoutrements brighten a wide-open room that aptly reflects the spaciousness of much of Coleman's music.

"I think my position is that I'm no more than a speck of dust in the sand," says Coleman, "and I'm trying to avoid being stepped on."

In that regard, however, Coleman has not been thoroughly successful, for virtually every concert he has played, every recording he has issued, and every unexplored musical avenue he has delved into has drawn at least a measure of derision. Though many factions of the music establishment have long since acknowledged that Coleman not only changed the course of jazz but opened it up to uncounted possibilities, he has been a walking target at least since the mid-1950s, when he began to unfurl his unconventional views of composing and improvising music.

Yet he seems to have been as unfazed by the assaults as he has been unimpressed by the accolades (which have included a MacArthur "genius" Fellowship in 1994 and Guggenheim Fellowships in 1967 and 1973), instead serenely sharing his unorthodox musical philosophy with any musician seeking it out.

Although artists famous and obscure have spoken of Coleman's efforts to instruct them in the self-styled musical language he long ago termed "harmolodics," Coleman himself recalls a recent encounter that sums up his approach to getting musicians to think differently.

"A young lady who is trying to make her debut professionally came by a couple of days ago, and though she makes a living doing something else, she also writes songs," says Coleman, seventy-three.

"So I said, 'Sing,' and she sang [music based upon] an F chord," a not exactly radical gesture that clearly would hold little appeal for a set of ears as restlessly inquisitive as Coleman's.

"So I gave her a newspaper, and I said, 'I want you to read the newspaper, and I'm going to play while you're reading,'" with Coleman presumably blowing unexpected pitches, bizarre melodic intervals, and chord-shattering phrases into his alto saxophone.

"And the more she was reading the newspaper, the more her voice became a song," meanwhile leaving the F major chord behind and slipping, unwittingly, into Coleman's more free-ranging musical terrain.

"And I said to her, 'You know what? You might not realize it, but when your voice sings . . . it's [now] coming out to make you sound like an individual.

"And I call that 'harmolodics.'"

In purely musical terms, Coleman's "harmolodics"—a linguistically suave merger of "harmony" and "melody"—represents a rebellion against the chord changes that have driven everything in Western music from the fugues of Johann Sebastian Bach to the pop songs of Elvis Costello. In Coleman's "harmolodics" the strictures of chord progressions are abandoned, allowing each instrumentalist in a band to pursue his own melody line. Instead of chord changes, then, the players use the particular interrelationships of multiple melody lines to forge a common musical language.

"It's like having a million melodies all at once," explains Coleman, "yet it's still a kind of unison."

In Coleman's hands, this approach produces a music that is often sublimely lyrical, though also often harmonically provocative. Love it or hate it, however, it continues to influence some of the most significant experimenters in jazz.

Just a few weeks ago, the inquisitive Chicago musician Ken Vandermark gave the Chicago Jazz Festival its most artistically significant performance while leading his new Crisis Ensemble.

"Yes, the Crisis Ensemble was named after [Coleman's] album *Crisis,*" says Vandermark, in an e-mail from Oslo (where Vandermark is on tour), referring to a characteristically adventurous Coleman recording of 1969.

"Ornette's use of 'fluid tonality' [another way of describing 'harmolodics'] has had a huge impact on the way I think about harmony in my compositions and playing," adds Vandermark, whose art embraces a broad range of techniques, many originating with Coleman. "Coleman's breakthrough with freeing harmony from a strict, repetitive structure has had a huge impact on the way improvisers have thought about tonality since the late 1950s. And his efforts to reduce the hierarchy between soloist and rhythm section also indicated a direction that free improvisers have built on since the late 1960s."

Indeed, as Vandermark suggests, Coleman rewrote the rules for improvising and writing jazz. The conceptual leap he made—from the extraordinarily complex chord changes of bebop giants such as Charlie Parker, Dizzy Gillespie, and Thelonious Monk to a postchordal language of his own device—not only changed the music but liberated it.

Like most aesthetic revolutions, however, this one earned its leader considerable fire.

In Los Angeles, in the mid-1950s, Coleman was hard-pressed to find musicians who would talk to him, let alone take his radical ideas onto a bandstand.

And in New York, in the early 1960s, revered swing trumpeter Roy Eldridge said, "I think he's jiving, baby"; trumpeter Miles Davis said, "If you're talking psychologically, the man is all screwed up"; and drummer Max Roach, after hearing Coleman play, "punched Ornette in the mouth," notes John Litweiler in his Coleman biography, *A Harmolodic Life* (William Morrow, 1992).

Even today, some observers hold serious reservations about the significance of Coleman's contributions.

"Free jazz is one of the things that anyone can do, because there are no rules to which you have to conform," says John McDonough, a veteran jazz critic who penned a famous anti-Coleman essay—"Failed Experiment"—in the January 1992 issue of *DownBeat,* where he serves as contributing editor.

"It's empty in the same way that when Sid Caesar does a [fake] Japanese or French dialect. It sounds authentic, but it says nothing."

Others, such as veteran Chicago jazz impresario Joe Segal, have had mixed feelings about different facets of Coleman's work.

"I've heard him make some great music—like when we had him at the Jazz Showcase [in 1975] with [bassist] Charlie Haden, [drummer] Ed Blackwell, and [saxophonist] Dewey Redman. I liked the tunes, because they had that Charlie Parker flavor.

"But [later] I heard him playing all-electric, and me and the other beboppers left at intermission, because it sounded like a big mess."

Early on, however, a select few musicians instantly perceived the melodic beauty that Coleman's ideas made possible.

"Don Cherry [the innovative trumpeter] told me about this alto player, Ornette Coleman, so I went to hear him, and Ornette takes out this white plastic alto saxophone, and I never had heard anything so beautiful in my life," recalled bassist Haden, in a conversation with the *Tribune* last year.

"When he walked out of the club, I ran back after him. I just thought he played like some revolutionary angel.

"So he invited me to come to his home—actually, it was his apartment, a little one-room shack with music on the floor and everywhere.

"And I'll never forget what he said to me: 'After we play the intro, listen to me, and we'll play what we want to play, not what we're supposed to be playing.' "

From these early collaborations with Haden, trumpeter Don Cherry, and bassist Billy Higgins, among others, came recordings that radically altered the direction of jazz. The bracing sounds of *Something Else! The Music of Ornette Coleman* (1958), *Tomorrow Is the Question* (1959), *The Shape of Jazz to Come* (1959), *Change of the Century* (1959), and *Free Jazz* (1960) signaled that jazz musicians content to play endless choruses on "All the

Things You Are" had permanently lost their position on the front lines of the music.

If this work sounded shocking to the uninitiated, it represented a great gust of fresh air to musicians with open ears and minds.

"I remember listening to those records when they came out, and it's true that a lot of people didn't seem to understand what he was doing," recalls Chicago tenor saxophonist Fred Anderson, himself an adventurous player.

"But I understood what Ornette was doing—he was coming right out of Charlie Parker, and it was good. It wasn't that he was trying to play like Charlie Parker. He was trying to find his own voice."

Parker, indeed, was the alto saxophonist Coleman most admired, but while generations of imitators tried to ape Parker's breakthroughs, Coleman chose instead to push beyond Parker's bebop revolution.

"I saw Charlie Parker play when I just got to L.A." in the early 1950s, recalls Coleman, "when I was really, really starving at that point. I couldn't even get in the nightclub, because of the way I was dressed.

"They said, 'Please, the customers don't want to see you like this.'

"So I spoke to him outside . . . he opened up ears to hearing another way of playing music.

"Jazz means two things: 'unknown' and 'present,'" says Coleman, explaining his view of the music that has defined his life.

"In other words, you [bring] something unknown into the present, right?

"Now I didn't call the music I was doing 'free jazz.' Someone [at the Atlantic record label] named it that, put a Jackson Pollock painting on it, and called it 'Free Jazz.'"

The phrase, which has stuck to postchordal jazz ever since, may have done a disservice to Coleman and his idiom, for it gave casual listeners the impression that, in this music, anything goes, anyone can play anything.

In reality, however, Coleman's fluid system of "harmolodics" requires musicians with uncommonly sensitive ears and nimble intellects, as well as audiences willing to embrace bursts of abstract instrumental color, utterly unpredictable phrase lengths, and a kind of democracy among players that allows a robust counterpoint to flourish.

So far as Coleman is concerned, this thinking-outside-the-margins approach to creating music was shaped early on, in Fort Worth, where the absence of Coleman's father and the tiny wages earned by his mother left the family shut out of mainstream society.

Even music seemed beyond his reach, at first.

"I don't ever remember hearing [classical] instruments like violins—I was always hearing people with guitars and blues and stuff like that, because there was segregation," says Coleman.

"The first time I saw a guy play a saxophone, I didn't know what it was. And someone told me it was a saxophone. So I asked my mother, and she told me that if I go out and make money I could buy myself one. So I made me a shoeshine box and went on the streets smelling feet.

"Until one day she told me, 'Look under the bed'—it took about three or four years—and I took it out and played it."

Or, more specifically, Coleman invented his own way of playing the instrument, since music education was not in the family budget. Long unfamiliar with the technicalities of keys, transpositions, and other nitty-gritty of the musician's art, Coleman conceptualized his own systems for how tones harmonize (and don't harmonize), leading, perhaps, to his homemade "harmolodics."

Ever since, Coleman has been relentless in his search for new sounds, venturing to study the musical rituals of Hopi Indians in 1962, to absorb the "healing powers" of the master musicians of Joujouka, Morocco, in the early 1970s, and to study practically every other culture to which he could obtain entree. These influences have continuously refreshed his art, inspiring epic pieces such as the jazz-meets-the-symphony *Skies of America* in the early 1970s, the quasi-classical "Freedom Symbol" suite (featuring a twenty-piece ensemble) in 1989, and the multimedia, multicultural social commentary of *Tone Dialing* in 1995.

Though these works have been praised and damned, Coleman remains undeterred.

"I'm drawn to what I can't see that represents God," says Coleman, who has put aside, he says, bitterness over race-driven arrests in his youth, beatings from fellow musicians early in his career in the South, and two brutal muggings from apparently random criminals in his adopted home, New York.

"I remember that I got my horn in the 1940s, and after I had some experience [on it], I discovered the word 'art.'

"And it seemed to me that art was anything that was created that didn't have to give in to anyone's influence. . . .

"That's one thing that I haven't done yet, and I'm not planning to."

September 21, 2003

~

The opening decade of the twenty-first century has been the season of recognition for Coleman, who has been showered with awards that he deserved decades earlier. In addition to the 2006 Pulitzer Prize in Music he won for his recording Sound Grammar, *he received a Grammy Lifetime Achievement Award in 2007 (though he never has received a Grammy for any recording); was installed in the Nesuhi Ertegun Jazz Hall of Fame, at Jazz at Lincoln Center, in New York, in 2008; and received the 2009 Miles Davis Award from the Montreal International Jazz Festival. More important, Coleman has remained an indefatigable source of some of the most tenderly phrased melodies that American music has produced. His harmolodic vocabulary may have shocked (many) listeners and scandalized (some) writers half a century ago, but compared to the sonic revolutions Coleman's music subsequently unleashed, his work today sounds lyrical, poetic, often fragile and usually disarming. Closing the thirtieth Chicago Jazz Festival in the summer of 2008, Coleman—standing before thousands of listeners—spun lines of silk on alto saxophone, produced atmospheric tremolos on violin, traced silvery arabesques on trumpet, and otherwise presided over a luminous night of music. It has taken a long time for most of the world to catch up with Coleman, who suffered the world's disapproval but imperturbably preserved the character of his voice.*

The Last Diva: Lena Horne

Survivor of a generation of singers whose virtuosity and style will not be heard again.

NEW YORK—Can the fetching woman seated just a couple feet away in a Manhattan recording studio—her manner so thoroughly youthful and engaging—possibly be entering her ninth decade? More important, can this soft-spoken, quick-to-smile woman be the same firebrand who defied Hollywood racism in the 1940s, anticommunist witch hunts in the '50s, and the foes of civil rights in the '60s? Apparently so, for Lena Horne, at eighty-one, not only has outlived her enemies, she now can laugh at them.

"In a way, it's all very funny, because so many of the things that happened were so ridiculous, you know?" says Horne, speaking with a slight southern lilt that evokes the years she spent growing up in Georgia. "You wouldn't be allowed to get on a particular bus, but you'd be asked to sign your autograph. Now that's funny."

Horne has good reason to laugh. Though she has conquered Hollywood and Broadway several times over, won more critical accolades than she can remember, and reminisced in two autobiographies, she finds herself in an unexpected chapter in an already remarkable life story.

Her recording career reignited in 1994, when she released her first album in more than a decade, *Lena Horne: We'll Be Together Again,* long after she had considered herself done with her public life. The live recording that followed shortly thereafter, *An Evening with Lena Horne: Live at the Supper Club,* won her a late-in-life Grammy Award (for Best Jazz Vocal), and her newest release, *Being Myself,* may be the best of the bunch. Certainly it's the most intimate and revealing.

"You have to realize that this is a woman who has experienced just about everything that can be experienced in the show business world, she has lived the legacy of American popular music going back to Bessie Smith through jazz and through blues," says Rodney Jones, who produced *Being Myself* and plays guitar on the album.

Jones does not exaggerate, considering that Horne made her stage debut at sixteen, in the mid-1930s, playing the Cotton Club in New York's Harlem.

"I think she feels that the historical Lena Horne is common knowledge, but this record is a chance to get a little more intimate glimpse of her," adds Jones. "And, for her, I think that's a freeing thing.

"Like many great artists, she was always subject to the whims of producers and record companies, and, to some degree, I believe she was imprisoned by her beauty," continues Jones, referring to the role of glamorous diva to which managers and executives consigned her.

"I think *Being Myself* was a chance for her to let out a part of her that people may not have known, and, remember, she's the one who picked the title for the recording."

Indeed, *Being Myself* is the bluesiest and most freewheeling recording in Horne's long career. From the drenched-in-irony opening tune, "Some of My Best Friends Are the Blues," to the soulful "Willow Weep for Me" to the bittersweet "What Am I Here For," the album offers a close look at the woman beneath the glittering facade.

The miracle, though, is that this recording—as well as the two excellent ones that led up to it—ever saw the light of day. In a youth-oriented culture, after all, record executives do not typically court female jazz singers who are pushing eighty.

Nor did Horne have any intention of returning to the spotlight. Having stopped touring and recording several years earlier, she agreed to make a single concert appearance in Lincoln Center's Avery Fisher Hall in 1993 to honor the late composer Billy Strayhorn, one of her closest and most sorely missed friends.

The glowing reviews persuaded Horne to return to the recording studio to make a privately financed tape, which was deposited (unsolicited) on the desk of Blue Note president Bruce Lundvall.

"They brought me a finished master, I loved it, I said I wanted it," remembers Lundvall. "When the record came out, she agreed to do two nights at Carnegie Hall, which I wanted to record, but she said that was too much pressure.

"So she agreed to do it in a smaller venue [the Supper Club, in New York], and the live record won a Grammy.

"Finally, last summer, right before her eightieth birthday celebration at Lincoln Center, she called me and said, 'Well, boss, I guess it's time for me to finish the [next] record,'" which she had started after the live CD.

"And when we finished it, she said she would like to do another one. That will make four new recordings from an artist who had decided not to record anymore."

The releases are important not only because of Horne's artistry and history but also because her glorious contemporaries—chiefly Ella Fitzgerald, Billie Holiday, Carmen McRae, and Sarah Vaughan—have passed on. Thus Horne stands as the last diva, a singer whose artistic lineage runs so deep into the traditions of twentieth-century jazz, blues, and pop that she has no living peer.

What other still-working female singer, after all, can claim to have learned her art in one of the most iconic places in black musical culture, the Cotton Club of the 1930s?

"It was great schooling for me—in fact, it's too bad we don't have places like that now," says Horne.

"Or maybe we have too many teachers. Today, I wouldn't know whether I should go to Sting or to one of the Monkees to get my schooling," adds Horne, ever ready with a quip. "But I had my schooling right there in the Cotton Club.

"I learned from Ethel Waters, Duke Ellington, Adelaide Hall, the Nicholas Brothers, the whole thing, the whole schmear. That was a great place because it hired us, for one thing, at a time when it was really rough [for performers of color]."

If there is a single theme that runs through Horne's life and her conversation, it is the restrictions that have been placed on black artists throughout the American experience. Perhaps her heightened awareness of the tragic side of American culture should come as no surprise, considering her lineage. Her grandmother, Cora Calhoun Horne, held key positions with the NAACP and the National Urban League; her grandfather was the first black member of the Brooklyn Board of Education; her uncle was an adviser on race relations to President Franklin D. Roosevelt.

But Lena Horne—born in Brooklyn and raised in various southern and eastern cities, thanks to an absentee father and a mother who toured as an actress—says she learned about the meaning of race in America from an authority on the subject, Paul Robeson.

"When I worked at Cafe Society [in the 1940s], that was the one place in New York that had no [color barriers], and he would talk to me," remembers Horne.

"He helped me come to an understanding about my people, and again to build up the kind of fierce pride I have about them now."

The lessons must have taken hold quickly, for after emerging a star in musical films such as *Cabin in the Sky* and *Stormy Weather* (both in 1943), Horne refused to take the roles of whores and maids routinely offered to black female actors at the time. As a result, she appeared only in musical segments of feature films, her footage excised for movie theaters in the South.

If her movie career stalled in the 1940s, it virtually ground to a halt in the '50s, when she was condemned in various anticommunist publications for her well-known friendship with Robeson. Yet she had no intention of severing her ties with him.

"I never had the great urge to be in the movies in the first place," she says today, "only because I saw that it was Tarzan or nothing, you know?

"I never fell for the myth. So when I saw the way things were going, I just got on out."

Nor did Horne's brush with Hollywood mark her first refusal to play the racial-political game. In a notorious incident during World War II, she triggered a contretemps while performing for troops at Fort Riley, Kansas. Looking into the audience, she realized that German prisoners of war were seated in front of black American soldiers.

"Accounts of what happened next differ," notes *Current Biography Yearbook*, but the military and Horne quickly parted company.

So exactly what did happen between Horne and the U.S. military?

"I just walked off the stage and went up and sang to the back of the room," says Horne, reveling in the moment.

"It happened a couple of times, and they finally said, 'Get her out of the USO.'

"I just reacted as Lena, you know, me. And my grandmother taught me about facing down, you know, looking people in their eyes and saying, 'I don't like it.'

"That's the reason people always used to say, 'You're a civic leader,' and all that, but, no, it's just me."

In 1960 she reportedly tossed ashtrays, plates, and a lamp at a customer in a Beverly Hills restaurant who had tossed a racial slur her way, and she spent most of the 1960s traveling through the South to appear at civil rights rallies.

But the controversies that perpetually swirled around Horne did nothing to diminish her popularity and may even have accentuated it, as she proved with acclaimed TV specials in the 1970s, a Tony Award–

winning Broadway show (*Lena Horne: The Lady and Her Music*) in the '80s, and now, surprisingly, a coda to her career in the '90s.

Having survived two marriages, the deaths of her second husband (musician Lennie Hayton, in 1971) and her son Teddy (of kidney failure, at about the same time), Horne clearly has faced her share of personal hurdles. (Her daughter, Gail Lumet Buckley, lives in New York and accompanies her to interviews.)

Today, says Horne, she has changed as an artist, her work onstage considerably different than before.

"I think, at some point, I began to like my audiences more," says the diva, long considered somewhat aloof as a stage and screen performer.

"I learned to enjoy the interplay with them, completely, and that only happened in the '80s. I was never really aloof, that was people's image of me, but it came about because I didn't ever think that I should be anything but perfect for the audience.

"I found out along the way that they like you a little imperfect."

Whether Horne will return to the stage is an open question, though she says sometimes "I feel one hundred."

Whatever happens, though, she endures as the last of an inimitable generation of singers whose virtuosity and style cannot be replicated. Like Ella, Billie, Sarah, and Carmen, she's known and revered around the world by a sweet, single name—Lena.

"Oh, I'd love to be thought that good," she says. "That's a compliment, but I'm not sure I'm the last.

"I certainly hope not."

June 7, 1998

Being Myself *turned out to be Horne's last recording, the singer thereafter returning to the shell of privacy she long coveted. Few were allowed into her circle of seclusion, but author James Gavin offered a sobering look at Horne's life and times and smoldering bitterness in* Stormy Weather: The Life of Lena Horne *(Atria, 2009), the most authoritative text on the subject. Her "final role," wrote Gavin, is "that of recluse." Horne died May 9, 2010, at New York-Presbyterian/Weill Cornell Medical Center, at age ninety-two.*

Von Freeman Is Chicago Jazz History

And the world discovers a legend can
continue to expand at seventy.

Never mind that the man noodling on the yellowed keys of his piano doesn't exactly look like one of the world's reigning tenor saxophonists, at least on this particular morning.

Having played until the early hours the night before, tenor legend Von Freeman is just getting his day started, which invariably means heading directly to the Starck grand in his small house on the South Side of Chicago. Wearing a pair of faded jeans and a purple T-shirt—a getup somewhat less swank than the fine suits, flashy ties, and dark glasses he typically sports on the bandstand—Freeman is playing strange, dissonant chords.

His piano is laden with music, his records are strewn all over the place, his every other word concerns music.

"I've even got chord progressions posted up on the wall in the bathroom—I think about this stuff all the time," says Freeman, whose gifts finally are making him an international name—on the eve of his seventieth birthday. Earlier this year, Steeplechase Records ventured to Chicago to record Freeman for a double-CD set due out later this year. A few days ago, Jazz Midwest, a Minnesota-based organization, presented him with its prestigious Jazz Masters Award. And in a couple weeks, he'll be ensconced at the La Villa Lounge in Paris, a chic club that booked him nearly a year ago for a birthday stint.

No doubt about it; Von Freeman's moment has arrived.

"I guess I'd have to say that I've been extremely lucky in the past couple of years," says Freeman, who has spent most of his life blowing tenor for "strip joints, taxi dances, vaudeville shows, comedians, jugglers, weddings, bar mitzvahs, jazz clubs, dives, Polish dances, Jewish dances, every nationality.

"I don't know why all this stuff is happening to me right now, because I'm surely not getting any younger. Maybe it's because in the past couple years all these [Chicago] clubs have been pairing me with those hard-blowing kids, like Ed Petersen and Eric Schneider [both incendiary tenorists].

"And those guys can play. So instead of laying back and just resting, I had to really come on strong and study some more and eat some more Wheaties.

"See, when you pass sixty, nine-tenths of this thing is stamina. Because you've got to be able to stand up and play, because nobody is going to have any mercy on you because of your age. They feel if you can't cut it, retire.

"So you've got to just lean in there."

The miracle is that Freeman has been doing precisely that for nearly all his life, long before much recognition or anything beyond subsistence pay was within reach. Somehow, says Freeman, who raised four children in the process, "I was able to eke out a living. Guess I was lucky."

That depends on how you define luck. Certainly Freeman was blessed as far as musical talent is concerned.

"Von was always a natural," says Freeman's younger brother, George, a noted guitarist.

"He always was able to catch on and hear things; he could pick up piano or horn or anything so fast, it was amazing."

And Von lucked out—as did George and their other brother, Bruz, an accomplished drummer—in that their father loved jazz.

"I got all this music by osmosis," says Von. "My daddy used to play trombone—not professionally, because he was a Chicago policeman. But he had records on all the time.

"And because he was detailed at the Grand Terrace Ballroom [a landmark club of the 1930s], he'd bring them all over to the house. Louis Armstrong used to come by from the time I was about three years old, and he'd always say to me: 'Hi, Pops.'

"Earl Hines came over, and Fats Waller played this piano of mine."

The reigning sound of the day was the tenor saxophone, with groundbreaking melodists such as Coleman Hawkins, Lester Young, and Ben Webster creating a new vocabulary for the instrument. So at age six, Freeman taught himself tenor.

"With this music, nobody else really can teach you or tell you that much," says Freeman. "You've got to perfect it yourself and find your own ideas of what you want to express.

"I did my first nightclub gig when I was twelve—my mother had to write a note for me. She wrote: 'Don't let him drink, don't let him smoke, don't let him consort with those women, and make him stay in that dressing room.'

"It was a club out in Gary, and I played seven nights a week. The guy who hired me said, 'Put something on your lip so you look a little older,' so I drew a mustache on."

By the time he was a teenager, Freeman was jamming with his friends at DuSable High School, where the feared-and-revered Captain Walter Dyett was building one of the country's premier jazz programs.

"Everybody in Chicago who had an instrument and wanted to play music back then tried their best to get to DuSable," says Freeman. "Like 'Jug' [Gene Ammons, the great Chicago tenorist]. He always had a beautiful tenor sound even then. He used to play in concert band, and he would wipe out all of the double-reeds.

"I guess Jug and I were like the two hotshots around school with solos and whatnot. And when Earl Hines left Chicago [in the late 1930s], King Kolax took a band in there and asked Jug and me to go in his band and maybe tour with him. This was a big break, and Jug left school and of course never looked back, just zoomed to the top."

Freeman, though, wasn't interested in the touring life, so he signed on with the Horace Henderson band in 1940, before being drafted. Artistically, that was a blessing in disguise, for it was in the navy band that Freeman found a kind of musical inspiration.

"I met this saxophone player named Dave Young, and, man, he had this sound that I had been looking for all my life," says Freeman.

"Because I loved Prez [Lester Young], but he didn't have that power. He had a relatively soft tone, though beautiful. And Coleman Hawkins had all this power, man, he could blow, you could hear him around the block, but he didn't have this floating thing of Prez's.

"But when I heard Dave Young, he had the power and the floating sound, like Lester, and that's what I wanted to try to get."

It must have rubbed off, for not long after Freeman left the navy in 1946, he and his two brothers quickly cohered into one of the most hard-charging units in Chicago jazz. Booked as the house band in the famous Persian Lounge, they backed virtually all the legends of the era, from Charlie Parker on.

"Actually, I had found out about Bird from my daddy after I got out of the service," says Freeman. "He said, 'You think you're a hotshot? Listen to this.'

"And he put on a Charlie Parker record, and I was sold.

"Playing with Bird was really beautiful, one of the few geniuses I have ever met in music. He just played what he wanted to play, and in jazz music, that's what you really try to do.

"Through any key, any idea, any tempo, Bird would just play."

Perhaps Parker's only equal in the nascent bebop language was trumpeter Dizzy Gillespie, "who was really identical to Bird in the things he could do on trumpet," says Freeman.

"I played with Roy [Eldridge] too, and he was the king of the trumpet, until Dizzy. He had this tone and this range, even though he was a little man, but just commanding."

By the 1950s, Freeman was becoming something of a master himself. Thus Miles Davis tried to hire him as replacement for John Coltrane.

"Actually, my mother got the phone call, because I was in New York playing with a blues band," recalls Freeman. "And she said, 'Well, he has four kids, and he's got a wife,' so Miles said he understood.

"That probably would have been my big break, but I missed it."

Maybe, but Freeman simply went about concentrating on his art rather than his career.

"What I was trying to do was to play something that was a little more sophisticated than just what everybody else was playing," says Freeman. "I've always tried to do that, no matter what anybody said, and people did criticize me.

"They said I played out of tune, played a lot of wrong notes, a lot of weird ideas.

"But it didn't matter, because I didn't have to worry about the money—I wasn't making [hardly] any. I didn't have to worry about fame—I didn't have any. I was free.

"So I'd spend a lot of time in Calumet City, playing behind a curtain—you know, strip places. And I learned a lot of different music there.

"It didn't hardly pay anything, but it was better than just laying around saying how great you were.

"And I'd be playing a lot of Bird tunes, and almost every night somebody sitting out in the audience would sit up and notice and say, 'What is that guy doing back there?' "

The sweet irony is that the utter musical freedom of this life probably made possible Freeman's musical accomplishments of today. Not beholden to any one style or any single audience, he developed a language that somehow fuses ornate ballad-playing of the 1930s, hard-hitting bop of the '50s, and chromatically dissonant explorations of the avant-garde. His volcanic sound and labyrinthine solos sound like no one else's.

In a way, Freeman's late-blooming fame comes at a perfect time, when his technique and his ability to improvise are at their peak.

"I'm not entirely happy with myself, but I'm kind of happy that my playing has improved in the last twenty years," says Freeman, who sometimes tours with his son, saxophonist Chico Freeman.

"And I hope my sound will improve some more.

"Basically, you've just got to pray and cry and suffer to try to find these ideas, because they're hidden. They're in the shadows, in the wind and in the breeze and in nature.

"And they're inside everyone. The art is bringing them out."

September 20, 1992

XIII

Panama's Vanished Music

Searching for the Missing Link of Jazz—
in Panama (in Three Parts)

A Culture with a Lost Past

Just as Spain, France, and Africa shaped the music of America, the same influences converged in Panama. So why has the country's musical heritage practically disappeared?

PANAMA CITY—A young woman swathed in a luminous green gown twists and turns onstage, as if possessed. As she sways across the proscenium, bending her body in sinuous and hypnotic ways, a small army of percussionists fires off a flurry of backbeats, their tempo accelerating as the tribal dance unfolds. Thousands in the audience, watching beneath a scorching afternoon sun, cheer loudly, their chants almost drowning out the accompanying jazz band, while the dancer continues to gyrate before them, her gestures inspiring further waves of adulation and exultation.

But the Panamanians egging on the performer aren't merely whiling away an afternoon at the Panama Jazz Festival, where the Bannaba Project—which merges ritual dance with modern jazz—is proving a certifiable sensation. More important, the locals are beholding their ancient past, attempting to connect with the origins of a Panamanian culture they're only beginning to rediscover and understand.

Their quest carries implications for the rest of the musical world, for it speaks to the origins of jazz and its precursors.

That's because Panama—like Havana and New Orleans—once stood at the crossroads of the slave trade, the Africans who were forcibly brought here, and elsewhere across the Americas, carrying with them the rhythms and techniques that eventually blossomed into jazz and its many offshoots.

But while the sounds of Havana and New Orleans have been celebrated around the world, the historic music of Panama has practically disappeared. Thanks to centuries of conquest by armies near and far, thanks to the often overweening cultural influence of the United States—which controlled the Panama Canal through most of the twentieth century—Panamanians have almost no record of a musical scene that may have rivaled New Orleans as a nexus of early jazz.

By trying to retrieve their musical heritage, through performance ensembles such as the Bannaba Project and through the fledgling Panama Jazz Festival itself, Panamanians are not only attempting to reconstruct their cultural legacy. Equally important, they're trying to find—through music—a sense of self-worth that has been battered through centuries of domination by foreign powers.

"We need to bring our self-esteem up, after all the stuff that has happened here," says Panamanian salsa star and movie actor Ruben Blades, who last year left Hollywood to become Panama's minister of tourism. [He stepped down in 2009, returning to his recording career.]

Speaking passionately about his country during lunch at Restaurante Martin Fierro, a short drive from his office in the capital's architecturally majestic but partly crumbling Old City, Blades believes that his compatriots are on a mission. Panamanians, he says, are trying to "understand our own music."

Adds Panamanian pianist Danilo Perez, chatting between sets at the jazz festival he created, "We have to help our self-image, and I think music does that.

"We have to erase the stereotype, the idea that Panama is mangos and bananas, that whole mentality.

"We have a lot of great talent here. The one thing we have is culture—but we don't know it."

Panama today indeed stands at a kind of crossroads. Having received control of its primary economic engine—the Panama Canal—from the United States on the last day of 1999 and having elected President Martin Torrijos last fall, the country finally stands poised to fully take hold of its future. Yet after centuries of living under the influence of Colombia, Spain, France, the United States, and other external forces, Panama has yet to find its own voice and identity, its sense of its cultural worth.

To do so, it has begun looking to a musical past that has barely survived. Only a few tantalizing fragments of Panama's sprawling musical history endure, in fact, to suggest that this isthmus—where the sun seems to rise over the Pacific and set over the Atlantic—once flourished as a cultural powerhouse. From the ancient chants and ritualized dances of the indigenous Kuna people (including the aforementioned dancer of the Bannaba Project) to the American-made recordings of Panama's first bona fide jazz star, pianist Luis Russell (who powered Louis Armstrong's great bands of the 1930s), Panama's musical roots run deep.

Moreover, the history of this country—which didn't become an independent nation until 1903—hauntingly echoes the origins of America's first city of jazz, New Orleans. Just as the cultures of Spain, France, Africa, and North America shaped the music of Louisiana, so too did these same influences converge in Panama.

The Spanish conquerors of centuries ago left behind their language, architecture, and European musical traditions, while the English traders who brought slaves here provided a critical element in the emergence of a distinct Panamanian music: the mystical, ancient sounds of Africa, borne by men and women in chains.

The arrival of the French, in the 1880s, to attempt to build a canal (a failed venture that cost 22,000 lives and nearly bankrupted France), and of the Americans in 1904, to construct the Panama Canal, completed the picture. Like Louisiana, Panama at the dawn of the twentieth century was poised to create a nascent jazz.

But with the exception of the music of Luis Russell, a Panamanian jazz genius who moved to New Orleans in 1919, at age seventeen, the first chapter of Panama jazz may have totally escaped documentation. If we are to judge by the accomplishments of Russell—who famously collaborated with such first-generation New Orleans jazzmen as clarinetist Albert Nicholas, drummer Paul Barbarin, and the great Satchmo himself—the initial wave of Panamanian jazz artists was formidable.

That a Panama-trained musician such as Russell, one of many Panamanian jazz pioneers, could hold his own alongside the first great jazzmen of New Orleans suggests that the Central American country may have been at the forefront of the music.

Unfortunately, Panamanians of Russell's vintage "had a chance to listen to the jazz but never the technology to record jazz groups here in Panama," says Ernesto Crouch, a Panamanian music historian and drummer who has been researching the subject for decades.

From the late nineteenth century to the early twentieth, when attempts to build the canal brought a wide swath of cultural influences here, Panama "was slums," adds Crouch, the country too poor and technologically undeveloped to try to document its own art.

"Even by the '30s, there were no recordings," says Francisco Buckley, a Panamanian music scholar who stands under a tent throughout the festival, in the Old City, selling copies of his recent book *The Salsa Music of Panama and Other Matters* (available only in Panama).

"But the people who heard this music, they remember," adds Buckley, who interviewed scores of musicians and listeners for his volume. In addition, he cites yellowed newspaper clippings that reference a jazz scene that thrived in the Panamanian provinces of Colón and Boca del Toros. For centuries Africans concentrated here, on the side of Panama facing the Atlantic and the United States, with the city of Colón emerging as the capital of a recognizably Central American brand of jazz.

The scene blossomed as Americans and others began work on the Panama Canal, in 1904—just when a New Orleans jazz pianist named Jelly Roll Morton began composing "King Porter Stomp," which would become a theme song for the new music.

The influx of American servicemen and civilians, as well as workers from across the Western Hemisphere, practically ignited Colón with the sound of jazz. The city became a kind of New Orleans of the Caribbean, its all-night bars, rowdy dance bands, and twenty-four-hour carnival atmosphere providing an ambience parallel to the Crescent City to the north.

Nearly forgotten musicians such as Samuel "Sam" Gooding, who led an eponymous band, and Professor Reginald Prescott, who fronted the Ambassadors of Jazz, thrived in Panama throughout the Roaring Twenties. They played rooms such as the Blue Moon and the Cotton Club, creating a music designed to entertain the American visitors, and others.

"Colón was a crazy place, because that was where most of the ships came in," says Buckley, who enthusiastically discusses the history of Panamanian music with passersby throughout the festival.

"The sailors would go around the clubs, and they brought music, they sometimes brought their instruments to play.

"If 1904 was the beginning of the American influence, by 1914, when the canal was completed, American servicemen were all over Colón.

"If the Panamanian musicians wanted to make money, they had to play what the Americans wanted to hear."

Moreover, only American armed services radio broadcast in Panama until 1937, when the country's first independent station went on the air, which meant that American big-band and small-ensemble music held sway throughout Panama during nearly the first four decades of the twentieth century.

But Luis Russell may be the only early-generation Panamanian jazz star whose music survives on recording, thanks wholly to his move to the

States. The entire world that produced him seems to have disappeared, having never been recorded in any form. Though Fred Ramdeen's and Henry Barlow's bands in the 1930s and Victor Reid's Aristocrats of Jazz and Eduardo Ralston's Royal Sultans in the 1940s are mentioned in old concert flyers and news reports, their music vanished with their era.

Not until the late 1950s and '60s did Panama begin recording its own artists, yet even these historic discs are difficult to find, because the country did not have the wherewithal to collate and archive its popular music.

Yet the occasional recording that has surfaced reveals a musical culture of extraordinary power, originality, and sophistication.

Though these LPs are difficult to find, pianist Perez—who has been collecting this music for a lifetime—spends an afternoon playing cassette tapes for a visitor in the Panama City apartment of his father, the singer and educator Danilo Perez Sr.

As the music booms through a couple of small speakers, Perez smiles, dances, and occasionally narrates, pointing out key passages in music that most of the world has never heard.

The sounds easily justify his enthusiasm. Listen to the roaring swing band of Armando Boza, the brilliant jazz-organ virtuosity of Avelino Muñoz, the calypso-meets-jazz vocals of Sylvia De Grasse, the Cuban-Panamanian mélange of pianist Papo Lucca's big band, and it's clear that music of this caliber could only have emerged in a culture in which jazz had thrived for decades.

Like its American counterpart, Panamanian jazz churned out hard-swinging rhythms, brilliant instrumental solos, and, sometimes, musical quotations from U.S. stars such as Charlie Parker, James Moody, and Ella Fitzgerald.

But Panamanian jazz also distinguished itself from the music of the States, offering a particularly Caribbean perspective on the art form. Generally more lyrical, more folkloric, and less rhythmically agitated than its American counterpart, Panamanian jazz—at least judging by those rare recordings of the 1950s—offered a hauntingly melodic approach to the art of jazz improvisation.

And though there's no mistaking in this music the sway of Cuba—its dance rhythms and song forms to this day influencing music across the Americas—the Panamanians in some ways withstood even the impact of Havana. By building performances on Panamanian folk tunes, invoking Panama's signature *tamborito* rhythm and employing instruments such as the *bocona*—a small, five-string guitar probably invented in Panama—as well as various indigenous drums, the Panamanians created a self-styled music that stands apart from anything else in Central America, or anywhere else.

Where the jazz ends and the folkloric tradition begins varies from one recording and one performance to another, just as it does in Cuba.

Yet the Panamanians have a cultural legacy to be proud of—if only they could flesh it out.

"One of the problems that we have in Panama is that we have no institution that keeps order or documentation of our music," says Ricaurte Villarreal, a virtuoso percussionist and folklorist who teaches at the University of Panama. As he speaks, he illustrates particular rhythms and pitch patterns on the traditional Panamanian drum he carries wherever he goes.

"So even the recordings from the '50s and '60s that do exist are very hard to find," adds Villarreal. "They are in private collections, not public."

Yet to those who heard this music as it was being forged, it left an indelible impression.

"It was a fascinating time to be in Panama when I was growing up, in the '40s and '50s," remembers Victor "Vitin" Paz, a legendary Panamanian trumpeter who eventually moved to New York before returning to Panama City five years ago.

Sitting on a bench in a Panama City park, occasionally noodling on his trumpet, Paz thinks back on music he heard more than half a century ago, its cadences clearly playing in his inner ear as he speaks.

"We listened to the Armed Forces radio, where we heard the American music—Harry James, Glenn Miller, Benny Goodman, Dizzy Gillespie, Cab Calloway.

"And then, from my house, I could hear the music coming out of the bars—Spanish music, Cuban music, Panamanian jazz. It was thrilling, like the whole world was coming together in Panama."

Inside the clubs, the Panamanian players were combining the fire and fury of American jazz with the smoldering melodicism and unhurried rhythms of the Caribbean.

"You could hear on alto saxophone Bat Gordon, who could blow like crazy in those days," recalls Carlos Garnett, who was born in the U.S.-controlled Canal Zone in 1938 and moved to the States in 1962, where he earned a sterling reputation, before returning home a few years ago.

At the Panama Jazz Festival, he galvanizes the crowd with the sheer sonic heft and musical complexity of his solos.

"And on trumpet there was Gene White, and on piano Victor Boa," adds Garnett, the latter having championed Panama's "tambo jazz," which embraces uniquely Panamanian rhythms. "All killer musicians."

Indeed, Gordon and White often were referred to as the Parker and Gillespie of Panama, while Boa's all-over-the-keyboard virtuosity evoked comparisons to no less than Art Tatum. Singer Barbara Wilson, meanwhile, was dubbed Panama's Ella Fitzgerald.

But that was only one facet of Panama's musical riches. Another was its extraordinarily rich and subtle folkloric music. It developed as blacks, Hispanics, and indigenous Panamanians intermingled, creating a huge but unwritten lexicon of intricate rhythmic patterns and motifs, as well as distinctly Panamanian drums (such as the *pujador,* the *repicador,* and the *caja santena*) and other indigenous musical instruments. The music of Panamanian antiquity still flourishes in the country's interior, where more than half a dozen tribes with roots in Africa have developed a seemingly infinite array of rhythms and improvisational forms.

But this music does not exist on recordings or in notation—it survives entirely in the hands and hearts of the men and women who perform it. If it were ever properly and systematically documented, it could offer a window on the roots of jazz and, perhaps, all African-derived music.

"The sadness is that not only does the world not know the beauty of Panamanian music—even we Panamanians do not," says the folklorist Villarreal, who has been spending his own time, buying his own recording equipment, and otherwise digging into his own pocket to try to capture the music of Panama's tribes before it disappears or transforms itself.

Since Blades became minister of tourism, last September, "I've been traveling through all the country, trying to understand what it is that we have," Blades says.

"I was stunned by the quality of what I was listening to. . . . I'm telling you, man, the thing is—it's hypnotic, it's got something that I thought was Haitian. But when you hear it, when you hear this stuff, you go, 'My God, the chords, what they're doing!'

"And the songs have very poetic names, like 'The Song About the Dance of the Long-Beaked Bird'—really complicated."

Though casual observers might say, "So what?"—who cares what Panama's jazz musicians invented in 1904 or their African tribes have been playing for centuries?—the answers mean a great deal to many people, starting with Panamanians.

An oft-tempestuous relationship with the United States may help explain why many Panamanians long to find a cultural profile of their own. The tensions date back to Panama's first days as a sovereign country, in 1903, when many Panamanians felt that they had been forced to pay too high a price for U.S. support of their bid for independence—American control of the canal, in perpetuity.

The presence of the American military in and outside the Canal Zone, where American soldiers enjoyed a higher standard of living than Panamanians, predictably did not sit well with locals. And a riot in 1964, when American troops killed and injured Panamanians protesting the removal of their flag from the Canal Zone, embittered many.

The U.S. invasion to oust Panamanian dictator Manuel Noriega in 1989 also nurtured tensions.

"It's very hard to be invaded by a foreign country and see people getting killed," says Javier Carrizo, president of the Purple Foundation for Art, an organization that has been championing Panamanian music for nearly two decades.

"There was too much killing, too much suffering.

"Music brings us back to life," adds Carrizo. "It tells us who we are."

March 6, 2005

"I've Got to Go Back Home"

Jazz pianist Danilo Perez's music soothes a nation in transition.

PANAMA CITY—Ten days after the United States invaded this Central American country to oust dictator Manuel Noriega, in 1989, a gifted Panamanian jazz pianist stepped onstage to calm the nation with music—or at least to try.

Several hundred Panamanians had been killed by the U.S. incursion, and though the locals were eager to be rid of Noriega, they grieved at becoming an occupied nation.

Unsure of their future, uneasy about their past—which had seen Panamanians subjected for centuries to the will of Spain, Colombia, the United States, and other foreign governments—Panama tuned in to Danilo Perez.

"It was a powerful moment—it taught me what music really means," recalls Perez, who played what is believed to be the first concert in Panama after the invasion, his music broadcast live nationwide.

"There was a lot of sadness, a lot of fear in our country," adds the pianist, seated in his parents' small but airy high-rise apartment, its balcony overlooking the lush terrain that separates the Atlantic Ocean from the Pacific.

"When they came that day to the performance, many people were crying.

"Psychologically, people needed to get out of here. They did it through music."

Specifically, they did it through Perez's music, his seductive merger of Panamanian rhythms and American jazz technique, perhaps the ideal balm for a Caribbean people facing foreign troops in their streets.

In effect, Perez's music helped bridge two cultures caught up in a violent clash, his art improbably finding common ground between the tiny country where he was born and the superpower to the north where he had moved just a few years earlier. Every note that Perez has played since then—and a great deal of what he performed before—has been dedicated to extolling Panamanian culture to the United States and to the rest of the world, through the international currency of jazz.

Indeed, if there is a single artist who has come to epitomize the robust sound and spirit of this country of three million people to the rest of the world, it is Perez, who ranks among the most accomplished jazz pianists of the under-forty generation.

Though it was pure coincidence that Perez had returned to his homeland a few hours before the invasion—for a concert engagement that had been planned months in advance—his appearance in Panama City proved fortuitous, not only for Panama but for him.

"I think that concert reaffirmed to Danilo his nationality, the fact that he could do something for his country in an incredible moment," says Javier Carrizo, a Perez friend and Panama jazz advocate who hastily arranged the impromptu performance on December 30, 1989 (the day after Perez's twenty-third birthday).

"It was a chance for Danilo to prove himself."

Though Perez was always fascinated by the music of Panama, says his father, Danilo Perez Sr., the postinvasion concert indeed appears to have transformed him. From that moment forth, championing the music and musicians of Panama has become something of an obsession.

"It's about pride," Perez says. "We want to show the world that Panama is not just a bunch of people walking around nude, you know?"

The postinvasion performance generated so much interest through the national broadcast that it was repeated the next day, but this was hardly the first time Perez has caught the interest of his country. Since childhood, he has been a much-talked-about figure in Panama City, showing nearly Mozartean precocity.

"When Danilo was a year-and-a-half old, I could name a particular song, and he would get me the right 45-rpm record from our collection—even though he didn't know how to read," recalls his father.

A retired educator, the elder Perez is revered in Panama as a singer, thanks to many decades of moonlighting with the best Panamanian bands. Seated on a living-room sofa beneath a portrait of the Last Supper, Perez Sr. urges his wife, Elizabeth, to bring from the bedroom a photo of the young Danilo riffing with a big band.

They recall that from age three Danilo was informally playing alongside various ensembles that featured his father; by eight he could repeat on a tiny, toy keyboard the often complex Afro-Caribbean music his father played at home on recordings; and by twelve he was gigging in Panamanian clubs.

This he accomplished even though his family for years was too poor to provide him with a working piano. After first noodling on the toy keyboard, Danilo at age eight graduated to a rotted-out spinet with one working octave.

Even so, he was accepted as a student at the prestigious National Conservatory, where he flourished.

"Danilo was the only student that I have had in my entire professional life that I never had to give a direction to twice," recalls Cecilia de Escalante, who taught Perez classical music at the National Conservatory until he left the country at age sixteen.

"He had total discipline, always," she says.

Yet he had something else too—an abiding interest in Panamanian music. To the young Perez, there was no hierarchical distinction between the music of the concert hall and the ballroom, between the minuets of Haydn and the merengues of his father's repertoire.

"I credit his father for this," says Patricia Zarate, a Chilean alto saxophonist who is Perez's fiancée and mother of their one-year-old daughter, Daniela.

After Perez won a scholarship to major in electronics and minor in music at Indiana University of Pennsylvania, he left Panama at age sixteen, a year and a half later enrolling at the Berklee College of Music, in Boston, arguably the most productive jazz campus in America.

"My mother went for two weeks crying," recalls Perez, age thirty-eight. "She was afraid of me not having a stability, a future.

"When I got to Berklee, it was scary. The level of playing was so high.

"So I started thinking, 'Maybe my mother was right. I've got to go back home.' "

Instead, Perez began practicing relentlessly, transforming himself from a promising pianist well-versed in Afro-Caribbean music to a full-service jazz musician capable of playing persuasively in various American styles. Some students began to joke, in fact, that as long as Perez wasn't speaking in his lilting Panamanian accent, listeners might have thought he was born in the States and never had left.

But in fact Perez was different from the other kids at Berklee, his fluency in a variety of Latin jazz idioms winning him spots with Paquito D'Rivera and with Dizzy Gillespie's United Nation Orchestra in the late 1980s, as well as record deals.

From the outset, his recordings stood apart from anything the young lions of 1990s jazz were creating, not only because of Perez's harmonic sophistication and extraordinarily fluid technique but also because of his deep ties to his Panamanian roots. Here was a jazz debut with a difference.

But if Perez is widely regarded as a driving force in Panamanian jazz, not everyone has applauded his efforts.

"We are not happy with him," says critic and broadcaster Ernesto Crouch, speaking to journalists in the restaurant of Hotel Miramar, the central gathering point of the recent Panama Jazz Festival.

Musically, says Crouch, Perez "is trying to do something funny, like pan-American jazz.

"And I say, 'What the hell are you talking about?' "

While experiments as original as Perez's are bound to provoke argument, the man seems fervently committed to his cross-cultural work. Though based in Boston, where he teaches, he has been returning to Panama with greater frequency in recent years.

"Right now, Danilo is in a period of his career where he's traveling a lot," says Zarate, his fiancée. "But he has such good memories of Panama—he spent his first sixteen years here.

"So I think eventually he wants to spend his time in Panama.

"He wants to work for the people of Panama."

March 10, 2005

Perez remains the single most visible and significant musician carrying the sound and impulse of Panamanian culture into jazz. In addition to the Panama Jazz Festival, which he continues to head, he released an illuminating recording of his Panama Suite *(Artist Share, 2008). Commissioned by the Jazz Institute of Chicago and unveiled in the summer of 2005, the three-part work bristled with freshly contemporary harmonies, contrapuntal instrumental dialogue, and, of course, the fiercely syncopated rhythms of Panama. If Perez's other 2008 recording, the decidedly more commercial* Across the Crystal Sea, *reflected more of arranger Claus Ogerman's aesthetic (easy listening) than Perez's, the CD at least showed Perez working persuasively in a quasi-classical concerto format. But perhaps Perez's most influential work unfolds with the Wayne Shorter Quartet, in which he performs alongside the saxophonist-*

composer, drummer Brian Blade, and bassist John Patitucci. The idiosyncratic harmonies and song structures of Shorter's compositions keep Perez at the leading edge of contemporary jazz. His Panamanian references may be less explicit here, yet they're at the core of his work.

Falling on Deaf Ears

Panama churns out talented young jazz musicians faster than the local scene can receive them. Will the rest of the world start listening?

PANAMA CITY—"One, two, three—hit!" the bandleader shouts, and the place begins to rumble.

Horns scream, saxophones shout, drums pulse, singers cry—wave after wave of glorious sound sweeps across the room, and before long passersby start peeking in, trying to find out what on earth is going on in here.

The venue is not a glamorous nightclub or a plush concert hall but, rather, a nondescript rehearsal room where young musicians in T-shirts and jeans are riffing beneath harsh fluorescent lighting for no audience but themselves (and the recently arrived gawkers).

No one in the world has heard of these young musicians—a rehearsal band led by the legendary Panamanian trumpeter Victor "Vitin" Paz—but they could hold their own in any jazz venue on the planet.

Unfortunately, these young Panamanians are all jazzed up with nowhere to go. Having recently rediscovered their country's deep roots in an Afro-Caribbean art form, they have embraced the music and, in some ways, have mastered it.

But their work is rarely heard outside this remote rehearsal space at the University of Panama.

"You can't imagine the talent we have here," says the band's twenty-eight-year-old pianist, Carlos Campos, who himself achieves dizzying virtuosity despite a dully thudding upright instrument.

"All the kids want to play jazz; the scene is growing all the time," Campos adds.

"But we have a lot going against us."

Indeed, the promising young jazz artists of Panama—which for roughly a century has been an incubator of jazz talent—find themselves in a precarious position.

They live in a country where jazz took root at the dawn of the twentieth century, just as it was blossoming in the United States, but eventually nearly vanished.

While America's jazz legends were celebrated around the world, Panama's were not even recorded until the late 1950s and early '60s, and most of its best artists left the country to pursue careers in the United States, Europe, and beyond.

So a culture that once played a starring role in the origins of the music practically lost touch with its own, distinctly lyrical brand of jazz.

In recent years, however, Panamanian-born giants such as Paz, salsa singer Ruben Blades, saxophonist Carlos Garnett, pianist Danilo Perez, and others began coming home to try to reawaken the art form in a country that's cash poor (at least by North American standards) yet talent rich. By organizing concerts, teaching master classes, and otherwise promoting the music to young artists, the Panamanian masters have succeeded surprisingly well in reigniting homegrown jazz.

The proof is plain to hear in the plush orchestral sound of Paz's rehearsal band, in the pianistic feats of Campos, and in performances across Panama City. From the high-flying virtuosity of guitarist Luis Bonilla during an outdoor concert in the Old City to the prodigious technique of eight-year-old percussionist Milagros Blades (no relation to Ruben Blades) in the Teatro Anayansi to the hard-hitting ensemble work of the youthful Panama Jazz Project in various venues, this city has started to swing again.

"Jazz is growing so fast in Panama," says Billy Herron, a twenty-six-year-old Panamanian jazz guitarist and aspiring record producer, between sets at the popular Take Five jazz club, in the Old City.

"Anywhere you go, you hear kids practicing trumpet lines from Miles Davis and Dizzy Gillespie and things like that."

Adds Carlos "Chale" Icaza, a jazz drummer and composer who two months ago moved back home to Panama from New York to get in on the action, "There is a rediscovery happening here. People are finding a pride in their country, and they're finding it in our music."

The confluence of seasoned musicians coming back to Panama and young talents learning from the elders suggests that Panama could rise again as a jazz power—if anybody outside Panama bothered to listen. If the world tuned in to the sounds rising up across this country, listeners would applaud artists who convey a melodic ardor and a folkloric grace that proves Havana isn't the only jazz powerhouse south of the border.

"We can play, but because we don't have a record industry here, who can hear us?" asks Campos, whose digital prowess and expressive power would keep him employed seven nights a week if he were in the United States.

"In Panama, the talented people don't have a chance."

That has long been the case in a country that for centuries found itself under the sway of the Spanish, the French, and, most recently, the United States, which started building the Panama Canal in 1904 and didn't relinquish control of it until the last day of 1999. Never as affluent as the outside powers that ran the country, Panamanians found their culture relegated to second-class status in their own land.

If artists such as Perez and Blades have proven surprisingly successful in helping Panama's young musicians rediscover their jazz roots, larger and more pressing issues have blocked them at the border.

For starters, the aforementioned lack of a recording industry, and a concert-promotion infrastructure to match, leaves Panamanians virtually unable to send their art outside the country. Unlike American and European musicians, who can cut and burn their own CDs relatively cheaply at home, Panamanians generally don't have this option. The computer and recording technology required is well beyond the means of musicians in a country where the per capita annual income is $4,020.

Worse, Panama's young musicians are virtually on their own when it comes to learning about their own music. Top-notch rehearsal bands, such as Paz's organization, are the exception, not the rule. The emerging Panama Jazz Festival, which gave young players a rare chance to hear such American heroes as tenor saxophonist Joe Lovano, drummer Jack DeJohnette, and bassist John Pattituci, has taken place just twice (in January and in 2003).

And the country's two major educational institutions—the National Conservatory and the University of Panama's School of Fine Arts—focus on European classical music while mostly sidestepping Panamanian jazz.

"The main challenge is breaking the educational model in Panama, which is based on the European conservatory tradition, not the Panama jazz tradition," says Javier Carrizo, a jazz activist and founder of the country's leading jazz organization, the Purple Foundation for Art.

As he sits on a plaza overlooking the rush of traffic in downtown Panama City, where stoplights are few and horns never stop honking, Carrizo bristles at the sad state of affairs.

"About three years ago, Danilo Perez wanted to give a free workshop for students at the conservatory," he says. "And the dean of the music school asked for his curriculum!

"This is like asking Sean Connery for his curriculum for teaching drama.

"In Panama [schools] they emphasize academics, not music."

Adds Perez, "Compared to the United States or Cuba, we are lacking education."

And that's not all that's sorely missing. During the recent Panama Jazz Festival, the French music producer Vincent Rousseau struggled to find adequate drums for visiting musicians to play and other instruments for locals who can't afford them.

"At a major festival, like Montreal's, you can get a drummer anything he wants—the exact size, brand, anything—they have a warehouse where they keep everything," says Rousseau, speaking over breakfast at a seaside hotel.

"Here, we have trouble finding a decent drum set. A good drum kit can cost $10,000 to $15,000, and they don't have that kind of money here."

So young talents in Panama find themselves with two choices: try to pick up the techniques of jazz on the fly—in rehearsal bands such as Paz's or at the occasional jazz festival or wherever else the music surfaces—or get out of Panama as fast as possible, as the country's jazz musicians have done for roughly a century.

Those who do often head to the Berklee College of Music, in Boston, where Perez studied and now teaches and where other Panamanians have ventured before launching careers in the States.

When they arrive at Berklee, or other U.S. music schools, they are astonished at what they didn't know about the inner workings of the music, despite their already high level of accomplishment as performers.

"At Berklee, they bombard you with so much information at once, they tell you all these things that you didn't know existed when you were still in Panama," says Luigie Gonzalez, a Panamanian composer-producer who's now based in Los Angeles.

He's speaking by phone during a break in producing a recording session, a career that he does not believe would have been available to him if he had stayed in Panama.

Like Gonzalez, generations of Panamanian musicians left the country throughout the twentieth century, and most never returned, leaving Panama a shadow of what it once was in world musical culture.

In recent years, however, that trend has begun to reverse, at least among a small but determined group of Panamanian masters who have made personal sacrifices to try to revive their country's indigenous musical culture.

Perez, who's based in Boston, spent much of the 1990s bypassing several high-paying international concert engagements to teach master classes for free in Panama and to perform in the Jamboree, a precursor of the Panama Jazz Festival he initiated two years ago.

Blades, who was thriving in Hollywood as a singer-turned-movie actor, last September returned home to become minister of tourism, which enables him to champion Panamanian music by targeting funds in its direction. Like Perez, he has paid a price, putting his lucrative film career on hold.

And artists such as trumpeter Paz, drummer Icaza, and saxophonist Garnett have moved back home, each for a different reason, but all with the hopes of helping to launch Panama's gifted but hard-pressed young players.

"When I left, in the 1960s," says Garnett, who went on to establish a stellar career playing with Miles Davis and others, "it was always with the intent to come back.

"I wanted to get knowledge and fame in the States, then come back and teach," adds Garnett, after playing an explosive set at the Panama Jazz Festival, his eruptions drawing some of the loudest ovations of the event.

"I've found that the young kids are getting a taste and a flavor of jazz, and they're hungry for it.

"But still, there are not enough clubs, not as much as there used to be when I left."

Even so, the talented young musicians and seasoned artists coming home seem to be forming a critical mass. With superb elder statesmen such as flutist Ibrahim Merel, percussionist-vocalist Antonio Bermudez, and singer Danilo Perez Sr. sharing concert stages and rehearsal rooms with a new generation of talent, Panama appears ready to reclaim not only its past but its rightful place in the jazz pantheon.

Perez Jr. already has begun making plans for next year's festival; pianist Carlos Campos is readying his application to Berklee; Icaza has formed a new band; and Garnett has gathered around him a formidable ensemble of twenty-something talents.

"We started this movement fifteen years ago," says Carrizo, the jazz organizer, "and now I think we see the start of the results.

"I believe Panama will become the jazz mecca of Central America, if we're lucky."

And if we are.

March 13, 2005

XIV

Farewells

Final Parting from the Masters

Legendary Farewell: Lionel Hampton

Jazzmen have long eschewed gloom for musical "home-goings."

NEW YORK—As the sun rose over Manhattan on Saturday morning, several musicians wearing crisp white shirts and impeccably pressed black suits and ties warmed up on their horns, their random notes piercing the early-morning quiet and quickly drawing a crowd outside the Cotton Club, in Harlem.

After a few minutes, trumpeter Wynton Marsalis—sporting the ebony bowler that tipped him as the leader of the band—called a tune, put his horn to his lips, and let out a glorious cry, while a horse-drawn carriage just ahead started rolling. It carried the body of jazz master Lionel Hampton, who died a week earlier at age ninety-four. For as long as anyone has played this music, jazzmen have taken their final journey this way, though more often in slow-and-easy New Orleans than in frantic Manhattan, which typically does not have time or space for such extravagances.

But Hampton—who grew up in Chicago, lived mostly on the road, and died in New York—deserved special attention. As the first jazz musician to champion the vibraphone and as a charismatic member of the first integrated band to perform publicly (Benny Goodman's quartet, in 1936), Hampton ranked as a genuine jazz legend. Even in a city crowded with celebrities, his death called for a grand gesture.

Not surprisingly, the spectacle of these splendidly attired musicians wailing their blues-tinged dirges while slowly marching in the middle of the street—oblivious to traffic lights and even to traffic—caused a stir. New Yorkers who had been watching from curbside fell in behind the band. Television crews and newspaper photographers, who had been tipped off that a New Orleans–style parade would proceed this morning, crowded in front of the parade and walked backward, so as to capture the action head-on.

As the funeral procession wended its way through the Morningside Heights neighborhood, the ancient strains of "St. James Infirmary" and "Flee as a Bird to the Mountain" rang out, performed just as black and Creole musicians have played this music for more than a century, the notes and chords and phrasings handed down through the generations.

This emotionally wrenching music awoke many of the locals, and as the band approached each block—bass drum pounding, clarinet squealing, trombone pumping almost without pause—folks got out of bed, opened the windows of their walk-up apartments, and leaned outside, half-dressed, staring at the proceedings in disbelief.

By the time Hampton's casket and Marsalis's musicians approached historic Riverside Church, the crowd had swelled to more than two thousand, church officials estimated. Meanwhile, the musicians played a searing version of "Just a Closer Walk with Thee," and though they didn't sing the words, you could practically hear the sublime lyrics coming out of their horns: "Just a closer walk with thee / Grant it, Jesus, is my plea," the song declared, beseeching Hampton's entry into the hereafter.

In case anyone missed the significance of the hymn, the preacher at Riverside Church spelled it out for a standing-room-only crowd (the kind that Hampton had always drawn).

"Officially, this is called a funeral service," said Reverend James A. Forbes Jr., senior minister at Riverside, "but really it's a service of 'home-going.'"

That belief—that life on earth eventually yields to a spiritual eternity—dates much farther back than even the jazz funerals, for it's rooted in the Dahomean and Yoruba cultures of West Africa, which African slaves brought with them to America. In New Orleans—where "music is as much a part of death as it is of life," jazzman Sidney Bechet once said—perhaps it was inevitable that death, immortality, and music would intermingle in the form of the jazz funeral. Any jazz musician worthy of the name wanted one.

"Every time one died, why 9 out of 10, there was always a big band turnout [on] the day that he was supposed to be buried," the New Orleans pianist and composer Jelly Roll Morton said in 1938.

"Never buried at night, always in the day. And, of course, a lot of times right in the heart of the city, the burial would take place," Morton continued. "Well, when the band would start, why we'd know that the man was fixin' to be buried. So, you could hear the band come up the street before they would get to the place where the gentlemen was to be taken in for his last rites, and they would play different dead marches."

On this morning, the band stopped playing once the casket had been placed at the altar and covered in a white-and-gold cloth. A variety of speakers took to the podium to praise Hampton, among them former President George Bush, tenor saxophone master Illinois Jacquet (who achieved his first great hit recording Hampton's "Flying Home" in 1942), and Representative Charles Rangel (D-N.Y.).

None, however, articulated the link between jazz and its spiritual undercurrent as eloquently as Representative John Conyers (D-Mich.).

"We have to ask the question, as we celebrate this great 'home-going': where did this music come from?" asked Conyers, who knew the answer all too well.

"It didn't come out of Africa," he continued, warming to the subject.

"It came out of the African experience in America—and out of that pain, out of that suffering, out of the church, came the music that became jazz."

Though he didn't say it, Conyers knew that Hampton, too, felt that pain, if only because he was a prodigiously gifted jazz musician who early in life was not allowed to enter through the front door of clubs where he was performing, was not allowed to drink from the same water fountains or stay in the same hotels as his white colleagues. Perhaps worst of all, he was not allowed to perform before the public onstage with the white musicians he admired.

But Hampton, with Goodman's help, defied the unspoken rule keeping black and white musicians apart, thereby opening a new era in race relations in America long before anyone heard of the great Jackie Robinson or the indomitable Rosa Parks.

Between speeches, some of the most exalted jazz musicians on the East Coast played a rousing number or two, among them Jacquet, pianist Hank Jones, and trumpeters Roy Hargrove, Jon Faddis, Clark Terry, and Marsalis.

When the speechifying ended, Marsalis and the band stepped to the front of the church nave and led the casket back outside.

But this time the music turned up-tempo, exuberant, and optimistic—the antithesis of the dark, mournful sounds that had first accompanied Hampton to the church. In this regard, too, the Hampton funeral mirrored age-old New Orleans traditions.

In an earlier era, once the horns started swinging, listeners assumed that the body had been "cut loose" so it could be taken to the cemetery for eternal rest and so the soul could be freed of earthly pains and travails.

"He's gone and everybody came back home, singing," recalled Morton.

"In New Orleans they believed truly to stick right close to the Scripture. That means rejoice at the death and cry at the birth."

The drummer inside Riverside Church banged his huge bass drum so hard it was a marvel the skin didn't tear, at which point the crowd in the church erupted into noisy conversation and laughter, as if the tension had been broken and Hamp had made his final passage. Here was what Morton called "the end of a perfect death."

Though the throngs followed the band and the casket outside, most folks couldn't yet bring themselves to leave the church grounds entirely. So they lingered in front, reminiscing about the great jazz musician who had been making music swing for as long as they could remember.

They recalled that Hampton played a controversial concert in 1957 that raised funds for several black South Africans who were charged with treason and lacked funds to hire attorneys. The cash that Hampton drummed up provided them a defense and spared them death. One of those men was Nelson Mandela.

"I came here to show respect to a man who did a lot more for this country than people may realize, even though he was famous just as a jazz musician," said Ronald Lonesome, a retired gentleman who said he lived in the neighborhood. He wore jeans and a purple T-shirt with the words "Harlem Lives" on the front.

"Hamp showed us what talent can do to bring people together," added Lonesome, "and even though I'll miss him, I don't think I'll ever forget him."

As the crowd milled outside the church, the casket carrying Hampton's body was eased into a black limousine bound for Woodlawn Cemetery, in the Bronx, where Duke Ellington and Miles Davis are also buried.

The band, meanwhile, paraded off into the distance, its lusty music becoming more faint with each step, until only the beat of the drum rumbled softly in the distance.

Then that, too, gradually dissolved into silence, the music no longer heard but—like Hampton's art—still resonating inside anyone lucky enough to feel it.

September 9, 2002

Sounding the Trumpet: Miles Davis

His last show in Chicago captured the man behind the myth.

Six weeks ago—on the steamy night of August 22—the late Miles Davis gave Chicago the next-to-last concert of his life. Although no one in the crowd at the south end of Grant Park could have known that Davis had but one more performance left to give (the next night at the Hollywood Bowl in California), he clearly was doing more than just playing at his peak: he was also facing down myths that had stalked him since he burst onto the national jazz scene in the mid-1940s.

Almost from the moment he arrived on Fifty-second Street in Manhattan—a capital of bebop immediately after World War II—Davis began accruing a reputation that would dog him wherever he went. Junkie, pimp, jailbird, artist, poseur, icon, wife abuser, derelict parent, visionary, fraud—often it was difficult to perceive how one person could inspire so much adoration and hatred alike.

During that last Chicago concert, Davis confronted part of his myth. For those who claimed that he was a poseur, never able to play bebop with the speed and virtuosity of the greatest instrumentalists, Davis offered some of the quickest, most brilliant trumpet playing this listener has heard.

For those who insisted that Davis was pervasively rude and arrogant, routinely performing with his back to the audience, on this occasion he walked straight to the edge of the stage, took off his signature shades, looked out at the crowd, waved, shook hands, and in every other way embraced his fans.

So perhaps it should come as no surprise that to those who knew him well, the private side of Miles Dewey Davis III, who died last week, was far different from the notorious public one.

"I first met Miles when he was a student in East St. Louis, and he was very timid, very introverted, extremely talented," recalls trumpeter Clark Terry, whom Davis called "my idol" in *Miles: The Autobiography.*

"I used to be buddies with Miles's teacher [Elwood Buchanan]," adds Terry, "and Buke kept saying to me, 'You gotta come over to school and hear this little Dewey Davis cat.'

"So one day, I went over there to hear him, and I was amazed that this shy, skinny little kid had so much talent and such a beautiful sound coming out of his horn."

Soon, though, folks in St. Louis were no longer joking about Davis. While still a teenager, he was sitting in with Billy Eckstine's legendary band, its lineup including Dizzy Gillespie and Charlie "Bird" Parker.

"When I heard Diz and Bird in B's band, I said, 'What? What is this!?'" Davis wrote in his autobiography. "The way that band was playing music—that was all I wanted to hear."

So Davis packed his bags and headed east.

"His daddy sent him to New York to study at Juilliard," Terry recalls with a chuckle, "but Miles—who always did things his way—he studied Bird instead."

By day, Davis dozed through his courses at Juilliard; by night, he played with Parker and Gillespie.

"I was rooming with Miles at the time, and we would be doing six or seven shows a night," recalls drummer Max Roach. "We would start playing at nine at night, and we literally would be finishing up at nine in the morning.

"The first set was always the most painful," adds Roach. "That's when Bird would tear us down. He would play the fastest, hardest, most difficult music in the world, and Miles and I couldn't keep up with him.

"So later we'd go home and practice some more and say to each other: 'Tomorrow we'll cut him, tomorrow we'll show him.'

"But it's like Miles once said: 'Bird died [in 1955] before we could get even.'"

From that brutally competitive world was born the myth of Miles Davis. Because he didn't summon the lightning virtuosity of Gillespie, for instance, the harshest critics considered him something of a poseur.

But, Roach argues, "Miles was one of the few trumpet players of the time—if not the only one—who dared not to copy Diz. Everyone else on Fifty-second Street did.

"And just because Miles played more lyrically and put more open space in his playing doesn't mean that he wasn't a great trumpeter," Roach adds. "I used to see him playing exercises on his trumpet out of clarinet books, which is impossible—except for Miles."

As Terry says, "It's true that Miles had trouble playing bebop in the beginning.

"But Miles became a great contributor to bop, but from his own viewpoint. See, Miles couldn't bring himself to copy anything. He had to come up with his own."

By 1949 Davis did just that, putting together a nonet unprecedented in jazz: French horn, trumpet, trombone, tuba, alto and baritone saxophones, piano, bass, and drums.

"It was a complete departure," says Roach, who played on the nonet recordings that later were combined on the historic *Birth of the Cool* LP. "And as history has shown, Miles was right on."

For Davis, the idea simply was to make "the instruments sound like human voices," Roach says, "and they did."

Although many listeners disparaged the seeming simplicity of Davis's music, "that was totally unfair," Terry says.

"Duke Ellington used to say, 'Simplicity is a very complex form,' and I think Miles fit very deeply into that. His music was like Mozart's—he said a lot with very few notes."

Tragically, at the very moment Davis was opening a new direction in jazz, he also was succumbing to a heroin addiction that would leave him without work for several years in the 1950s. As he acknowledges in his autobiography, he supported his drug habit by pimping, stealing, and swindling. At one point, Terry had allowed Davis to sleep in Terry's hotel room, while Terry went on the road with Count Basie. After Terry left, Davis grabbed his property and sold it at a pawn shop for cash.

"That was really painful for me," Terry recalls today. "I got very angry at first. But then I thought about it and said to myself, 'The cat is just sick and can't help himself.' "

Yet despite Davis's incredible transgressions, despite his self-confessed misogyny and the desperate state of his health from the drug-ridden 1950s onward, at least one miraculous fact cannot be denied: Davis continued to create some of the most alluring new sounds in jazz.

By the mid-1950s, he was recording exquisitely atmospheric tone poems with arranger Gil Evans in the *Sketches of Spain* and *Porgy and Bess* albums; in the mid-1960s, he was off in another direction, throwing out the rules of harmony to develop music on "modal" scales; and in the early 1970s, Davis was redefining jazz yet again with albums such as *In a Silent Way* and *Bitches Brew,* each blending jazz and electronic music in a new kind of "jazz-fusion" that caught fire around the world.

Even at this new peak of fame, however, Davis would again puzzle his fans, retiring for fully five years in the 1970s. During that time he rarely left his apartment, indulging his vices.

"I can only guess that he ran into some kind of brick wall," says Roach, who, with Gillespie, was one of the few visitors Davis saw. "Maybe he was bored with what he had been doing musically.

"And he was having a lot of physical pain at the time—from his hip operations.

"But when Miles finally got through that hermit period, I think he said to himself: 'I don't care what anyone says, I'm going right on into rock.'"

That move, which dominated everything Davis did in the 1980s, drew some of the ugliest criticism of his career.

"I don't know why people were so upset about Miles getting into rock," Terry says. "I always used to tell people, 'Who are we to tell Miles Davis how he should play?'"

But Davis's defiance of jazz convention, as well as his much-chronicled beating of third wife Cicely Tyson, often made his notoriety more prominent than his musical accomplishments.

"A lot of people started to think he was ugly and evil and mean, but that was a facade," Terry insists. "Once you got past that, you found a real pussycat. Like a few years ago, Miles called me when he heard I was sick.

"And he said to me: 'Man, you die on me and I'll kill you, I swear it.'

"That was Miles. Like nobody else."

October 6, 1991

An Underrated Legend: Ella Fitzgerald

The depths of her artistry remain misunderstood.

To this day, she remains universally celebrated but widely, and sadly, misunderstood.

The death of Ella Fitzgerald, Saturday at age seventy-eight, did nothing to shatter the myths that have hovered over her art since at least the 1940s. The obituarists, like uncounted critics before them, invoked patronizing clichés in describing Fitzgerald as a "technician," an "innocent," a "girlish" performer who veered far from "the emotional fray" of a song.

To those who judged Fitzgerald's art strictly by its dazzling surface, perhaps these descriptions sufficed. Certainly no singer before or since had ever reeled off such brilliant, fast-flying passages; no jazz vocalist had ever matched Dizzy Gillespie's mercurial trumpet passages with such apparent ease and fluidity.

But the blinding virtuosity of much of Fitzgerald's work prevented many listeners from understanding that there was a deeper and more profound artist—a genuine interpreter of song—at work here. By frequently comparing Fitzgerald unfavorably to Billie Holiday, an austere singer whose stripped-down vocal lines avoided technical virtuosity at all costs, observers missed the message underneath Fitzgerald's voluptuous sound.

Listen closely to Fitzgerald's mournful, drenched-in-blue reading of "Angel Eyes" (from 1957), her sensual, nearly erotic account of Cole Porter's "All Through the Night" and "I Love Paris" (1955), her whimsically comic style on the Gershwins' "Let's Call the Whole Thing Off" (1959), and there's no question that Fitzgerald understood the great American songbook better than those who criticized her performances of it.

"As an interpreter of popular songs she is limited," notes the *New Grove Dictionary of Jazz*, though adding that she is "unrivaled in her rendition of light material." Faint praise indeed.

How, then, does one explain the singer's yearning, crying tone in "You Won't Be Satisfied" (1946), her starkly broken lines in "I Didn't Mean a Word I Said" (1946), her slightly tipsy, thoroughly vulnerable stance in "One for My Baby (and One More for the Road)" (1960)? These tracks may be overshadowed by such technically stunning recordings as "Flying Home" (1945) and "Airmail Special" (1952), yet they're just as important, if not more so, in defining the artist.

Fitzgerald, of course, was not alone among jazz musicians whose technical accomplishments were held against them. The nearly orchestral pianism of Art Tatum, the shimmering keyboard work of Oscar Peterson, the virtuoso trumpetry of Wynton Marsalis, all have been held up as evidence of these musicians' presumed shortcomings as interpreters and thinkers.

In Fitzgerald's case, this benighted point of view seemed all the more egregious, because she was far from the "natural" or "born" artist that her detractors labeled her. On the contrary, her art was hard-won, with the singer transforming herself from naive beginner to master musician through unrelentingly hard work.

Once again, the proof is in the vinyl. The recordings she made with the Chick Webb Orchestra in the mid-1930s, such as "I'll Chase the Blues Away" and "I Want to Be Happy," show a nascent singer of limited vocal and emotional range utterly lacking in the melodic invention and scat virtuosity that were yet to come. The characteristic exuberance already is there but none of the sensuality of sound or sophistication of phrasing.

Not until the 1940s, when she came under Gillespie's spell, did Fitzgerald begin to flower into the supreme jazz diva.

"After Chick [Webb], I used to go and jam with Dizzy, and that's how I learned my bop," Fitzgerald told me in 1991. "Back then, they used to have places where you could just go and jam, you know?

"Although they'd be sort of seedy after-hours spots, it was still the place to be.

"So I used to follow Dizzy, travel a couple places with him, and I guess I was just thrilled with what was going on [in Gillespie's bebop band] and I tried to do it.

"I just tried to do what I heard the horns in the band doing."

Yet even after Fitzgerald had taken bebop vocalizing to unprecedented heights, she did not stop inventing new ways of singing. By offering up *Songbook* albums (beginning in 1955) devoted exclusively to the music of Cole Porter, Harold Arlen, Duke Ellington, the Gershwins, and so on, she found untapped layers of musical meaning.

So much, in fact, that lyricist Ira Gershwin once remarked, "I had never realized just how good our songs really were until I heard them sung by Ella Fitzgerald."

That a singer of this stature just a few years earlier had been forced by Decca to record such treacle as "Melinda the Mousie" and "My Wubba Dolly" indicates how badly she had been misperceived.

"I always feel that Norman [Granz] saved me," said Fitzgerald in the 1991 interview, referring to the impresario who bought out her Decca contract so that she could record the *Songbook* albums on his fledgling Verve label.

"He had the idea that maybe I could sing something besides just straight jazz songs. And bless him, he had the idea for me to try to do the songbooks, and I guess people were surprised to hear that I could sing something besides just pure jazz.

"I thank Norman so very much; otherwise, where would Ella be?"

Perhaps the ultimate proof of the depth of Fitzgerald's artistry came toward the end, in the summer of 1991, when she played her last Chicago-area concert at the Ravinia Festival in Highland Park. Though she took the stage gingerly, with the help of her accompanist, though her pitch range had shrunk and her voice lacked the luxuriance of old, she turned in a startling performance, producing clicks and pops and other novel effects in Gillespie's "A Night in Tunisia," offering guttural growls and even a shriek or two in Porter's "It's All Right with Me."

The voice may have been frail, but the spirit was freewheeling and airborne.

"Through the years, when I look back and think about all I've been through, I sometimes ask myself, 'Was it worth it?'" Fitzgerald said on the eve of that performance. Surely she referred to the personal price she had paid to tour the world tirelessly as a solo artist: two brief, failed marriages (one to bassist Ray Brown, which produced her only child, Ray Jr.).

"Then I look at all these things in my [California] home," she added, referring to her National Medal of Arts, Grammy Awards, honorary doctorate degrees, and, of course, a silver trophy for her famous "Is it live or is it Memorex?" ad.

"And I say to myself, 'Well, my gosh, maybe it was worth it.'

"I'm grateful to see all these awards and things, because it makes me feel like somebody loved me."

June 19, 1996

A Free-Form Life: Sun Ra

Sun Ra: He came, and went, ahead of his time.

In jazz, as in any art, the true heroes are not necessarily those who receive the most publicity. On the contrary, in a musical world increasingly dominated by MTV, international ad agencies, and billion-dollar record-media conglomerates, the lone voice of the visionary artist seems all the more precious and vulnerable.

For that reason, among others, the recent death of bandleader-composer Sun Ra represents a setback for those who value musicianship over hype, art over commerce. Ra, who died May 30 in Birmingham, Alabama, apparently at age seventy-nine, never achieved household-name status, even though he came of age when the big jazz band still belonged to mainstream American culture. Lacking the tuneful accessibility of a master such as Duke Ellington or the straight-ahead commercial appeal of a Count Basie, Ra spent his career well outside the warmth of the popular-media spotlight. Worse, he considered himself the object of ridicule to the end, largely ignored by the wide public he deserved and taunted by those in his own profession.

"I still face plenty of opposition," he recently told me. "When I was in England four months ago, I worked with an Indian drummer who was magnificent. But when he told his fellow musicians that he was playing with the Arkestra [the name of Ra's band since the 1950s], they asked, 'Why would you want to play with a band like that? Why not work for a real one?'

"So that's how many musicians feel. They still don't get it."

That's how it always was for Ra. Born in Birmingham in May of 1914 or 1915, depending on which history book you believe, Herman "Sonny" Blount came to Chicago in the late 1930s at the invitation of bandleader Fess Whatley. In a short time he was working for the first of the great swing bands, the Fletcher Henderson organization.

But "even when I was playing the Club DeLisa [the jazz room that once thrived on south State Street] in the '40s, I had to be careful, because I was dealing with something that was really ahead of its time.

"When I was playing [keyboards and arranging] for Fletcher Henderson at Club DeLisa, I had a lot of trouble. The band members kept saying I was too 'different.' And when I went to play the Club Morocco in Canada [in the 1950s], I got fired because the man said I was playing God's music. He asked me to change my style, which I refused to do, so they paid me off and told me to get out."

What was so radical about this music? At the time, just about everything.

No sooner had the first crude electronic keyboards come onto the market in the early 1940s than Ra, still known as "Sonny" Blount, acquired one and built his music around it.

"I felt we were moving into a different age—a 'space age,' and I used that term years before people started reading it in the newspapers," Ra recalled.

"So I realized I needed something besides just a piano. My arrangements were always colorful, almost symphonic, so that's why I turned to electronic keyboards."

By the 1950s he had pushed to the front of the avant-garde, leading his Chicago big band into "free-form" compositions, nontriadic harmonies, and epic, seemingly rambling structures. Not content merely to sit at a bandstand churning out one overplayed tune after another, he enriched his show with gyrating dancers and garbed his musicians and himself in fabulous turbans and capes.

Renaming himself Sun Ra, his band the Arkestra, and his idiom "space music," he became a kind of mystic, musically contemplating the universe fully a decade before the flower children of the 1960s proclaimed the dawning of the Age of Aquarius.

But Ra's innovations were not purely of the social kind. While Miles Davis was being justly honored for his "cool" style of the 1950s and John Coltrane was emerging as a leader for his fevered, postbop experiments, Ra was light years ahead. Somehow, he was able to merge standard swing-band ideas with fiercely dissonant passages and outlandishly ornate rhythms.

The unfettered "free jazz" experiments of Ornette Coleman and Cecil Taylor, the percussion innovations of Chicago's avant-garde of the 1960s, and the internationally recognized achievements of Chicago's AACM (Association for the Advancement of Creative Musicians) all owed to Ra's breakthroughs.

Yet the journey was tough, especially when it came time to pay the bills. Thanks largely to the remarkable devotion of Arkestra virtuosos such as alto saxophonist Marshall Allen and tenor saxophonist John Gilmore, who moonlighted in more traditional jazz bands to help bring in money to keep the Arkestra afloat, Ra at least was able to keep working.

By the 1960s he had headed to New York and, later, Europe, where he and his Arkestra proselytized relentlessly on behalf of his beloved "space age."

To many listeners, it was all a big gag, a gimmick to draw attention to a big band that had difficulty attaining it. Yet, in retrospect, Ra's tenacity in pushing his unorthodox view of music and the world seems anything but self-promotional. Surely a cannier salesman would not have endured the slurs Ra did. No less than former Chicago avant-gardist Muhal Richard Abrams, for instance, once confessed that when Ra had been in Chicago, "I was one of the people who tended to make fun of what you [Ra] were doing. Now I find out we have to do those same things."

Indeed, only from today's vantage point is it possible to understand the revolution Ra helped launch half a century ago. Listen to such vintage Ra recordings as *Sound Sun Pleasure, Holiday for Soul Dance, Monorails and Satellites,* and *Purple Night* (all recently reissued on Evidence), and you will hear a bandleader coaxing music of the past into the future.

The unabashed merging of African chant, classic jazz rhythms, and exultant passages of dissonance document just how much a visionary Ra was.

Of course, no one understood the substance and depth of Ra's seemingly far-out experiments better than he. Despite the resistance he endured, even from musicians, he was unwilling to surrender.

Just last year, having suffered a series of strokes, Ra brought his Arkestra back home to Chicago, the band turning in one of the most volcanic, virtuosic jazz-band performances of the season at the Oak Theatre.

"The musicians, the ones who are academic, they still want to hold onto the past, they want to hold onto the one thing they know how to do," Ra told me at the time.

"But people want something fresh and new.

"And all I'm saying is that the space age is here to stay—and nobody can really run away from it."

June 13, 1993

Favors's Spirit Will Live On Through Music

Bassist's funeral draws musicians singing praises.

A brilliant alto saxophonist played a searing blues lament. A jubilant gospel choir unleashed exuberant rhythms and cries. A stream of formidable musicians sang the praises of a fallen colleague.

If a funeral can provide insight into a man's life, it was clear on Thursday that bassist Malachi Favors—who died last month at age seventy-six—made a deep impact on musicians and audiences who were drawn to the plush, mystical beauty of his sound.

The very size of the crowd that packed Love Community Church, in south suburban Hazel Crest, and the stature of the artists who paid homage to Favors said a great deal about his importance to music in Chicago and beyond. For here were jazz stars and cultural scholars, literary figures and everyday working Chicagoans, all buzzing before the services began about how much Favors had meant to them.

"He was the first person I ever played with in Chicago," said George Lewis, the visionary musician-educator who won a MacArthur Foundation "genius grant" in 2002 and flew in from California to pay his respects.

"The thing about Malachi and the other guys that founded the AACM," continued Lewis, referring to the Chicago-based Association for the Advancement of Creative Musicians, "was that they were able to analyze their situation and take action."

The innovative black musicians of Favors's generation realized that jazz in the early 1960s had been marginalized—or worse—by the commercial music industry in America. Rather than pack up their instruments and go home, however, they organized, presenting concerts in churches and schools, releasing recordings on obscure independent labels, and finding their first great acclaim in Europe.

The band that most eloquently heralded the future eminence of the AACM was the Art Ensemble of Chicago, which caused a sensation on the Continent beginning in 1969. In this breakthrough band, Favors—joined by reedists Roscoe Mitchell and Joseph Jarman, trumpeter Lester Bowie, and drummer Don Moye—showed the way for a new jazz avant-garde. Wearing ceremonial African garb, playing ancient and modern instruments, drawing on time-honored African ritual and groundbreaking musical techniques, the Art Ensemble—and the many AACM bands that followed—revivified a jazz world that seemed spent or reduced to recycling past triumphs.

Favors, who graduated from Wendell Phillips High School and attended Wilson Junior College, was at the forefront of this movement.

"What Malachi and the other guys discovered—this new way of approaching improvisation—was a stunning revelation to someone like me, who didn't have a clue," continued Lewis.

"Basically, Malachi and the others said, 'We think we have found a way.'

"Malachi, in particular, had a clear focus on what he and the Art Ensemble and the AACM were trying to do, and that information was shared freely."

That was a critical difference between the first-generation AACM players and many jazz musicians of earlier generations, who often found themselves competing ferociously with one another for engagements, management, and record deals. In the early days of the twentieth century, in fact, musicians often were so protective of their hard-won musical knowledge that some covered the valves of their horns with a handkerchief so that other players could not steal their fingerings. Many artists declined to publish their tunes, for fear of losing control of the music that was at the core of their livelihoods.

AACM musicians such as Favors, however, took a radically different tack, collaborating with colleagues on staging concerts, booking tours, and documenting their music—and bearing the financial risk.

"I prided myself on never joining the armed forces," Moye told the crowd. "Little did I know that when I joined the Art Ensemble I had signed up for boot camp."

Indeed, Favors and his Art Ensemble colleagues did not take their work lightly, recording and touring prolifically. Albums such as *A Jackson in Your House* and *Urban Bushmen* became instant classics of a new jazz language.

If trumpeter Bowie was the brash, extroverted personality that pushed the band into oft-outrageous sonorities and practices, Favors was its spiritual center, his self-effacing personality and deep well of sound representing the noblest, most introspective facets of the Art Ensemble in particular, and the AACM in general. His adopted surname,

"Maghostut," an African word meaning "I am your host," poetically expressed his desire to serve his listeners.

As Thursday's funeral service unfolded, Favors's colleagues found it difficult to quantify their loss.

Percussionist Kahil El'Zabar, who toured the world with Favors and Ari Brown on saxophone in the Ritual Trio, called Favors "the closest thing we will ever see to Malcolm X, the closest we will ever feel to the energy of Mahalia Jackson."

Chicago poet Haki Madhubuti said, "We have just lost a hurricane."

And multi-instrumentalist Douglas Ewart called Favors "one of our most profound messengers."

Some of the most evocative commentary came from the music, with Mitchell alternating between blues exhortations and avant-garde eruptions in a startling alto saxophone solo, the Friendly Temple Choir offering hope and celebration, and Ari Brown setting aside his horn and sitting down at the piano to produce inspired, sweetly diatonic chords.

Finally, in a brief film tribute, the great Favors could be seen speaking for himself, his amazing bass underscoring his own muted commentary.

Nearby, his open casket contained an American flag (he served in the U.S. Army during the Korean War) and his bow, clenched in his hand.

"I'm just going to keep playing till the Lord says stop," Favors said on the film.

But his music and his life clearly will echo long beyond that.

February 8, 2004

Spirit of Dorsey's Songs Fills His "Home-Going"

Several thousand Chicagoans and out-of-towners jammed Pilgrim Baptist Church on Thursday night and sang exultantly for the funeral service of gospel legend Thomas A. Dorsey, who died Saturday at age ninety-three.

Massive choirs, brilliant vocal ensembles, pianists, organists, saxophonists, gospel stars, politicians, and everyday churchgoers affirmed that the spirit of Dorsey's music survives him.

With hands waving, bodies swaying, feet tapping, and eyes often tearing, the congregation celebrated Dorsey's life's work. Strangers locked hands as the jubilant sound of gospel—a genre that Dorsey created in Chicago in the 1930s—filled the immense sanctuary of Pilgrim Baptist. This was Mr. Dorsey's church, and it was in this nearly century-old edifice—at Thirty-third Street and Indiana Avenue—that he introduced the jazz-influenced sound of gospel in 1932.

Chicagoans who took the pulpit were generous but accurate in their tributes to Dorsey.

"We all know that Professor Dorsey was the father of gospel music," said Mayor Richard Daley. "He alone, single-handedly made Chicago the gospel capital of the world. . . . He will always remain a Chicago treasure."

Alderman Shirley Coleman (Sixteenth) said, "Those songs that Dr. Dorsey wrote have carried us on. . . . We thank Dr. Dorsey, and we know that there will be 'Peace in the Valley,'" referring to one of Dorsey's most beloved gospel songs.

Several speakers noted the proximity of the deaths of Dorsey and another great African American leader, former U.S. Supreme Court Justice Thurgood Marshall, who died Sunday.

"Only you, God, would put two giants in front of us [by having them die at the same time]—Thurgood Marshall and Thomas Dorsey," said Reverend L. J. Anthony. He noted of the congregation, "They came from across the nation and the world to say thank you, Lord, for Dr. Dorsey."

Dr. Elmer L. Fowler added, "If there wasn't a Thomas Dorsey, there wouldn't be an Elvis Presley or a Duke Ellington or a Cab Calloway."

Reverend Clay Evans said, "This man will live on and on and on. And we will join together when we get to heaven. . . . Hallelujah."

During the service, saxophonist Arthur Scales played Dorsey's "Today," his high-pitched cries drawing shouts of approval from the congregation. The crowd was similarly moved when Scales recalled meeting Dorsey when Scales was nine years old.

"I remember asking him," Scales recalled, "'Professor Dorsey, does it really make any difference what instrument you play for the Lord?'

"And he let me know that it doesn't matter what instrument you play, as long as you play it wholeheartedly and to the Lord and not unto men."

In addition to the spoken tributes, telegrams have arrived at Pilgrim Baptist from President Bill Clinton, Atlanta Mayor Maynard Jackson, and the Atlanta City Council. An Illinois Senate resolution, read by Senator Margaret Smith (D-Chicago), acknowledged Dorsey's honorary doctorate degrees and other awards.

And several speakers noted, "This is not a funeral—it's a home-going."

The tribute to Dorsey seemed fitting, for his role in the creation and evolution of modern gospel music cannot be exaggerated.

Born on July 1, 1899, in Villa Rica, Georgia, Dorsey moved to Chicago as a teenager, drawn here by the city's thriving jazz scene. Ma Rainey, one of the era's reigning blues divas, engaged Dorsey as her piano accompanist in the mid-1920s, when he was known around town simply as Georgia Tom.

All the while, however, Dorsey was writing religious songs as well, but unabashedly applying blues and jazz techniques to them, a major innovation. In 1932, when Dorsey's wife and infant died during childbirth, the composer abruptly gave up the jazz life and turned to religion.

The first song he wrote after the tragedy, "Precious Lord, Take My Hand," became a personal statement of faith and, eventually, one of the most universally performed of all gospel songs. From this point on, Dorsey was remarkably prolific, writing more than a thousand songs, including such staples of the repertory as "When I've Done My Best," "Search Me, Lord," and "There'll Be Peace in the Valley."

More than that, though, Dorsey became a tireless proselytizer for the new, jazz-tinged music he called "gospel," centering his activities at the same Pilgrim Baptist Church where the funeral service was held.

Beginning in the early 1930s, he staged gospel concerts in Chicago and beyond; published songs and sold them door to door himself; and personally trained several generations of Chicago gospel singers, among them such giants as Roberta Martin, Sallie Martin (no relation), and Mahalia Jackson.

It was the eloquence of Dorsey's music, in combination with the pervasiveness of his salesmanship, that launched the new music.

"Thomas Dorsey was the one who brought the gospel sound into church, even though the church resisted at first," said veteran gospel impresario Sid Ordower. "It wasn't easy for him. The churches didn't want to hear about the new music.

"But it had to catch on because Dorsey wrote music that the people wanted to hear. He was able to bring his musical background—which was jazz and blues—into the religious music so that people would not only accept it but feel it in their bones.

"That music of his was so beautiful that it actually brought people into the church. That's the sign of a great composer."

January 21, 1993